Jamie McGuinness left university mid-way through studying engineering, to discover the world. After prospecting for gold in the western deserts of Australia, training huskies in Sweden and selling Trans-Siberian train tickets in Hong Kong, he finally found his place in it – as a Himalayan trekker.

To satisfy a yesteryear sense of exploration, for much of the year Jamie can be found in Nepal leading treks and climbs or exploring the forgotten corners of the country. His latest project is publishing trekking information for less frequented regions of Nepal on the Internet. When not in Nepal he can be found surfing or skiing in New Zealand.

Trekking in the Everest Region
First edition: 1993
This third edition: 1998

Publisher
Trailblazer Publications
The Old Manse, Tower Rd, Hindhead, Surrey, GU26 6SU, UK
Fax (+44) 01428-607571
Email: trailblazer@compuserve.com

British Library Cataloguing in Publication Data
A catalogue record for this book is available from the British Library

ISBN 1-873756-17-8

Editor: Anna Jacomb-Hood
Series editor: Patricia Major
Cartography and index: Jane Thomas

A note from the author: When I wrote the first edition of this guide in 1992 I began
with a few (unwritten) fundamental philosophies. I didn't want to recommend any
lodges. Instead I have either listed all of them by name, or simply stated the number
at a particular place. I have seen first hand the change in fortunes a recommendation
in a guide book can have on hill lodges. Second was to cover virtually every route and
track in the region so that you have the choice of where to go, rather than being forced
to go where information is available. Probably 80% of trekkers still stick to the main
routes but at least the choice is theirs. It was also my hope that this info would spread
trekkers to equally deserving areas. Third, I have tried to write for everyone, from the
first time visitor, to the Nepalophile. My fourth aim is to allow the book to act as a
vehicle for the local peoples and the organisations involved with conservation and
development. My fifth aim was to have enough trail detail so that at any confusing
junction, the answer would be in here. However, it is only with this edition that the
Salpa-Arun route is covered in sufficient detail, and a few very noticeable omissions
have been fixed: the first trail junction out of Lukla, getting out of Jiri and routes for
wandering around Namche. An apology to anyone who had a more adventurous trek
from the Arun than they bargained for.

Printed on chlorine-free paper from farmed forests by
Technographic Design & Print (☎ 01206-303323) Colchester, Essex, UK

TREKKING
IN THE
EVEREST
REGION

JAMIE McGUINNESS

TRAILBLAZER PUBLICATIONS

For Suzanne

Acknowledgements

Once again I am particularly grateful to the people of Nepal, who did much more than simply help with the research for this guidebook; living in their country has provided me with a diverse insight into life itself. The Sherpas and the mountains, especially of the Khumbu, hold a special place in my heart.

In Kathmandu, I should like to thank Dr Tom Deitz and Dr David Shlim for pointing the medical section in the first edition the right way. Wendy Brewer-Lama provided thoughtful and expert eco-tourism input and kept me up to date with the new Makalu-Barun National Park and Conservation Area project.

My frequent sojourns in Kathmandu have been immeasurably more entertaining with the assistance of the delightful Mr Puru of Hotel Karma and many of the hotel's guests. The staff at the Ministry of Tourism and the Department of Immigration also deserve special mention for so graciously allowing me to stay so long in Nepal.

In the Khumbu, Lhakpa Sonam Sherpa provided much historical information, numerous naming corrections and Nga Gyalgen Sherpa of Chourikharka provided accurate detail for that region. Urken Sherpa from Khumjung and Dole gave historical details and advised on the correct names for selected places in the Gokyo Valley, and has more to tell yet. Nima Wanchuk, the Sagarmatha National Park warden, discussed many excellent tourism ideas, and might soon have a budget to begin implementing them. Shailendra Pokharel, assistant warden and Bung Sector manager provided much of the material for the section on Bung and the Makalu-Barun National Park and Conservation Area. Gabriel gave additional info on the pass just north of the Tsho La and Kangchung Nup, and together with Russell, entertained us with tales of what trekking was all about in the '70s. Also thanks to many Khumbu lodge owners whom I have stayed with, for all their warm welcomes and uncomplicated hospitality. Many people have accompanied me to the region: thanks to all the group members who were so tolerant while I ran off to check something for this book, and for the good company. It is partly with the help of groups that I have been able to visit this region no less than 15 times. On perhaps half these treks Gyalgen from Traksindo has carried, organised and most of all entertained. Pasang, with an equally unquenchable smile and also from Traksindo, is set to become a second star sherpa.

Each year the volunteer doctors staffing the Himalayan Rescue Association posts share their accumulated knowledge on altitude sickness and the region with infectious enthusiasm and deserve a thousand thank-yous not just from me but from all trekkers who have visited the posts. Sue and John Heydon suggested the major improvement of listing normal symptoms for the AMS section, and provided homely hospitality.

I am also particularly grateful to Kerry Moran, James F Fisher, Margaret Jefferies and Stanley Stevens whose eloquent and appreciative works on Nepal immeasurably broadened my insight.

Thanks also to Jane Thomas for drawing and updating the maps and Anna Jacomb-Hood for editing the text. The publisher updated the list of overseas trekking companies, had the difficult job of selecting the photos and provided material for the Kathmandu and Nepal chapters, part of the minimum impact trekking and the language section.

Along the trails in the Khumbu there are so many Nepalis that I'd like to thank by name but the vast majority are more easily recalled by their smiles and helpfulness, as too are the many foreign trekkers I met.

A request

The author and publisher have tried to ensure that this guide is as accurate and up to date as possible. However things change quickly in this part of the world. Prices rise, new lodges are built and trails are rerouted. If you notice any changes or omissions that should be included in the next edition of this book, please write to Jamie McGuinness at Trailblazer Publications (address on p2). A free copy of the next edition will be sent to persons making a significant contribution.

Updated information is available on the Internet at **www.webfoot.co.nz/nepal-treks/**

CONTENTS

INTRODUCTION

PART 1: PLANNING YOUR TREK

What is trekking?
First time trekker 9 – Trekking in the Khumbu 10

With a group or on your own?
Teahouse trekking 10 – Commercial guided treks 13
Trekking companies 15 (UK 16, Continental Europe 17
USA & Canada 17, Australasia 18)

How long to go for
Time planning 19

Route options
Getting to Namche 21 – Routes above Namche (Lobuche
Gokyo and Chukhung) 24 – Other options 27 – Other activities 29

Budgeting
Costs in Kathmandu 32 – The trekking budget 32
Currency 33

When to go
Seasonal conditions 34 – The Kathmandu climate 37

What to take
Factors affecting equipment selection 38 – Equipment list 39
Renting or buying equipment in Nepal 45 – Adventure trekking
equipment 46 – Recommended reading 49 – Maps 50

Health precautions and inoculations
Medical conditions 52 – Inoculations 53 – Medical insurance 54

PART 2: NEPAL

Facts about the country
Geographical background 55 – Historical outline 56
Economy 58 – Development 59 – The people of Eastern Nepal 59

Practical information for the visitor
Visa and trekking regulations 61 – Getting to Nepal 61
Local transport 64 – Language 65 – Electricity 65 – Time 65
Money 65 – Post and telecommunications 66 – TV, newspapers
and magazines 66 – Holidays and festivals 67
Food 68 – Drink 68 – Things to buy 68 – Security 69

INTRODUCTION

The Solu-Khumbu region of Nepal has been a magnet for mountaineers, adventurers and travellers ever since its opening to foreigners in the 1950s, and with good reason. They may primarily be drawn by a desire to see the world's highest mountain but Everest is only one of a myriad of beautiful peaks in the area and there are many other attractions here.

Passing through populated areas, a trek in Nepal is very different from a wilderness hike in the USA or New Zealand, or a randonaire route in the European Alps. The hills in Nepal are the life and soul of diverse ethnic groups, the most famous of which are the hospitable Sherpa people. What further sets trekking in Nepal apart is the low cost and the ease with which a trek can be arranged. There can be few countries where you can set off for a month-long walk carrying no food or shelter yet be 100% sure that every day you will be able to find these essentials, and on a budget of just a few pounds or dollars a day. Alternatively, if you want an organised trek with an entourage of guides, cooks and porters to transport you back to the time of pukka sahibs and memsahibs, this can be quickly arranged with competent staff for a very reasonable cost.

Three areas in Nepal have become popular with trekkers, for their scenic attractions and their established network of local lodges for accommodation and food. As well as the Everest region, there's the Annapurna region, north of Pokhara, which may have a greater range of terrain and cultures but receives three times as many trekkers as the Everest region. The third area is Langtang, north of Kathmandu, which is quieter but there are no mountains over 8000m here. What sets the Everest region apart from these two other areas is the fact that, once above Namche and Lukla you are right among the mountains, continuously above 3000m/10,000ft with many chances to ascend above 5000m/16,400ft.The greater Khumbu (Everest) region also has immense scope for exploration.

One of the world's classic long trekking routes, the first part of the trek to Everest crosses ridge after ridge of painstakingly-terraced hills populated by subsistence farmers. Mediaeval villages cling to the hillsides with mysterious *gompas* (Buddhist monasteries) above them. Rural life, unchanged for centuries, surrounds the trekker, thought-provoking and very different from the Western way of life. You soon settle into the trekking life-style leaving the world of portable telephones and fax machines far behind and rediscovering simple pleasures like the enduring glow of a sunset, the magic of flickering flames and the bliss of sleep to soothe naturally exercised muscles.

Namche, the capital of the Khumbu and a focal point for trekkers, is juxtaposed between the old and the new with traders well versed not only in the various types of Tibetan *tsampa* but also in the different brands of titanium ice screw. From the alpine valleys above Namche, the scenery is awesome: Ama Dablam, Machermo, Cholatse and numerous other peaks while the 8000 metre giants, Makalu, Cho Oyu, Lhotse and Everest command respect for their sheer height.

The highest mountain on earth has several different names. To the Western world it became Mt Everest in 1865 but to the Tibetans and the Khumbu Sherpas it has always been Chomolungma. The Chinese have wisely used the local name (transliterated as Qomolangma). Much more recently the government of Nepal has given it the name Sagarmatha. In this guide, it's referred to as Everest only because this is the name most readily recognised by readers. I personally prefer the original name, Chomolungma.

PART 1: PLANNING YOUR TREK

What is trekking?

I see fields of green and skies of blue and I think to myself, 'Oh, what a wonderful world'.
Louis Armstrong

And there are few more wonderful experiences than trekking in Nepal.

A Himalayan trek is an altogether different experience from a week's backpacking in the Rockies or bushwalking in Tasmania. Rather than a wilderness walk, this is a hike through a countryside free from roads. The paths are timeless pilgrimage routes, trails between villages caught in a time warp, or tracks to high grazing pastures. It is by no means an untouched landscape but it is an incredibly beautiful natural world. Only higher up in the alpine valleys are the villages left behind, replaced by herders' huts. Higher still are the ice castles of the Himalaya.

The practical aspects of trekking are surprisingly easy. In the villages and along the way are lodges and teahouses where meals are ordered from menus in English. Alternatively, on a trekking tour three-course meals are served by your crew. Without the need to carry food and camping equipment, backpacks are light, and if you have a porter you need carry only your daypack. So trekking is really little more than a pleasurable ramble through attractive villages amid incredible mountain scenery.

The satisfaction of trekking is in the process; most trekking days are not particularly long so there is time to spot wildlife, take photographs, chat along the way and relax over lunch or a reviving cup of tea.

FIRST TIME TREKKER?

For the first time trekker, however, the prospect can be daunting as well as thrilling. There are challenges: the first is the physical effort required. Although you'll hopefully be lightly laden, hill-climbing still requires plenty of effort. Pleasure can be had from frequent rests to admire the scenery which, even after a mere 10 minutes, alters satisfyingly and often dramatically. Take comfort, too, in the frequent teahouses which are often strategically placed. The second challenge is the discomfort of sickness. This is the developing world and no matter how careful you are you may experience an upset stomach or some bowel problems, though these are usually minor and seem very trivial compared to the whole wonderful experience.

To enjoy the Himalaya you don't have to be the tough outdoor type. Like rucksacks and cameras, trekkers come in all shapes and sizes and with widely differing aspirations. Trekking is physical but certainly not beyond the majority of people. Bring along a traveller's curiosity and a sense of humour, and before you know it you'll relish the thought of another trek.

TREKKING IN THE KHUMBU

Trekking is usually a wonderful experience but a reality check is in order. You're heading into an extreme mountain environment. It can snow unexpectedly at any time. Emergency facilities are limited: most villages don't even have a phone. You will also be at extreme altitude and experience its discomfort and problems. Foolhardiness or ignorance about acclimatisation (see p236) can and does still kill, although it is entirely preventable.

With a group or on your own?

Nepal, long suspicious of foreign influence and colonial powers, began opening its borders only in 1948. The first tourists (as opposed to mountaineers and researchers) arrived in 1955 but it was not until 1965, when Colonel Jimmy Roberts set up Mountain Travel, that the first commercial treks began. The concept was similar to the expedition approach used by mountaineers, with guides, porters and tents. These holidays proved to be a great success and essentially the same format is still used today by most trekking companies.

Alongside this self-sufficient approach to trekking is a second locally-based tourism industry catering to the needs of a different type of visitor. Along the main trade routes the hill peoples of Nepal traditionally had a code of hospitality towards travellers. It was only a matter of time before small groups of adventurers started using this, staying in the basic teahouses and lodges. In 1964, 14 foreigners visited the Khumbu but by the 1970s the numbers were rapidly increasing. Now more than 10,000 people trek this way each year, staying in the much improved lodges and teahouses along the routes.

The trekking infrastructure in the Solu-Khumbu has now developed to a stage where many options are possible: from a full-scale expedition with tents and porters to an independent trek using the local lodges and carrying only a sleeping-bag and jacket. It is simply a case of choosing the option most appropriate for you.

TEAHOUSE TREKKING

Dotted along the main trails the privately-owned teahouses and lodges cater specifically for independent trekkers. They can provide anything from a cup of tea to a full meal and a bed so, for the entire trek, there's no need to carry food or shelter. Teahouse trekking, as it's usually called, is easy to organise: just a day or two planning and bureaucracy-bashing in Kathmandu, and away you go. It's also cheap: luxuries aside, US$10/£6.50 a day easily covers food and accommodation.

The level of comfort and facilities in the lodges has improved greatly. Many once infamously smoky and rather too authentically-mediaeval inns are now modest hotels which generally offer better facilities than the expedition approach.

As well as being economical, teahouse trekking gives you the freedom to alter your schedule and stop where you wish. This is particularly handy if you are sick for a day or two or you feel like a rest; commercial group treks have to push on. The freedom to explore is, however, limited by the location of lodges and the restricting geography of the region. In practice most trekkers follow a few standard routes and similar itineraries, as do the trekking companies. This means that during the peak season the lodges in popular stopping places are crowded, although a meal and bed can always be found.

The main difference between the approaches is the style of interaction with the local people. Staying in a lodge provides the rewarding opportunity to mix with your Nepali hosts, many of whom speak reasonable English. How much you interact depends on you; some trekkers seem happy to spend all their time only in the company of other trekkers. On an expedition-style trek, although being self-sufficient removes the enjoyable need to interact with the villagers, this is redeemed by the crew, an often substantial team who look after, entertain and add local colour to a guided trek.

Trekking alone
Although there are few risks in trekking alone in the Khumbu it's always safest to trek with a friend or two. Many people come to Nepal alone and then find trekking partners in Kathmandu. You can advertise on, or scan, the noticeboards around Thamel, especially at the Himalayan Rescue Association (HRA) office. You'll also meet lots of other trekkers at the Department of Immigration as you get your permit. Other alternatives are to hire a porter-guide through a trekking company or try to join an existing group.

Unless trekking during the monsoon or off the standard routes you constantly meet other trekkers in the lodges or on the trail. While you can remain by yourself most people end up walking in small groups and staying at the same lodges. This process often begins on the bus out to Jiri, or on the flight to Lukla, and more friendships evolve during the rest of the walk, one of the special joys of Nepal trekking.

Villagers will often ask how many people you are trekking with and if you're trekking alone but want to be cautious you can always say your friend is just behind; violent crimes against foreigners are still rare. As a woman you are slightly more vulnerable and locals do caution against hiking alone. Many lodges, however, are managed solely by the woman of the household while her husband is away, and women sometimes herd cattle and collect leaves alone or walk just with their children. Dressing sensibly and behaving modestly is essential. When stopping for the night, check that there is another woman staying there or pick busier lodges; if heading off the main routes you should definitely team up with someone else.

Is a guide or porter necessary?

Assuming you will be taking this book with you, there's no need for a **guide** of the human kind on the established trekking routes. The lodges are impossible to miss, route finding presents few problems and basic English is widely understood. However, trekking with some local people can be an enlightening, entertaining and rewarding cultural exchange.

Hiring a **porter-guide** is an option that gives you the advantages of both the independent approach and the group trek. You retain control with the opportunity for the greater insight and interaction that a guide can provide, and you have your load pleasantly lightened. A porter-guide should speak reasonable English, know the region and carry 10-15kgs plus their equipment. Usually they are younger and aspiring to become a full guide or sirdar. They are happy to work for one person or a small group or if you have several loads to be carried you could hire an additional porter to accompany the group. See p86.

A cheaper option is to hire a normal **porter**, who will probably speak little English but know the route well. Once at a lodge they tend to look after themselves but on the trail they can be helpful, especially in route-finding and deciding on a lunch stop. You shouldn't feel the least bit guilty if you do hire a porter-guide or a porter. For US$5-15/£3.30-10 a day, it directly benefits the local economy and it can be an enjoyable cultural exchange (see p87 for details).

Trekking the wild way

For climbers and experienced trekkers the region has an incredible amount to offer. At any major village on the main trekking routes you can pick up enough food (provided you're not a fussy eater) to disappear into the wilderness for a week so the scope for exploring off the beaten track is immense. The main decisions boil down to selecting exactly what gear to take and deciding if you have enough experience for some of the wilder route options.

Commercial teahouse trekking

Recognising the improvements in lodges, some trekking companies now also offer teahouse style treks. While a dining room is a vast improvement on an often frigid dining tent and the bedrooms have more headroom than a tent, you pay dearly for the privilege compared to doing the same thing independently. The advantages are that everything is already arranged in Kathmandu and the length of the trek is fixed. The quality of the trek then rests on the leadership: a good Western leader backed up by a local sirdar or guide is a powerful combination. Many companies, however, particularly if the group is small, provide only a local guide and you are equally as likely to land a good one hiring through a Kathmandu trekking agency as through the foreign trekking companies. Often, the best local leaders form their own trekking companies or work as expedition sirdars.

COMMERCIAL GUIDED TREKS

The traditional idea of trekking evokes images of armies of heavily-laden porters catering to the every needs of a few pampered sahibs and memsahibs. Sherpas pitched the tents and kitchen staff served magnificent dinners on tables complete with table linen. This is still, in fact, the basic format of the ordinary commercial or package trek, but the scope of trips on offer is increasingly varied.

What you're paying for

The expedition style is a pleasant routine suited to those who enjoy being looked after and, with everything planned in advance, is perfect for people with limited time. Normally the package includes airport pick-up, a guided tour plus a day or two in Kathmandu, hotel accommodation, and everything while trekking.

What sets one company above another is the quality of the trek leaders. The better companies will always provide a Western leader (who is also always backed up by a local sirdar), or an exceptional local leader. Treks operated by more ordinary companies will be led by a guide or sirdar who may have excellent organisational abilities but be less able to act as a cultural interface between trekkers and Nepalis. They are also likely to lack medical training, although many companies carry a first aid kit. A few guides also have little understanding of altitude sickness. Whatever they may say,

❑ **A day in the life of a group member**
You're normally awoken with 'bed tea' followed by hot washing water. Sufficiently encouraged, you're expected to rise and pack your kit bag before a hearty breakfast. As you consume this the tents are struck and the porters set off, halting at around 10am for their traditional twice-daily meal of *dal bhat* (rice and lentils).

On the trail after breakfast, you carry just a day pack containing little more than your camera and jacket. Sherpas are on hand to assist and accompany you and the sirdar or leader sets a measured pace with occasional tea stops and breathers. While you leapfrog with the porters the kitchen crew races ahead to prepare the lunch. This is an ample and leisurely affair usually with time to explore around a village, play a hand of cards or read.

Camp is established following the afternoon's walk, sherpas erect the tents and the cooking crew is busy once again, preparing a three-course dinner. Some camp sites now have a kitchen shack and even a rough dining room that the crew will also sleep in. Most trekkers turn in early. The two-person tents are comfortable enough and slightly warmer than the dormitories of the high-altitude lodges, but space is at a premium. After a good day's walking sleep comes quickly.

the hard reality is that 95% of companies don't have sensible acclimatisation plans. One large company justified this to me by saying that although they do have many people coming down with AMS, the majority of people were satisfied with their trek.

A selling point for companies is the independence that trekking with tents allows. In reality, on the standard trails porters prefer to stay in the villages so the group is just as reliant on these as is the teahouse trekker. Off the main trails, however, and in the true wilderness areas, the expedition approach is the best and only alternative for a group.

Adventure treks
A few professional trekking companies offer itineraries that would be difficult or expensive for an individual to organise. These are expeditions that would need a supreme amount of confidence to tackle alone; their experienced leaders make climbing the easier trekking peaks and crossing the tougher mountain passes relatively safe for newcomers to the Himalaya.

Trekking peaks and expedition peaks
In 1981 the government of Nepal streamlined group climbing permit applications for 18 mountains which it calls '**trekking peaks**'. The name is not well-chosen for some of these peaks are challenging technical climbs but a handful are 6000m or 20,000ft peaks within the ability of the experienced hill-walker/hiker (with a guide). This form of recreational mountaineering took off at the end of the 1980s and expeditions can now be organised at a similar cost and within a time frame similar to a less adventurous trek.

The best professional operators offer full expedition-style treks with experienced mountain guides and staff with medical training to ensure a safe trek. **Expedition peaks** are now also on a few company programmes, Ama Dablam (6856m) is popular and several even offer guided attempts on Cho Oyu and Everest.

Arranging a guided trek in Nepal
Armed with the addresses of trekking companies in Nepal a number of people have tried arranging a trek by letter, email or fax from their home country. Some have had success, others experience frustration. In fact it's better simply to arrive in Nepal and start making arrangements there. You won't be met at the airport but that's about all that will be missing. Allow a couple of days comparing companies, then a few more for the trekking company to get a crew and supplies together, and you'll be ready to go. Complications do arise if you wish to fly in to begin your trek as the crew may have to walk in, taking longer (chartering a helicopter is an option) but if time is so important consider a package trek booked in your home country.

This approach is cheaper than a packaged tour. You are not paying for office services in your home country, which may amount to more than the actual trek cost, or a set standard of luxury that you may not entirely desire. Other advantages are greater flexibility on the choice of itinerary and changes en route. Try to talk to other trekkers who have used a company's services: some pretend to specialise in everything (trekking, rafting, climbing) rather than sticking to what they do best.

Climbing trekking peaks (see above) can be arranged on arrival in Kathmandu but unless you are an experienced climber who would prefer to lead and be responsible for safety you are better booking with a competent adventure trekking company. The reason for this is that there are many cowboys in this industry; skilled guides are likely to have been booked in advance and hard to find at short notice.

If your intention is to join a group trek arranged on arrival, you must be prepared to wait. The majority of pre-arranged treks are organised by foreign tour operators and are considered exclusive: bookings via the overseas agent only. There are a few companies that advertise set trekking dates but these usually depart even if only two people book. Sometimes, although not always, this is just a different way of advertising trek-organising expertise.

TREKKING AGENCIES OUTSIDE NEPAL

Some companies offer a general range of treks while others specialise in climbing and adventure treks. Brochures usually stress the level of experience required for treks and climbs advertised. Don't, however, lose sight of the fact that although trekking is made easier by the need to carry only a day pack, it is still your legs that do all the walking. Don't be afraid to quiz the company on who is leading the trek, their group numbers policy, and on the detailed itinerary. All profess to following comfortable acclimatisation rates but the hard reality is that many don't. They may have a good safety record, saving people before it's too late, but many itineraries cause undue and unnecessary discomfort.

Costs

US companies quote land-only costs. For the shortest treks that fly to Lukla and explore as far as Tengboche, they charge US$1500-2000. The longer standard treks start at US$1900 but most are around US$2500 and climbing treks cost US$2600-3000. US companies that offer UK or Australian operated treks are usually a little cheaper.

In the UK, trek costs are generally quoted including return airfares. Treks start from £1400 with most around £1700 and the longer climbing treks ranging between £1800 and £2300. US companies (bar one) don't operate in Europe because they are not competitively priced; the Australian and UK markets, however, seem to mix well.

Australian companies quote air and land costs separately. A return flight to Nepal is around A$1700. Short treks are A$1300 and upwards, and the standard treks are from around A$2000 to A$3000. Trekking peak expeditions cost A$2500-3500.

Trekking agencies in the UK

● **Activity Adventures Worldwide** (☎ 01494-448901) 67 Verney Ave, High Wycombe, Bucks, HP12 3ND. Agents for Mountain Travel & Sobek Expeditions (see: Trekking agencies in the USA).

● **Classic Nepal** (☎ 01773-873497, fax 01773-590243) 33 Metro Ave, Newton, Derbyshire, DE55 5UF, feature a good mix of standard routes and adventure treks.

● **Encounter Overland** (☎ 0171-370 6845, fax 0171-244 9737) 267 Old Brompton Rd, London SW5 9JA, offers guided treks in the region.

● **Exodus Expeditions** (☎ 0181-675 5550, fax 0181-673 0779) 9 Weir Rd, London SW12 OLT, have a wide range of guided treks with accommodation in tents or tea-houses.

● **Explore Worldwide** (☎ 01252-319448. fax 01252-343170) 1 Frederick St, Aldershot, Hants GU11 1LQ, offers a number of treks.

● **Guerba Expeditions** (☎ 01373-858956, fax 01373-858351) Wessex House, 40 Station Road, Westbury, Wilts BA13 3JN, leads small group treks in the region. Agents for Peregrine Adventures (Australia).

● **Himalayan Kingdoms** (☎ 01179-237163, fax 01179-744993) 20 The Mall, Clifton, Bristol BS8 4DR, have several treks in the region. Their expeditions section (☎ 01142-763322) organises more ambitious adventure trekking and mountaineering holidays.

● **KE Adventure Travel** (☎ 017687-73966, fax 017687-74693) 32 Lake Rd, Keswick, Cumbria CA12 5DQ) offers treks and trekking peaks including Mera.

● **Naturetrek** (☎ 01962-733051, fax 01962-736426) Chautara, Bighton, Nr Alresford, Hampshire SO24 9RB offer bird-watching tours in several regions of Nepal including the Everest area.

● **OTT Expeditions** (☎ 01142-588508, fax 01142-551603) 62 Nettleham Rd, Sheffield S8 8SX, specialises in trekking peaks and mountaineering expeditions.

● **Roama Travel** (☎ 01258-860298, fax 01258-861382) Shroton, Blandford Forum, Dorset DT11 8QW specialise in individual treks.

● **Sherpa Expeditions** (☎ 0181-577 2717, fax 0181-572 9788) 131a Heston Rd, Hounslow, Middx TW5 ORD, have over 20 years experience in Nepal and a wide range of guided treks.

● **World Expeditions** (☎ 0181-870 2600, fax 0181-870 2615) 4 Northfields Prospect, Putney Bridge Rd, London SW18 1PE feature a range of standard treks.

Trekking agencies in Continental Europe

● **Austria Okistra** (☎ 0222-347526) Turkenstrasse 4, A-1090 Wien. **Supertramp Reisen** (☎ 01222-5335136) Helferstorfer St 4, A-1010 Wien.

● **Belgium Andersreisen** (☎ 013-33 40 40) Refugiestraat 15, 3290 Diest. **Connections** (☎ 02-512 50 60) Kolenmarkt 13, rue Marche au Charbon, 1000 Bruxelles, with branches in Antwerpen (☎ 03-225 31 61), Gent (☎ 091-

23 90 20) and Liege (☎ 041-22 04 44). **Joker Tourisme** (☎ 02-648 78 78) Boondaalsesteenweg 6, Chaussée de Boondaal 6, Brussel 1050 Bruxelles. **Divantoura** (☎ 03-233 19 16) St Jacobsmarkt 5, 2000 Antwerpen. **Roadrunner** (☎ 03-281 16 50) Belgielei 209, 2018 Antwerpen. **Divantoura** (☎ 091-23 00 69) Bagattenstraat 176, B-9000 Gent.

● **Denmark   Inter-Travel** (☎ 33-15 00 77) Frederiksholms Kanal 2, DK-1220 Kobenhavn K. **Marco Polo Tours** (☎ 33-13 03 07) Borgergade 16, 1300 Kobenhavn K. **Topas Globetrotters** (☎ 86-89 36 22) Skaersbrovej 11, 8680 Ry.

● **Germany   Explorer** (☎ 0211-379 064) Huttenstrasse 17, 4000 Dusseldorf 1. **SHR Reisen** (☎ 0761-210 078) Kaiser Joseph Strasse 263, D-7800 Freiburg.

● **Iceland   Icelandic Student Travel** (☎ 01-615656) V/Hringbraut, IS-101 Reykjavik.

● **Ireland   Maxwells Travel** (☎ 01-779 479) D'Olier Chambers, 1 Hawkins St, Dublin 2.

● **Italy   CTS** (☎ 06-46791) V. Genova 15, 00184 Roma.

● **Netherlands   NBBS** (☎ 071-22 1414) Schipholweg 101, PO Box 360, 2300 AJ Leiden. Branches in Groningen (☎ 050-126 333), Amsterdam (☎ 020-20 5071), Utrecht (☎ 030-314 520) and Rotterdam (☎ 010-414 9822). **De Wandelwaaier** (☎ 020-622 6990) Herngracht 329, 1016AW Amsterdam. **Terra Travel** (☎ 020-275129) Singel 190H, 1016AA Amsterdam. **Royal Hansa Tours** (☎ 050-127799) Stoeldraalerstraat 11, 9712 BT Groningen.

● **Norway   Terra Nova Travel** (☎ 47-2 42 14 10) Dronningens Gate 26, N-0154, Oslo 1. **Eventyrreiser A/S Adventure Travel** (☎ 22-11 31 81) Hegdehaugsvn 10, 0167 Oslo.

● **Spain   Banoa (Bilbao)** (☎ 94-424 00 11, fax 423 20 39) C/Ledesma, 10-bis, 2°, 48001 Bilbao. **Banoa (Barcelona)** (☎ 93-318 96 00, fax 318 00 37) Ronda de Sant Pere, 11, àtic 3ª, 08010 Barcelona. **Expo Mundo** (☎ 03-412 59 56) Diputacion, 238 Stco, 08007 Barcelona.

● **Sweden   Aeventyrsresor** (☎ 08-654 1155, fax 08-650 4153, email info@aventyrsresor.se) Fleminggatan 68, PO Box 12168, S-102 24 Stockholm. **Himalayaresor** (08-605 5760) Box 17, S-123, 21 Farsta.

● **Switzerland   S.S.R.** (☎ 01-242 30 00) Backerstr. 52, CH 8026, Zurich. **Suntrek Tours** (☎ 01-462 61 61) Birmensdorferstr. 187, CH-8003 Zurich.

Trekking agencies in the USA

● **Above the Clouds Trekking** (☎ 508-799 4499, fax 797 4779, email sconlon@world.std.com) PO Box 398, Worcester, MA 01602.

● **Adventure Center** (☎ 510-654 1879, ☎ 800-227 8747, fax 654 4200) 1311 63rd St, Suite 200, Emeryville, CA 94608 – agents for Explore (UK).

● **Geeta Tours & Travels** (☎ 312-262 4959) 1245 West Jarvis Ave, Chicago IL 60626.

● **Geographic Expeditions** (☎ 415-922 0448, ☎ 800-777 8183, fax 415-346 4435) 2627 Lombard St, San Francisco, CA 94123.

● **Himalayan Travel** (☎ 800-225 2380, fax 203-359 3669) 2nd Floor, 112 Prospect St, Stamford CT 06901 – agents for Sherpa Expeditions (UK).

● **Journeys International** (☎ 313-665 4407, ☎ 800-255 8735, fax 665 2945, email info@journeys-intl.com) 4011 Jackson Rd, Ann Arbor, MI 48103. Also includes some treks specially for families.

● **Mountain Travel & Sobek Expeditions** (☎ 510-527 8100, ☎ 800-227 2384, fax 510-525 7710, email info@mtsobek.com) 6420 Fairmount Ave, El Cerrito, CA 94530. Wide range of upmarket treks.

● **Overseas Adventure Travel** (☎ 800-221 0814) 349 Broadway, Cambridge MA 02139 offer a number of treks in this area.

● **Safaricentre** (☎ 310-546 4411, ☎ 800-223 6046, fax 546 3188, email info@safaricentre.com) 3201 N Sepulveda Blvd, Manhattan Beach, CA 90266 – agents for Exodus (UK).

● **Wilderness Travel** (☎ 510-558-2488, ☎ 800-368 2794, fax 510-558 2489, email info@wildernesstravel.com) 1102 9th St, Berkeley, CA 94710.

Trekking agencies in Canada

● **Canadian Himalayan Expeditions** (☎ 416-360 4300, ☎ 800-563 8735, fax 416-360 7796, email treks@chetravel.com) 2 Toronto St, Suite 302, Toronto, Ontario M5C 2B6. This is one of the few Canadian companies that run their own treks, rather than acting as agents for other companies.

● **Travel Cuts**, also agents for Exodus (UK), have offices in **Edmonton** (☎ 403-488 8487) 12304 Jasper Ave, Edmonton, Alberta, T5N 3K5, **Toronto** (☎ 416-979 8608) 187 College St, Toronto, Ontario M5T 1P7 and **Vancouver** (☎ 604-689 2887) 501 602 West Hastings St, Vancouver BC, V6B 1P2.

● **Trek Holidays**, agents for Explore (UK), have offices in **Calgary** (☎ 403-283 6115, 336 14th St NW, Calgary, Alberta T2N 1Z7), **Edmonton** (☎ 403-439 9118, 8412 109th St, Edmonton, Alberta T6G 1E2), **Toronto** (☎ 416-922 7584) 25 Bellair St, Toronto, Ontario M4Y 2P2 and **Vancouver** (☎ 604-734 1066, 1965 West 4th Ave, Vancouver BC V6J 1M8.

● **Worldwide Adventures Inc** (☎ 416-221-3000, fax 416-221-5730, from USA ☎ 1-800-387-1483) 36 Finch Avenue, West Toronto, Ontario, Canada M2N 2G9 – agents for World Expeditions (Australia).

Trekking agencies in Australia

● **Adventure World** has branches in **Adelaide** (☎ 08-231 6844, 7th floor, 45 King William St, Adelaide, SA 5000), **Brisbane** (☎ 07-3229 0599, 3rd floor, 333 Adelaide St, Brisbane, Qld 4000), **Melbourne** (☎ 03-9670 0125, 3rd floor, 343 Little Collins St, Melbourne, Vic 3000), **Perth** (☎ 09-221 2300, 2nd floor, 8 Victoria Ave, Perth, WA 6000) and **Sydney** (☎ 02-9956 7766, toll free 008-221 931, 73 Walker St, North Sydney, NSW 2059).

● **Ausventure** (☎ 02-9960 1677, fax 9969 1463) Suite 1, 860 Military Rd, (PO Box 54) Mosman, NSW 2088. This long-established adventure travel company offers a comprehensive range of treks.

● **Classic Adventures** (☎ 02-9264 5710) Level II, 456 Kent St, Sydney. Agents for Mountain Travel & Sobek Expeditions (USA).

● **Exodus Expeditions** (☎ 02-9552 6317) 81A Glebe Point Rd, Glebe, NSW 2037 – agents for Exodus (UK).
● **Outdoor Travel** (☎ 03-9670 7252, fax 9670 3941) 382 Lt Bourke St, Melbourne, Vic 3000 – agents for Sherpa Expeditions (UK).
● **Peregrine Adventures** is a Nepal specialist with branches in **Melbourne** (☎ 03-9663 8611, fax 9663 8618, 2nd floor, 258 Lonsdale St, Melbourne, Vic 3000) and **Sydney** (☎ 02-9241 1128, 5th floor, 58 Pitt St, Sydney, NSW 2000) and offers a good range of treks.
● **Peregrine Travel** (08-223 5905) 192 Rundle St, Adelaide, SA 5000.
● **Summit Travel** (☎ 09-321 1259) 1st floor, 862 Hay St, Perth WA 6000.
● **World Expeditions** (☎ 02-9264 3366, ☎ 1-800 811 469, fax 9261 1974) 3rd floor, 441 Kent St, **Sydney** NSW 2000. Branches also in **Melbourne** (☎ 03-9670 8400, fax 03 9670 7474) 1st Floor, 393 Little Bourke St, Melbourne Victoria 3000 and **Brisbane** (☎ 07-3216 0823, fax 07-3216 0827), Shop 2, 36 Agnes St, Fortitude Valley, Queensland 4006. The main competition for Peregrine. As well as range of standard treks, some climbing expeditions are offered.

Trekking agencies in New Zealand
● **Adventure World** (☎ 09-524 5118, 0800-652 954, fax 520 6629) 101 Great South Rd, Remuera, PO Box 74008, Auckland – agents for Explore (UK).
● **Suntravel** (☎ 09-525 3074, fax 525 3065), 407 Great South Rd (PO Box 12-424), Penrose, Auckland – agents for World Expeditions (Australia).
● **Venture Treks** (☎ 09-379 9855, fax 770 320) PO Box 37610, 164 Parnell Rd, Auckland – agents for Sherpa Expeditions (UK).
● **Himalaya Trekking** (☎ 06 868 8595, treks@clear.net.nz), 54a Darwin Rd, Gisborne.

How long to go for

If time is the ultimate luxury then a trekking holiday should be a decadent one. The more time you have in the mountains the better. It takes a day or two to leave the road culture behind and to adjust to the trekking lifestyle and exercise.

If you only want to sample trekking rather than eat the whole pie, a week to ten days is a good length. Anything less is just a walk.

Time planning
Arriving in Nepal, it's best to allow a minimum of two whole days in Kathmandu (ie three nights). Don't under-estimate how long it takes to adjust to the different time zone and climate. If arranging a trek on arrival,

three or four full days are better. Note that government offices are closed on Saturday (but open Sunday) and there are numerous public holidays. Try to have at least one day in Kathmandu at the end of a trek in order to clean up and do last minute shopping. More time is all too easily filled by exploring the Kathmandu Valley.

For the trek itself allow a day or more than the quickest itineraries suggest. Getting to the starting point of a trek can take a day or just a couple of hours and buses do sometimes breakdown. Once on the trail, especially on a longer trek, allow a day or two for inclement weather or a gloriously lazy day for eating and reading. Although many people have never been hiking for more than four or five days at home (or indeed never been hiking at all) two weeks in the mountains of Nepal fly by all too quickly. Avoid the trap of planning a whole itinerary down to the last minute.

Allow four days to a week between treks if you're doing more than one. You'll need time to wash everything, organise yourself again and have a couple of lazy Kathmandu café days.

Route options

Since ancient times caravans have followed trade routes across many parts of Asia. The advent of motorised transport brought great changes but these developments passed Nepal by until the 1950s. The first road link, the Rajpath, between Kathmandu and India was opened only in 1956 but road construction is now a government priority (rail is impractical). With much of the countryside being not far off vertical, only the low-lying Terai and the Himalayan foothills have been penetrated but the roads are still very rough.

The rest of the country still relies on the footpaths and mountain trails that form an age-old surface transportation network across the country. So extensive is this network that it's easy to plan some weird and wonderful routes in wild and isolated areas. However, only a few major routes are suited to trekkers wanting to stay in lodges, but what routes some of them are!

Planning
Most people start planning with the intention of seeing Everest. Basically this entails going to the Khumbu region and up a hill to view the mountain. So the majority of trekkers fly to Lukla, trek to the top of Kala Pattar, then fly out of Lukla. This standard route is popular with reason but options are much broader. All routes to Everest pass through **Namche** (except a few tough options mentioned later) so first it's a question of getting there. If you plan to fly one way then flying out is best since the walk in gives helpful acclimatisation (the process of getting used to altitude, see p236). If flying in and out, flying in to Phaplu rather than Lukla is more sensible.

GETTING TO NAMCHE

The main options plus approximate time to walk to Namche are:

Bus to Jiri (1 day) then walking (6-9 days)

Flying to Lukla (2 days, plus 1 extra acclimatisation day)

Flying to Phaplu (4-6 days)

Flying to Syangboche (not recommended)

Bus to Hille (1 day) then walking (9-12 days)

Flying to Tumlingtar then walking (7-10 days)

From Jiri – the expedition route

Jiri, a day's journey by bus or taxi from Kathmandu, is the usual starting point for trekkers who prefer to walk in. This route is often called the expedition route because it follows the trek that the majority of expeditions took in, although when Everest was first climbed the trail began on the edge of the Kathmandu Valley.

This route (see p129) features numerous pleasant lodges and teahouses catering for trekkers. While during peak season the regions above Lukla are congested, the Jiri approach never feels crowded; most trekkers on this route are individuals rather than groups. It's surprisingly strenuous with the route crossing three large ridges but this is a rewarding walk that prepares you for the higher altitudes ahead.

❏ **TIMEFRAMES – KATHMANDU TO KATHMANDU**

Overall times required for a trek at normal pace with acclimatisation days and including buses and/or flights (counted as a day) are given below. Don't forget to allow an extra day or two so that you have the flexibility to cope with a delayed flight or a day of sickness. For sample itineraries see Appendix A.

Fly in and out of Lukla:
- **Quickest Everest view** (to Namche with a day trip there): 5-6 days
- **To Tengboche Gompa:** 7-9 days
- **Khumbu culture** (time around Thame, Namche, Tengboche): 10-12 days
- **Everest Base Camp** (actually Kala Pattar): 13-16 days
- **Gokyo Lakes:** 12-14 days
- **Explore the Khumbu** (Gokyo, Kala Pattar, Chukhung): 18-21 or more days
- **Attempt Island Peak** (or another peak close by): 18-21 days
- **Mera Peak:** 19-23 days

For flying in to Phaplu instead of Lukla add 4-6 days
Note if Syangboche exit flights are allowed again this will save a day.

Walking into the region
- **Expedition route** bus to Jiri, trek to Kala Pattar, fly from Lukla: 20-22 days
- **Exploring the Khumbu** Jiri, look up the main valleys the fly out of Lukla: 23-28 days
- **Expedition route plus walking out** via Salpa-Arun to Tumlingtar: 27-30 days

Sun Kosi rafting beginning: add 8-9 days
- Arun-Salpa fly to Tumlingtar, Kala Pattar and fly out from Lukla: 22-25 days
- **Tilman-Shipton route** Hille Salpa-Arun to Kala Pattar, fly from Lukla: 24-28 days

Flying to Lukla (2850m/9350ft)

This is the most popular starting point because it's only one and a half day's walk from Namche. However, the risk of altitude sickness is double that of alternative routes unless at least one extra acclimatisation day is scheduled. Trekkers in organised groups should particularly note this; see p224. In the past there were nightmarish flight-booking queues but the problem has now largely been alleviated with the introduction of private airlines. Most group treks begin and end here.

Flying to Phaplu (2350m/7710ft)

If you wish to fly, flying to Phaplu is an under-used route and yet the most sensible choice. It saves what some consider an arduous day on a bus (ie to Jiri) and a few days walking. Compared with flying to Lukla, it allows a safer and more gentle introduction to altitude and reveals a richer cultural variety with the added bonus of being able to visit Junbesi and Chiwang Gompa. The government has recognised the potential and introduced tourist priority flights but trekking companies have yet to adapt. Flying to Lukla saves that extra day or two, all-important in today's package trek market. See p193.

Flying to Syangboche (3700m/12,139ft)

There are no scheduled flights to Syangboche, the airstrip just above Namche. The runway here is too short for all domestic aircraft bar one. Instead it is used by charter and cargo helicopters. From 1994-1996 the airstrip was used for commercial helicopter flights. Now only cargo or small helicopter charters are allowed to use it.

Arriving directly at Namche, at 3450m or 11,319ft, is a dangerous altitude to fly to directly without previous acclimatisation.

The Salpa/Arun route from Hille/Basantpur or Tumlingtar

This route was used the first few expeditions into the Khumbu. Compared with the Jiri to Namche walk, the number and height of the hills on this route are similar but the overall distance is slightly greater. Route-finding is more challenging and many lodges are a half or full day's walk apart so it's better attempted by trekkers with some experience. It was, until 1992, a little-trekked route because of misleading information about lodges and trails. More recently a Makalu-Barun National Park project (see p114) has assisted locals in improving the lodges. See p195 for more details on the route.

Walking from Hille or Basantpur first involves a rough 24-hour bus ride from Kathmandu, then a short but hot two-day walk to Tumlingtar airport. If the on-again, off-again huge Arun III hydro scheme up-river is ever begun the road will be extended along the ridge above Tumlingtar, saving a day and a half's walking. Flying directly to Tumlingtar is cheap and relatively reliable and generally the better option. A variation on this route is to begin from Bhojpur (see p211). Few tourists come this way and the facilities are less than basic.

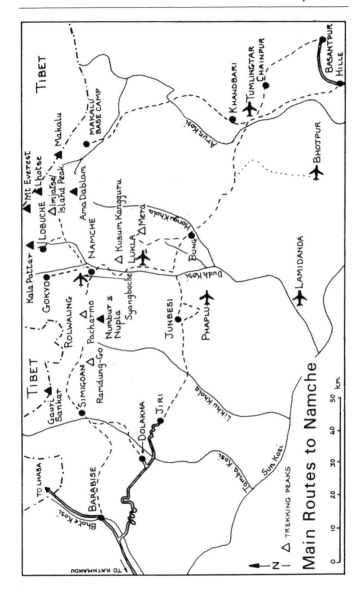

Main Routes to Namche

❏ **Salpa-Arun or Jiri?**

Previously the decision was easy to make: the Jiri route had superior facilities and the route is straightforward while the Salpa-Arun route had far more basic facilities and there was a high probability of getting lost. Now although the facilities from Jiri are still better, on the Salpa-Arun little hardship is required, though there is much less choice and the distances between some lodges are still relatively long. Getting lost is less likely now along the Salpa-Arun but it is still a slightly longer route and equally strenuous.

In all other ways each advantage is matched by a disadvantage. Culturally, the Arun has a greater variety but fewer people speak English so it is perhaps less accessible. Scenically, the Salpa-Arun has more variety, beginning in low country but this first stretch is always hot and sweaty. Taking the Salpa-Arun route in ties in perfectly with a Sun Kosi rafting expedition.

If the decision is still difficult, flip a coin or walk one in and the other out.

THE ROUTES ABOVE NAMCHE

Altitude sickness

The key to planning an itinerary above Namche is awareness of altitude sickness: going up too fast causes a medical condition serious enough to kill you. The higher the altitude, the less oxygen there is in the air. On the summit of Kala Pattar (5554m/18,222ft), for example, there is 50% less oxygen than at sea level. Your body needs several days to adapt to this phenomenon so for a safe trek it is absolutely essential that you allow sufficient time for acclimatisation.

The doctors at both the Khunde Hospital and the HRA Pheriche clinic stress that in virtually all of the cases they treat, the patient has ascended faster than the guidelines. In a surprising number of cases trekkers were forced to ascend too quickly by the itinerary set by the group. Sometimes this has been because a delayed flight in has meant they have had to cut a vital acclimatisation day. See p236 for more information.

The choices

There are four main valleys (see opposite), each spectacular and worthwhile exploring. The upper Bhote valley is closed to trekkers at present but a day or overnight trip from Namche to Thame, in the lower section, gives useful acclimatisation and is a good introduction to the Khumbu. The Gokyo Valley is particularly beautiful and offers incredible potential for exploration. The popular standard route to Lobuche and Kala Pattar is also spectacular and the Chukhung valley offers good exploring and climbing. There are also several high passes that can be crossed in between the major valley systems for a greater challenge.

The amount of time spent above Namche varies with your ambitions. To spot Everest from the top of Kala Pattar, or Gokyo Ri in the Gokyo Valley, a minimum of nine days must be allowed (Namche to Namche). This

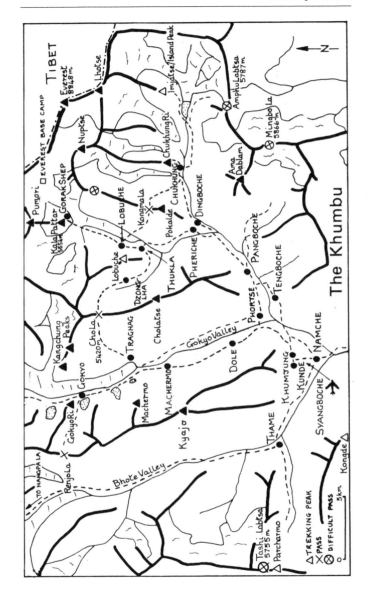

includes several consecutive nights spent at the same point while ascending, essential for adequate acclimatisation. Lovers of grand mountain scenery and explorers, however, could spend weeks wandering up the high valleys above Namche, only returning to hunt down a hot shower and Namche cuisine. In addition to incredible scenery wherever you trek, staying in quieter lodges and spending time with Sherpas and other local people is all part of a rewarding experience. It is this that separates trekking in Nepal from trekking in wilderness areas in Western countries.

Lobuche vs Gokyo

Years ago, heavy marketing for treks to Everest Base Camp excluded other less goal-orientated options. This is still reflected in the brochures of many trekking companies which barely mention a trek up Gokyo valley. It is, however, well worth considering but it makes choosing an itinerary limited by time difficult.

The pros and cons The views from Kala Pattar (near Lobuche and Everest Base Camp) are fantastic. Although only the upper part of Everest can be seen, spectacular sheer mountains and glaciers entirely surround you. For the fit, climbing another of Pumori's spurs offers more extensive views of Everest in similarly-inspiring terrain. Most people don't end up visiting Everest Base Camp since the trail there is rough and the only view is of the fearsome icefall.

From Gokyo Ri the mountains are just as spectacular but not so close with views extending into the distance. Close to Gokyo there's a more extensive view of Everest than from Kala Pattar or Gokyo Ri and it doesn't even require climbing a hill, but from there the other mountains are not as impressive so the overall effect is not as satisfying.

Trekking to Gokyo has the advantage of taking one day less and also the highest sleeping altitude is 4750m vs Lobuche's 4930m. If you plan to spend only a single day at one or the other, Lobuche is possibly the better option because the views are great from nearby Kala Pattar and the walk is perhaps more spectacular. If you have three or four extra days the options broaden. Having been to one of either Gokyo, Lobuche or Chukhung you should now be acclimatised sufficiently so that you no longer have to plan with this in mind. The distances in the Khumbu are not in fact very great with each valley only being a day or two apart. Deciding between visiting Chukhung en route to Lobuche or going to Lobuche first and then Gokyo, is such a difficult choice you might as well add a couple more days and visit all of them. Examples of itineraries are given on p223 and can be joined together to create even more interesting combinations.

Gokyo and Lobuche

If you plan to visit both, but not Chukhung, it may be slightly more sensible to visit Gokyo first since the maximum sleeping altitude there is slightly lower. Crossing the Tsho La (see below) between the valleys takes most people two days while walking around the bottom route via Phortse take two to three days. If you plan to visit Chukhung as well then beginning with Gokyo or Chukhung makes equal sense. Gokyo and Chukhung offer many days worth of side trips while Lobuche/Gorak Shep is more limiting.

Chugima La/Tsho La The Tsho La/Cho La (p186) is a tempting option when contemplating visiting both Gokyo and Lobuche valleys but the conditions must be good. This normally takes two days. The walk around via Phortse is less alpine but probably as rewarding while taking a day longer.

LEAVING THE REGION

Flying out
The majority of trekkers fly out of Lukla. Although the walk from Namche to Lobuche or Gokyo takes a week going up, the return trip takes most trekkers only two days, then one more to Lukla. It is no longer possible to fly out of Syangboche.

Walking in and out
The most obvious route is to walk from Jiri to the Khumbu, then exit via Tumlingtar or Hille/Basantpur. It is slightly better attempted in this direction because the Jiri route is a more gentle introduction to trekking. However, retracing your steps to Jiri is not a boring alternative; returning, the views are different and the seasons change the colours of the countryside. You'll get a warm welcome from lodges you return to, and being wiser to the ways of the land you'll probably find this part of the walk more rewarding than before.

OTHER OPTIONS

Other non-technical routes into the Khumbu
The standard routes (Jiri and the Arun) are the most logical and direct, reinforced by chains of lodges. However, walking from Barabise to Jiri is feasible, as is flying into Lamidanda, Okhaldhunga, Bhojpur (p211) or Taplejung, or trekking up from the Okhaldhunga road to the south. These alternatives are not on difficult or dangerous trails but they traverse hot low country and lack lodges, so they are better attempted after acquiring some Nepalese trekking experience.

Technical passes into the Khumbu
There are four challenging 5700m+/18,700ft+ passes that drop into the Khumbu and require mountaineering competence. The tough and dangerous **Tashi Labtsa** is at the head of the Rolwaling Valley and can be reached from Barabise or Dolakha. If you're trekking with a group, a climb of the trekking peak Ramdung-Go is usually included as acclimatisation and to ensure that you are capable of the crossing. The **Mingbo La** and **Amphu Labtsa** are technically difficult and isolated, and are generally only crossed in conjunction with climbing the trekking peak Mera (6476m/21,246ft) or crossing a

couple of 6100m/20,013ft passes from Makalu Base Camp. Generally it's better to visit the Khumbu first and acclimatise properly, then exit via one of the high passes. Read the detailed route descriptions on pages 190, 191 and 214 for 'scare' factors.

The **Nangpa La** (5716m/18,753ft) is the highest and one of the more arduous trading passes in the world. It links Tibet with the Khumbu but is closed to foreigners.

The high passes of the Khumbu and the trekking peaks are better attempted during the October to end of December season. Later the numbing cold and increasing snowfall make these already tough propositions highly dangerous or impossible.

Trekking peaks

These are dotted around the Khumbu, Rolwaling and Hinku areas, and present satisfying objectives. Their level of difficulty varies considerably but they are not all the exclusive domain of tough mountaineers. A couple are little more than a high altitude walk requiring an ice-axe and crampons plus

---

❏ Cultural treks

The Salpa-Arun and Solu-Khumbu regions are perfect areas for a culture-orientated trek. In many ways time is the most important factor. Taking a Sherpa guide and staying in lodges gives you an immediate introduction to a local house (ie their lodge). If the lodge isn't busy you can sit at the kitchen fire and chat with the owner. This is more easily accomplished off-season from Namche and above. Thame and the small settlements en route, Upper Pangboche and Phortse are less frequently visited villages. Below Lukla the main trails aren't heavily trekked and there are not many trekkers in the shoulder season, eg late September, December through March and mid-May to mid-June. You can get off the tourist-frequented routes by either taking an expedition crew, or, if you have the right guide, simply by staying in people's houses. But be warned the food will be simple, hygiene will be marginal at best, and there may be little privacy. Perhaps the best way to experience the culture is to briefly live it, eg help with the harvest.

There are some loops that take you off the main trekking routes. For a sample of **Rai culture** consider staying in Bung or Gudel for at least several days and visit a few of the villages nearby, eg Cheskam. There is a route south of the main trekking route, via Somtang, to or from Phaplu.

Phaplu and the surrounding region is barely visited by trekkers. There are several interesting old and new gompas and Salleri is the district headquarters, the real Nepal, although half modern. Chialsa is a **Tibetan enclave**, as is Thubten Choeling, north of Junbesi. Trekking up from Okaldunga to Phaplu would be an experience. Around Bhojpur, Dingla, Tumlingtar, Khadbari and Chainpur is a mainly Hindu region. Trekking to the Rolwaling Valley is rewarding and it is possible to exit via a different route. You will have to camp a few nights but the hardy could mostly stay in local lodges and people's houses.

For all the ideals involved in taking a cultural trek, it is difficult to really experience or get deeply into the culture especially without speaking the language. It helps to read as much background information as possible, particularly anthropological papers. Few guides, however, are adept at explaining their culture.

rope for the snow fields. See the individual descriptions beginning on p226. For competent alpinists and serious mountaineers there is endless potential limited only by the government regulations.

Alternative treks

The psychological omnipotence of Everest is so great that few people contemplate trekking in this region without the aim of seeing it from close quarters. However, apart from the star attraction there are other areas that offer fantastic trekking amid stunning mountains. These all require a degree of self-sufficiency and camping out. Many would be particularly suited to the classic style of Nepal trekking – a crew to carry the excess, and a few Sherpa companions to round the experience. Going without local support is for the tough and experienced and even so a porter for some sections would be invaluable. The best suggestions are:

● **Exploring above Junbesi**, to Dudh Kund (Milk Lake) below the holy mountain of Numbur and in the Lumding Kharka area, below Kongde and Nupla. This could be combined with the trek to Namche.

● **South of the Rolwaling valley** hides untold exciting possibilities – high kharkas and ridges littered with mountains a touch under 6000m/19,685ft. Several circuits are possible over unused passes.

● **The Hinku and Hongu valleys** offer challenging and remote treks amongst mind-blowing mountains. A circuit including Mera would be attractive.

The Barun and Makalu region

This is an isolated area with only a fraction of it used for grazing and expedition access to Makalu. Otherwise it's impenetrable forest topped by savage mountains. A trek to **Makalu Base Camp** is the only feasible option; a description of this route was included in earlier editions of this guide but can now be found on the Internet at: www.webfoot.co.nz/nep al-treks/.

❏ OTHER ACTIVITIES

Nepal now offers a lot more than just trekking. Unless your schedule is tight, these activities don't need to be planned in advance, just remember to allow some extra time.

Chitwan National Park wildlife safari (3-4 days)

Fancy shaking trunks with an elephant or sipping exotic cocktails under a crimson sunset? How about wildlife spotting by dugout canoe and elephant-back or watching rhinos forage in the savannah from the breakfast table? Royal Chitwan National Park is one of Asia's premier game parks, a mix of jungle, grasslands and river plains teeming with wildlife, including the endangered **royal Bengal tiger**, the rare **Gangetic dolphin** and the much more common **one-horned rhino**. Safari Asian style is quite different from Africa. The game, although abundant, is often more elusive. Also it is better hidden in the long elephant grass and jungle undergrowth, hence the advantage of spotting by elephant-back, from canoes and from *machans* (hides or blinds). However, you'll see lots of game and there's a special thrill finding it in its natural environment. (Continued on p30).

Chitwan National Park (cont)

There are two ways of enjoying Chitwan: staying inside the park or outside. Sauraha, the travellers' haunt outside the park, is the cheaper but less satisfactory alternative: the elephant ride to go rhino spotting is short so most game spotting is done on foot (and by climbing trees if a rhino charges) or by jeep. And in the cosmopolitan village, you miss the absolute serenity of the morning and evening jungle. Inside the park, the wildlife resorts (packages from US$140) provide a secluded, peaceful, relaxing and comfortable place to stay. The activities are well-planned and the service is superb. Each has its own fleet of dugout canoes, jeeps and elephants who are handled by guides who know the wildlife's habits and who can usually spot the game long before you do. The resorts make the Chitwan Experience a brilliant way to begin or end a holiday in Nepal. If you're around in early December, Tiger Tops (fax +97-1-414075, email tiger@mtn.m os.com.np) hosts an annual **elephant polo tournament**.

Bardia National Park (4-8 days)

Lost in Nepal's Wild West, Bardia is almost undiscovered compared to Chitwan, only because it is either inconvenient or expensive to access. Here four or five-day safaris penetrating well into the park are better. Access is from Nepalganj, a US$99 flight (one way) or a gruelling 14-18 hour night bus journey. From Pokhara, flights cost US$60 and the bus journey is the same length.

Other more remote parks are **Kaptada National Park**, a middle altitude forest plateau which can only be trekked into (seven to 14 days total) and the **Royal Suklaphanta Wildlife Reserve** which is close to Mahendranagar. The reserve is a grassland area with the occasional tiger and wild elephant, and is rich in rare swamp deer. It's a gruelling 30 hours by bus or US$142 flight from Kathmandu.

Rafting (2-12 days)

While Nepal is famous for its mountains it should also be world-famous for its white water. Huge mountains mean big, steep rivers which are perfect for rafting and kayaking. For thrill-seekers no trip to Nepal would be complete without a white water expedition. Believe it or not, almost every trek in Nepal could be rounded off with a rafting expedition. Costs are US$15-65 per day.

For a cheap and gentle introduction try the Trisuli. Almost every rafting company run trips on this river (two to four days) for most of the year. If you know you will enjoy the thrills and spills go straight for a river with a higher scare factor. The Bhote Kosi (two days) and the Marsyangdi (five days) are steep, technical and fun. For the ultimate experience, try the massive waters of the Karnali (eight to nine days plus three travelling) and the Sun Kosi (eight to nine days plus two travelling), which have rapids that will make even the coolest cucumber gulp in disbelief. Another world-class river is the exhilarating Tamur (Kanchenjunga region) with its magic trek in and 130 rapids in 120km. For a shade off full throttle consider the cultural Kali Gandaki (five days, out of Pokhara). There's also kayaking: Kayak Clinics come highly recommended – just ensure the instructors are qualified.The high water season, for those with no fear, is late September-early October and May. Trips run into November then begin again in March and taper off by late May. Wherever you go, safety should be paramount. Take a look at Peter Knowles' *Rafting: a consumers' guide*, available in Kathmandu. There are only three Thamel companies to run big rivers with; **Ultimate Descents**, **Equator Expeditions** and **Himalayan Encounters**. For more information on all the rivers of Nepal see Knowles & Allardice's excellent *White Water Nepal*.

Mountain biking (1-4 days)

The hills around the Kathmandu valley have many roads. Most of these should be called four-wheel drive tracks, though for some even this title is fanciful. However they are perfect for mountain biking. Trips can be organised through **Himalayan Mountain Bikes** or **Dawn till Dusk** in Thamel. A minimum of two, sometimes four people is required.

Biking/motor-biking around the valley

Cycling used to be the most pleasant way to see Kathmandu but now with the dust and pollution few people cycle there for pleasure. However, once outside the city limits it's a different story; see a detailed map of the valley for ideas. Clunky Indian mountain bikes (better kept on tarmacked roads) cost US$2-4 a day while motorbikes go for around US$10 a day plus petrol.

Mountain flight

If you've just got to see Everest but don't like the idea of the high altitude trek, take a breathtaking close-up of the Khumbu from a mountain flight (US$99). During the autumn peak season highly rated mountain flights around the Annapurna Circuit also operate out of Pokhara. Taking any other domestic flight is, if the weather's perfect, also spectacular.

Balloon flight

The latest adventure activity to lift off in Nepal is hot air ballooning (US$195). Piloted by a colourful Australian, the hour or so flight is exhilarating, peaceful and somewhat random; you land where the gods have taken you.

Pokhara

Beside a lake gazing up at the huge Annapurna range, the delight of Pokhara is that there's nothing to do besides enjoying the cafés. It is also a good base to begin or end Annapurna treks and ties in well with trips to Chitwan National Park and rafting the Trisuli, Seti and Kali Gandaki.

Visiting Tibet

If you already have a Chinese visa, you can usually cross the border as an individual. On the other side, since there are (officially) no buses, you often have to hire a landcruiser (minimum US$60 per person) to Shigatse. This also gets around random permit problems. The easier and quicker way is to book one of the eight-day fixed departure tours in Kathmandu. These drive to (or from) Lhasa stopping at most points of interest along the way. The budget versions cost US$480-600, including the US$190 flight back, with departures Saturdays and Wednesdays. They run from March through to mid-November. There are four or five operators in Thamel with little to distinguish them. Most trekking and travel companies organise through them too.

Visiting Bhutan

The Land of the Thunder-dragon is a particularly rewarding destination. The friendliness of the people and the smooth organisation come at a price; around US$200 a day whether trekking or travelling. Visits take time to arrange; a minimum of two weeks but starting at least three months in advance is better.

A second trek?

Trekking can be addictive! Around 20% of trekkers do it again in the same holiday. Trekkers also have one of the highest tourism return rates in the world; an amazing number of people just keep coming back year after year.

Budgeting

The price of material progress is too often to replace a smile with a worried frown, the god being money instead of inner peace **Tom Weir**

Nepal is undoubtedly one of the cheapest countries to travel around. It's possible to survive on US$5/£3.50 a day but for under US$15/£10 a day you can live really quite comfortably. There's also a tempting array of services and souvenirs to mop up any excess funds.

COSTS IN KATHMANDU

Your choice of hotel will largely determine the amount spent on basics. A spartan double room with communal bathroom facilities goes for US$2-5/£1.30-3.50 a night, and with attached bathroom US$5-10/£3.50-7. A pleasant 1 or 2 star room is about US$20/£13. The 4-5 star hotels are not quite to international standards but at around US$110/£70 a night neither are their prices.

Food is of a more uniform price. If you avoid the ten most expensive restaurants, meals are US$1-5/£0.60-3.50, so US$5-8/£3.50-5.30 a day is plenty. What you spend on drinks depends on your poison: large bottles of beer and double nips of cheap spirits are around US$1.50-2/£1-1.30 while soft drinks cost less than US$0.50/£0.30.

For a budget traveller, around US$100/£65 a week is adequate for cheap hotels, good food, sightseeing, visa extensions/trekking permits, and other necessities such as chocolate, bicycle hire, newspapers and a quick call home. It is the avoidable one-off expenses, such as flights, rafting trips and quality souvenirs that will have a large impact on your budget plans. With much less than US$100/£65 per week careful budgeting is required.

THE TREKKING BUDGET

Independent trekkers

Once it was difficult to spend even US$5 a day but there are now double rooms and extensive menus in lodges, tempting trekkers to spend more. Around US$10/£6 a day per person gives you good food and accommodation, plus a few treats. Lodges charge under US$1/£0.70 for dormitory accommodation while doubles go for US$1-4/£0.70-2.60, and main courses

---

(**Opposite**) A smiling welcome is assured from most lodge-owners.

are around US$1-2.50/£0.70-1.75. Chocolate, beer and Coke are not so cheap but even with an excess of these luxuries spending more than US$15/£10 daily would be a challenge. At the tight end it is still possible to trek in relative comfort on US$6/£4 a day on the trail.

There are, however, other things than day-to-day survival to allow money for: extra films, souvenirs and, most importantly, emergency situations. Many trekkers visit the doctors at Khunde or the HRA post and the doctors report that often budget trekkers don't have enough cash on them. If you twist an ankle you may need to hire a porter to carry your pack. In an extreme situation emergency evacuation could be required.

It's best to take perhaps US$100-200/£70-130 more than your budget. You will most likely spend this in Kathmandu upon your return; if heading to India it can easily be converted to Indian rupees. To take advantage of the leftover mountaineering gear sold in Namche you'll need lots of rupees, and sometimes dollars.

If you're planning to organise a guided trek on arrival in Nepal or to hire a porter see p88 for the costs.

Commercial treks

With all the money paid up front it's simply a case of following company guidelines and allowing for the few extras. While trekking there are no expenses bar the odd bottle of beer and tips for the crew so just allow for souvenirs, extra film and bars of chocolate.

Currency

US, Canadian, Australian, Hong Kong and Singapore dollars are accepted, plus all the main European currencies, cash and travellers cheques (any major brand although only American Express has an office in Kathmandu). Major credit cards are accepted by star-class hotels, in some shops and for cash advances at a few banks. Eurocheques and Post Giros are not accepted. As in the rest of Asia some US$ cash is handy.

Nepal's once thriving black market is slowly being eroded by more realistic exchange rates and currency regulations, and by banks opening exchange counters where tourists need them. There are, however, still plenty of touts who will take you into a shop and exchange dollars for rupees at marginally more favourable rates. You should, however, be aware that exchanging money on the black market does nothing to help the country's balance of payments.

For rates of exchange see p65.

(Opposite)   Top: Most of the larger lodges now have energy-efficient stoves which incorporate a hot water system. **Bottom:** Whether you're taking off or landing at Lukla airstrip (see p147) the experience is always exhilarating.

When to go

Trekking the standard routes in the Khumbu is possible and can be pleasant at almost any time of the year; just tailor your route and your expectations to the prevailing seasonal conditions. However, for climbing and crossing high passes the classic trekking time (October to December) is best, followed by April to early June a distant second. Some years winter falls of snow can be surprisingly light and, providing you can cope with the numbing cold, exploring and climbing is possible. Other years a heavy fall in October, November, March or April all but stops climbing and closes passes until the fall partially clears. During the depths of winter and the monsoon some areas are all but inaccessible and finding willing crew is difficult because of the greater risk involved.

The post-monsoon season (October and November edging into December) offers the clearest weather and stunning views but since it's also the busiest time many lodges are full. The winter perils are of an elemental kind – cold and the occasional snow fall at altitude but for the well-prepared, trekking is still rewarding. Winter thaws to the spring reawakening: the flowers bloom, leaves sprout and the rhododendrons blossom for the March to May trekking season. During this increasingly warm period the afternoons are hazy unless there's been a shower of rain to clear it away. By the end of May and into June it's hot and the approaching monsoon occasionally rattles its sabre. When this does arrive, in the middle of June or the beginning of July, everything flourishes under the life-giving rain. Except at high altitudes, leeches abound and coupled with the humidity are enough to put off all but the most determined trekkers.

SEASONAL CONDITIONS
One constant is the lack of wind. Although Everest expeditions are frequently hampered by high wind, in the trekking regions anything more than a stiff breeze is rare. As the morning sun strengthens, thermal currents waft up but the evenings are often so still that outside a candle will stay lit. On Kala Pattar, high passes and trekking peaks the wind sometimes whistles, but is often more noisy than blustery.

Early Autumn (mid-September to mid-October)
The monsoon has dwindled but a few tail-end clouds and showers (or short-lived snow at altitude) must be expected. Locals and trekkers simply take cover in the nearest teahouse and wait the afternoon shower out. There's also a chance that the monsoon may not quite have ended, staging a dramatic return for a few weeks. The Jiri to Namche section is either hot and sweaty

under the fierce sun or cloudy, while higher up it's pleasant with cool but mostly frost-free nights. If you skip the lower country, this is a particularly pleasant and under-trekked season. The whole country is lush, a verdant green at this time.

The approach of winter (mid-October to Christmas)
This is classic trekking time, famed for clear skies and fantastic fine weather. Early October through to late November is also the busiest period with most lodges and camp sites brimming with trekkers.

The long fine periods are occasionally broken for day or two by a front sweeping overhead causing high cloud or cloud banks that roll up the valleys, then usually clear at altitude with the sunset. The odd stronger front brings a spot of wet weather as well but it is impossible to tell (even the locals can't) whether a front contains rain. Barring unusual conditions during this trekking season perhaps two or three periods of showers and drizzle, or short-lived snow at altitude, can be expected.

Tengboche begins receiving frosts in October and by November at altitude evenings are chilly. During a cold clear snap in the up-valley lodges (Lobuche, Gokyo and Chukhung) a water bottle beside your bed will partially freeze overnight and the lakes above 5000m/16,404ft begin to freeze. Shorts can still be worn above Namche on windless days by the determined; but light pants feel more comfortable. December is probably one of the most pleasant months for trekking because statistically it is the driest month of the year and the vast majority of trekkers have already headed down. The shorter winter days are cooler but on the walk in you'll still sweat on the hills. Above Namche it is cold but a thick down jacket, good sleeping bag and lots of hot drinks can ward the cold off effectively.

Winter (January through March)
New Year usually brings a week or so of disturbed weather and frequently this is the snowfall that puts a stop to the easy pass-hopping and climbing or at least brings more challenging conditions. This almost regular fall is followed by more winter storms breaking the fine periods. Two closely spaced storms can lead to snow drifts above Namche. A bad year will see the high lodges snowed in for a few days and a sudden rush on plastic boot rentals in Namche. The shaded snow has no chance of melting while the rest of the snow patchily clears over a week or two. In other years there'll be only light falls that burn off quickly in the sunny spots. Air temperatures stay around 0°C/32°F during the warmer days, and nights are all below 0°C/32°F and can even hit -30°C/-22°F at 5000m/16,404ft. All the high altitude lakes sport ice thick enough to skate on and many (for example Gokyo lake) will not thaw until May. Early March has a reputation among the Sherpas as being colder than December, and with snow lying around, trekking is more challenging. Below Namche, down to an altitude of about 2600m/8530ft, periodic snow falls and ice can occasionally be expected. Flights to Lukla are sometimes disrupted by snow during January and February but only for a day or so.

Early summer (April to early June)

The second trekking season commences at the end of March and continues into May with the atmosphere becoming increasingly hazy. The fine periods will be broken by lots of cloud rolling up the valleys during the afternoon, often bringing drizzle that clears during the evening. On the trekking peaks and above this is a pattern of daily light powder snow that shortens the useable part of the day. Also, a torrential pre-monsoon downpour is possible though rare. The temperatures warm up considerably and by the end of April it's hot at low altitudes and sometimes on the warm side higher up. The rain, sun and warmth spark a flourish of growth with rhododendrons painting the hillsides, beginning in late February at lower altitudes and blooming ever higher during March and April.

In May the middle hills are sweltering although if you start walking early, rest in the heat of the day and sometimes walk in the late afternoon you can minimise the discomfort. The low altitude haze and occasional cloud reduces the strength of the sun, however. In the high country, May into early June is an under-utilised trekking time. While the weather may be less stable than November-December, the warmth, lushness and the comparative lack of other walkers mean it is still great trekking.

The monsoon – (late June to early October)

The monsoon usually hits the eastern Himalaya around mid-June, although very occasionally it be as much as a month early or late. Below 3000m/9843ft it's oppressive, muddy and leeches abound but flights still operate (on an irregular schedule: planes may not be able to get to Lukla for as many as 15 days in a row) so it's possible to avoid the worst areas. There are frequent showers, mainly in the afternoon and at night, and occasional heavy deluges, especially in July. Everybody dives under the nearest shelter to drink tea and wait it out. Infrequently these cloudbursts create dangerous flash-floods and mud slides which can put paid to the day's walking.

Above Namche the days are warm and the nights are frost-free although short-lived snow can fall on Kala Pattar and even down as far as Chukhung. Rainfall is uneven with the southernmost mountains bearing the brunt; this is the reason the glaciers on Numbur and in the Hongu/Hinku are so big. Above Namche is a partial rain-shadow area and consequently in the higher reaches of the main valleys the rain is reduced to occasional showers and drizzle. The rain pattern is not regular; it might be misty and rain every afternoon for a week, then clear for a couple of days. Slippery trails can be a problem, particularly for porters. The monsoon always eventually manages to find its way into tents; better to stick to teahouse trekking.

Overall, the almost perpetual cloud cover is more of an annoyance than the drizzle. The views are stunning when they clear but you often wait days for this to happen; although Kala Pattar does clear more frequently. The rewards of this season are lush green valleys carpeted by small flowers, although this is also true of late May and early June. If you're the kind of person who likes wandering, rather than trekking to a schedule, it's a wonderful time to observe the other way of life of the Sherpas, the monsoon cycle of agriculture.

By September the monsoon is in retreat. Usually the rains stop around mid-September but they sometimes cease as early as the beginning of the month or as late as early October. Although the monsoon conditions in the Bay of Bengal may have finished, the unsettled pattern of cloud and periodic drizzle usually continues into early October.

Every few years during October (although this has occurred as late as early December) the remnants of a Bay of Bengal hurricane unload in a torrential downpour lasting a day or two. At altitude this falls as deep snow that generally clears rapidly.

Climatic statistics for Tengboche (3867m/12,687ft)

In October an average night minimum of -4°C/24°F and an average day maximum of 10°C/50°F can be expected.

For January the average night minimum is -9°C/16°F and the average day maximum is 4°C/39°F.

Average monthly rainfall for Tengboche is as follows:

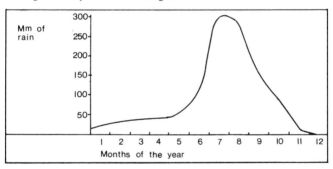

THE KATHMANDU CLIMATE

At the moderate altitude of 1400m/4600ft, the capital's climate is quite mild. The monsoon showers keep the temperature down to the high 20s°C/80s°F during summer, although it's quite humid and uncomfortable if it does not rain.

By the end of September the tropical temperatures cool and by late October the evenings are a little cold for just a shirt. The early winter days are sunny and agreeable, the evenings require a thick jacket and there's the occasional frost. From Christmas onwards a morning fog often settles on the valley making rising early a challenge. This also disrupts flights but by 10 or 11am schedules are back to normal.

Visiting Kathmandu is pleasant during any of the seasons although spring and autumn are the most popular, and crowded, times.

What to take

FACTORS AFFECTING EQUIPMENT SELECTION

If you plan to stay only in lodges then camping equipment (tent, foam pad, stove, food, cutlery, plate and mug) is not needed. For the trek in (if you are not flying), regardless of the season, you'll want mainly cool loose clothes for the warm days. Above Namche the days are cooler and a set of inter-changeable warm/windproof layers is best. These layers will also do for sitting around in the high lodges from late April to October but at other times a thick down jacket for cold mountain tops and fridge-like lodges is essential. An important key to staying healthy is sleeping well and warmly so that your body doesn't waste energy trying to keep you warm. Don't skimp on your sleeping bag.

During the main trekking season, October to December, it is nearly always dry so you need one set of clothes, ie only what you can wear at once (plus an extra shirt and a change of underwear). During late winter into April clothing may get wet so an extra thermal or light fleece might be appreciated.

All this can add up to a lot of equipment and since you (or a porter) must carry it all consider carefully how to keep it to a minimum. On domestic fixed-wing flights a strict 15kg limit is enforced; on helicopters the allowance is 20kg with modest charges for extra baggage.

> ❏ **The bare necessities**
> What to take is simply a question of what is essential. I met some Tibetans travelling without yaks over the 5716m/18,735ft Nangpa La. We looked at each others' lunches (my biscuits and their *tsampa*) and then compared rucksacks: my fancy expedition-sized pack versus their grubby day-packs. One Tibetan unpacked the rest of his bag to show me what the essentials were: gloves, an extra pair of socks and shoes (Chinese shoes are not known for durability), a jersey and grass (for starting yak dung fires). After lunch into the bag went a 2kg sack of tsampa, a stomach of butter, a brick of tea, spoon, cup and the ancient teapot, and on top went the all-too-thin bedding roll. A hat was already on his head and his jacket pockets held a knife and lighter. They laughed as I shouldered my 20kg backpack and followed them.
>
> Assuming you will be staying entirely in lodges, confident trekkers can get away with very little equipment. **For Sept-Oct and May-June**: 50 litre backpack, T-shirt, thermal top for evening wear, light down jacket (or a thick thermal plus fleece top), rain jacket, mid-weight longjohns, light trekking pants.
> **For Nov to May**: 60 litre backpack, 2 thermal tops (one for walking, one for the evening), down jacket (thicker is better), good breathable rain jacket (gore-tex or similar), thick longjohns, light trekking pants, optional snow gaiters.

The layering principle

If you wear a number of thinner layers of clothing you can simply shed a layer if you get hot or add a layer if the temperature drops. In spite of the fact that this keeps your clothing dry (more comfortable and much warmer than if wet) you still see many people wearing a fleece jacket and dripping with sweat during the day. Of course the layer next to your skin will probably get wet with sweat so you should carry an extra T-shirt. When you stop, change the wet top for a dry one and then put an extra layer or two on to keep warm. This is a good principle for walking during the day but cold Himalayan nights require another. Forget the layers and simply put on dry thermals and the thickest down jacket you can find. Down is comfortable over a large range of temperatures, so even during a mild evening, thick jackets are still functional.

What to sleep in when it's cold

Surprisingly, if you put on all your clothes to go to bed you feel constricted and not a lot warmer. Using a sleeping sheet and thermal underwear is better and if that's not enough put your down jacket over your sleeping-bag. Alternatively, wear the down jacket but with only a T-shirt or thermal top on underneath. What keeps you warm is trapped air not the materials themselves. Pull the draw-cords tight and ensure your head is well insulated.

Foot care

Your feet will be doing far more work than they're probably used to so take great care of them. The rest of your body has the luxury of changes of clothes but your feet are confined to a single pair of boots that must cope with the extremes of heat and cold. So air them, and your socks and boots, frequently – lunch in the sun is an ideal time. Consider changing your socks more than once during the day and wash your feet and socks, if nothing else, at least every few days. If you feel a hot spot or a blister developing, you should stop immediately and cover it with tape before it's too late to prevent damage.

EQUIPMENT LIST

● **Sleeping-bag** – essential. A down bag is lighter and more compact than a synthetic one of the same warmth. From late April to the end of October a three season bag (700g of good down) is adequate. For the cold months, November to March, take particular care to choose a warm four season bag (900g+ of high quality down). When buying a down bag look for good and even thickness; the down should be fluffy and light. A muff around the top of the bag makes a big difference to overall warmth.

In Kathmandu you can easily rent ordinary sleeping-bags and there are also a few good down bags. Trekking companies often provide bags but if you already have a good one it's worth taking it instead. There are also fleece liners for approximately US$15 that can boost a tired bag's warmth.

● **Sleeping-bag liner** (cotton or silk). Saves washing your sleeping-bag, adds warmth and can double as a towel. In Kathmandu, these can be easily and cheaply made up from light cotton. Light-weight silk is harder to find and the more easily available imitation silk is not as good.

● **Rucksack/backpack** It's important to have a comfortable one. The feature that will help most in this respect is a good waist band – it should fit snugly without riding up your stomach (which interferes with breathing). At the same time it must not sit too low and touch your walking muscles. Small backpacks are neat and look trendy but are not really big enough. For winter, a larger pack is preferable since gear does not have to be tightly compressed and this makes packing easier. Group trekkers will need only a day pack but once you put a down jacket, wind pants, camera and water bottle in, plus more odds and ends, you need a big one, 30 litres or slightly more and a proper waist band will make it far more comfortable.

● **Boots** One of the most important things for ensuring a happy trek is having comfortable feet. Carrying a backpack places a greater load on your feet than normal so rigid supportive boots will feel more comfortable in the long run. It's possible to trek in running shoes but the new generation light-weight trekking boots are far superior. Trekkers seem to get away with these boots even in winter but this can be dangerous during a snowfall. Sturdy but fairly light all-leather boots are better for cold weather (although they must be treated with waterproofing agents between January and the end of the monsoon).

When choosing boots look for good ankle support, plenty of toe room (essential for the long descents), a stiff sole (helps prevent tired feet by lessening twisting), and the boots should not be too heavy. Check the inner lining – leather is good and Cambrelle (which can destroy the bacteria that cause foot odour) is even better. Light-weight trekking boots generally have good shock-absorbing qualities but some foams can actually be crushed if too heavily loaded. Leather boots, even with Sorbothane heel inserts, transmit shock via the outer edges so some extra shock-absorbing insoles are a good idea and will leave your feet feeling less tired at the end of the day. The Spenco range is best but sometimes hard to find. Boots must be worn in before trekking and this should include some steep hills.

For independent trekkers weight and space are of prime importance so a single pair of comfortable boots is generally enough. If trekking with a group, another pair of shoes for relaxing around camp can be useful. In cold weather down bootees are an option worth considering.

● **Socks** Most of the time your feet will be warm or even hot while walking so quality cotton mix sports socks are fine. Three to four pairs are enough. It's during some evenings and a few cold days that you will need good warm socks. Light-weight trekking boots generally fit snugly so wearing two pairs of socks at the same time (originally used in stiff boots to prevent blisters) is not practical. Instead a single pair of thick high quality socks is quite adequate, with an extra pair in reserve.

● **Down jacket** This is essential during the cold months. Find one of bumwarming and hand-warming length, big and thick with a hood. If trekking during the warmer months you will not need it until above Namche and even then a hat and a jersey or fleece combined with a rain jacket may well be adequate.

● **Down pants/trousers** – a luxury that may be appreciated above Namche from December to March by group trekkers who are camping.

● **Wind/rain jacket** – essential. High up, if the sun is shining, it can be wonderfully warm. When a breeze picks up the true air temperature becomes apparent and wind protection is a necessity. Since it rarely rains all day – or even at all in peak season – having an expensive, totally waterproof jacket is not necessary. When it starts raining everybody simply takes cover in the nearest shelter. Plastic ponchos are only of use during the monsoon.

● **Jersey/Fleece top/Polarplus top** Opinions vary – when it's cold people with down jackets consider down essential, but those with only fleece say it's adequate. Fleece is no substitute for a down jacket in real winter, however. From May to October, the wet times, fleece is a better choice. Kathmandu is a great place for buying luxuriously thick wool jerseys but they are very heavy to take trekking.

● **Shirt/blouse** T-shirts are popular but thin long-sleeved cotton shirts/blouses are more versatile: the collar protects the back of your neck and the sleeves can be rolled up or down. Take two so that you have a dry one to change into after trekking.

● **Underwear** Along the trail into Namche washing every day or two is never a problem. Higher up, when it is cold, the inclination to change your underwear and wash may occur less frequently. Four to five pairs is plenty. (When

---

❑ **Don't under-estimate the cold**
Above 4000m it is cold year-round but from November through to April it is *very cold*. While many Canadians, Americans and Scandinavians understand the cold, most Brits, Kiwis and Ozzies will rarely have experience of such low temperatures. High altitude winter temperatures are as cold as or colder than your freezer at home (which is normally set at minus 18°C). There is another factor that conspires to cool you: the lack of oxygen. For it is largely oxygen in the blood that keeps fingers and toes warm: when bottled oxygen was first tested on Everest in the 1920's the first effect noticed was that everyone felt warmer. The trick at altitude is to carefully manage and regulate your body temperature. If possible avoid getting sweaty and damp and the moment you start cooling down add some layers. At the end of the day, when your energy reserves are low is the most critical time: having a snack, or at least a hot drink helps. It is far easier to stay warm than get cold and try to warm up again.

Ranulph Fiennes and Mike Stroud crossed Antarctica they took only one pair each for over 100 days!) If you frequently wear a sports bra bring two, otherwise what you normally wear is fine.

● **Thermal underwear** Longjohns and a top are essential unless substituted by fleece for the warmer times, and in winter thermals should be used with fleece. Mid-weight or expedition thickness is best.

● **Pants/trousers** Light material, loose and dark-coloured is best. These are easily bought in Kathmandu. Cotton/polyester travel pants or rock-climbing baggies in nylon or cotton/nylon mixes are best. Jeans are not practical; they are restricting and cold when damp.

● **Fleece pants/trousers** During the warm seasons these are good to have but not really needed since longjohns with walking pants/trousers over the top will do. In winter they are essential.

● **Windproof/waterproof pants/trousers** If your trekking pants are partly windproof an additional pair isn't needed. They may, however, be useful during winter.

● **Warm hat** This is essential.

● **Sun hat** You need something to protect your head in hot sunny weather, particularly from April to the end of October.

● **Mittens/Gloves** – essential except during the monsoon. The hand-knitted gloves available in Kathmandu are fine. If you already have ski gloves these will do. In very cold conditions a pair of thin liner gloves is invaluable.

❏ **Dress standards**

These vary considerably around the country. Kathmandu is the most liberal and culturally diverse place though Western women will find dressing modestly attracts far less attention. The well-off (locals and foreigners) are expected to dress conservatively, casual but clean. Along the regular trekking routes the Nepalese are used to (though have never understood) the comparatively odd and occasionally indecent ways in which Westerners dress, but in less frequented areas locals may still be quite shocked. Even with the Khumbu Sherpas' familiarity with foreigners, you will rarely see more than their head and forearms. Being dressed in a culturally acceptable way gains you much greater respect among the local people, a fact that many trekkers have commented upon.

For men, shorts are more or less acceptable although often you will be looked upon in a strange way because the only Nepalese who wear shorts are the porters (for the caste conscious, a low caste). T-shirts are OK, but singlets, running shorts or cycle pants, despite the fact that some porter-guides wear them, are going too far; bare chests are rude.

For women double standards exist. Long baggy shorts are worn although a skirt that falls at least to the knee, or light baggy trousers, are definitely more appropriate. A T-shirt is the minimum for modesty but Lycra pants invite unwarranted attention.

● **Gaiters** Leggings that protect from the ankle to the knee are useful in Nepal only when it has snowed heavily. On the main trails, after a large fall of snow a path is cleared quickly so if you can wait you can survive without gaiters. Off the main trails or when climbing, they are essential.

● **Towel** Doesn't need to be big. Quick-drying sarongs are the best. A T-shirt makes a reasonable substitute (and gives it a little wash into the bargain).

● **Bathing suit** – only useful while walking along the Arun, where the water is less than glacial in temperature.

● **Insulating pad** – not needed unless you plan to spend a night or two outside.

● **Water bottle** A one-litre water bottle is essential and should be leakproof, tough and able to withstand boiling water.

● **'Green tea'** (pee) bottle The effects of altitude test even the largest of bladders. Particularly in winter, when staying in double rooms, this luxury will be appreciated!

● **Sun screen** – essential. The ultra-violet (UV) concentration increases around 4% for every 300m gain in altitude and snow reflects 75% of UV. Apply frequently and extensively at higher altitudes even on cloudy days.

● **Sunglasses** These are essential and must be able to protect against UV. For prolonged high altitude sojourns side pieces are useful but ski goggles are not. If you wear prescription glasses it's best to get a pair of prescription sunglasses made. Alternatively detachable dark lens have proved adequate.

Contact lens wearers report problems with grit and pollution in Kathmandu but few problems in the hills except cleaning them in cold conditions. To prevent the cleaning solution from freezing it's best kept in your sleeping-bag on very cold nights. Also bring your glasses.

● **Torch/flashlight** – essential. A quality torch is invariably better, as are Western-quality batteries. Head torches are particularly handy for group trekkers in tents. Independent trekkers may get by with a cheap Kathmandu torch.

● **Ski pole** Useful for stiff descents on rough terrain. One for each hand is unnecessary. The telescoping variety is best.

● **Umbrella** Most useful during late spring and the monsoon through to the end of September, an umbrella is great protection against the sun and, coupled with a good rain jacket, is essential for surviving the monsoon. Available in Kathmandu.

● **Pack cover** – useful from January to the end of September. A large, carefully cut plastic bag can be a reasonable substitute. Both are available in Kathmandu; you can also buy plastic bags in main villages on the trail.

❑ **Old clothes needed by Kathmandu charities**
If you have a little space in your luggage there are a couple of worthy local charities that would be very grateful for some old clothes.

Kumbeshwar Technical School in Patan was set up to cater specifically for the very low caste groups. It incorporates a small orphanage, a primary school and a technical school where carpet weaving and carpentry are taught. High quality sweaters are on sale in the showroom here. The principal is Karuna Khadgi (☎ 536483).

Child Workers in Nepal (CWIN) is a charity working for the rights of children and the abolition of child bonded labour (16% of children in the country are bonded labourers). They also run a 'Common Room' to support the 1000 children who live on the streets of Kathmandu. Clothes are always needed; children's clothes are best but they can alter adults' clothes. They can also make use of any medicines you may have left after your trek. CWIN is near the Soaltee Holiday Inn in Kalamati. It's run by Gauri Pradan (☎ 271658).

● **Toiletries** This is where you can really save some weight. There is no need for a half litre bottle of shampoo; chances are you will only wash your hair a few times. Finding hot water for a shave is not always easy and there are no plugs for electric razors. The smallest size of toothpaste sold is perfect for a month. Don't forget your deodorant ('the trekkers' shower'). Natural antibacterial mineral crystals are available, but hard to find, in Asan Tol market.

● **Toilet paper** Available on main routes so start with only one roll.

● **Lighter** – essential for burning used toilet paper and handy for lighting candles in lodges.

● **Moisturiser** A small tube for sensitive or well cared for skins is useful as the air is dry and the sun harsh.

● **Lip balm with sunscreen** Essential to prevent chapped and blistered lips, this should be used frequently especially above Namche, and even on cloudy days.

● **Tampons/sanitary napkins** The supermarkets in Kathmandu always have limited stock, Namche generally has some but they're unavailable elsewhere.

● **Pre-moistened towelettes ('Wet-ones')** Handy for group trekkers but bulky for individuals.

● **Camera** If you bring one always keep it with you. Thieves are well aware of the value of cameras so check your insurance policy to ensure your camera is fully covered. A modern compact, especially with a zoom lens, is light and convenient. Today's auto-everything camera places high demands on batteries which sometimes give out in the cold so take a spare set. Bring some cleaning equipment as lenses get dusty. While compacts are good, bigger cameras are better. Bring several zoom lenses (or a 28-200mm) for complete flexibility; a telephoto lens (to 200mm or more) is essential for close portraits and landscape detail and a wide angle lens (from 24mm) is great for getting it all in.

Cameras with zoom lenses mostly have smaller apertures so faster 200ASA or even 400ASA film makes it easier to take shots in lower light. Disposable cameras come in two varieties, panoramic and normal. In the panoramic version the picture is blown up to give the illusion of length but quality is lost as a result. Standard disposables don't suffer this problem and, used in the right light, produce surprisingly good results.

● **Film** Kathmandu stocks a wide variety of print, black and white, and slide films (Kodak, Fuji, Konica, Agfa) at competitive prices. The Kathmandu laboratories do a reasonable job developing print film and enlargements are exceptional value. Unfortunately the quality of black and white and slide film developing is not so good.

● **First aid kit** See the medical section, p245.

● **Water purification kit** – essential, see p235.

● **Reading matter** Owing to the lack of night light and the social nature of trekking, there's not much time for reading. One paperback is usually enough and this can be exchanged in Namche or with another trekker.

● **Diary** Many people like to write a diary while they trek.

● **Money pouch/belt** Most people find wearing one while trekking a hassle and keep it buried in their pack until they stop for the evening.

If you plan to stay exclusively in lodges or are trekking with a group then a tent, foam pad, stove, cutlery, plate and mug are not needed.

Modern equipment aside, in Kathmandu it's possible to buy a thick jersey, cotton thermal underwear, socks, and hit the trail having spent little money. Whatever else you don't already have can be rented.

RENTING OR BUYING EQUIPMENT IN NEPAL

In Kathmandu

There's a great variety of rental equipment here which saves buying expensive specialised gear. Easy-to-rent items include down jackets, down pants, sleeping-bags, insulating pads, ice-axes, crampons and ski poles. Also available (although stocks often run low) are water bottles, stoves, fuel bottles and backpacks.

Many items can also be bought here, for less than in the West. You can rely on finding lightweight trekking boots (mainly HiTec brand, and only a few models), thick down jackets, locally-made rucksacks, inferior down sleeping bags, good quality head torches and their batteries, Maglite torches, fleece jackets (little variety, though), woollen mittens, gloves, socks and hats, jerseys, low quality longjohns, large 'porter' or duffel bags, telescoping ski poles and sunglasses. To check if sunglasses are UV protective, look on the inside of the lenses for a purple film, the coating necessary on cheap plastic lenses to protect your eyes.

The items that are better brought from home include high quality socks, boots, thermal underwear, liner gloves, fleece and good quality rain gear.

Increasingly, equipment is being made in Nepal. While much of it is serviceable, the quality is much inferior to outdoor equipment from home. Disturbingly, local manufacturers have chosen to copy Western labels but these fakes are generally easy to pick out from the originals. The stitching is uneven, the webbing and fabrics feel inferior and are less well colour-coordinated, logos are on plastic labels and the designs are less innovative. All locally made Gore-Tex jackets and pants are definitely not made from Gore-Tex; and you can be sure that all brown 'The North Face Made in USA' labelled backpacks and sleeping bags are fakes – real North Face gear has the name on zip rings and pops, machine-embroidered logos and labels difficult to duplicate. Similarly, real Lowe and Wild Country rucksacks were once common but now are mostly fakes. If using a locally-made rucksack take a sewing kit. Dental floss (with several large needles) is the strongest and easiest to use thread.

Locally-made sleeping bags use either Russian or Korean down, offering reasonable quality, although since it is untreated it often smells after a while. Local 'down' is not worth buying.

In Namche

If you are flying in and out of the Khumbu then it's safer to rent most of the equipment you require in Kathmandu. Comparing daily rates, renting gear in Namche tends to be marginally more expensive than in Kathmandu; but you don't have to carry it up or pay for the time it's not in use. You can rent sleeping-bags, down jackets, down pants and down boots. Gloves and hats can also sometimes be rented or more usually bought. Quality socks and thermal underwear are usually unobtainable.

Left-over expedition equipment is also available for sale or rent, sometimes enough virtually to equip a serious expedition with high quality gear – ice-axes, crampons, plastic boots, climbing hardware, tents, down suits, the latest Gore-Tex clothing and more. The only problem is you never know exactly what will be there, and in what sizes. Some of this amazing equipment is dumped by expeditions to save the cost of having it carried out and some comes from the high altitude porters who must by law be given full equipment. This is often worth many times their minimal wages so it's a valuable part of their income. The prices are not dirt cheap but are generally cheaper, often quite significantly, than in the West.

ADVENTURE TREKKING EQUIPMENT

Group trekkers are provided with extensive lists. Climbers and experienced adventure trekkers planning to camp out frequently really need to plan carefully: too much is horribly heavy unless you recruit a porter, and too little is limiting.

If trekking alone, or in a small group without a full trekking crew, it's really worth employing a porter who has trekked the route before. Not only will all your packs be lighter (often making the difference between an enjoyable trek and an endurance test) but experienced porters know the bivvy caves, the local herders, the track details and the latest on where you can find supplies in unusual places.

In Namche it's possible to rent or buy everything necessary to climb a trekking peak: harnesses, snow stakes, ice screws, ropes, crampons, plastic boots, tent etc. There's also left over expedition equipment for sale (see above).

High altitude – October

Day temperatures rarely drop below zero, except above 6000m, so good fleece and thick thermals are enough though thick or light down jackets are still handy. Although the weather is mostly fine you should be prepared for a fall of snow. Leather boots are quite adequate for 6000m peaks and the high passes in fine weather; however, most people attempting trekking peaks do wear plastics.

High altitude – November and December

Day temperatures range from 10°C/50°F to -10°C/14°F and at night you can expect -10°C/14°F to -25°C/-13°F .

● **Day wear for climbing** should include thin/mid-weight longjohns plus semi-windproof trousers, T-shirt or mid-weight top with expedition weight top (or fleece) and a Gore-Tex shell for more demanding conditions. Liner gloves (thin and not windproof) are essential, backed up by something more substantial. The higher you go the better your mittens must be. Semi-windproof pants can be enough without carrying extra Gore-Tex pants, even to 6500m.

● **Boots** This is the most difficult choice. You have to be planning a lot of pass-hopping and peak-bagging in rough country to wear plastics the whole time above Namche. Walking from Jiri in plastics is absolutely out of the question. Tough well-insulated leather boots backed by full gaiters (eg Yeti) are more manageable, even for a single trekking peak or high pass in reasonable conditions. Insulating shock-absorbing inner soles can make the world of difference to the comfort of big boots. The often hard to find Spenco range is the best. Foot care is incredibly important and should never be neglected. If there is only one part of you that you wash in weeks at high altitude, it should be your feet.

● **In the evening** you'll need a substantial down jacket, thin balaclava, and perhaps thick longjohns or fleece pants. Down pants are a luxury.

● **At night**, for several people a tent might be comfortable but a bivvy bag will do. However, if your sleeping-bag is exceptionally warm even a bivvy bag is superfluous (provided you have an emergency space/survival blanket for an unexpected snowfall). If using a Thermarest self-inflating mattress, an ultra-lite with a very thin back-up pad is a comfortable combination, otherwise a thick foam pad will suffice.

High altitude – January to mid-April

Be prepared for extreme cold. Light down jackets or, better, thermals with fleece, and expedition-weight longjohns are comfortable to walk in. Plastic boots above 4000m/13,123ft are good for trekking, with some trekking crews and lodge owners wearing them; and they are essential for climbing. If trekking in leather boots use full gaiter protection and take care to keep them dry. A tough tent is essential. You must be prepared for savage cold and snow-storms. Above 5000m/16,404ft a cold clear night can put thermometers off the scale.

Frostbite is something to be aware of. For hands, tough liner gloves are invaluable. Take great care of your feet: lacing boots tightly compresses the lining and the socks that are meant to keep your feet warm and restricts vital circulation. Inner boots may need lacing only around the ankle. The soles suck heat out and insulating inner soles are invaluable. A single extra layer of material around the whole boot (like a stuff sack) can make a big difference on the coldest mornings when wearing crampons.

High altitude – Mid-April and May

The warmer conditions are tough with soft, wet and often deep snow. Bring an alarm clock for early starts and a few novels for long snowy afternoons. Tents and clothing should be waterproof and plastic boots are still best for climbing. Gore-Tex pants/salopettes and fleece are in their element; carry plenty of spare dry clothing and perhaps some camp shoes.

General gear

● **Stoves** Kathmandu and Namche have 'Blue Gaz' and most other canisters, with matching stoves for rent. Dirty, low quality kerosene is available in small quantities at virtually every lodge, and there is a reasonable chance of finding petrol at two or three lodges above Namche. Petrol is easier to light and significantly cleaner than kerosene. All fuel should be filtered.

● **Water bottles/bags** A total capacity of three litres per person is useful for camping.

Climbing gear

See the trekking peak descriptions for recommendations. For a first trip in the Himalaya, many climbers strongly advise beginning with a trek and a light climb or exploration rather than focusing on the vertical. With this approach you need technical gear basically just for walking on glaciers.

Don't neglect your crew's equipment

While you may have the latest and best equipment your crew certainly will not. Sirdars usually have reasonable gear although it is worth checking their climbing gear and sleeping bag. The sherpas and kitchen hands are less well-equipped and generally appreciate cast-offs, perhaps a Kathmandu fleece or a good piece of clothing as part of the tips. Porters have nothing and appreciate clean serviceable clothes of any sort and especially old running shoes or boots. See p86-88 for notes on employing and looking after crew.

RECOMMENDED READING

Kathmandu has the world's best selection of books on Nepal and the surrounding mountain areas. Prices can be below normal cover prices so it's also an attractive place to buy them. The Thamel area boasts many second-hand bookshops with hundreds of cheap paperback novels.

Guidebooks

For exploring the Kathmandu Valley and the rest of the country there's a wide range available. Apa's *Nepal Insight Guide* has beautiful coffee-table photos and an informative text but is, however, of limited use as a practical guide. Apa also have a *Kathmandu Insight Guide* covering the Valley and a *Kathmandu* city guide suitable for a flying visit.

Lonely Planet's *Nepal* is an exhaustive guide to the Kathmandu Valley with good practical information and ideas on what to do after your trek. Moon Publications' *Nepal Handbook* is a literate in-depth guide to the country and the *Rough Guide to Nepal* has interesting background information and a chatty style. Footprint's *Nepal Handbook* is particularly strong on culture and history.

If you fancy another trek, Lonely Planet's *Trekking in the Nepal Himalaya* and Stephen Bezruchka's *Trekking in Nepal* (particularly strong on cultural and environmental information) give useful overviews of the options. For greater detail see *Trekking in the Annapurna Region* and *Trekking in Langtang, Helambu & Gosainkund*, also from Trailblazer.

Trekking Peaks of Nepal by Bill O'Connor is the standard but dated reference for climbing these 'limited bureaucracy' mountains.

Trekking/mountaineering books

Hundreds of expedition accounts have been published but many are of interest only to avid climbers. The books that I particularly enjoyed are listed below.

Bill Tilman and Eric Shipton are names closely linked with much of the early exploration of the Himalaya and Karakoram. It's incredible, even judged by modern standards, the ground they covered and the peaks that they conquered. Their second legacy is a series of books written in elegant prose with vivid and interesting descriptions that twinkle with penetrating insights, often curiously and hilariously funny. Their individual books have been reprinted in several volumes. Eric Shipton's *The Six Mountain-Travel Books* (The Mountaineers, Seattle, 1985) includes two books about Everest: *Upon That Mountain* and *The Mount Everest Reconnaissance Expedition 1951*. HW Tilman's *The Seven Mountain-Travel Books* (The Mountaineers, Seattle, 1983) includes *Everest 1938* and *Nepal Himalaya*.

Everest by Walt Unsworth (Oxford Illustrated Press, 1989) is a climbing history capturing the hopes and fears of the attempts on Everest.

Everest: the best writing and pictures from 70 years of human endeavour, edited by Peter Gillman (Little, Brown & Co, London 1993) features interesting historical snapshots of the climbing of Everest.

Cho Oyu by Favour of the Gods by Herbert Tichy covers the first ascent of Cho Oyu. With only three members this was not the usual grand expedition, and neither is the book written in the traditional heroic style.

Nothing Venture Nothing Win by Sir Edmund Hillary is an interesting autobiographical account of his adventures including the scaling of Everest. His *Schoolhouse in the Clouds* offers an insight into the development of the Khumbu and other Sherpa areas.

Sherpas: Reflections on Change in Himalayan Nepal by James F Fisher is an interesting and readable investigation into the changes in the Khumbu that tourism and schooling have brought, with perceptive feedback from local people.

Into Thin Air: A Personal Account of the Everest Disaster by Jon Krakauer is the compelling story of how so many climbers died (and some miraculously lived against the odds) on two commercial expeditions in 1996.

MAP RECOMMENDATIONS

This guide specifically includes many maps, enough to cover a normal trek to the Khumbu from Jiri or Lukla. However for identifying the many surrounding peaks and features, detailed topographic maps are invaluable and virtually essential for exploration off the beaten track.

The **Schneider 1:50,000 series** published by Freytag-Berndt und Artaria, Vienna covers the entire area in beautiful four-colour topographic maps. The *Khumbu Himal* is the most useful for all trekking, exploring and climbing from Namche to the north. *Tamba Kosi* covers Jiri to Junbesi (and the approaches to the mountains south of the Rolwaling but not the range itself), including from Dolakha. *Shorong/Hinku* includes the trekking routes from Junbesi and Lukla to Namche as well as north of Junbesi, the Hongu (the area surrounding Mera peak) and the eastern Arun trekking route from

---

❏ **Useful Web sites**

For updates to this guide check **www.webfoot.co.nz/nepal-treks/books_ter 3_update.html** or **www.trailblazer-guides.com**.

Other sites which can be helpful for planning a trip include the following:
● The Nepal section at **www.south-asia.com**.
● Check **www.bena.com/nepaltrek/index.html** for links to many Nepal sites.
● The best online health information is on CIWEC Clinic's section on Kathmandu's concise page: **www.bena.com/nepaltrek/ciwec/ immune.html**.
● At Lonely Planet's site (**www.lonelyplanet.com**), you can leave messages for other travellers on their 'Thorn Tree'.
● Also see Himalaya Trekking's site at **www.webfoot.co. nz/nepal-treks**.

Lukla/Kharikhola to the Surkie La. *Dudh Kosi* covers Phaplu to Junbesi, and also from the Rumjatar and Lamidanda airports up the Dudh Kosi. *Rolwaling Himal* includes the area from the Tashi Labsta to Simigoan and the Tamba Kosi, and is useful for exploring the Rolwaling range. *Lapchi Kang* covers from the Tamba Kosi to Barabise. These maps are available in Kathmandu (Rs700-950).

Look out for the new 1:50,000 topographical series of maps being produced by the **Nepal Survey Dept** with assistance from Finland (FinnAid). The surveys for the east of the country were done in 1992 (ie more recently than surveys for the Schneider maps above), contours are shown for every 40m and print quality is good. In Nepal they're available for Rs80 from Maps of Nepal, near the Everest Hotel. In the UK they can be ordered from books through the UK distributor, Cordee.

The **National Geographic Magazine** (USA) published a beautiful map of the area surrounding Everest but, unfortunately, it does not cover the Gokyo valley, or even below Pangboche. Inserted in the 1988 centennial issue, it was the most accurate and detailed 1:50,000 map ever made. Use it for the Amphu Labtsa, Mingbo La, Sherpani Col and climbing around Chukhung. It's stocked by most bookshops in Kathmandu.

Also readily available in Kathmandu are several cheap **general maps** covering either Jiri to Kala Pattar or Lukla to Kala Pattar. Even up-dated '98-99' editions are loaded with minor inconsistencies but they are adequate for trekking. One of the better brands is **Nepa Maps**.

Health precautions and inoculations

The physical aspects of trekking

Trekking means walking almost every day for four to seven hours, often for three weeks or more. Many people begin only moderately fit but generally cope well and end the trek feeling amazingly healthy. A few find the reality of continuous walking difficult. If you lead a sedentary life then plan an exercise programme well before you go. Brisk walks are a good start, building up to include walking up and down hills with the boots you plan to wear trekking, to introduce your body to the rigours of hill walking. Jogging and aerobics are reasonable substitutes. Muscles strengthen fairly quickly, although painfully if you overdo exercise. Stretching should be included in your training programme: once you've warmed up stretch gently, without bouncing, holding each pose for 20-30 seconds.

It is important to realise that while trekking you can be a long way from help. Sometimes you will have to be your own doctor, there is no other choice. However, the Khumbu region is better endowed with medical facilities than anywhere else in rural Nepal. There's a hospital at Kunde (an hour above Namche) staffed by two Western doctors. The Himalayan Rescue Association post at Pheriche is staffed by two more Western doctors and open during the two busy trekking seasons.

MEDICAL CONDITIONS

Anyone with heart, lung and blood pressure abnormalities or a continuing medical condition should have a check-up and get a medical opinion before setting off.

● **Older people** Many recently-retired people have made it to the top of Kala Pattar (5554m/18,222ft) so age need not be a barrier. The older you are, the more important prior fitness preparation is.

● **Young children** Caution should be exercised when taking children trekking. Younger people can be slower to adapt to altitude, and very young children have difficulty in communicating exactly how they feel. No studies have been undertaken so cautious doctors recommend the safe maximum for pre-teenage children is 3000m/9843ft. However a number of young children have made it to the top of Kala Pattar. Trekking with children can be very rewarding and bring you closer to the locals. You share a common bond for there are few people without children in Nepal. Little legs are easily carried by a porter when tired, and Sherpanis are good babysitters.

● **Teenagers** There is no evidence to suggest that teenagers adapt to altitude more slowly than adults. However they do appear to be more at risk. This is likely to be because of competitiveness and a will not to give in, and also because some school groups treat the trek as an outward bound exercise, with everyone carrying their own backpack. Organisers of such groups should allow an extra day or two over the most conservative itineraries and be particularly watchful.

● **Asthma** is no reason to avoid trekking. Except in polluted Kathmandu there are fewer irritants in the air so most asthmatics actually feel better while trekking. Look after your medication – wear your inhaler on a chain around your neck or keep it in a pocket. There is still the normal risk of a serious attack so brief your companions on what to do.

● **Diabetes** If it is well controlled diabetes is no reason to avoid trekking. You cannot afford to lose the medication so keep it with you at all times and warn you friends on the procedures in case there's an emergency. Your increased energy expenditure will alter carbohydrate and insulin levels so it's very important to monitor your glucose levels frequently and carefully and to keep blood sugar levels well controlled.

● **High blood pressure** Blood pressure will fluctuate more and be higher than usual while on a trek. You should seek the advice of a doctor who is aware of the history of your condition.

● **Previous heart attacks** Studies have yet to be conducted but it is likely that the level of exertion required on a trek is more significant than the altitude factor. Get the advice of your doctor.

● **Epilepsy** There is a moderately increased risk of a seizure at altitude but not a reason to stop you trekking. Your companions must be briefed on all the relevant procedures.

● **Pregnancy** Complications are common especially in the first pregnancy. Sometimes sophisticated care is needed so it's probably not a good idea to go trekking while pregnant. The effects of reduced oxygen at high altitude on the foetus have not yet been studied.

INOCULATIONS

...she also probably suffers iodine deficiency (though she has no goitre), which might explain why she has had only one completely normal child out of seven. Four of her children died at or near birth; of the surviving sons one is a cretin, one is profoundly deaf and therefore also dumb, and one is normal.
Jim Fisher on health conditions before the opening of Khunde Hospital

The majority of Nepal's population has no access to doctors or modern medicines so the health situation is extremely poor. Disease and malnourishment are rife and even sickness easily cured by medicine often leads to death without it. Visitors arriving with immunisations, healthy bodies and access to clean water are much less at risk. A bout of diarrhoea, however, is almost inevitable, no matter how careful you are.

There are no official immunisation requirements to enter Nepal but the following should be considered. The best people to consult about the vaccinations currently recommended are clinics specialising in travel medicine. They will have access to more up-to-date information than a normal general practitioner.

● **Hepatitis A** Usually passed on in contaminated water; immunisation is considered a must by most doctors unless you have had hepatitis A before. The new vaccine is Havrix and a full course will give up to ten years protection. A cheaper alternative is a gamma globulin injection which should be given just before departure and be repeated every 4-6 months while travelling. Although this is a blood-based product there is no chance of contracting AIDS from this immunisation.

● **Hepatitis B** This disease is avoidable since, like AIDS, it's passed by unsafe sex or contaminated blood products. A vaccine is available.

● **Meningitis** Occasional cases of meningococcal meningitis occur in Nepal. It is an often fatal disease but the vaccine is safe and effective and should be obtained.

● **Cholera** The World Health Organisation no longer recommend this vaccination. It is only partially effective and often causes a reaction. The risk of travellers acquiring cholera in Nepal is extremely low.

● **Typhoid** is prevalent in Nepal. There are now a variety of vaccines and one should be obtained.

● **Tetanus-Diptheria** This vaccine is recommended if you have not had a booster in the last 10 years. Many doctors advise a tetanus booster every time you intend to travel for any length of time.

● **Polio** If you escaped immunisation as a child a series of vaccinations is recommended. If you have not had a booster as an adult, one may be required. Check with your doctor.

● **Measles, mumps and rubella** If you did not have these diseases (or the vaccinations) as a child you may need a vaccination.

● **Japanese Encephalitis B** This disease is transmitted by mosquitoes and there have been sporadic outbreaks in the Terai (lowland Nepal) and India. Western doctors based in Kathmandu suggest the vaccination only for people visiting the Terai for extended periods.

● **Rabies** This deadly virus is transmitted by the bite of an infected animal, usually a monkey or dog. The risk of being bitten is minimal, probably greatest in Kathmandu since some of the street dogs are certainly rabid. A vaccination is available but even if you've had it you'll then need a follow-up course of two further injections. If you've not been vaccinated and are unlucky enough to be bitten, a series of injections is available only from the CIWEC clinic in Kathmandu and should be started within a week.

● **Malaria** Carried only by the lowland *Anopheles* mosquito, malaria exists in the Terai in Nepal (ie below 1000m/3281ft), and across much of the rest of rural Asia. There's no risk in Kathmandu or while trekking (except possibly at low altitudes during the monsoon). If visiting Chitwan or going rafting close to the monsoon season then consider taking tablets to protect against malaria. The drug of choice for different areas changes as resistance builds up in the parasite. If you have just visited a malarial area, for example India or Thailand, then it's vital to continue taking your medication for the recommended length of time.

The first line of protection, however, is to avoid being bitten. The *Anopheles* mosquito is active only between early evening and dawn so you should cover up well between these times and use mosquito repellent on any exposed skin.

If you are behind on any of the immunisations listed above, they can be safely obtained at clinics in Kathmandu.

MEDICAL INSURANCE

A combined travel/medical insurance policy is a sensible choice for any traveller and a requirement for most tours booked in your home country. Since trekking may require helicopter rescue which is not always covered by general travel schemes, trekking companies have specially-tailored policies. Independent trekkers should register with their embassy which will be contacted if helicopter rescue is required. Forms are available at the Himalayan Rescue Association in Kathmandu. Note that a rescue mission does not take place unless there is a guarantee of payment by a trekking company or your embassy (see p246).

See p234 for a detailed discussion of staying healthy on the trek.

PART 2: NEPAL

Facts about the country

GEOGRAPHICAL BACKGROUND

Perilously placed between the Asian superpowers of India and China, Nepal is a land-locked rectangle roughly 800km by 200km (500 by 120 miles). It straddles the hills and mountains between the enormous Ganges plain and the high Tibetan plateau. In the south is a narrow strip of flat land known as the Terai. Rising abruptly from this are the small Siwalik hills and the Mahabharat range. Between are broad valleys, the Inner Terai, which were once infested with malaria. Thanks to DDT spraying in the 1950s that threat has been eradicated and this rapidly developing area is now the fertile bread basket of Nepal. The wide band of steep middle hills sheltered the older centres of population – Kathmandu, Pokhara and smaller towns like Jiri. To the north are the majestic Himalaya, including Kanchenjunga, Makalu, Lhotse, Everest, Cho Oyu, Manaslu, Annapurna and Dhaulagiri – eight of the ten highest peaks on the planet.

The Himalaya

As well as being the world's highest mountains, the Himalaya are also the youngest. What fascinated early explorers was the fact that they did not form the continental divide. This is, in fact, to be found further north on the Tibetan Plateau. The Himalaya were formed by the collision of two continental plates, with the Indian plate being forced under the edge of the Asian plate, pushing up part of the Tibetan Plateau into jagged mountains. However, as fast as the Himalaya rose, the rivers to the north cut their southern paths faster, which accounts for the great depth of many of the valleys in the region. The patterns of formation can be seen on many rock faces, especially the Lhotse-Nuptse wall (where distorted sedimentation lines are quite obvious) and from Kala Pattar (where continuation of the yellow band near the top of Everest can be seen in Changtse/Bei Peak, the mountain to the north in Tibet).

> ❏ **Earth Mother**
> When geologists first came to Nepal Sherpas were horrified to see them breaking rocks and digging holes without first apologising to the land. Sherpas perceive the earth as mother earth: the soil is her flesh, the rocks her bones, the water her blood. They depend on her for their lives and when they die their flesh becomes one with the earth.

CLIMATE

Nepal is at the same latitude as Florida and Cairo so the climate in the lowland areas is hot with temperate winters. The trekking areas are, however, well above sea level and consequently temperatures vary considerably. The climate comprises distinct seasons but with an important additional feature: the monsoon. This moisture-laden wind amasses in the Bay of Bengal and sweeps up across India to spend its forces on the Himalayan mountain chain between late June and mid-September. It does not rain continuously or even every day. Rather there may be a couple of heavy downpours during the day that usually last less than an hour, keeping the summer heat down to bearable levels. Sometimes it rains only at night. After the monsoon retreats, the climate is dry and sunny for the remainder of the year. Autumn is renowned for clear skies and pleasant temperatures. By winter the high hills take on dry brown shades and the mountains are occasionally dusted with fresh snow. The colourful spring, March to May, is punctuated by the odd shower of life-giving rain but the heat builds up until the monsoon relief arrives. The trekking seasons are detailed on p34.

HISTORICAL OUTLINE

Facts and fables

Nepal's early history is clouded in folklore and legend. One story relates how the Kathmandu Valley, then a huge sacred lake, was emptied through a channel cut by the stroke of a god's sword. The Chobar Gorge, which drains the valley, indeed fits the description and geologists maintain that the soil in the valley gained its renowned fertility as a lake bed.

At the time of the Buddha, in the second half of the 6th century BC, the Kirati ruled the Kathmandu valley. They were a Mongol race whose descendants include the Rai and Limbu now settled in the east of Nepal. Buddhism spread slowly and the arts and architecture developed under the 28 successive kings. Around 300AD the Indian Licchavi dynasty invaded Nepal, introducing the caste system and Hinduism, which intermingled with Buddhism, a process continuing to this day. Around 900AD power struggles enveloped the valley and it was not until 1200AD that the Malla dynasty became established. The caste system was rigidly defined and (although there was occasional infighting that laid the towns of the valley to waste) trade, cottage industries and the enduring Newar culture blossomed. The 1400s left the wealth of architecture, carving and sculpture that surrounds the Durbar Squares in Kathmandu, Patan and Bhaktapur. Known then as Kantipur, Lalitpur and Bhadgoan, respectively, these three cities divided into separate flourishing but quarrelsome kingdoms in 1482 on the death of Yaksha Malla.

Unity, treachery and extravagance

In 1768 Prithvi Narayan Shah of Gorkha (a princely kingdom between Kathmandu and Pokhara) conquered the Kathmandu valley and began the Shah dynasty that continues by direct blood line to this day. He started by consolidating the many individual kingdoms that now form the basis of Nepal. His successors, although 'honourably defeated' in the 1814 war with British India were able to resist colonial domination, a fact that the Nepalese are proud of to this day.

Overall control by the Shah dynasty was undermined by the rich nobles whose constant struggle for power often led to violence. However, in 1846, unequivocal control was seized by Jung Bahadur Rana who killed all the ministers and high officials in what became known as the 'Kot Massacre'. He declared himself Maharajah and the founder of a second line of Nepalese kings. To ensure continuity of the line his family married into the Shah dynasty and other high caste families. Jung Bahadur Rana alone fathered over 100 children. He and his heirs effectively ruled the country, although the King, kept in seclusion, was the highest authority. The Rana family amassed incredible wealth, visible in the numerous European-style palaces (inspired by Jung Bahadur's visit to Europe) which now house various government departments in Kathmandu. This feudal dynasty held Nepal in its grip for over a century until 1950 when the puppet king Tribhuvan escaped to India.

The post-war period

Following the end of the Second World War much of Asia was in turmoil. Newly independent India, and China, both seemed to have their hungry eyes on the tiny neighbour that divided them. Political discontent and fear were growing in Nepal.

Now known as the father of democracy in Nepal, BP Koilara managed to undermine the Ranas' control, and India assisted in engineering the return to power of King Tribhuvan in 1951. Keen to establish its independence as a country in its own right and not an Indian vassal, Nepal quickly invited foreign countries to open consulates in Kathmandu. Thus ended more than a century of isolation.

The panchayat system

In 1955 King Tribhuvan died and was succeeded by his son, Mahendra. The constitution was reformed and in 1957 the people of Nepal voted in the Nepal Congress Party with a decisive majority. However, bribery and corruption played a large part in the country's first elections and continued in the new government. This gave King Mahendra the excuse to step into power and at the end of 1959 he arrested the entire cabinet. He took direct control himself, later instituting the *panchayat* system. Under this system the locally-elected leaders of village councils nominated the candidates for higher posts, all ultimately under the King. In theory, this was quite a reasonable system and was endorsed by the new Eton-educated King Birendra (still the reigning monarch) when his father died in 1972.

Democracy established

Corruption and self-interest prevailed and popular discontent spread again, erupting in 1979 with rare violence in Kathmandu. The panchayat system was put to the test by public referendum and survived, but only just. Its days were numbered and the government's inability to solve a serious trade dispute with India in 1990 and its continued persecution of the opposition caused public protest. Meetings dispersed with bullets became riots and the palace was surrounded by machine-gun toting soldiers.

The soldiers were supposedly there to protect the King but soon let it be known on which side their sympathies lay, as did the foreign aid donors. Cornered, the King lifted the ban on political parties in April 1990. He agreed to become a constitutional monarch and a temporary government was formed.

In 1991 the promised elections were held. The Nepal Congress Party (symbol: the tree) won, putting the Communist Party (the sun) in the role of opposition party.

Congress versus communists
After the elections the new government announced considerable changes. The price of subsidised foods (eg rice) was freed to stimulate production. Tourism was targeted for development and the Nepalese rupee gently floated on the open market, dealing a death-blow to the flourishing black market.

Expecting the promised improvements and a rise in living standards to come quickly once the democratic machine was in place, Nepalis soon lost confidence in their new government. The opposition parties were quick to take advantage of this, stirring up riots in which several people were killed. The government itself was torn by internal dissent and Nepal's second general election was called 18 months early, in November 1994. The communists took power, ruling in a coalition government under the leader of the United Marxist-Leninist Party, Man Mohan Adhikari.

Nepal's experiment with communism lasted till September 1995 when Adhikari's party lost a vote of no-confidence in parliament. Since democracy's inception the two main parties have been fighting a surprisingly equal battle with neither one nor the other able to gain easy control of the house. The consequence of not having a party with a clear majority in government has been unproductive political bickering. One can only hope that this feuding doesn't descend into vindictive violent politics like many of Nepal's near neighbours.

ECONOMY

Nepal's rural backwardness may be attractive to tourists but the mediaeval way of life is not easy for most Nepalese. In the past tenant farmers, the majority of the population, paid crippling taxes to landlords in a vicious semi-feudal system. The 1964 reforms sought to redress this by land redistribution and reducing rental to a (still unbearable) 50% of the crop. They were only partly successful. Even now 90% of the population lives off the land with the majority existing at subsistence level. It's a simple, hard life virtually without money, the reason that the average annual per capita income is so low – around US$150. This legacy means the prospects for the farmers' children are indescribably bleak. Nepal's astronomic birth rate and a lack of new arable land are the main problems. The ever-expanding population has been partly absorbed by the Inner Terai but the amount of arable land available per person continues to drop. Crop yields have increased but cannot keep pace with demand so Nepal has become a net food importer. There are dire predictions about the decline of land fertility and the destruction of the forests; already there are food and firewood shortages. Without development miracles this situation can only get worse.

Nepal is barely industrialised. Demand for jobs far outstrips supply resulting in exploitative wages and appalling working conditions. With no manufacturing base all machinery and construction materials must be imported which means paying hard currency or Indian rupees, and earning these is difficult. Of the few exports, the majority go to India since reliable and cheap shipping is problematic for greater distances. The hard currency earners are carpets, tourism (250,000 people a year), and Nepalese working overseas, particularly the Gurkha soldiers. Foreign aid programmes are, however, big business in Nepal and a third of government funding comes from this source.

DEVELOPMENT

There is no doubt that considerable development is needed in Nepal, if only to avert tragedy. The root of the problem is the spiralling population growth. Nature's harsh natural balance was upset by the introduction of a few simple life-saving measures such as oral rehydration salts and basic hygiene principles. The five million people that lived in Nepal in 1950 have multiplied to 21.5 million, and this population is expected to double in the next 30 years, with catastrophic results.

It's difficult to get the message of birth control across to Nepal's peasant farmers when to them more hands are an asset and extra children an insurance against others that may die. Obviously education and health care are a good start. If you are secure in the knowledge that your children will live (their health protected by vaccines and clean water) and believe that their quality of life may be better (with education) you will be more interested in trying to limit the size of your family. Electricity and roads provide opportunities for diversification from agriculture and a move to a more cash-orientated society, where the benefits of birth control become more obvious.

Such massive changes don't happen overnight, certainly not in Nepal, despite vast quantities of foreign aid.

THE PEOPLE OF EASTERN NEPAL

A cultural bridge between Tibet and India, Nepal is a colourful patchwork of ethnic groups, castes and clans. Although officially the only Hindu kingdom in the world, tides of history have also deposited Buddhists and even a few

Muslims and Christians. Unlike in India the caste system is not institutionalised and is generally only observed by the beneficiaries, the higher castes.

Newars, with their rich urban-based culture and separate language, are the traditional inhabitants of the Kathmandu valley, responsible for much of the famous architecture and art. Outside Kathmandu they are mainly merchants, particularly shop owners. **Brahmins** are the high Hindu priestly caste rather than an ethnic group. Traditionally they earn money from performing religious rituals and must avoid being polluted by people of a lower caste. Many now work in the government and in business. In the hills they are often little better off than the lower castes and intermarriage has taken place.

Sherpas (see p105), Kirat (Rai and Limbu) and Tamangs are the ethnic groups most commonly encountered on the Everest trek. **Rais** are found south of Solu and Pharak, particularly in the area between the Khumbu and the Arun. The villages of Bung and Gudel are exclusively Rai and you'll also meet them at the Namche Saturday market. Usually stocky and short, the Rai have Mongoloid features, a round face and a tanned but fairly light skin and they wear light-coloured clothing. The diet staples are rice, maize, wheat and millet, mixed with a variety of vegetables. The Rais are well represented in Gurkha battalions of the Indian and British armies. **Tamangs** are people of the middle hills and very often act as porters. The women are distinctive with nose jewellery that hangs over their lips while the men wear a rough sleeveless woollen tunic when it is cold. They are Buddhists and like the Sherpas have their roots in Tibet.

RELIGION

Nepal describes itself as a Hindu Constitutional Monarchy. Official statistics state that 89.5% of the population is Hindu, 5.3% Buddhist, 2.7% Muslim, 2.4% shamanist and animist, 0.1% Jain and 0.04% Christian. Since being Hindu and Nepali-speaking can confer greater employment opportunities and higher social standing, it's likely that there are more Buddhists and fewer Hindus than these figures suggest.

The long tradition of religious toleration has led to a blurring of distinctions, especially between Hinduism and Buddhism. You'll see Buddhist prayer-flags fluttering over a Hindu temple and statues of Hindu gods in Buddhist *gompas* (monasteries). In fact, many Hindu deities have their Buddhist counterparts.

❏ **Buddhism – the Four Noble Truths**
1. Life is suffering.
2. The cause of suffering is thirst or desire.
3. Ending desire ends suffering.
4. And this means taking the Noble Eightfold Path: right view, right thought, right speech, right action, right livelihood, right effort, right mindfulness and right concentration.

Practical information for the visitor

VISA AND TREKKING REGULATIONS
Visas
All visitors require a visa for Nepal, easily obtained at the airport or border on arrival (passport-sized photo no longer required) or at Nepalese embassies abroad, sometimes the more expensive option.

At the airport a single entry visa valid for 15 days costs US$15 and a 30-day visa costs US$25, payable only in US$ cash. A double entry visa costs US$40 for an initial 30 days for the first visit and provides another 30 days on re-entry. Similarly, a multiple entry visa for US$60 is valid initially for 60 days. All visas can be extended in Kathmandu.

Trekking permits
To go trekking you need a trekking permit, obtainable from the Department of Immigration in Kathmandu. For the first month of a permit you're charged the equivalent in Nepalese rupees of US$5 per week, and for the following months, the equivalent of US$10 per week. In addition you need a permit (Rs650-1000) to enter the national park.

If trekking through a trekking agency they will organise the permit, national park entrance fee and visa extensions as required. For trekking peak permit costs, see p226.

Visa extensions and trekking permit applications
Visa and trekking permit applications are accepted at the Department of Immigration, conveniently located in Thamel. It's open Sunday to Friday, 10.30am to 12.30pm, closed Saturdays and the main public holidays. If you apply in the morning you can usually collect your permit/extension in the afternoon of the same day. Visa extensions cost US$1 per day (paid in equivalent Nepalese rupees), for up to a maximum of five calendar months in one year. Visas for children under 10 years old are free.

Leaving the country
Immigration officials will fine you if your visa has expired by more than one day. When leaving by air you're entitled to cash back into hard currency only 15% of the rupees for which you have encashment receipts. For those heading to India excess Nepalese rupees are easily converted into Indian rupees.

GETTING TO NEPAL
By air
The quality airlines that fly into Kathmandu are Thai and Singapore Airlines. Other carriers include Pakistan International Airlines, Indian Airlines, Royal

Nepal, Bangladesh Biman, Aeroflot and Dragonair. Apart from Royal Nepal and Indian Airlines, which operate daily flights into Kathmandu, most airlines have only two flights a week.

● **From the West** For the cheapest flights check the travel advertising section of the major papers. From the UK the cheapest return ticket is on Bangladesh Biman at around £400. The fastest flight from London is on Royal Nepal which touches down only in Frankfurt and the Gulf. Lufthansa also flies between Kathmandu and Frankfurt, with connections to London.

● **From India** On Indian Airlines there are daily flights between Kathmandu and Delhi (US$142/£90) or Varanasi (US$71/£45). On Tuesday, Thursday and Sunday there are flights between Kathmandu and Calcutta (US$96/£60). Royal Nepal also operates flights between Patna and Kathmandu, and Kathmandu and Delhi.

● **From Thailand** Since the border with Burma is closed the only way is to fly. There are direct flights or the cheapest combination is to fly from Bangkok to Calcutta, then take surface transport.

● **From Tibet** The surface route is the more interesting but you can fly between Kathmandu and Lhasa for US$190/£125. See p31.

See p71 for information on arrival at Kathmandu airport.

Overland from India

From Delhi or Varanasi the most convenient border crossing is

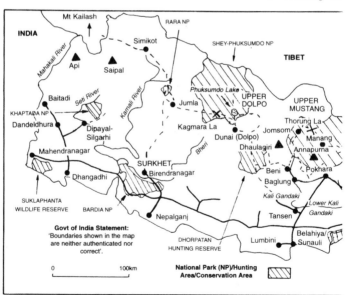

Sunauli/Belahiya, reached via Gorakhpur. There are no through buses; whatever the agents in Kathmandu or Delhi may say you have to change at the border. It's not difficult to arrange your own tickets along the way and doing it yourself gives you the option to stop where you want to. Doing the trip from Delhi to Kathmandu all by bus is for masochists only and can take up to 60 hours. It's better to travel between Delhi and Gorakhpur by train (approximately US$4/£2.50 in 2nd class) then take a local bus for the three-hour journey to the border at Sunauli.

Immigration is staffed from dawn to dusk although the border does not physically close at night. If you arrive late simply walk across and stay at the better hotels on the Nepalese side, then visit immigration the next morning. Without a visa and entry stamps you'll encounter many problems in Kathmandu. Buses to Kathmandu (US$2/£1.30, 12 to 14 hours) leave from 5am to 9am for the day service and from 4pm to about 8pm for the night buses. For much of the way the route follows the Trisuli River and the scenery is an impressive introduction to the hills of Nepal. The road is being rebuilt over large sections and consequently is rough.

From Calcutta the usual route is via Patna to the border at Raxaul/Birganj. From there the direct Hetauda-Naubise road is narrow so buses take the longer route via Mugling to Kathmandu. The border crossing at Kakarbhitta, near Darjeeling, is open but the road is particularly rough and often washed out during the monsoon.

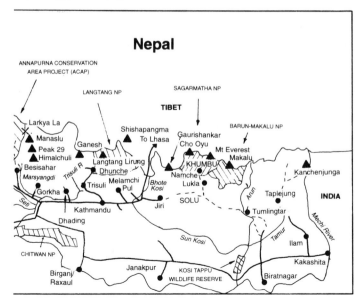

LOCAL TRANSPORT

● **Air** Nepal has an extensive domestic network to make up for the lack of roads. With at least six competing airlines, services are efficient but basic. Since radar is not used bad weather can postpone flights, sometimes for several days. Tickets can be bought direct from the airline offices; travel agents, however, can normally get them for the same price, saving you a taxi trip. Fares must be paid in hard currency, cash or travellers' cheques, not rupees. For more details see p89.

In 1992 Asian Airlines pioneered the use of the large MI-17 Russian helicopters in Nepal. Designed for the military, they can carry around 26 people or 3500kgs of cargo and are big enough to drive a jeep into. Delivered new, these helicopters were flown all the way from Russia to Nepal loaded with spares and crew. Everest Air and Nepal Airways soon followed suit with used versions of these workhorse helicopters. At present all the pilots and flight engineers are Russian, and exceptionally experienced, while the co-pilots and flight attendants are Nepalese. There are plans to replace the Russians with Nepalese once training is complete. Currently these helicopters are used only for cargo and charter flights.

● **Long distance buses** Services are run using sturdy Indian buses that cope well with the rough roads. Night coaches are for masochists and better avoided since sleep is impossible. The day buses are often filled to bursting point and feature a variety of seating, mostly unsuitable for long legs. The spectacular scenery can, however, make up for the lack of comfort. It's important to realise that you pay to get from A to B, whether you have a seat or not. A few tourist coaches have been organised. These cost a little more and are much less crowded. See a travel agent for tickets.

● **Taxis** are plentiful and cheap to use. All are now required to have meters and to use them. Don't accept any stories about meters being broken or needing recalibrating.

● **Hiring a vehicle** is best organised directly with a taxi driver for a taxi, or through a travel agent for mini-buses.

● **Local buses**, usually large Mercedes vans that have seen better days, these are cheap and unbelievably crowded.

● **Tempos** are small three-wheeled vehicles. There are two types: auto-rickshaws which are black and yellow, and fixed-route tempos with enough space in the back for eight Nepalis, or a single foreigner with a backpack!

● **Cycle-rickshaws** are found in all major towns and bargaining is required before you depart.

● **Bicycles** are a convenient and cheap way to get around Kathmandu. Standard bikes and mountain bikes are easily hired in the Thamel and Freak Street areas. The place would make a perfect bicycle city if it weren't for the pollution and the lack of road rules.

(**Opposite**) Namche women dressed in their finery for an important wedding.

LANGUAGE

Nepali, a Sanskrit-based language similar to India's Hindi, is the country's official language. For approximately half the population Nepali is not the mother-tongue, ethnic languages such as Sherpa and Newari being widely used in local areas. Nepali is the medium for schools but English is also taught and you'll meet a surprising number of children who know at least a few English words. In the tourism industry English is the main language, although it is by no means fluently spoken. In the main trekking areas it's quite possible to get by speaking only English.

It is handy to learn a few phrases if trekking without a guide (see p248). Learning more is rewarding and will provide many amusing reactions. Simple spoken Nepali is not difficult and most Kathmandu bookshops sell small phrase-books.

ELECTRICITY

The electricity grid covers only the major towns and cities, and power cuts are frequent. The supply is 220V and 50Hz using old-type round-pin sockets (two-pin and three-pin). Rural Nepal has no electricity, apart from a few very small-scale private or foreign aid hydro-schemes. On a trek it is impossible to recharge batteries for video recorders, other than with a solar panel because even if a village has electricity, the power is rationed to a few bulbs per house and turned on only for the evening. An efficient new system is now operational in Namche, facilitating the recharging of batteries here.

TIME

Throughout the year, Nepal is 5 hours and 45 minutes ahead of Greenwich Mean Time (GMT), and 15 minutes ahead of India (as a show of independence).

❏ Rates of exchange	
US$1	Rs63
UK£1	Rs106
Can$1	Rs45
Aus$1	Rs42
NZ$1	Rs38
DM1	Rs35
FF1	Rs11
C HF1	Rs43
NG1	Rs31
IndRs1	Rs1.60

MONEY

The Nepalese rupee (Rs) comes in banknote denominations of 1, 2, 5, 10, 20, 50, 100, 500 and 1000 rupees. It's divided into 100 paisa but as a tourist you will seldom have to deal with anything less than a rupee. There's a nickel coin worth a rupee and some aluminium coins for lesser denominations. Rates of exchange vary depending on whether the exchange is an official

(Opposite)   Top: The stupa at Bodnath (Baudha) in Kathmandu is one of the largest in the world and the centre of a large community of Tibetan Buddhists.
Bottom: Musicians at a festival in Kathmandu.

government transaction or a transaction being made by a tourist in a commercial bank, and there's also a third, black market, rate.

Changing money

This is supposed be to done at your hotel or at a bank, not on the (now small) black market. Ensure you are given a receipt and some change is useful, in particular Rs100 bills.

Tipping

Once virtually unknown in Nepal, this custom is spreading through the tourism services. Tipping hotel and restaurant staff is not necessary but if the service was good a 5% tip, or the small change, will be appreciated. Tipping trekking crews is now normal and the companies offer guidelines.

POST AND TELECOMMUNICATIONS

The Nepalese postal system is slow. Airmail letters to or from Europe, USA and Australasia usually take around two weeks but can take up to a month; surface mail takes three to six months. The best addresses to have mail sent to are the star-class hotels, American Express or the communication centres in Thamel, which also have faxes. The Poste Restante service in the GPO consists of large boxes for each letter of the alphabet that contain hundreds of letters and anybody can look through them although it's rare for ordinary letters to go missing.

Kathmandu is blessed with a good telephone system and international calls and faxes can be sent and received with ease. The international dialling code for Nepal is +977 followed by 1 for Kathmandu.

Many communications agencies in Kathmandu now offer e-mail and Internet services.

TV, RADIO, NEWSPAPERS AND MAGAZINES

Kathmandu has TV news in English at 9.15pm followed by the BBC TV World Service. Satellite TV on the Star TV network from Hong Kong is available in larger hotels.

Radio Nepal's shortwave transmissions reach the whole country. News in English is broadcast at 8am and 8pm, followed by the general weather forecast; note that they have a hopeless record in predicting huge snow storms. Try Voice of America's Lhasa forecast or the BBC. Recently, commercial radio stations have been allowed on the airwaves. The music is more modern but few reach out of the Kathmandu valley yet.

The local English-language dailies are the *Rising Nepal* and the (rather better) *Kathmandu Post*. The *Rising Nepal* is still obsessed with the comings and goings at the royal palace; international news is usually confined to a few columns. The paper gives a rosy and vague outline of what the government is currently up to and also includes odd titbits, like the state of the New

Zealand economy. The *International Herald Tribune*, *USA Today*, and the *Asian Wall Street Journal* are sold everywhere as are magazines including *Time*, *Newsweek*, *Far Eastern Economic Review*, *Business Week*, *The Economist*, *Stern* and *Der Spiegel*. There's a plethora of Nepali magazines, many advertising tourist orientated services and interests. One that is worth looking out for is *Himal*, a quarterly Himalayan development and environmental discussion magazine. The British Council has a reading room with a variety of magazines and papers.

HOLIDAYS AND FESTIVALS

Government office and business hours are 10am to 5pm. On Saturdays government offices (including the trekking permit office) and banks are closed but you can still change money in larger hotels. Everything re-opens on Sundays, except the embassies. Souvenir shopping and sightseeing are possible every day although all museums are closed on Tuesdays.

Nepal is a land of colourful festivals and these are celebrated with fervour, especially by the less well-off masses. Dates are generally determined by the lunar calendar so fall on a different day each year. The following will be of particular interest to visitors:

● **Dasain** (Durga Puja) is a 10-day October festival – the most important of the Hindu year – which commemorates the victory of the good Lord Rama over Ravana, the demon king of Lanka. Rama, an incarnation of Vishnu, is venerated by Hindus as the paragon of all virtues, so the victory symbolises the ultimate triumph of good over evil. This is a time of family reunion and consequently results in total chaos as everybody heads home. On days eight and nine there's a mass slaughter of buffaloes, goats and chickens. Vehicles are blessed by having their wheels doused in blood. Government offices are closed for at least three days.

● **Tihar** (Deepavali) is a five-day Festival of Light that takes place in late October or early November. Amongst the symbolism is an acknowledgement of the value of brothers and sisters, dogs and cows. Children go from house to house singing and dancing and are given a little food or money. At the height of the festival on the third day people light their homes with candles to welcome Lakshmi, the goddess of wealth.

Sherpa festivals

● **Mani Rimdu** is the popular three-day Sherpa festival held at Tengboche in November and at Thame in May. Monks perform ceremonies and dances, both serious and fun. It is a major social occasion.

● **Losar** Tibetan New Year is celebrated during mid-February. It is a time to receive new clothes (making them is a winter job) and raise new prayer flags.

● **Orsho** is a rite to protect the crops and takes place at the start of April.

● **Ch-rim**, to rid the land of evil spirits, occurs twice a year. The rite is enacted first after potato planting, then again after the harvest when the livestock returns from the summer pastures.

● **Dumji** is an important five-day festival that takes place during the monsoon, over the anniversary of the Khumbu's patron saint, Lama Sange Dorje. The gods are requested to subdue the evil spirits of the village. A group of eight families (different each year) lays on the feast. There are separate festivals in Namche, Thame and Khumjung.

● **Buddha's birthday** falls in May and the **Dalai Lama's birthday**, particularly celebrated by Tibetan refugees, is on 6 July.

FOOD

Despite the ethnic mosaic the local cuisine is not particularly inspiring (unless you stay with well-off Nepalese friends). Standard Nepalese fare, *dal bhat*, consists of rice, lentils and a few vegetables. It can become monotonous but is certainly cheap and filling – your plate is topped up until you've had enough. In the Khumbu, potatoes form a major part of the Sherpa diet.

In response to trekkers' requests the restaurants of Kathmandu (and along some trekking routes) experimented with foreign dishes with surprising success. There's now an incredible variety of non-Nepalese cuisines at these places. Authenticity is not a strong point but you can eat passably Mexican, Italian or Thai food. There are excellent restaurants in Kathmandu specialising in tandoori and other styles of Indian food. 'Buff' (buffalo) steaks are a feature of many menus, beef being outlawed in this Hindu kingdom, although some restaurants manage to import it. The range of Tibetan food includes *momos* (meat or vegetables encased in dough and steamed or fried), and meat soup known as *thupka*.

The cakes and pies can be a real delight. These vary from restaurant to restaurant but many are wholesome and just as Mum would make them. The vast choice includes apple pie, apple strudel, cheese-cakes, chocolate cakes, lemon meringue pies, cinnamon rolls and banana cream pie.

DRINK

All water should be treated (see p235) before it is safe to drink. Plastic bottles of mineral water are available, but from an environmental point of view drinks such as Coke are better since the glass bottles they come in are returnable. Several types of beer are brewed, some under licence from foreign companies. *Chang* is locally brewed beer produced by villagers.

THINGS TO BUY

In Kathmandu and at a few of the larger centres along trekking routes, shops selling souvenirs and handicrafts abound. They offer Newari art, Tibetan *thangkas* (paintings of religious symbols and figures done on cloth), jewellery, bronze Buddhas and Hindu deities. Boys wander around the streets of Thamel pestering you to buy khukri knives, chess sets and Tiger Balm. Carpets come in a great variety, many with modern designs in vegetable-dyed pastel shades. Luxuriously thick, they are made mainly in Kathmandu from a blend of New Zealand and Tibetan wool. When buying jewellery finding quality silver is not easy and you should beware of glass 'rubies' and dyed concrete-dust 'turquoise'.

Hand-knitted jerseys/sweaters and clothing are made in the distinctive styles of the regional cultures and are popular with travellers. In Kathmandu, embroidered T-shirts are a speciality. There's a wide range of motifs to choose from and they look good on fleece jackets too.

Bargaining

Throughout Asia, bargaining is a part of life, although trekking exposes you to few situations that require bargaining. Most lodges have a menu with fixed prices that really are fixed – where you eat or stay is your choice. Buying at markets or from a farmer or hiring a porter may require some negotiation. As a foreigner (incredibly wealthy in comparison to most Nepalese) you start at a disadvantage and this will be utilised. Bargaining need not be aggressive – it's better to treat it as a game with smiles and jokes. After a price has been agreed it must be honoured. Once the transaction is complete that is the end of the matter, all is forgiven and forgotten. Harbouring resentment comes across as a small-minded Western attitude.

SECURITY

Kathmandu is safer than most Western cities. Violent crime is virtually unknown, and it is safe to take taxis, cycle and walk the streets and alleys at night, although women may be safer in a group. Despite the relaxed atmosphere in hotels, staff are honest, rooms have barred windows and managers are security-conscious, keeping an eye on who goes in or out. In the cheaper hotels other travellers are a greater risk, if anything. The better hotels have security boxes for valuables and all will store luggage safely while you trek.

Around town adept pick-pockets work crowded local buses. The usual ploy is to distract you with conversation or by pretending to be interested in your watch. Pick-pockets have a field day at busy festivals, as the queues of foreigners outside the American Express office the following day testify. Keep your travellers' cheques and money in a pouch or money belt and never let your camera or other valuables out of your sight.

The trekking regions were once crime-free but as the population is exposed to the wider ways of the world, occasional cases of theft now occur. Violent attacks are almost unheard of in the Solu-Khumbu although the tents of trekking groups are occasionally slit during the night and valuables disappear. The trekking crews are trustworthy, although if you lend gear, you will have to ask for it back. In the crowded lodges during high season occasionally the odd thing goes missing, generally a camera or valuable trekking equipment, but in a quiet lodge things are absolutely safe.

You are incredibly wealthy by local standards so don't flaunt your gear or openly display large quantities of money and camera equipment. You should show that you value and care for all your belongings.

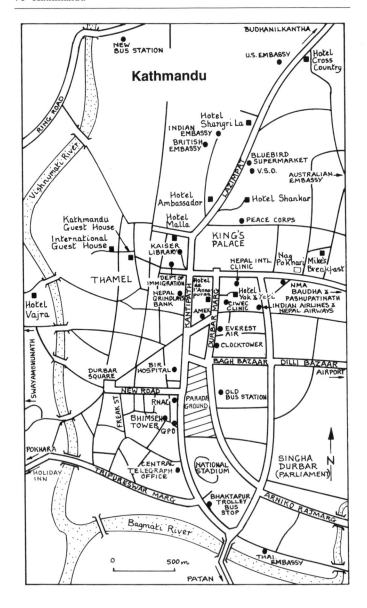

PART 3: KATHMANDU

The city

Nepal's capital, Kathmandu (population 560,000), is a fascinating city which rose to prominence in mediaeval times. You should allow a few days at the beginning or end of your trek to see the sights and explore its narrow alleys. In any case all trekkers to the Everest region must pause in Kathmandu for at least a night or two to get their trekking permits.

ARRIVAL AND DEPARTURE

By air
● **Arrival** Tribhuvan International Airport is a 20-minute drive from the centre of Kathmandu. There's a bank in the Immigration Hall (ensure you're given a receipt) and 30-day visas are available for US$25.

Downstairs is the luggage carousel. Customs don't generally offer problems for tourists (although valuable items like video cameras may be noted in your passport for re-export).

Through Customs is the quiet main hall where the tourist information booth gives out free copies of *Travellers' Nepal* (in which the star-class hotels advertise heavily) and a free map of Kathmandu, both well worth picking up. The hotel reservation counter deals with star-class hotels, making reservations and organising a free taxi service. The pre-paid taxi counter organises transport into town for Rs200 for the whole car or Rs100 per seat if you're travelling alone. You can do this yourself perfectly easily if you're prepared to bargain with the taxi drivers outside, and it should cost around Rs150-200 for the whole taxi. Plans to restart the government-run airport bus service have not, as yet, come to anything. The pre-paid taxi desk operates a coach for Rs70, when they can get enough passengers together.

Outside the building is a chaotic scene similar to any Third World airport forecourt. Boys eagerly try whisking away your luggage to one taxi, while taxi drivers pull you to another offering discount hotel rooms. Travellers usually head for Thamel or Freak Street for budget accommodation. Taxi-drivers recommend the marginally more expensive Thamel hotels (where they can get commission) but it's easy enough to find your own hotel when you get to either of these places.

The several routes to town pass through narrow streets lined with crumbling red brick houses. You know you've arrived in Thamel when, after driving by a few roundabouts, you see the Department of Immigration on the right and the road ahead narrows to a jumbled mass of vehicles. This is as good a place as any to get out. Alternatively, ask for the Kathmandu Guest House, to land yourself in the centre of it all.

● **Departure** If you leave Nepal by air, a departure tax of Rs700 (Rs600 for India and SAARC countries) is payable in local currency only, as you check in at the airport. In the bank here you can reconvert up to 15% of the remaining rupees for which you have exchange receipts.

By land
Most buses (except buses for the Everest region) terminate at the new main bus station which is in the north of the city. If you're coming into Kathmandu by bus it's worth asking the driver to drop you off as near Thamel as possible. From the bus station, however, there are frequent shuttle buses (Rs2) which pass by the northern end of Thamel on their way to the old bus station near the clock tower. If you're arriving on a blue and white Sajha bus, note that they arrive and depart from just outside the GPO.

ORIENTATION

Greater Kathmandu, which includes Patan as well as Kathmandu itself, lies at about 1400m/4593ft. The Bagmati River runs between these two cities. The airport is 6km to the east, near the Hindu temple complex of Pashupatinath, with the Buddhist stupa at Baudha 2km north of Pashupatinath. The other major Buddhist shrine, Swayambhunath, is visible on a hill in west Kathmandu. The third city in the Valley, Bhaktapur, is 14km to the east.

Within Kathmandu, most hotels and guest houses and the Department of Immigration (for trekking permits) are to be found in Thamel, north of the historic centre of the city, Durbar Square. Freak Street, the hippie centre in the '60s and '70s which still offers some cheap accommodation, is just off Durbar Square. Some of the top hotels and the international airline offices are along Durbar Marg which runs south from the modern royal palace.

WHERE TO STAY

Hotel areas
● **Thamel** Most travellers find Thamel the most convenient area to stay in, although it's now largely a tourist ghetto. Everything you could want is available here, with over 100 guesthouses and hotels (from $1/£0.65 to $90/£60 per night), good restaurants, souvenir shops, book shops, communication centres and travel agencies. It's also close to the Department of Immigration, for trekking permits and visa extensions.

● **Freak St** In the halcyon days of the '60s and '70s when Kathmandu was a major stopover on the hippie trail, Freak St, just off Durbar Square, was the place to hang out. Although the hash dens are now all closed it still retains a quaint, almost timeless charm. Its 15 or so hotels and restaurants are all in the rock bottom to cheap bracket.

● **Other areas** Away from the intense tourist scene are other small hotels scattered throughout Kathmandu. In Patan, there are a couple of budget hotels off Patan's Durbar square and also a few good three to four-star hotels. Baudha and Swayambhunath have a scattering of simple hotels favoured by Buddhists and travellers.

Prices

Prices given here are for the high season (Oct-Nov/Mar-Apr) for single/double rooms, with common (c) or attached (a) bathrooms as indicated. You may be able to get a discount of anything up to 50% on the prices below outside the high season, depending on the length of your stay. Many hotel owners quote their prices in US dollars; you pay in rupees, though. Given the changing rate of inflation in the country, this is a sensible idea so US dollars are also used here. The dollar/pound exchange rate hovers around US\$1.60=£1.

Budget guest houses (US\$5/£3 or less)

In Thamel there are around 40 places to choose from in this price bracket, and in some you'll even get an attached bathroom for this price. A few hotels have triple or quad bed rooms. Check that the hot water works and try to get a room that faces away from the roads – Kathmandu is plagued by noisy dogs and honking taxis. The cheapest hotels tend to be in Narsingh Camp (behind Pumpernickel Bakery), in Chetrapati, a suburb adjoining Thamel, or hidden in the outskirts of Thamel.

Freak Street is one of the few places in the world where it is still possible to find a room, admittedly small, for one US dollar a night. A slightly larger budget widens the choice considerably. The majority of hotels are on the main street but looking down alleys nearby yields more.

Cheap hotels in Thamel (US\$6-15/£3.50-9)

Most Thamel hotels offer a range of rooms, the majority falling in this price bracket. The hotel should provide clean sheets, blankets and a desk while the better will supply towels and toilet paper and perhaps be carpeted. Little features to check are: is there a vent or window in the bathroom, a clothes line and a rooftop garden? Features aside, when choosing a hotel, go by the reception staff – are they friendly and helpful or lackadaisical? Most people new to Kathmandu begin looking at hotels in the heart of Thamel. However, there are plenty of hotels in every direction, none of which are more than a few minutes walk from the centre.

The best known of the hotels in Kathmandu must be the long-running *Kathmandu Guest House* [82] (☎ 413632, 418733), a Thamel landmark. Popular with groups, it's bursting in the high season. They have a few rooms from US\$6-8/\$8-10 (c) but most accommodation here is US\$17/20 or more in the new wing.

Moderately-priced hotels

There are numerous reasonable hotels in the US\$15-30/£10-15 price range. Most have attached restaurants. All rooms have attached bathrooms with hot water, and in the more expensive rooms a TV and perhaps and air-conditioner/heater. Some hotels have a few de luxe rooms in this price range too.

Thamel Accommodation In **ascending order by price** for singles/doubles with common (c) or attached (a) bathroom. Prices in US$ but payable in rupees.

01 Frugal GH $1.50/2 (c)
02 Norling GH (221534) $1.50/3 (a)
03 MK GH (212866) dbl: $2 (c), $3 (a)
04 Pheasant Lodge (417415) $2/2.50 (c)
05 Cosy Corner (426467) $2/2.50(c) $5 (a)
06 Continental GH (221446) $2/3 (a)
07 Fortune GH (411874) $2/3 (c & a)
08 Hotel Potala (419159) $2/3 (c)
09 Friendly GH (414033) $2/3 (c)
10 Mini Om GH (229288) $2/3 (c)
11 Buddhist GH (241456) $2/3 (c), $5 (a)
12 Hotel Silk Rd (212224) $2/3 (c), $4/6 a
13 White Lotus GH (224563) $2/3(c)$3/5 (a)
14 Hotel Star (411004) $2/3 (c) $6/8(a)
15 Everest GH (222231) $2/3 (c), $3/4 (a)
16 Hotel Kathmandu Holiday (220334) $2 (c), $3/4 (a)
17 Pooja GH (416657) $2/3 (c), $3/5 (a)
18 Mt Blanc GH (222447) $2/3 (c), $4/5 (a)
19 My Mom's House $2/3 (c), $4/5 (a)
20 Guest Palace GH (225593) $2/3c, $5 a
21 Plover Nest (220541) $2/4
22 Souvenir GH (410277) $2/4 (c), $8 (a)
23 Chitwan Tulasi (416120) $3/4 (c)
24 Hotel The Earth (229039) $3/4 (c), $7/8 (a)
25 Htl Yeti (414858) $3/4 (c) $7/8 (a)
26 Kunal's (411050) $3/4 (c), $5 dbl (a)
27 Fishtail Home $3 dbl (c), $4 dbl (a)
28 Green Peace Ktm GH (426817) $3 (c), $5 (a)
29 Yak Lodge (224318) dbl: $4 (c) $5 (a)
30 Htl Florid (416155) $5 (c), $8 (a)
31 Hokkaido GH (426051) $4/6 (c)
32 Skala (223155) $2/4 (c), $4/6 (a)
33 Gurkha Soldier GH (230666) $2/3 (c)
34 King's Land GH (417129) $3/4 (c)
35 Blue Sky GH (426550) $3/5 (c)
36 New Orleans (425736) $3/5 (c)
37 Polo GH (242356) $3/4c, $4/5a
38 Namaskar GH (421060) $4/5 (a)
39 Orange GH (410182) $2/4 c, $4/5 (a)
40 Pumori GH (424270) $2/4 (c) $4/6 (a)
41 Fuji GH (229234) $4/5 (c) $6/9 (a)
42 Gorkha (214243) $3/5 (c), $4/6 (a)
43 Rainbow GH (417157) $3/5 (c), $3/6 (a)
44 Bharati Home (224986) $4/6 (a)
45 Tourist GH (418305) $4 (c), $6 dbl (a)
46 A-One GH (229302) $4 (c), $6 (a)
47 Tibet Peace GH (415026) $3/4 (c), $4/7 (a)
48 Marco Polo (227914) $4-10 (c,a)
49 Tara GH (220634) $3/4 (c), $5/8 (a)
50 Htl Puska (228997) $3/5(c),$4/6(a)
51 Ktm Peace GH (415239) $4/5 (c), $6/12 (a)
52 Holy Lodge (416265) $3/5 (c), $7/10 (a)
53 Dolpa GH (224367) $4/5 (c) $6/7 (a)
54 Shangri-La Guest House (250118) dbl: $5 (c) $10 (a)
55 Earth House (418197) $4/6 (c), $6/12 (a)
56 Base Camp Hotel (212224) $4 (c), 7(a) dbl

57 Valentine (425051) $4/6 (c), $8 dbl (a)
58 Deutsch Home (415010) $4/5 (c), $7/10 (a)
59 Shiddartha Guest House (227119) $5(c), $7/10/12 (a)
60 Hotel Shakti (410121) $5/7 (c), $16/18 (a)
61 Htl Iceland View (416686) $8/12 (a)
62 Lhasa GH (226147) $5/6 (c), $8/12 (a)
63 Hotel Horizon (220904) $6 (c) $20 (a)
64 LP GH (412715) $6/7 (c), $8/10 (a)
65 Down Town GH (224189) $5/10(a)
66 Thahity GH $5/10 (a)
67 Mustang GH (426053) $5/8 (c), $10/15 (a)
68 Hotel Elite (227916) $4/8 (c), $12/20 (a)
69 Mt Annapurna GH (255462) $5-15 dbl (a)
70 Htl Jagat (227701) $5/10 (a)
71 Htl Mt Fuji (413794) $8/12 (a)
72 Htl Himgiri (250048) $6/10 (a)
73 Acme GH (414811) $4-10 (c) $6-20 (a)
74 Holyland GH (411588) $6/10 (a)
75 Hotel Namche Nepal (417067) $3-8 (c), $5-20 dbl (a)
76 Universal GH (240930) $8 (c), $8/10 (a)
77 Damaru GH $4/6 (c), $6/12 (a)
78 My Home(231788) $10/14 (c) $14/18 (a)
79 Capital GH (414150) $4/5 (c) $7/8 (a)
80 Tibet Rest House (225319) $6/9 (c), $8/12 (a)
81 Hotel White Lotus (249842) $4/8 (c), $10/14 (a)
82 Kathmandu Guest House (413632) $6/8 (c), $17/20 (a)
83 Hotel Bikram (417111) $6/10 (a)
84 Trans Himalayan GH (214683) $7/15 (a)
85 Sagarmatha GH (410214) $4-8 (c), $10/20 (a)
86 Potala Tourist Home (410303) $6/10 (c) $12/15 (a)
87 Villa Everest (413471) $7/16 (c), $30 (a)
88 Shakya GH (410266) $7/10 (c), $10/12 (a)
89 Htl Nana (418633) $8/10 (a)
90 Mustang Holiday Inn (249041, fax 249016) $8-20/10-30 (a)
91 Potala GH (220467) $8-10/15-20 (a)
92 Pilgrims Htl (416910) $8/10 (c), $15 (a)
93 Tibet Cottage (226577) $8 (c), $12 (a)
94 Yeti Guest Home (419789) $4/6 (c), $8/12 (a)
95 Thorong Peak Guest House (224656) $8/12 (c), $14/18 (a)
96 Tibet GH (214383) $9/10 (c), $13/15 (a)
97 Newa GH (415781) $12/17 (a)
98 Prince GH (414456) $7/10 (a)
99 Hotel Shree Tibet (419902) $10/15 (a)
100 Khangsar GH (216788) $8/10 (a)
101 Sherpa GH (221546) $8 (c) $10/15 (a)
102 Hotel Lily (414692) $8/12 (a)
103 Htl Greeting Palace (417212) $10/15 (a)
104 Hotel New Gajur (226623) $12/16 (a)
105 Hotel Pisang (220097) $12/15 (a)
106 Hotel Norling (240734) $10/20 (a)
107 Hotel Sonna (424806) $5/11 (a)

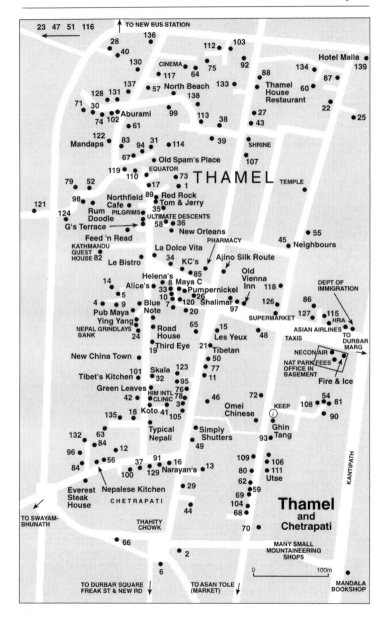

TO NEW BUS STATION

23 47 51 116

28
40
130
136
112 103
CINEMA
117 64 75 92
137 57 North Beach 133 88 Thamel House Restaurant
128 131 138 60
71 30 99 113 38 27
74 102 Aburami 61 43
122 Mandaps 83 94 31 114 39 SHRINE
67 Old Spam's Place 107
119 110 EQUATOR
79 52 17 73 THAMEL TEMPLE
98 Northfield 89 Red Rock 1
121 124 Rum Cafe Tom & Jerry
Doodle PILGRIMS 35
G's Terrace ULTIMATE DESCENTS 55
58 36 45 Neighbours
Feed 'n Read New Orleans
KATHMANDU PHARMACY
GUEST La Dolce Vita
HOUSE 82 Le Bistro 34 KC's Ajino Silk Route
14 85 Old Vienna Inn 118 DEPT OF IMMIGRATION
Alice's 8 Maya C
5 33 Pumpernickel 126 86
4 9 10 26 127 115
Pub Maya Blue 7 120 Shalimar 97 SUPERMARKET HRA
Ying Yang Note 20 ASIAN AIRLINES TO DURBAR MARG
NEPAL GRINDLAYS 65 15 48 TAXIS
BANK 24 Road Les Yeux NECON AIR
House 19 21 Tibetan NAT PARK FEES OFFICE IN BASEMENT
Third Eye 50 KEEP Fire & Ice
New China Town 123 77
101 Skala 11 54
Tibet's Kitchen 32 95 108 81
Green Leaves 76 78 46 72 90
42 HIM INTL 3 KEEP
18 Koto 41 105 Omei Chinese
135 Ghin Tang
132 63 93
96 84 12 109 106
84 56 37 91 16 80 111
100 129 Narayan's 13 62 Utse
Everest Nepalese Kitchen 29 59
Steak CHETRAPATI 69
House 104
44 68
THAHITY 70
CHOWK Thamel and Chetrapati
66
2 MANY SMALL MOUNTAINEERING SHOPS
6 0 100m
TO SWAYAM-BHUNATH
TO DURBAR SQUARE TO ASAN TOLE MANDALA
FREAK ST & NEW RD (MARKET) BOOKSHOP

Typical Nepali
Simply Shutters
49

Hotel Malla 134 139 87 22 25

Helena's

KANTIPATH

108 Imperial GH (249339) $12/15 (a)
109 Htl Blue Diamond (226320) $12/15 (a)
110 Hotel Garuda (416340) $9-20/13-25 (a)
111 Hotel Utse (226946) $13/20 (a)
112 Htl Gauri Shankar (417181) $14/19 (a)
113 Hotel Karma (417897) $10/15 (a)
114 Htl Tashi Dhargey (415378) $15/20 (a)
115 Hotel Tilicho (410132) $15/25 (a)
116 Htl Moonlight (419452) $10-25/14-35 (a)
117 Hotel Buddha (413366) $15/20 (a)
118 Htl MM Internatl (411847) $20/30(a)
119 Hotel Mona (422151) $15/20 (a)
120 Hotel Excelsior (411566) $18/22 (a)
121 International GH (410533) $16/19
122 Hotel Mandap (413321) $18/24 (a)
123 Htl Tashi Dhele (217446) $15/25 (a)

124 Hotel Shikhar (415588) $10/14 (a)
125 Hotel Lantipur (414850) $10/15 (a)
126 Hotel Tridevi (416742) $12/15 (a)
127 Tibet Holiday Inn (411453) $10/15 (a)
128 Hotel Rimal (410317) $15/20 (a)
129 Hotel Tayoma (244149) $15/30 (a)
130 Hotel Tenki (425905) $15/20 (a)
131 Hotel Blue Ocean (418499) $15/25 (a)
132 Nirvana Garden H (222668) $18/25 (a)
133 Hotel Thamel (417643) $18/25 (a)
134 Htl Norbu Linka (414799) $20/30 (a)
135 Hotel Pyramid (246949) $20/30 (a)
136 Hotel Manang (410993) $50/60 (a)
137 Htl Marshyangdi (414105) $30/40 (a)
138 Htl Vaishali (412968) $90/100
139 Hotel Malla (410320) $110/132

Three-star standard hotels

Around the three-star standard are two well-managed traditionally built hotels. *Hotel Vajra* (☎ 272719, fax 271695) was conceived and paid for by a Texas billionaire, and built by Newar craftsmen, with wall-paintings by Tibetan and Tamang artists. Rooms are US$14/16 for singles/doubles with wash-basins, US$33/38 with attached bathroom and US$53/61 for rooms in the new wing. It is located near Swayambhunath. The traditionally decorated *Summit Hotel* (☎ 521894) in Patan is popular with expeditions seeking peace. Prices range from US$20 to US$75. Both have a pleasant atmosphere nice gardens, restaurants and thoughtful amenities.

Close to each other in north Thamel are the *Hotel Marsyandi* (☎ 414105) and *Hotel Manang* (☎ 410993), both popular with trekking groups.

Four- and five-star hotels

Until its unfortunate demise in 1970, the top place to stay was the Royal Hotel. Its success was largely due to its proprietor, the legendary White Russian émigré, Boris Lissanevitch. It was the country's first Western hotel, opened in 1954 in a wing of the palace that is now the Bahadur Bhavan. Virtually everything for it had to be imported from Europe, shipped to India and then carried in by porters. Staying here you'd be guaranteed to meet interesting people and many of the mountaineering expeditions made it their Kathmandu base.

Now the most popular is *The Yak & Yeti* (☎ 413999, fax 227782), with rooms from US$130/160 to US$450 for a suite. The Yak & Yeti Bar with its excellent Chimney Restaurant was moved here from the Royal Hotel when it closed. Close by, the new *Hotel Durbar*, four-star, is less train station-like than its bigger neighbour.

The *Soaltee Holiday Inn Crowne Plaza* (☎ 272550, fax 272205) is probably the best of the big hotels, although it's not so well located, being in the west of the city, in Kalimati. Rooms range from US$150-675. It's popular with Indians, mainly because it has the best casino on the sub-continent.

Back on Durbar Marg is the *Hotel de l'Annapurna* (☎ 221711, fax 225236) with rather ordinary rooms from US$125/135-300, a large pool and

> **❏ Water alert**
> Kathmandu has an ongoing water shortage. Most tourists won't notice this since
> hotels have huge tanks to get around times when supplies are low. However to
> help ordinary Kathmandu-ites who aren't as lucky:
> *When it's yellow, it's mellow, when it's brown, flush it down*
> **Sue Behrenfeld** (USA)

seedy casino. With similar prices US$105/115, *Hotel Sherpa* (☎ 227000, fax
222026) opposite is better. The *Hotel Malla* [139] (☎ 410620), a minute
north of Thamel, is pleasant with rooms from US$100/110. It has a fitness
centre and swimming pool. In the same price range is the *Hotel Kathmandu*
(☎ 418494) along Maharajganj, in the far north of the city. The best value in
this group is the *Hotel Shangri La* (☎ 412999, fax 414184), in Lazimpat,
with rooms from US$100/115. All five are popular with groups.

The quietly located Indian-owned *Hotel Vaishali* (☎ 412968, fax
414510) is Thamel's first four-star hotel. Rooms are from US$90/100
although travel agents can offer substantial discounts.

Probably the best hotel in Kathmandu is *Hotel Dwarika's* (☎ 470770, fax
471379), which has opted out of a star classification. If Kathmandu is a living museum, this is the ultimate place to experience it. The red brick buildings are lavished, inside and out, with ornate panels lovingly restored from
old Kathmandu houses. Every room (US$110/125) is an individual work of
art, and the restaurants' offerings are similarly exotic.

Worth avoiding are the inconveniently-located *Everest Hotel* and the
overpriced *Hotel Shankar*.

Note that all star-class hotels add a 10-14% government tax to the bill.

WHERE TO EAT

Kathmandu's restaurants are renowned amongst travellers throughout South
Asia for their ability to serve passable approximations of Western dishes.
You will, however, probably be more appreciative of Kathmandu's apple-pie
and enchilada cuisine after a trek rather than on arrival direct from the West.
It's surprising how quickly you forget how things really supposed to taste!
The cost of meals in restaurants doesn't vary as greatly as hotel prices. Most
main courses cost less than US$3/£2, often much less.

Be especially careful about what you eat before you set out on your trek;
you're more likely to pick up a stomach bug in a Kathmandu restaurant than
in the hills. A test on the quality of the tap water in Thamel showed it to contain more than ten times the WHO recommended safe maximum level of fae-
cal matter. The better restaurants are serious about hygiene but don't believe
all restaurants that tell you their salads are washed in iodine. Similarly filtered water is not reliably clean; stick to bottled or hot drinks. Unless otherwise indicated the restaurants described are in Thamel (see map p75).

Breakfast

Even the smallest guest houses now offer breakfast and snacks either as room service or in their own snack bars. Most of the Thamel restaurants have set breakfasts that can be good value but there are a few places worthy of special mention.

The *Pumpernickel Bakery* does a roaring trade in cinnamon rolls, bagels and other pastries and cakes. There's a pleasant garden behind it and the noticeboard here is a good place to track down trekking partners. *Brezel Bakery*'s roof top offers competition especially with its quick service.

For many years the place to go for a relaxing start to the day has been *Mike's Breakfast*. You breakfast on authentic American (hash browns, pancakes and syrup, fresh coffee with free refills etc) and Mexican fare in a garden, serenaded by the sounds of the ex-Peace-Corps owner's classical record collection. The main branch is in Naxal (north east of Thamel) but there's a second branch, the *Northfield Café*, by Ultimate Descents' office.

In *Hotel Garuda* the attached restaurant offers some mountaineers' favourites, including the Scott Fisher Special and a Hillary Breakfast. The cinnamon-flavoured fruit curd is so good that one is never enough. You get the morning papers to read; and the kitchen is clean. The *German Bakery*, in a small alley just north of Mandaps, is cheap and relaxed.

Lunch and dinner

● **Western** The cheapest restaurants in Kathmandu serving 'Western' fare are in and around Freak St.

The *Jasmine Restaurant*, just off Freak St, still has a nice mellow atmosphere and does veg fried rice for Rs25. The *New Mandarin* (in reality almost as old as the hills) is as popular as ever, breakfast costs Rs28. In the Annapurna Lodge, the *Diyalo Restaurant* offers main courses from Rs45-85 and shows free videos in the evening. The *Oasis Garden* is more expensive but does, as the name suggests, have a pleasant garden. Steak and chips are Rs85. Opposite, the *Paradise Vegetarian Restaurant* is probably the best place to eat in Freak St. Their crêpes with garlic cheese are recommended but will set you back Rs75.

Back in Thamel, restaurant prices can be much higher, but there are still places where you'll get a cheap meal that's reasonably filling. *Helena's* is a popular place, main dishes are Rs80-200, there's good cappuccino and a wide range of cakes and pies. *Narayan's*, in Chetrapati, is also popular, especially for dessert. The *Road House Café* is a rather self-consciously cool terrace-diner with a have-a-go-at-anything menu. The food's ordinary but the music, usually live, is mellow. For a refreshingly different menu and good music don't walk past *New Orleans*. Their chicken burrito with chips and salad is Rs90 and a Mississippi mud cocktail with real Baileys in it is Rs110. You can sit by the fire or in the quiet garden at the new *North Beach*, by Hotel Vaishali, and enjoy real burgers and an original American menu .

Many places have steaks on the menu, usually (but not always) buffalo steak. It's often served as a 'sizzler' and arrives in front of you on a heated cast-iron plate doing just that. The enduring *Everest Steak House's* speciality is a wide range of real beef fillet steaks, beginning from Rs140. If you have the appetite of a yeti try the Rs600 chateaubriand (better split between two to three people). *The Third Eye* is also good and, in the back room you can recline on the cushions while you eat.

KC's Restaurant & Bambooze Bar is as much a Thamel institution as the Kathmandu Guest House. The food's good but prices are distinctly up-market. A sizzling steak from the people who introduced the 'sizzler' to Kathmandu now costs Rs195; and if that doesn't fill you up you can round off your meal with their cheeseboard (yak, mozzarella and cottage cheese with wholewheat bread and pickles Rsl00). Another Kathmandu institution recommended for its food is the *Rum Doodle*. Enjoy a real fire without guilt: the logs are made from crushed rice husks. Lemon grilled chicken goes for Rs170.

Most of the video restaurants around Thamel show Hollywood's latest but feature unmemorable food and low quality recordings. The exception is *Red Rock* near Old Spam's Place.

G's Terrace is a Western-Nepali joint venture and authentic Bavarian cuisine is served in this pleasant roof-top restaurant. There's Bavarian home-made potato soup with sausage and specialities like French pepper steak in cognac and cream. Most main dishes are over Rs200. *Old Vienna Inn* serves Austrian cuisine for similar prices. In their attached deli the salami rolls (Rs42) are delicious and can be eaten there or on the run.

There are several more delis and sandwich spots: try a cream cheese bagel from *Titbit* in Hotel Garuda. The *Delicatessen Center* on Kantipath is distinctly upmarket, stocking a surprisingly wide range of imported cheeses and other delicacies, at unsurprisingly high prices. The *Hot Shoppe* has opened a branch in Thamel: chicken quiche (Rs45) and pastries make the perfect take-away lunch.

Many of Kathmandu's top restaurants are in the Durbar Marg area and in the five-star hotels there are some excellent Western-style restaurants, some run by Western chefs. The buffet lunch or dinner at the *Yak & Yeti* costs Rs537 including tax.

Lazimpat has a wide range of good if slightly expensive restaurants catering to the large expat community around there.

Nepal isn't the place to suffer a Mac Attack; McDonald's hasn't arrived. The alternatives are *Nirula's* and the cleaner brighter *Wimpy*, both on Durbar Marg. Beefburgers are out of the question, mutton burgers being the less tasty alternative.

● **Nepali and Newari** There are many cheap local Nepali places out of Thamel that serve dal bhaat or momos, usually for less than Rs50. In Thamel the *Nepalese Kitchen* has a range of superior dal bhaat specials (Rs80-165) and live music several times a week. The *Typical Nepali Restaurant* does the same in a typical building. You won't miss the typically dressed tout outside either. The upmarket *Bhanchha Ghar* (meaning Kitchen House) in

Bagh Bazaar offers wild pork or dried deer meat to accompany drinks and the dinner menu is similarly exotic. Imitating this is *Thamel House Restaurant* (☎ 410388) set in a renovated 100-year-old Newar house. Main dishes range from Rs80-130 and the nine-course set meal costs Rs450.

● **Tibetan** restaurants are amongst the cheapest places to eat in Thamel. By Equator's office is *Lhasa*, run by a Tibetan family. Momos are Rs35. The *Tibetan Restaurant* in the same building as the Lovers' Nest Guest House is excellent value and is run by friendly Tibetans. You can get a plate of ten momos here for Rs15; buffalo chowmein costs Rs20. Under the Kingsland Guest House, *Tashi Deleg* is popular and also does Western food that's good value. The best-known Tibetan place here is *Utse*, at the hotel of the same name. The pingtsey soup (meat soup with wontons) is excellent, as are their momos (vegetable, mutton, buffalo or pork) which cost Rs37 for ten. Given a couple of hours' notice, they will prepare a complete Tibetan banquet (Rs860 for four people). *Tibet's Kitchen* in the Sherpa Guest House has an open-plan kitchen and food is similarly clean and fresh.

● **Indian** Mughal/tandoori dishes appear on many menus but can be disappointing and unlike what you would expect in a good restaurant south of the border. Serving good Indian food has made *The Third Eye* popular but *Mandap's* is better, even if the menu is limited. Delicious chicken tikka masala, with a nan bread or rice is Rs162. *Feed n' Read*, behind Pilgrims book shop does decent southern Indian dosas for Rs40-50, the perfect lunch.

The grimy *Shalimar Restaurant* does chicken masala that's good value at Rs35; chicken tikka costs Rs75 and the chef is from India. On Durbar Marg, there's the *Amber Restaurant* which is popular with local people.

The top Indian restaurant is the Hotel de l'Annapurna's *Ghar-e-kabab* (☎ 221711). It specialises in the rich cuisine of North India, main dishes are around Rs200 and there's live music in the evenings. You may need to book.

● **Mexican** People rave about *Northfield Café* (a branch of Mike's Breakfast); it's the only place for a tostada. It is also one of the most hygienic Thamel restaurants. The attached *Jesse James Bar* serves free corn chips and salsa with drinks.

● **Italian** Many restaurants serve pizza and pasta but one place stands way above the rest, however. *Fire & Ice Pizzeria & Ice Cream Parlour*, just opposite the Department of Immigration, has to be experienced to be believed. Run by an Italian woman who's imported her own computer-controlled Moretti Forni pizza oven, some of the best pizzas on the subcontinent are now turned out here – to the sound of Pavarotti. Prices range from Rs170-290 and there's wine by the glass for Rs130. *Northfield Café* turns out the next best pizzas, and at half the price. For authentic pasta try *La Dolce Vita*.

● **Chinese** Most restaurants have spring rolls and chowmein on their menus although what appears on your plate is usually unmemorable. The

New China Town Restaurant above the ANZ Grindlays exchange branch is the best in Thamel. Although the Garuda's hotel restaurant only has two chop sueys in the Chinese section of the menu, they are crispy, fresh and clean. Probably the best Chinese restaurant is the *Mountain City* at the Malla Hotel, just north of Thamel.

● **Thai** *Ying Yang*, opposite the Third Eye, is Thamel's best restaurant. The speciality is Thai but there is also Western cuisine. They take credit cards. *BK's Thai* is good for its moderate price and their continental food compares well with their neighbours, KC's and Helena's.

● **Israeli** Catering to the large number of Israeli visitors that the country is attracting, *Aburami* opened in 1992. The food is quite authentic and good value. Hummus with chapattis costs Rs48, Israeli salad and felafels with chapattis is Rs94, and they do some of the best chips in town. They put on special meals for Jewish festivals.

● **Japanese** There are several Japanese restaurants, and all serve fairly authentic dishes at almost authentic prices. *Koto*, towards Chetrapati, is the most conveniently located. You're greeted with warm towels, and the dishes are works of art.

● **Vegetarian** All restaurants have some dishes for vegetarians who are sick of dal bhaat. *New Nirmala* has brown bread, garlic toast (Rs8) and excellent cream of spinach soup for Rs35. Tofu lasagne al forno is Rs89. *Skala Vegetarian Restaurant* is set in a pleasant garden and has an imaginative menu (herb roulade with mushrooms and brown bread for Rs80).

If it's Indian vegetarian food you're after, try the *Foodsmen Maharaja Restaurant* tucked away near Hotel My Home. The owner, a Sikh, supervises the production of Punjabi cuisine. A cheese paratha is Rs18, egg curry Rs35. On Freak St, *Paradise Vegetarian Restaurant* is an excellent place.

● **Desserts** After a long trek there's hunger enough in the stomach for a substantial dinner *and* dessert. In Freak Street *the* place is the long-running *Snowman*. It's been renovated, leaving it sterile compared to its hippie past, but the desserts are still astounding value at Rs20. The crème caramel is undoubtedly the best in Kathmandu. Back in the Thamel area *Narayan's*, in Chetrapati, has a window filled with cakes and pies that taste as good as they look. *La Dolce Vita's* tiramisu, served in a cocktail glass is addictive, as is *Rum Doodle's* excellent rum raisin cheesecake (Rs50). Suffering ice cream withdrawal? At *Northfield Café* try the chocolate or the brownie sundae (Rs95) at your peril! Alternatively try a banana split at *Nirula's*.

NIGHTLIFE

Rum Doodle Restaurant & 40,001ft Bar is a Kathmandu institution, with yeti prints on its walls inscribed by the members of many mountaineering expeditions. As well as a wide range of drinks (hot rum punch at Rs70, for example) the food here is good; main dishes are Rs120-200. The **Tom & Jerry Pub** is noisy and popular, an old favourite. There's a rooftop terrace, pool tables and satellite TV. **Pub Maya**, **Old Spam's Place** and **Maya Cocktail Bar** are all similar. New bars seem to pop up every week or two, many with live music although there is no real disco in Thamel yet.

Several of the best Thamel rafting companies put on slide shows with free rum n' coke to tempt you. **Chris Beall's slide presentations** offer good unbiased advice for trekkers about to head into the hills. The shows cost around Rs250 and are held in the Kathmandu Guest House when he's in town

The Kathmandu Guesthouse has a large screen **video disc cinema** with seating for around 25 people. The quality comes at the modest price of Rs100. Hotel Sherpa and Hotel d'Annapurna (both in Durbar Marg) and the Shankar Hotel (off Kanti Path) put on **cultural shows**. The French Cultural Centre occasionally sponsors a play, jazz night or mime act and details are advertised.

The top hotels all operate **casinos**. If you recently flew into Nepal you're entitled to Rs100-worth of free coupons at the Soaltee Holiday Inn casino. There's a shuttle bus (also free) that leaves Thamel and major hotels every hour, 8pm to 11pm.

SERVICES

Banks

Larger hotels can change money at reception. In Thamel there are several authorised money-changers but their rates, like the hotels, are not quite as good as the banks.

Rastriya Banija bank has an exchange counter at the Department of Immigration; in the shopping centre opposite is the Himalayan Bank; Nepal-Grindlays also has an exchange office in Thamel. In Kanti Path, east of Thamel, Nabil Bank offers some of the most competitive rates in the city; the main branch of Nepal-Grindlays is also here.

The **American Express** office (☎ 226172, open Sunday to Friday 10am-1pm and 2-5pm) is by the Hotel Mayalu.

Credit card withdrawals are best made at ANZ-Grindlays, either branch. Rupees or US$ travellers' cheques are the two currency options.

Bookshops and libraries

Kathmandu has some of the best bookshops on the sub-continent, including many small second-hand shops where you can trade in your novel for another. Most international news, computer and fashion magazines are regularly available.

The Kaiser Library, Kaiser Shamsher Rana's private collection, is worth visiting as much for the building as for the 30,000 plus musty volumes. This Rana palace is now the Ministry of Education and Culture, just west of the modern royal palace. The British Council Reading Room on Kanti Path is open to all and has the main UK newspapers and plenty of magazines, although they're all a week or more old.

Communications

The GPO is a 20-minute walk south of Thamel, on the corner of Kanti Path and Prithvi Path. This is where to go for Poste Restante mail. When sending a letter don't put it in a post-box but ask them to frank it or the stamps may be removed and resold. Sending mail is far more easily attended to by the numerous communication centres in Thamel which take letters to the GPO for franking each day.

The cheapest place to make an international phone-call (minimum three minutes) is at the Central Telegraph and Telephone Office, opposite the national stadium at the southern end of Kanti Path. Since this is a 30-40 minute walk from Thamel most people make their calls at one of the **communication centres** dotted around Thamel. They provide excellent services for a modest charge above the normal rates, and don't impose a three-minute minimum on phone calls. You can make international calls, send and receive faxes and, at the better places, send and receive email cheaply, and even access the internet for approximately US$5 an hour. The business centres in the big hotels are generally much more expensive for the same services.

Embassies
● **Australia** (☎ 411578), Bansbari
● **India** (☎ 410900), Lainchaur
● **Israel** (☎ 411811), Bishramalaya House, Lazimpat
● **New Zealand** (Honorary Consul ☎ 412436), Dilli Bazaar
● **Sweden** (☎ 220939), Khichapokhari
● **Thailand** (☎ 420410), Bansbari
● **UK** (☎ 411590), Lainchaur
● **USA** (☎ 411179), Pani Pokhari

Medical clinics

CIWEC (☎ 228531, open Monday to Friday 9am-12 noon, 1-4pm) is an exceptionally competent clinic which is located just off Durbar Marg, near the Hotel Yak & Yeti. Consultations cost US$35 or equivalent in any currency. **Nepal International Clinic** (☎ 412842, open Sunday to Friday 9am-5pm) is also excellent and consultations cost US$30 or equivalent. It's opposite the Royal Palace, slightly east of Durbar Marg.

Cheaper clinics in Thamel include **Synergy** (☎ 413503), who are better at advertising than consultations; **Everest International** (☎ 411504) on the Thamel Chowk; and **Himalaya International** (☎ 225455) near Hotel Utse.

Trekking equipment rental

There are perhaps 20 shops with a wide variety of equipment so you can afford to be selective and shop around. Large deposits are required: money of any sort or valid airline tickets but credit cards should not be trusted to anyone.

WHAT TO SEE

A virtual living museum, the Kathmandu valley is crammed with sights and it's well worth setting aside several days to take some of them in. The most popular attractions are mentioned below. Aimless wandering through the narrow streets also has its rewards, though. Amongst the colourful confusion you'll come upon numerous temples, stupas and other holy places.

Swayambhunath

From this huge stupa on a hill in the west of the city, the all-seeing eyes of the Buddha overlook the entire Kathmandu valley. It's also known as the Monkey Temple and dotted around it are several other shrines and temples. There's a pilgrims' rest house, a Buddhist library and *gompa* (Buddhist temple) as well as a Hindu temple dedicated to the goddess of smallpox. Behind on a smaller hill is a favourite temple for children, dedicated to Saraswati, the goddess of learning. Walking (half an hour from Thamel) or cycling through the colourful streets is the most pleasant method of reaching the hill.

Pashupatinath

Beside the sacred Bagmati River, this is one of the most revered Hindu temples on the Indian subcontinent. Entry to the main temple is barred to non-Hindus but there are numerous other shrines in this large religious complex. Dedicated to Shiva, the destroyer and creator – stone linga fertility symbols are everywhere. Cremations take place on the banks of the river, providing a morbid tourist attraction. You'll see lots of sadhus, saffron-robed holy men, who perform various feats here (including rock-lifting – with their penises no less!). Pashupatinath is on the eastern outskirts of Kathmandu, easily reached by bike or taxi.

Bodhnath (Baudha)

One of the largest stupas in the world, Bodhnath is surrounded by a thriving Tibetan community. Prayer wheels line the mandala-shaped base. These must be turned clockwise, the direction in which you should walk around the stupa. There are lots of souvenir shops as well as Tibetan restaurants and a few guest houses. Close by are a variety of Tibetan gompas. When visiting you should leave a small donation.

Patan

Once a separate city-state, this ancient historical centre is now a southern suburb of Kathmandu. It's an architectural feast, at the centre of which is Durbar Square. Temples abound and it is best to explore on foot or by bicycle. The outskirts of the town are beautiful and semi-rural, the most desirable residential area for wealthy Nepalese and expatriate staff.

Bhaktapur

Compared with Kathmandu and Patan, the other cities in this mediaeval trio, time has stood still in Bhaktapur. Wandering round the narrow streets and temple-filled squares is fascinating and schoolboys act as surprisingly knowledgeable guides. They'll want some baksheesh (Rs30 or so, though they'll try for more). Staying here overnight, especially during a festival is well worthwhile.

It's 14 km from Kathmandu and you can get here by taxi, mini-bus or trolley-bus. You can also cycle here although the pollution on the outskirts of the city is horrific. Hiring a mountain bike to combine with a steep ride to Nagarkot makes for an adventurous expedition.

Nagarkot

Perched on the eastern rim of the encircling hills, the Himalaya from the Annapurnas to Everest are visible from Nagarkot on a clear morning. It's a popular overnight excursion although the exploring possibilities on foot or by mountain bike warrant more time. There are plenty of cheap lodges, and buses from Bhaktapur leave every hour or so. A tourist mini-bus leaves outside the Kathmandu Immigration office at 1.30pm and early morning sunrise tours are easily arranged by travel agents or with a taxi driver. Close by is Dhulikhel, another favourite viewing spot. Just off the Arniko Highway this is also easily reached.

Dakshinkali

Sacrificial blood flows freely on Tuesdays and Saturdays for the goddess Kali at this temple. Like hungry hyenas tourists jostle to take red-splashed photos and a few turn vegetarian. It is 20km from Kathmandu, an uphill cycle ride. Buses leave from just east of the GPO in Kathmandu.

SIGHTSEEING TOURS

One of the more competent operators is Gray Line. Bookings can be made through travel agents and hotel receptions. Half day guided tours cost around US$5/£3. Many travel agents and hotels also organise their own tours. To get the most from these ensure you will be accompanied by a qualified guide.

Trek preparation in Kathmandu

KATHMANDU ENVIRONMENTAL EDUCATION PROJECT

The Kathmandu Environmental Education Project (KEEP) raises environmental awareness among trekkers and the trekking industry. They have an information centre and library in a new location on the corner of the lane that leads to the Mustang Holiday Inn.

HIMALAYAN RESCUE ASSOCIATION (HRA)

The HRA was founded in 1973 with the primary aim of saving lives in the mountains by alerting trekkers to the dangers of altitude sickness. It's largely due to their unfailing efforts (passed into guidebooks) that the death toll from altitude sickness is now very low. Their office is worth visiting for advice and the library. They also have forms here so you can register with your embassy. Unless you're trekking with an organised group, you're advised to do this since your embassy's assistance is necessary if a helicopter rescue is required for you.

In addition to the Kathmandu information centre the HRA has two medical posts, one at Manang (in the Annapurna region) and the other in the Khumbu at Pheriche (see p169). They operate only during the peak trekking seasons, however, from early October to early December, and March to April.

ORGANISING A GUIDED TREK IN KATHMANDU

If you're planning to organise a trek with porters, tents and a cook along a standard route to the Khumbu it's worth pointing out that the better lodges here offer a competitive standard of service. As an alternative to the full organised trek you could hire a porter-guide or porter and use the lodges and their facilities. The expedition trekking style is, however, best suited to lightly-trekked routes, remote areas and for climbing trekking peaks.

Trekking companies in Nepal

All trekking agencies in Nepal must be owned by Nepalese nationals so foreign companies have to operate through them. A few have a Western operations manager indirectly in charge. Despite the small offices, most trekking companies are well practised at organising treks; a few have yet to perfect the art though. Try to talk to another foreigner who's been on one of the treks organised by the company before signing up.

Trek personnel

A **sirdar** (trekking guide) is an organiser rather than a trained specialist of history and culture; guides as such don't exist for the trekking regions. He (virtually never she) will speak English and carries only his personal equipment. The older Sherpa sirdars are generally more knowledgeable about the region but few guides are expansive; displaying their culture is not a widely understood tourism concept.

The sirdar, who is often the leader as well when there is no foreign representative, hires and/or supervises the porters, the sherpas (who are not necessarily from the Sherpa clan, and distinguished by the lack of a capital 'S'), and is usually in charge of the money. It is therefore a powerful position and a good sirdar will ensure the trek functions in a trouble-free manner. A bad sirdar can cause endless problems. The **sherpas** are the sirdar's assistants, general helpers who erect and pack the tents, serve the meals, and help in any way they can. They ensure nobody gets lost and carry bags if the members tire. Most speak some English. The **cook** is another key figure, heading a small army of kitchen helpers.

A **porter** is a load-bearer, who generally speaks little or no English. The standard trekking company load is 30-35kg/66-77lbs but if you are doing the hiring then a more gentle 20-25kg/44-55lb will leave a spring in your porter's step and flexibility about the stages.

Operating independently from the above personnel there is the **porter-guide**, usually someone who is not experienced enough to be a sirdar, but speaks some English and wants to try their luck at making more than the usual paltry wage. Since few people hire only a guide, they are willing to carry your backpack, leaving you with just a day pack. By asking around you may be able to find a porter-guide in Lukla but they are scarce in Jiri.

Yaks and **zopkios** (sterile cross between a yak and a lowland cow) are also load-bearers and are usually used in the Khumbu instead of porters, especially by large groups. Yaks are normally used only above Namche while zopkios are to be found from Lukla and above. They carry double the load of a porter, 60-70kg/132-154lbs, for double the cost. Normally the minimum number you can hire is three, with a **yak driver** to look after them.

Costs At present the official minimum charge for a fully organised trek (all food, tents and crew) is US$20/£13.50 per person per day, for which you get a simple, often quite adequate level of service. US$30-40/£20-27 per person per day should provide a reasonable standard of service. The top companies charge around US$35-80/£23-60 a day for slightly better food and slicker service. The cost also depends on the number of people in the trekking group, and there are often discounts if there are more than a few people.

Ensure it is clear exactly what you are paying for and, more importantly, what is not included. All the wages for the crew must obviously be included, and all food plus tents, but are bus tickets, taxes and the National Park entrance fees additional? Decide also on the rates for extra days, for example if you decide to trek for longer, or if the flight is delayed.

HIRING GUIDES AND PORTERS

When looking for a porter/porter-guide, follow your instincts. A pleasant manner is more important than fancy clothes, and in fact for porters, the older and scruffier, the more reliable. Mutual respect is important so don't be afraid to show who's boss. They are being paid comparatively well and the working conditions are less demanding than a normal porter's job. By hiring somebody you take on the responsibility of an employer. One couple who had previously hiked a lot in the Rockies said, 'It was like having a child with you'. Others find the experience rewarding and at the very least it makes getting up the hills easier. Trekking personnel look after themselves in most situations, finding food and lodgings (and often assisting you in this task), but when it comes to snow conditions with the risk of frostbite and snow-blindness, they are notoriously naive. Usually it is you who will have to take preventative action and pay for hired boots and jackets and sunglasses for porters.

Hiring in Kathmandu Trekking companies are happy to arrange crew but be clear what the charges include. You normally pay a daily rate to the trekking company and then pay for the crew's food and lodging on the trail. A few guides are adept at running up huge bills so it's sensible to establish what they will be eating. Most will, however, prefer dal bhaat, the standard cheap Nepali food. Setting a daily allowance for food is a good idea: perhaps Rs150 to Rs200 in the lower areas and Rs250 to Rs300 in the higher, more expensive, regions. An alternative arrangement to agreeing to pay for the crew's food is to pay a higher food-inclusive daily rate.

Since you will be spending a great deal of time together, talk to the guide beforehand, perhaps even go out for a meal with him and if you have real doubts, ask for someone else. With porters, if they are going to high altitudes, insist on knowing the arrangements for gear hire. No matter what's agreed, once you're up there the crew often lack the right gear.

The daily rates for guides are US$6-12/£4-8, the higher rates being the norm. Rates for porters are slightly less, normally around US$5-8/£3.50-5.50 but prices vary considerably between the many agencies. Some trekking companies exploit their employees mercilessly. The crew may often receive no more than standard wages but must hire cold weather gear themselves and pay for food which is progressively more expensive higher up.

Guides wanting work (or touts who have contacts) can often be found outside the Department of Immigration.

Hiring on the trail At Lukla, guides, porters and porter-guides are usually easy to find. At Jiri only porters are readily available. Lodge owners often know who is looking for work. Families with young children or a group of women trekking together may be able to hire female staff.

Independent porter-guides can be hired for Rs200-300 a day plus food, or for an all-inclusive rate of Rs400-600. Bargaining is often required. Bear in mind that for menial jobs in Kathmandu the wage is Rs1000-2500 a month. Note that if you hire through a trekking company all staff are fully insured while those hired independently on the trail are not. Also, many people have mentioned that with hiring locally the rates are often high and work out to be similar to what was obtainable in Kathmandu though a trekking company.

MONEY FOR THE TREK

Provided you're not planning to buy a ticket at a rural airport (payment in hard currency only), it's best to take your entire budget as cash in Nepalese rupees since the only bank in the region is at Namche. About a quarter of the total amount should be in medium and small denomination notes. The most frequently used notes are Rs100 but busy lodges can usually break down Rs1000 notes. For the Arun, Makalu and Rolwaling areas it's safest to have all the money you'll need for that section in denominations of 100 rupees and less.

LUGGAGE STORAGE

Most hotels will store whatever you want to leave behind. There's normally no charge if you'll be staying on your return. Things are quite secure; a few hotels also have safety deposit boxes.

GETTING TO THE KHUMBU

By air

Arranging air tickets to airports in the trekking regions (particularly Lukla) used to be a trick best left to travel agents or trekking companies. But at the end of 1991 the government allowed the formation of private air companies in order to provide much-needed competition for the inefficient state-run Royal Nepal Airlines Corporation (RNAC). Now, with several airlines flying planes and helicopters, tickets to Lukla are easy to arrange, except perhaps in peak season.

Schedules and costs Airlines quote their prices in US$ but tickets can be paid for in most hard currencies (ie not Nepalese rupees). Prices and the airlines that fly the routes are as follows:
● **Lukla:** US$83 (RNAC, Asian, Lumbini, Gorkha).
● **Tumlingtar:** US$44 (RNAC).
● **Biratnagar:** US$77 The eastern hub for Tumlingtar, Bhojpur and Phaplu. (RNAC, Necon Air, Nepal Airways).
● **Phaplu:** US$77 direct (RNAC, sometimes Gorkha and Asian).
● **Bhojpur:** US$77 direct (RNAC only).
● **Syangboche:** (Charters only).
● **Mountain flight:** US$99 (Everest, Necon, Buddha).
The flight timetables and airlines flying the route on a particular day change frequently so it's still worth using a travel agent, particularly during peak seasons. You can contact the airlines direct, however: **RNAC** (☎ 220757), **Nepal Airways** (☎ 420421), **Asian Airlines** (office in Thamel), **Buddha Air** (☎ 418864), **Lumbini Air** (☎ 272903), **Necon Air** (☎ 472542).

RNAC tickets for Lukla can be bought directly at the RNAC head office (☎ 220757) near the GPO, but other tickets must be purchased at their domestic sales office (☎ 223453, Thapathali).

Nepalis (ie your trekking crew) get significantly cheaper fares and so airlines are reluctant to carry them: Lukla Rs1500, for example.

Buying tickets at a rural airport On some flights tourists are given priority over locals. The fare must still be paid in hard currency. You are safest using US$ cash or travellers' cheques. Change and refunds are given only in Nepalese rupees.

By bus

Most bus rides are long and uncomfortable but stops are made for drinks and meals. Roadside stalls sell biscuits, fruit, sweets and soft drinks. Restaurants serve little more than dal bhaat and are not too hygienic. It's wise to be cau-

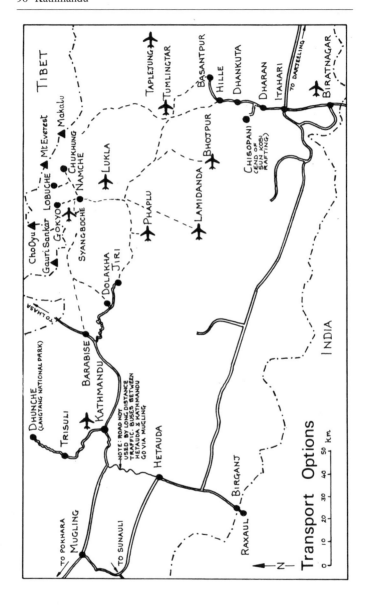

Transport Options

tious, especially at the start of your holiday. Buses for Jiri, Dolakha and Barabise still use the old central bus station near the clock tower, not the new bus station north of Thamel.

Jiri Approximately 12 buses a day leave Kathmandu's old bus station for Jiri (around US$2, 10-12 hours) between 5.30am and 7.30am. This route is worked intensively by thieves. Your backpack must be locked away or within sight for the whole bus journey. From Jiri the last bus leaves at around midday. You may be able to get a lift back on privately-hired transport returning to Kathmandu, more comfortable than the buses. Ask around at the lodges in Jiri.

Dolakha There are three direct buses a day, the first of which leaves at around 6am from the old bus station in Kathmandu. Otherwise you can catch any bus heading to Jiri and get off at Charikot (around US$1). It takes less than an hour to walk down to Dolakha from there. For the return journey the direct daily bus leaves Dolakha at 5am.

Hille/Basantpur The road that goes north from Dharan to Dhankuta and Hille is in the process of being extended and now goes as far as Basantpur. Kathmandu to Hille takes around 24 hours although it'll take less time when the road is finished. At present it's one of Nepal's more uncomfortable night-bus journeys. It certainly gives an interesting insight to life in the hot Terai and, given the right frame of mind, the ride can even be fun.

Check to see if the direct bus to Hille is running. If not, book to Dharan (around US$4, night buses only, leaving Kathmandu's new main bus station from 4pm) then change for Hille. It's better to book a seat a day or two ahead, at the main bus station or through a travel agent, and ask for a seat near the front. Buses between Dharan and Hille leave in the mornings. An alternative route is to Itahari first, then Dharan and Hille.

For the return journey the last bus for Dharan leaves Hille at around 3pm. The Dharan-Kathmandu buses leave in the late afternoon but if you miss these catch a bus to Itahari then one of the buses passing through from Kakarbhitta to Kathmandu.

Barabise There are frequent buses leaving Kathmandu's old bus station between 5am and 4pm for Barabise (under US$1, seven hours). The buses generally stop at the office on the west bank in Barabise.

Tourist vehicles
A special tourist mini-bus to Jiri with tickets sold through travel agents is sometimes operated. Beware of unscrupulous agents who will sell a standard bus ticket as a tourist bus ticket – in reality you end up on the local bus. Otherwise it's possible to hire a taxi or mini-bus and spread the cost between a group of trekkers. You pay for the vehicle to return as well.

PART 4: THE EVEREST REGION

Mountaineering history

EVEREST

Meantime let us count our blessings – I mean those thousands of peaks, climbed and unclimbed, of every size, shape and order of difficulty, where each of us may find our own Mt Everest. HW Tilman *Mount Everest 1938*

The search for the world's highest mountain

In 1808 the Survey of India began the daunting task of mapping the whole of the subcontinent. One of the goals was to discover if the Himalaya was indeed the highest mountain range in the world, as had previously been suspected. Already challenging, the project was made even more difficult by the fact that Nepal and Tibet, wary of foreign intervention, were closed to outsiders.

By 1830 the survey had reached the border between India and Nepal. Unable to cross into Nepal, surveyors resolved to continue the project from the plains. A baseline the length of the range was marked and in 1847 surveying of the northern peaks began, using trigonometrical calculations based on the heights and distances of known points. Conditions were terrible: malaria was rife and monsoon rain eroded the observation towers each year.

Until the mid-19th century it was thought that Kanchenjunga, in Sikkim, at about 28,000ft (8534m), was the highest peak in the range. In 1856 calculations published by the Survey of India revealed that a mountain on the border between Nepal and Tibet was higher. This mountain was designated 'Peak XV' and its height stated to be 29,002ft (8839m); Kanchenjunga was 28,156ft (8582m).

The accuracy of this first survey is astounding, considering the fact that the mountains were measured from survey points 108 miles to 150 miles away from the peaks. In their calculations surveyors had to take account of the earth's curvature and the changing air density, which bends light. It's a sad fact that a survey made from the same points would not be possible today. Dust and air pollution are now so bad that it's rare to be able to make out even the second foothills of the Himalaya from the plains. The present accepted height of Everest is just 26ft (8m) higher: 8848m/ 29,028ft, from an Indian survey taken in Nepal in the 1950s. It's interesting to note that when National Geographic made their much lauded 1:50,000 map of Everest, instead of re-measuring the mountain they used its accepted height as a base for all the other altitudes on the map.

The naming of Everest

It was not until 1865 that Peak XV was named. The accepted method of naming peaks at the time was to use the local name if one could be found. The first map of the area, made in the 1700s, marked this peak as **Tschoumoulancma** but the Surveyor General, Andrew Waugh, chose to name Peak XV **Mount Everest** after his predecessor, Sir George Everest, who oversaw the great survey of India.

This appropriately grand appellation stuck in the West, but Tibetans and Sherpas have always used some variation of the name used on the 18th century map. The Dalai Lama, giving permission for the 1921 Reconnaissance Expedition, called it **Chha-mo-lung-ma**, the name adopted by the Chinese (but transliterated as Qomolangma or Chomo-lungma). This is also the name that the Sherpas use. Difficult to translate directly, it is usually said to mean: 'Mother Goddess of the World'. Sherpas sometimes translate it as 'Home of the Goddess of the Wind' or 'Home of the God or Goddess that Looks After Mothers'. (Makalu is said to be the home of the deity who protects daughters).

The Nepalese name is an even more recent creation than the English designation. They call it **Sagarmatha**, which has been variously translated as: 'Forehead Touching the Sky', 'Head in the Sky', 'Head above All Others' or 'Churning Stick of the Ocean of Existence'.

The Dalai Lama permits the first Everest expedition

Once Everest had been identified as the world's highest mountain nearly three-quarters of a century were to go by before an expedition could be set up to reach the area. The main interest was originally from the British but Nepal and Tibet were suspicious of this colonial power's intentions. Nepal already had a British Resident living in Kathmandu, installed as a permanent observer after they had lost the 1814 war to the British, and one resident foreigner was more than enough. Tibet's capital Lhasa had been a closed city for more than a century but in 1904 Francis Younghusband led a British expedition which fought its way through Tibet, killing many Tibetans, ostensibly to negotiate trade links between the two countries. For more than a decade the Dalai Lama withheld his permission for a British party to make an attempt on Everest. However, eventually he yielded to British demands and the first expedition was mounted in 1921. It was organised by the Royal Geographical Society with climbers from the Alpine Club and was followed by further attempts in 1922 and 1924.

1921 Reconnaissance Expedition

The first expeditions were remarkable for a number of reasons. Many of the most promising young mountaineers had been lost in the battles of the First World War so the average age of members of the reconnaissance expedition was an almost geriatric 44. Although composed of experienced mountaineers, their experience was of European mountains half the height of Everest. Very little was known about the effects of altitude and their equip-

ment and clothing, although the best available at the time, would seem totally inappropriate by modern standards. It was not a strong team and only six
of the nine members reached the base of the mountain after the long walk
from Sikkim.

A major figure in the first expeditions was George Mallory. With his
mountaineering partner, Bullock, he first spent a tough month exploring the
area to find the easiest access to the mountain, the hidden East Rongbuk
Glacier. It was immediately obvious that summer, the monsoon period, was
not the most favourable time for climbing. But despite this and their
appalling equipment, three Sherpas and three climbers reached the North
Col, 6990m/23,000ft. By the end of the expedition a thorough exploration of
the Tibetan side of the Everest Massif had been made, and Mallory had even
peered into the Western Cwm, as he named it, from the Lho La.

Frozen spaghetti on the 1922 Expedition

The 1922 expedition, led by Brigadier General Bruce, arrived before the
monsoon and boasted a thirteen-member team (including a film crew) and
rather superior food supplies. As well as champagne and caviare there were
tins of Heinz spaghetti which, like most of the other foodstuffs, froze solid
at the higher camps.

They may have been better fed but the team members were still woeful-
ly under-clothed. A famous picture of Mallory and Norton, high on the
mountain, shows them dressed in wool trousers and jackets with little room
for more than a jersey or two and long-johns under this. They sported
medum brimmed hats and, aside from the goggles, ice-axes and rope, would
not have looked out of place strolling in an English park on a winter's morning. A series of camps was established. Camp IV was set up on the North Col
and the primitive Camp V at a height of over 7600m/25,000ft. Although
experience showed that this was too low for a serious attempt on the summit, the first attempt was launched from here. Nevertheless, Mallory, Norton
and Somervell reached a height of 8150m/26,800ft without oxygen, before
descending, all slightly frostbitten.

The second attempt was by Finch, accompanied by Bruce's son. Spurred
on by hot tea and the discovery that using oxygen at night aided warmth and
sleep, they climbed to 8320m/27,300ft. For Bruce this must have been especially satisfying since this was his first climbing trip. It was also the first time
that oxygen had been used on Everest and some members of the group were
very much against it, maintaining that its use was most unsporting.

The third attempt ended prematurely, 200m below the North Col with a
fatal avalanche. Nine Sherpas were caught and seven of them killed. The
Everest toll had begun.

'Because it's there' – the 1924 Expedition

It is immaterial whether or not George Mallory coined the immortal phrase:
'Because it's there', when asked in 1923 why anyone would want to climb
Everest; it's for his pioneering contribution towards its conquest that he

should be remembered, and the fateful 1924 expedition was to be his last.

Team members were still inadequately clothed; they had no down clothing. Each climber was given a clothing allowance of £50 to kit himself out. Norton boasted wind-proof overalls and a leather, fur-lined motorcycle helmet plus the usual all-too-thin layers, hardly sufficient against temperatures as low as -40°C (-40°F).

Early storms battered the group forcing them to retreat to Rongbuk Monastery. Here they received the Lama's blessing which they'd imprudently not bothered to seek out when they'd first arrived in the area. The freak weather patterns held up stocks of oxygen sets, leading to a shortage at Camp IV on the col but, despite this, Camp V was established. Camp VI was set at an altitude of 8170m/26,800ft, with Norton and Somervell staying there overnight. They set off early the next morning but Somervell was overcome by a serious coughing attack. He had developed frostbite in his throat and almost choked on a lump of his own frostbitten flesh which he later coughed up, giving him much relief. Norton was forced to struggle on alone and, labouring up steep ground covered with powder snow, reached a record altitude of 8570m/28,126ft, a phenomenal achievement. One has to wonder how much further Norton would have been able to climb if he had had an oxygen set.

That evening, with Norton suffering from snow-blindness and Somervell also out of action, Mallory chose the young and relatively inexperienced Irvine to accompany him the next day. Odell who was older and more acclimatised might, in fact, have been a better choice. Sherpas climbed with Mallory and Irvine up to Camp VI, returning to report that apart from the stove rolling off the mountain, all was well. Next morning the weather was not perfect, and it is assumed that Mallory and Irvine left late. Odell climbed from Camp V to Camp VI studying the geology of the rocks along the way, and through a brief hole in the clouds saw the two climbers ascend a step. Initially he was inclined to think it was the second step before the summit but later suffered doubts. This was around 1pm so the climbers were far behind their schedule: Mallory had intended to be at the second step by 8am. A snow storm blew up and then cleared two hours later leaving the ridge and the summit cone fully visible but there was no sign of Mallory or Irvine. The night was also clear and a watch was kept on the ridge to the summit. However, they were never to be seen again.

Their disappearance began endless conjecture as to whether or not they reached the summit before they died. Subsequent climbers have remarked that Odell's description of where he saw them fits the third and final step better than the second; climbers are still easily visible at that point. If this were the case Mallory and Irvine quite possibly made the summit. To the day he died Odell wasn't sure which step he saw them on but thought it likely that they attained the summit. Their bodies have still not been recovered. This is not surprising since later expeditions have tackled the final stage of Everest up the face, rather than along the ridge, which was the route they used. In

1975, however, the Japanese Women's Everest Expedition was followed a few days later by a Chinese group. As one of the Chinese passed a Japanese climber he made it clear that the body of a British climber had been found at 8100m/26,575ft. If this were indeed true, the body could only have been Mallory's or Irving's. But the mystery continues because the very next day the Chinese climber himself disappeared in an avalanche.

Telephones on Everest – The 1933 Expedition

It was not until 1933 that another attempt was made. This boasted technical innovations: radio and, from Camp III to Camp IV, a telephone line. It was a strong team but bad weather interrupted the process of setting up intermediate camps, putting the expedition behind schedule. Nevertheless, they equalled Norton's altitude record, climbing without supplementary oxygen on bad snow.

British institutions like the Royal Geographical Society and the Alpine Club considered Everest their own preserve, jealously guarding it from attempts by outsiders. They were not amused by the announcement, in 1933, by the wealthy adventurer, Maurice Wilson, that he would climb Everest alone. He bought a light aircraft and flew himself from Britain to India. Despite having no previous climbing experience he managed to get as far as the North Col before succumbing to the cold. His body was found by the next group of climbers.

The 1935 Reconnaissance Expedition

Led by Eric Shipton, this was the first of several expeditions to be headed by this famous explorer-mountaineer. He was known for his ability to think quickly and he preferred to travel light, living off the land, which was a major departure from the normal expedition approach. Since eggs were the most accessible source of protein they regularly appeared on the expedition menu, and Shipton notes that 'though many of them were rather stale we consumed enormous quantities. Our record was 140 in a single day between four of us, and many times our combined party of seven put away more than a hundred.' (*Upon that Mountain*).

One of the Sherpas taken on was an enthusiastic nineteen-year-old named Tenzing Bhotia (later Norgay), who proved to be ambitious and strong. Amongst the other team members was Dan Bryant, a cheerful Kiwi. The expedition had instructions not to climb Everest but the monsoon broke late so there would, in fact, have been time for a serious attempt that season. It was, however, a surprisingly successful climbing expedition in other respects, with an impressive total of 26 peaks over 6095m/20,000ft climbed by the seven-man group, and all for a total cost of a mere £1500.

(Opposite): Mt Everest (8848m/29,028ft) and the Khumbu Icefall seen from high on Pumori's slopes.

Monsoon stops play

The following year the 1936 Everest attempt, for which the 1935 expedition had been preparing the way, was unfortunately washed out by the early arrival of the monsoon. The 1938 low-budget expedition was led by HW Tilman (recounted in his *Mount Everest 1938*). Having learnt lessons about the monsoon from previous expeditions, they arrived early but to no avail. The monsoon broke three weeks earlier than it ever had previously. Still, they continued, even trying a different route but snow conditions for the last 1000m steadily worsened.

Nepal at last

In 1948 the Kingdom of Nepal for the first time opened its doors a crack but only to parties interested in scientific research. Tilman was not a scientist (he claimed that he 'had hitherto refused to mingle art with science') but he compromised his principles and squeezed in a year later. He was allocated the Langtang area, which to his delight was marked 'unsurveyed' on his map. Later he was lucky enough to be invited to visit Namche, walking in from Dharan via the Arun River. He made the first ascent by a foreigner of the now famous Kala Pattar.

The 1951 Reconnaissance Expedition

After the Chinese invasion of Tibet the northern route to Everest was sealed off with the closure of the border. An expedition, led by Shipton, was dispatched to reconnoitre an alternative, southern route through newly-opened Nepal. Although Shipton had turned down many suitable applicants for the team in Britain, recalling New Zealander Dan Bryant on the 1935 Expedition, in a moment of weakness he accepted a request from the NZ Alpine Club for two unnamed climbers to join the team. They were George Lowe and Edmund Hillary. It was to be the first time that a party had climbed after the monsoon, the traditional season being in the 'lull before the storm'. They arrived in Namche at the end of September and climbed to the Western Cwm. In spite of the danger from the Khumbu Icefall it was clear that the southern route up Everest was indeed feasible.

1952 – the competition closes in

Time was running out for the British and what they chauvinistically considered their exclusive 'right' to the area. In 1950 the first 'eight-thousander' (8000m peak), Annapurna, had been conquered by the French. After the British 1951 Reconnaissance Expedition to the Khumbu, there came an unwelcome piece of news: the Swiss had been given permission to make an attempt on Everest in 1952 and the British would have to wait until the following year. A French attempt was scheduled for 1954. Surprisingly, the

---

(**Opposite**) **Top:** Porters usually carry their loads in the traditional *doko* (conical basket). The top of a pass, in this case Salpa Bhanjyang (3349m), is the perfect place for a rest. **Bottom:** With keen eyes, the chances of spotting a musk deer are good.

Swiss almost agreed to a joint Anglo-Swiss expedition (obviously wanting to make use of Shipton's wide experience of the mountain) but the details could not be worked out to everyone's satisfaction. The Swiss chose Tenzing Norgay as their sirdar. He held them in high esteem because it was with two of the Swiss expedition members that he had successfully climbed a peak in 1947, his first despite 12 years climbing with expeditions.

The trek to base camp took 23 days from the newly-opened airfield in Kathmandu. They established five camps between Gorak Shep and the head of the Western Cwm and conclusively proved that it was a feasible route. Tenzing and Lambert climbed to just below the south summit but could go no further. It was realised that an additional camp and further logistical support were needed for an attempt to succeed. Their second attempt after the monsoon was dogged by bad luck, bad planning and the ferocious high-altitude winter winds.

Preparations for the 1953 British Everest Expedition

The Swiss attempts gave the British a chance to prepare properly. Training included an expedition to Cho Oyu in 1952, led by Shipton. Although they failed to reach the summit (see p102), the expedition was of great value: as a result important refinements were made to oxygen sets and clothing.

In planning the 1953 expedition internal politics played a large part. Though Shipton had led many previous expeditions and had immense popularity with the public, some members of the Alpine Club committee felt that he might not be the right man to lead an expedition of such size and under such pressure. This would surely be the final chance for them to reach the summit first. Diplomatic to the last, Shipton agreed that he was indeed happiest climbing with the minimum of encumbering resources and it was decided that John Hunt, an army officer, should lead the expedition which would be run on military lines. Strangely, most of the committee had never met Hunt, and he had been turned down for the 1935 Everest expedition on health reasons.

'We knocked the bastard off!' – success in 1953

The 1953 expedition was an all-out assault. It was decided that oxygen was to be used to the limit of its advantages, for aiding sleep and climbing – anything to conquer. With all this equipment the walk-in was on a grand scale: the first of two groups of porters numbered some 350 people. Since the only currency accepted in the hills at the time was silver coins it took several porters just to carry the wages. There were 13 climbers, with Tenzing Norgay added to the climbing ranks, plus a reporter and cameraman.

The team spent two weeks climbing in the Khumbu area to aid acclimatisation before tackling the Icefall. It was while forging a route through this monstrous obstacle that Hillary and Tenzing first got to know each other and Tenzing demonstrated that he could match the very competitive Hillary. Once the camps in the Western Cwm were established sickness took its toll, setting back the schedules. However, after a 13-day struggle, Camp VIII on the South Col was established. Evans and Bourdillon made the first summit attempt from this camp although it was too far away to allow a safe return if they did succeed. In the event snow conditions deteriorated and one of the oxygen sets caused problems, so the climbers settled for the south summit. This was less than 100m/328ft below the real summit, but at that altitude, even with oxygen, the climbers estimated it to be three hours away.

The second assault was better planned. A higher camp, Camp IX, was established and Hillary and Tenzing rested here for the night, drinking quantities of hot lemon and even eating a little. At 6.30am on 29 May, they began the climb. They reached the south summit by 9am, and the snow conditions past this first critical point were good. What is now known as the 'Hillary Step', a 13m/43ft barrier, was overcome by chimneying up a gap between a cornice and the rock wall, a dangerous but necessary move. The summit, only a short distance away, was reached at 11.30am. In the words of Hillary:

I looked at Tenzing and in spite of the balaclava, goggles and oxygen mask all encrusted with long icicles that concealed his face, there was no disguising his infectious grin of pure delight as he looked all around him. We shook hands and then Tenzing threw his arm around my shoulders and we thumped each other on the back until we were almost breathless. *The Ascent of Everest* John Hunt

By evening they had struggled down to the South Col where Hillary told his team mate: 'Well, George, we knocked the bastard off', though this was not exactly what was printed in the press at the time!

Chinese attempts on Everest

The pressure bubble burst with the success of the British expedition. It was some time before further attempts were considered as now the other unclimbed 'eight-thousanders' commanded attention. The Swiss climbed Everest after their conquest of Lhotse in 1956. In 1960 the Indians came

---

❑ **The Himalayan Trust and Sir Edmund Hillary**

The Himalayan Trust is a charity that has helped local people set up almost thirty schools, several hospitals and construct many bridges and runways in the Solu Khumbu. Many years on, the positive results are obvious and the region is far ahead along the development road compared with the rest of rural Nepal. Its phenomenal success is the result of sound principles and dedicated staff. Sir Edmund Hillary deserves the highest praise for his selfless efforts. Almost every Himalayan Trust school, bridge and hospital bears the stains of Hillary's sweat and he still returns to Nepal virtually every year to continue the work. Villagers soon saw him as the one person who could realise their local projects. It is the fact that these were projects initiated by the people themselves (rather than imposed by the government or a distant aid agency) that has been the key to their success. Development has happened at the village pace. Involvement of the local people in their projects has been another reason for their success. As far as possible, villagers must provide land and labour although the Trust provides the bulk of finance required for materials. This degree of local involvement ensures that bridges, hospitals and schools are well cared for. In addition, more than 50 scholarships are awarded each year for further education, with priority for girls.

close to success and at the same time the Chinese attempted the pre-war route via Tibet. It was a mammoth affair, mounted on a grander scale than any previous attempt. Success was announced but no photos could be produced and the expedition account, after being suitably embellished by the propaganda department, made entertaining reading but was inconsistent with the mountaineering thinking of the time. We join them on the second step on a four-metre wall:

Each one made several attempts but fell back each time. They looked at each other for inspiration. Time was marching on mercilessly, and according to the weather-station forecast, it was the last day of the fine weather period... Then Liu Lien-man had an idea that the "courte echell" (short ladder) technique might help, so crouching down he offered his companion a leg-up. Ignoring the biting cold and the danger of freezing, Chu Ying-hua took off his high-altitude boots and his eider-down stockings to make the climb easier.... It had taken them five full hours to overcome this obstacle.... dusk came and an icy wind howled dolefully. The three members of the Communist Party of China, Wang Fu-chou, Chu Ying-hua and Liu Lien-man, discussed the situation and it was decided to leave Liu Lien-man behind and press on. *Mountaineering in China* (People's Physical Culture Publishing House)

They claimed to have left a plaster bust of Chairman Mao Tse-tung near the summit. Although the attempt was ridiculed by the Western media (this was during the Cold War) it's now considered that the expedition did succeed in reaching the summit.

Sydney Wignall, in his book *Spy on the Roof of the World* suggests another reason for the attempt. In 1955 he gained permission to climb Nalkanbar, on Nepal's far western border with Tibet. In fact they planned to make a clandestine attempt on Gurla Mandhata, 7800m. They made the mistake of confiding in Tibetan traders, whom they later found out could only cross the border with a Chinese spy among them, who ensured they said only good, entirely fictitious things about the invaders. They were soon caught and taken to Taklakot. They were interrogated for two months. In desperation to please his captors, Sydney told them that Hillary and Tenzing had placed a sort of nuclear-powered radar capable of seeing all the way across Tibet to Lop Nor (where, unbeknown to him, the Chinese were developing their first nuclear weapon). Among his interrogators was the General in charge of Tibet. He appeared technologically naive. Later, after a diplomatic hiatus they were released but were only allowed to return over a route known to be impossible in winter. Much to the dismay of the Chinese the mountaineers

---

❏ The Everest industry

During the main season, counting both sides of the mountain, there will be approximately 600 people camping, around 200 people attempting the climb and some 1000 plus tents on the mountain at any one time, not to mention fax machines, computers, satellite phones and cappucino machines. Historically approximately 10% of climbers attempting the mountain actually succeed, although with the advent of commercial expeditions this ratio is increasing.

Adapted from *Outside* magazine

succeeded in returning; as a result it was proved the Chinese had been lying since they had announced that they had released them a month earlier in a different region. Sydney brought valuable information out, which unfortunately was ignored by India. The Chinese invasion of Indian Aksai Chin (Ladakh) should not have been a surprise at all.

There were rumours of another Chinese attempt in 1966 in which 24 climbers died but Chinese officials refused to discuss the incident. In 1969 it was claimed that three surveyors reached the summit without oxygen or additional support; and in 1975 another Chinese team was said to have reached the summit. Proof of their success was found by Doug Scott and Dougal Haston of the 1975 British South-West Face Expedition. On the summit they came upon a red Chinese tripod.

Recent attempts on Everest

More than 300 mountaineers have now stood on the summit of Everest and it continues to attract attention. New routes are attempted, such as the southwest face and the west ridge from Lho La. Different mountaineering methods have been applied and in 1978 Reinhold Messner and Peter Habeler reached the summit without the use of oxygen. Messner went on to make a successful solo climb without oxygen in 1980 and has since soloed all 14 of the world's 'eight-thousanders'. Recently Hans Klammerlander repeated Messner's climb solo from 6400m to the top in a staggering 17 hours, and without oxygen. Partly using skis he managed to return to his high base camp in less than 24 hours total. Other summiteers have relied on bizarre methods to gain media attention. In 1970 an intrepid Japanese adventurer actually skied part of the way down and, in 1988, Frenchman Jean-Marc Boivin jumped off the summit with a paraglider!

As of early 1998 the record for the most successes on Everest is held by Ang Rita Sherpa, who had summitted an amazing 10 times, and only once with oxygen. In fact Ang Rita has climbed 19 times on 8000m mountains, one more than Messner. Appa Sherpa, who at present has climbed the mountain eight times, is chasing this record.

1996: The best guides or not, Everest is still the limit

In 1996 some high profile deaths and some surprising survival stories put Everest is the world headlines again. Rob Hall, a kiwi guide who had summitted Everest three times previously, and Scott Fisher, who had summitted previously without oxygen, were the respective leaders of two commercial groups of climbers. Due to some bickering between the climbing sirdars ropes up the Hillary step were fixed very late, creating a bottleneck. Unheralded, a light storm caught the late climbers unaware. A group made it down to the 8000m South Col, only to lose the way, forcing them to spend the night huddling together for their lives. In a brief early morning clearing a few struggled into camp. Rescuers dragged a couple more climbers back but left Beck Weathers and Yakuso Namba, who were badly frost-bitten and barely alive, to die. Amazingly, in the morning Beck suddenly awoke and staggered into camp. After a heroic rescue effort including a 6000m helicopter landing, he survived losing a hand, fingers and his nose to frostbite. Yasuko died on the col.

Meanwhile high on the mountain a similar struggle was happening. Rob Hall and Andy Harris, New Zealand guides, valiantly struggled with Doug Hansen, on his second attempt at the mountain with Rob Hall and Adventure Consultants. By morning only Hall was left, and he knew he was in deep trouble. By the wonders of modern communications he was able to talk with his wife in New Zealand, seven months pregnant. Jan had climbed Everest with Rob previously and immediately understood that death was clawing at her partner's back. Two sherpas attempted a rescue in bone-chilling conditions and climbed to 200 vertical metres below Hall before being driven back. Hall, by this stage was badly frost-bitten and even oxygen and dexamethasone weren't enough. He died by the south summit.

Scott Fisher and a reckless Taiwanese, 'Makalu' Gau made it further down the ridge to approximately 400m vertical metres above the South Col before giving up. When sherpas found them the next morning, although both were alive, only Gau revived. The sherpas, who could only manage one person at this altitude, had to leave Fisher to die.

The deaths may have shocked the world but in fact that season climbers got off relatively lightly, as John Krakauer in Into Thin Air, his first hand account of the disaster, point out. Historically approximately one in four summitters had died, whereas in 1996 only one in approx seven summitters died.

Walt Unsworth's book, *Everest,* and Peter Gillman's similarly-titled book are highly recommended for more information on the history of climbs on the mountain.

CHO OYU (8201m/26,906ft)

The name Cho Oyu is almost certainly Tibetan in origin and is transliterated in several ways. My favourite is Chomo Yu which means 'Goddess of Turquoise', the colour the mountain often assumes at sunset when viewed from the Tibetan side.

The 1952 British attempt

In 1952, while the Swiss were attempting Everest, Eric Shipton led a British expedition to Cho Oyu. They failed to reach the top probably because Shipton was unwilling to build a supply line up the mountain on the Tibetan side. Tibet was now in the hands of the communist Chinese and Shipton was wary of doing anything that might jeopardise the planned 1953 Everest Expedition. In 1951 he'd been caught by the Tibetans on the wrong side of the border. Quite prepared to hand over everything he possessed (Rs1200) when they brandished their swords and demanded a ransom, he was soon amused to discover that his ever-faithful Sherpas had bargained the final sum down to a mere Rs7!

Herbert Tichy's style of mountaineering

An Austrian attempt on Cho Oyu was launched in 1954, led by Herbert Tichy. The decision to climb was made on the spur of the moment after a conversation with a Sherpa, before Tichy had even seen the peak. The team consisted of three Austrians and seven high-altitude Sherpas but their prospects did not look good. One of the Austrians had previously been shot through the lung, another suffered severely from sciatica and Tichy admitted to smoking a lot and drinking 'without reluctance'. In addition, the attempt was launched after the monsoon, without oxygen, with little equipment and less than Rs1000-worth of food. At that stage in the history of Himalayan mountaineering, success had occurred only on well-equipped pre-monsoon expeditions.

On the walk in, Tichy soon noticed that changes were afoot in the area: 'We followed in the tracks of other expeditions – notably Everest expeditions. They had rubbed off the bloom which I was still able to enjoy in the west of Nepal the year before: they had also spoilt the market (four eggs for a rupee instead of 10) and the villagers treated us with that mixture of interest and condescension people bestow on a travelling circus' (*Cho Oyu by Favour of the Gods*). Tichy's relaxed approach to climbing left much time for merry-making with friends in the Khumbu. On one such occasion he notes that the Sherpa porters had done full justice to the parting from their friends and their families and when 'we overtook our proud array we saw that some of our Sherpanis were so drunk that their male companions had to carry them and their loads as well. This predicament was taken as a great joke' (*Cho Oyu by Favour of the Gods*).

1954 – Austrian success

The walk up to Base Camp, slightly north of the Nangpa La (just inside Tibet), was accomplished with only 27 porters. Camp IV was established at 6980m/22,900ft, ten days from Base Camp, but then disaster struck. In savage winds with the temperature below -35°C. Tichy made a desperate dive to save one of their tents and suffered frostbite on his fingers. The climb had to be temporarily abandoned. Nevertheless nine days later he and his companions set off again, spurred on by meeting a Swiss expedition that had been rebuffed by Gauri Sankar and had just arrived with the similar intention of attempting Cho Oyu. A storm pinned the Austrians down for two days before they could return to Camp IV. However, on the following day, 19th October 1954, Tichy, Sepp Jochler and Pasang Lama made the summit.

For Pasang Lama the ascent was all the more remarkable, indeed the stuff of legends. Having returned to Namche to pick up more supplies, at Marulung (4150m/13,615ft), a day's walk from Namche, he heard of the Swiss plans and so raced, heavily loaded, in a day up to Base Camp. Then, even more remarkably, the next day he ascended with a load to Camp IV and on the following day climbed to the summit.

MAKALU (8475m/27,805ft)

British/American 1954 Expedition

In the line-up for attempts on Everest, the French had been allotted the year following the British. The same order was established for Makalu (8475m/27,805ft), with the British and Americans given permission for the spring of 1954 and the French scheduled to follow them. The French were naturally not keen to follow in the wake of a British success (as on Everest) and the results were anxiously awaited. With a strong team that included Hillary, it looked as if success on Makalu was likely. However, the summit was not reached. Interestingly the expedition took approximately 250 porters over the Mingbo La, West Col and East Col to Makalu Base Camp.

1955 – French success

The French were spurred into action with an autumn reconnaissance and gear-testing trip. Chomo Lonzo (7790m/25,557ft), just inside Tibet, and Makalu II (7640m/25,065ft) were both climbed from the Nepalese side.

The 1955 attempt was a classic assault of the mountain, superbly organised, kitted with the best of equipment and conducted as if the pride of the country was at stake. They were prepared for the worst and ready to make repeated attempts. However, perfect weather allowed all the expedition members, as well as some of the Sherpas, to reach the summit of Makalu between 15 and 17 May. Now around 100 foreign mountaineers pass through Tashigoan to attempt Makalu, Makalu II, Baruntse or Chamalang each year.

❏ Conquering the world's top ten peaks

The world's ten highest mountains were all climbed in a relatively short span of frenetic mountaineering activity between 1950 and 1960. The heights, and dates for the first climbs, are given below:

1	Everest/Sagarmatha/Chomolungma	8848m/29,028ft	29 May 53
2	K2 (Pakistan/China)	8611m/28,251ft	31 July 54
3	Kanchenjunga (Nepal/India)	8586m/28,169ft	25 May 55
4	Lhotse (Nepal/Tibet)	8501m/27,890ft	18 May 56
5	Makalu (Nepal/Tibet)	8463m/27,765ft	15 May 55
6	Cho Oyu (Nepal/Tibet)	8201m/26,906ft	19 Oct 54
7	Dhaulagiri (Nepal)	8167m/26,794ft	13 May 60
8	Manaslu (Nepal)	8156m/26,758ft	9 May 56
9	Nanga Parbat (Pakistan)	8126m/26,660ft	3 June 53
10	Annapurna (Nepal)	8091m/26,545ft	3 June 50

In comparison to these, the heights of the highest peaks in some Western countries are rather less impressive

USA: Mt McKinley	6194m/20,320ft
Canada: Mt Logan	5961m/19,524ft
France/Italy: Mont Blanc	4808m/15,771ft
Switzerland/Italy: Matterhorn	4478m/14,692ft
New Zealand: Mt Cook	3754m/12,316ft
Australia: Mt Kosciusko	2228m/7310ft
Britain: Ben Nevis	1343m/4406ft

LHOTSE (8501m/27,890ft)

Lhotse was so named by one of the British expeditions in the 1920s; no local name for it could be found. It is Tibetan for 'South Peak' and Lhotse Shar is the south-east peak of Everest.

The 1956 Swiss Expedition

In the spring of 1952 the Swiss had climbed to 250m/820ft below the summit of Everest before being forced back. In 1956 an expedition was mounted with permission for Lhotse (at that stage the highest unclimbed mountain) as well as Everest. It was a very well planned and provisioned expedition and the team worked well together. A cautious acclimatisation programme was followed, with many rest days at Tengboche and Pheriche. It's interesting to note that in an effort to make the route through the Icefall safer, explosives were used!

Success came on 18 May, when Ernst Reiss and Fritz Luchsinger, using oxygen, fought their way up the steep slopes in unsettled weather to the summit. The second goal was also attained and four climbers reached the summit of Everest on the same expedition.

The people

THE SHERPAS

Years of living in their villages left me well aware that Sherpas are no more strangers to greed, pride, love of power, jealousy or pettiness than other mortals. They seem still, for all the close familiarity, a singularly appealing people. Stanley Stevens *Cultural Ecology and History in Highland Nepal* (University of California)

The mountaineering exploits of the Sherpas on foreign expeditions since the 1920s brought them clearly into the world spotlight. Sherpa Tenzing's conquest, with Hillary, of Everest in 1953 was a fitting tribute to the part played by Sherpas in the history of mountaineering, not just in the Khumbu but in many parts of the Himalaya. Although the lure of Everest has brought crowds of foreigners to their land, they seem to have weathered the cultural invasion surprisingly well. Theirs is an ancient culture which Westerners have learnt to respect, indeed admire, for its tolerance, comradeship and many other positive values.

Origins

Shar-pa is Tibetan for 'Eastern People' and the first Sherpas were almost certainly migrants from 1300km away in Kham (north-east Tibet) possibly fleeing from Mongol incursions. It's thought that they tried settling in a number of places en route but were consistently driven on, crossing the Himalaya about 500 years ago over the Nangpa La. Migration occurred in several successive waves with large numbers of people arriving in the late 1800s and early 1900s and another major migration in the 1960s after the Chinese invasion of Tibet. Settlements first appeared in the mid-1500s on both sides of the Lamjura Pass (Junbesi and north of Kenja), where Sherpas still live today. The Thame and Pangboche gompas were established later, possibly during the 1670s, although it's likely that the area had been populated previously. It's thought that the Khumbu was used for pastures by Rai shepherds before the Sherpas arrived; the Dudh Kosi is known as 'Khambu' by Rais today. The Sherpas have always considered the Khumbu a Be-yul or hidden valley, free from the troubles of the outside world.

Agriculture

The crop with the highest yield in the Khumbu is the humble potato and about 75% of the cultivated area is planted with them. Growing enough, however, is not easy and most families have always supplemented their income, originally by trading with Tibet and now mainly through tourism. Their agricultural methods are quite sophisticated even though their tools may be primitive. Land holdings are scattered and several crop varieties are used in order to minimise the risk of blight and other diseases. The soil is not naturally very fertile but large quantities of organic fertiliser (compost, human waste and animal manure) have worked well, according to soil scientists. Women and children do much of the work but the roles aren't rigidly defined. Up until the 1950s all ploughing was done by hand with four men to a plough but now animals are used. The men tend to the animals and are also occupied with trade, often leaving their wives to manage the entire affairs of the household.

The Sherpas of Pharak and Solu live at lower altitudes and the milder climate enables them to grow a wider range of crops. In Junbesi, many of the vegetables served to trekkers are grown locally. Apples thrive in this area and apple pies and jams are on every lodge menu. Yaks, naks (female yaks) and crossbreeds, are kept high in the mountains away from the villages. Their milk that was once made into butter and traded with Tibet to keep the monastery lamps burning is now sold to local cheese factories. Sherpa trade in this area is now mainly with passing trekkers.

Diet

As one might expect, potatoes are eaten at almost every meal, although the well-off also eat rice. Potatoes are usually boiled and once they've been peeled (the skin is never eaten) they're dipped in salt and a chilli sauce. Savoury pancakes, made from a mixture of buckwheat (the non-sweet variety) and grated potatoes, are eaten with butter and chillis. However, the great Sherpa favourite is shakpa, a thick soup made with whatever comes to hand – usually potatoes(!), a few other vegetables and sometimes chewy balls of wheat flour.

With potatoes being a staple, it's not surprising that the Sherpas are connoisseurs of the varieties that are suited to the Khumbu. Trekkers also consume huge quantities of potatoes, not because there are no alternatives on the menu but because they're surprisingly tasty. If you show an interest, the lodge owner may show you the different types. The highest yielding variety (commonly served to trekkers) is not considered quite as tasty as some of the older types.

The Sherpa diet is fairly healthy. Naks and dzums (a yak/cow crossbreed) provide dairy products and meat is occasionally eaten, dried or fresh. In the past the diet lacked only iodine, a deficiency of which causes goiters and cretinism. The situation was quickly solved by the first doctor at Kunde hospital. Now the majority of salt in Nepal, instead of coming from Tibet, is naturally iodised sea-salt from India.

The Sherpa House

Unlike the Tibetan house, which is flat-roofed and built around a courtyard, the Sherpa house features a roof adapted for the monsoon rains and has no courtyard. Although it does bear a superficial resemblance to the Tibetan house, the Tibetan architectural style is reserved for gompas.

The size of a house is a sign of prosperity. In the Rolwaling there are still many single-storied houses, whereas in wealthy Namche there are now even

---

❑ A year in the Khumbu

Many trekkers have mistakenly come away with the impression that Sherpas don't seem to do anything in the Khumbu apart from looking after trekkers. This is not the case. The Sherpa calendar of activities is governed entirely by the seasons with a short cultivation period. It's most fortunate that the main trekking season occurs at the end of the harvest.

April-May After the fields have been prepared, the potatoes are planted, followed by barley and buckwheat. These are labour-intensive activities.

May-June Traditionally, this is a time of trading. The high passes to Tibet are open for a short while after the winter snows have melted and before the snows of the monsoon arrive. It's also the season of yak-shearing and calving.

June-July The fields are weeded: a laborious job that may have to be done several times.

June-September After calving, the yaks and naks are herded up to the high summer pastures to protect the crops and save the grass lower down for the spring. Summer is the time of butter, cheese and curd production.

September-October These are the busiest months. At the high pastures hay is cut, while in the villages the potatoes are dug up and the barley and buckwheat harvested and threshed. Once this is completed the cattle can return to the villages. It's also the breeding season for cattle and the beginning of the trekking season.

November-March The long, cold winter months are filled with spinning and weaving, collecting firewood and feeding the animals by hand. It's also a time for trading, not only with Tibet, but also Kathmandu and trips to the capital are also made to beat the cold and visit friends. Losar, the Tibetan New Year which usually occurs in February, is the main festival.

some four-storey hotel 'sky-scrapers'. However, the majority of Sherpa houses consist of two levels. The ground floor is for stabling cattle and is a storage area for grain, animal fodder, firewood and tools. It's also where the *chang* (home-brew made from rice or barley) is fermented. The upper level of the house is usually an open living-room, sometimes with the kitchen partitioned off.

Roofs are made of slate or wood, though slates are now being replaced by corrugated iron sheets. Walls are usually stone with huge wooden beams running between them to support the floor. In some of the older houses, the beams can be up to 25 metres long which gives some idea of the size of the trees in the forests that once covered this area of the Himalaya.

The layout of the interior is dictated by tradition. The west wall is for a shrine with Buddha images, candles or butter lamps and pictures of the Dalai Lama and the King and Queen of Nepal. Beneath the sunny south-facing windows are long benches, often covered with thick Tibetan rugs. The southeast corner is for the master bed, usually the only bed, in which the whole family sleeps. If there are visitors for the night, they sleep on the carpeted bench seats. The sunless north wall is windowless and lined with shelves displaying the valuable kitchen-ware. The long tea-churn for making salt-butter tea should always be near the stairway. Many tea-churns are cherished family heirlooms, passed down from generation to generation.

The Sherpa view of life

Most Sherpas are followers of the Nyingmapa ('Red Hat') sect of Tibetan Buddhism, the most ancient and least reformed of the four major Tibetan sects. It developed out of the tantric practices introduced by the Indian Padmasambhava (Guru Rinpoche or 'precious teacher') and is combined with older beliefs of the Sherpas: the Bon-po religion and animism. Spirits

---

❏ Prayers for the world

In addition to general good conduct, repeating *mantras* (prayer chants) is an important means by which to gain *sonam*. Most common is the mantra *Om Mani Padme Hum*, meaning 'hail to the jewel in the lotus', the jewel being the Buddha.

The more times a mantra can be repeated, the better, so Tibetan Buddhism has evolved many ingenious labour-saving methods to mass-produce these prayers. **Prayer wheels** are filled with a long paper roll inscribed with mantras that are activated by turning the wheel. They come in many forms, from the portable hand-held device so admired by tourists, to huge wheels that with a single turn repeat astronomical numbers of prayers. There are also water-powered prayer wheels, and multicoloured fluttering **prayer flags**, printed with mantras, infuse the winds with prayers to travel the world. The mantra may be carved onto a **mani stone**, which benefits both the carver and the person who has paid for the work. Large numbers of these stones are piled up into the mani walls you see along the trails.

Note that you should always pass to the left of a mani wall and walk clockwise (the direction in which prayer wheels must always be turned) around Buddhist shrines and monuments.

and demons (*lu*) inhabit the springs, trees and rocks, and there are detailed rites for protection and exorcism.

As Buddhists, Sherpas view life as an endless cycle of rebirth into a world of suffering. Escape (*nirvana*) is possible only by accumulating a series of 'good' lives. The measure of good and evil is *sonam*. By carrying out virtuous deeds you gain merit, but sinful acts reduce the total at a rather unequal rate. One sin is far more powerful than a few good deeds so constant work is required to keep ahead. If you fall far behind you may not even be born human again: monastery dogs are considered reincarnations of the not-so-studious monks. The meritorious who have finally escaped may return to assist their brethren as reincarnate head lamas, such as the Lama at Tengboche.

All forms of life are treated with respect since to kill something is regarded as one of the greatest demerits. However, Sherpas relish meat and to eat it is no sin as long as the consumer was not responsible for the animal's death. The Sherpas' approach to life is remarkably unpuritanical and considerably more liberated than that of the Hindu Nepali. There is no caste system and women (Sherpanis) are treated much more equally. In most cases it is the Sherpani, rather than the Sherpa who controls the family finances.

Mountaineers, sirdars and porters

Sherpas are well known for their dedicated service to mountaineering expeditions, first as porters and sirdars and later also as participating climbers. The part they play in many expeditions has often been behind the scenes but it is nonetheless crucial for that. On the 1922 Everest attempt, six Sherpas climbed to Camp VI (8170m/26,800ft) from Camp V 800m below, merely to deliver thermos flasks of beef-tea to the sahibs after a storm.

Shipton, who always took Sherpas on his long and unbelievably wild treks in the Himalaya and Karakoram thoroughly admired them:

'One of the most delightful things about the Sherpas is their extraordinary sense of comradeship. During the six months we were together, I never detected any sign of dissension among our three....This quality of theirs is due largely, I imagine, to their robust sense of humour. It hardly ever failed. Each enjoyed jokes against himself as delightedly as those who he perpetrated. Two of them would conceal a heavy rock in the load of the third, and when, after an exhausting climb, this was discovered, all three would be convulsed with mirth....They were forever laughing and chatting together as though they had just met after a prolonged absence.' *The Six Mountain Travel Books*, Eric Shipton

Even today, Sherpa high-altitude porters still play a vital role in many expeditions, and the opportunity for mountaineering training has spawned local heroes. Sungdare Sherpa was one among many. He climbed many mountains, often at great speed (Cho Oyu, 8201m/26,905ft, in 18 hours), and had attained the summit of Everest five times before he died a premature death (not as a result of a mountaineering accident). The majority of Sherpas who work for expeditions do so for money, however, and consider the risks a trade-off for income. Ang Rita, ten times summiteer, says simply that expeditions keep paying him more and more so he can't refuse. Most admired now, apart from the mountaineers, are the sirdars and trekking company directors who have broken through Hindu caste barriers to become some of the most successful business-people in Nepal.

Coping with development

The Sherpas' liberal and positive outlook on life combined with the head-start they were given through the Himalayan Trust (see p99) have enabled them to develop and adapt at a far quicker rate than most peoples in Nepal. Although community spirit is strong, individual endeavour and achievement through hard work are respected. There is little resistance to change that is obviously beneficial. If a new strain of potato, for example, proves to be an improvement on a previous type, it will be widely adopted.

Change in the Khumbu has been rapid but not overwhelming. Houses are bigger, smarter and less picturesque but their basic design and the style of construction are still close to time-honoured methods. The diet is generally healthier and more varied but an increase in sugar consumption has led to a greater incidence of tooth decay, especially among children. The worldliness of the Sherpas has undoubtedly increased with the steady stream of visitors and themselves travelling overseas but they are nonetheless still delightful people and can be entertaining hosts if you have time to spend with them.

THE RAI

At Namche's Saturday market the squat, almond-eyed people are Rais. A surprising number work in the fields and even in the lodges of the Khumbu. Trekking via Salpa-Arun, you pass through many Rai villages.

Rai can be easily distinguished by their attire and accessories. The women wear a large round nose ring through the left nostril, while another ring hangs from the middle of the nose over the mouth. The musical clang of this ring with the tea cup is a constant melodic reminder of her wealth. They favour a wraparound patterned lungi (tight skirt). The men often wear a wool vest called *lukunis* and always carry a khukri, a large knife used for cutting firewood, splitting bamboo and cleaning fingernails.

Origins

Rai, with the similar Limbu ethnic group, are collectively referred to as Kirat. They are considered the original inhabitants of Nepal. Having first lived in the Kathmandu Valley these people moved eastward – possibly from the second century on. Once in the east, the Rai were later confronted by the Sherpa, and were pushed still further east. However, mythology also relates how the mongoloid (Tibetan-style people) descended from seven brothers, Sherpa, Rai, Limbu, Tharu, Tamang and various Tibetan groups.

There are many Rai sub-tribes but the Kulung Rai consider themselves the original inhabitants of the Majh-Kirat area (what is now called the Makalu-Barun Conservation Area). The main concentration of this sub-tribe live in Bung and Gudel.

Religion

The religion of the Rai ethnic group is called Mudum; although somewhat influenced by Hinduism and Buddhism it retains much of its originality in its animistic heritage through oral myths, ceremonial dialogues and ritual recitation. Oral myth transmission is preserved by priests, shamans and elders. Natural spirits make the basis for the Mudum religion, including the 16 gods of the forest. Mudums worship in the home whereas Sherpas worship in gombas and Hindus in temples. For the Rai, the cooking area is considered one of the most sacred places in the home where three stones are placed to represent the stages of marriage. One stone looks in the direction of where the father sits (called *Pakalung*), one stone looks in the direction of where the mother sits (*Makalung*) and the third stone looks outside the house (*Sabelung*). A bowl (*dampay*) is kept on a shelf near the cooking area; it is filled with local beer (*chang*) four times a year and is used to bless the stones. If a new stove is built in a home, the original is not destroyed but kept as the place of worship.

Another important divinity resides in the main pillar of the house – a myth relates how a god or goddess became very angry with his child and tried to kill it by the fireplace in the courtyard and at the bottom of the door but could not. Finally he tried by the main pillar and the child died. Soon he was filled with deep remorse for killing the innocent child in a fit of rage so he blessed him to become the protector divinity of the house.

A Rai family has one major ceremony (*puja*) a year which takes place in the fall. A holy man (*dhami*) is hired for one full day to bless the home. The puja begins outside during daylight hours. The dhami sits and chants next to offerings of food, alcohol and tree branches while a feast of chicken and millet is prepared. In the evening, the ceremony is moved inside to the cooking area where the family is blessed and another chicken, also blessed with rakshi and rice, is sacrificed for the second feast of the day.

Agriculture and work

The life of the Rai is deeply rooted in their natural surroundings. Living at a lower elevation than the Sherpas, Rais have access to a greater variety of natural resources, such as bamboo – seven different species are found in the surrounding area. Being strong, versatile, and fast growing, it is highly valued and can be made into over 50 different domestic articles. A keen eye can spot some of these items including mats, vessels, hunting and fishing implements, toys and musical instruments.

Economically, the needs of locals are not met by subsistence farming forcing many young men to seasonally migrate to other regions for additional work. Some men work in the Khumbu or on farms in the Terai, while others go to fruit orchards in Bhutan or join the Indian army. Many also join the forces of the trekking business. Being less of a celebrity than the Sherpas, most Rai are left with the less glamorous job of porter where a day's work often only earns the day's food. Still, mixed groups of them often treat the work as a non-stop party.

Values

A study of the Rai reveals an appealing culture. They have a long tradition of reciting Mandhums, poetic expressions of legends, mythology, history and stories. Some explicitly deal with the various taboos: promiscuity after marriage, incest, and bad/unequal treatment of women – the problems that every society faces. Several stories altruistically tell of the dangers of polluting the environment, especially the water in the lakes. They share community values and are gentle people but they are also said to have a quick temper and to be fast with a khukri without caring about the consequences. Similarly their relaxed attitude – spend and enjoy today, forget about tomorrow – is a minor cultural impediment to long term development.

National parks

SAGARMATHA NATIONAL PARK

Set up to control the environmental impact of the increasingly large numbers of tourists visiting the Khumbu, Sagarmatha National Park was officially gazetted in July 1976. For the first six years, the New Zealand government, through the National Parks Service of New Zealand provided training, management and guidelines. In 1979 it was declared a World Heritage Site by UNESCO in recognition of its rich cultural heritage and magnificent scenery. The park's area is around 1200 sq km encompassing the entire

❑ **Sagarmatha Pollution Control Committee (SPCC)**

Founded in 1991 with technical and financial support from the World Wildlife Fund (WWF) this is managed by local staff and an elected committee. Currently the Ministry of Tourism allocates a portion of peak fees to assist with keeping the region clean.

At the beginning of the programme 30 tonnes of rubbish was removed from Everest Base Camp. Every year, in conjunction with the Nepal Mountaineering Association (NMA), the trekking peak base camps of the region are cleaned. The 1997 monsoon clean-up netted an astonishing 2.8 tonnes of rubbish left behind by trekking companies and members.

Another of SPCC's main functions is policing expedition rubbish. Expeditions are now required to separate their rubbish into burnable, non-burnable and gas cylinders. Burnables are taken to the Lukla incinerator, non-burnables must be returned to Kathmandu, and gas cylinders (including oxygen) have to be returned to their country of origin. In one year 13 Everest expeditions created 2.6 tonnes of burnable rubbish, one tonne of non-burnables (tin cans and glass mainly) and used half a tonne of gas cylinders. In addition 1.6 tonnes of toilet waste was carted from base camp to be properly disposed of at Gorak Shep.

For more details have a look around their information centres in Lukla and Namche.

watershed of the Dudh Kosi with the boundary being a virtually impenetrable ring of mountains. The numbers of foreign visitors has been steadily increasing: from around 5000 people in the 1981-2 season (Nepali calendar year) to around 10,000 during the 1990-1 season. During 1996-7 approx 17,500 foreigners visited the park. The local Sherpa population numbers approximately 3500, and the national park staff around 60. There are more than 200 government civil servants living in the park.

Policies

Initially, there was local resistance to the park owing to worries that the people might be forcibly resettled, as had happened when Rara Lake National Park (west Nepal) was created. To allay such fears village areas were excluded from the park. There have inevitably been clashes of interest between villagers and park management. Villagers are unhappy at not being able to farm new land or even work existing terraces that had previously been abandoned. The view of the park management is that as land becomes more valuable, every bit must be protected if possible. The relatively well-educated people of the Khumbu now have a slow rate of population growth and the land at present in use already generates a surplus of crops.

Many of the park's policies have been accepted by the villagers once they've been seen to show positive returns. The management of forest resources is a good example. Local forests were once protected by the collection of firewood in different section on a yearly rotation. The nationalisation of forests partially broke this system down, then the influx of starving Tibetan refugees escaping from the Chinese invasion took a heavy toll on the forests and environment in general. Then large expeditions turned firewood into a valuable cash crop, all adding up to a devastating result. A complete ban was placed on the cutting down of trees when the park came into being: a move that is now respected as the most sensible course of action. As well

❏ Environmental dilemmas

Making environmentally-friendly regulations for the trekking industry involves complex factors. Consider this classic example. Soft drinks, mineral water and beer are luxury items consumed mainly by trekkers. They are carried over great distances but in the process considerable value is added which benefits the local economy. There's a returnable deposit on soft drink (but not beer or mineral water) bottles so, close to Jiri, the bottles are collected. However, by the time an empty Coke bottle reaches Namche it is no longer economic to return it for the deposit so it is discarded. Safe disposal is possible, and the SPCC (see opposite) has begun ferrying some bottles out of the area, but in practice glass tends to end up everywhere. A secondary problem is that soft drinks start to enter the local market with disastrous consequences for teeth, particularly in a country that has few dentists. So, should bottled drinks be banned from the park, or banned from some areas, with the consequent loss of income to porters, shop-keepers and lodge-owners? The park warden believes that canned drinks are a lesser evil but these are currently more expensive and less widely available than bottled drinks.

as organising reforestation schemes, the National Park is involved in the construction of facilities for trekkers (toilets), controlling rubbish disposal and raising local environmental awareness.

Until recently the national park was given no funds other than for wages; your park fee simply went into the always empty state coffers. Now 40-50% of your fee goes directly to the park for park-managed projects. As of 1997 it was still being decided how the money due would be split among the parks: Chitwan is by far the biggest earner, while Kaptada received just 13 trekkers during 1995-6.

MAKALU-BARUN NATIONAL PARK & CONSERVATION AREA (MBNPCA)

The park was gazetted in 1991 and formally inaugurated in 1992, with a total area of 2330 sq km, of which 830 sq km is a conservation or buffer-zone area. Encompassing the region from close to the Arun river to Sagarmatha National Park, including the Hongu/Hinku or Mera Peak area, it was initially formed to set up the systems of environmental protection that would be needed if the planned 'Arun III' hydro-electric scheme went ahead. This massive project would require an access road that would open up a previously isolated area. The project is on hold again.

Policies

Recognising that the government doesn't have the funds to efficiently manage and develop the region, the Mountain Institute has been allowed to work alongside national park staff for a trial period until the end of 1999. Funding has come from the United Nations Development Program's Global Fund; SNV, the Dutch government's development program which focuses particularly on community-based and local government development, and IDRC, a Canadian research fund. It is extremely ambitious and impressively managed. The brief is:

● **Manage flora and fauna** Motivate and educate with meetings and workshops. A patrolling process has been set up with the locals.

● **Grazing management** User groups have been formed with the idea of promoting a long term approach. Burning is gradually being restricted.

● **Promote eco-tourism** Lodge management training courses with the emphasis on retaining the simple family-run lodges but with better hygiene and a better understanding of trekkers' wants.

● **Participatory education** Non-formal women's literacy and motivation classes, kindergarten programs called *nanny bari* or 'children in the fields'.

● **Applied ecology research** The region has huge untouched valley systems worthy of study.

● **Village initiated programs** They provide structured support, and often finance, for whatever the villagers approach them on, including drinking water schemes and technical assistance for community forests and tree-planting.

● **Natural resource management** This focuses on sustainable use. To this end they have sponsored a carpenter training program, thinning and pruning, and forestry management. They hope to set up a kerosene depot sometime.

● **Entrepreneurship and gender empowerment** Help to implement income-generating local industries such as paper-making, poultry and pig farming, improved water mills and lots of training courses. And you wondered where your National Park and Conservation entry fee went!

Some people like to argue 'but do the people really want or need this development?'. Before the Bung post was set up the villages in the region were asked whether they wanted to be in the conservation area and therefore have development help available. Over a series of village meetings the villagers were asked to decide. Bung and Cheskam decided to join, while Gudel didn't want to. Now a couple of years into the project, Gudel has reconsidered and would also like to be part of the project. Makalu-Barun is working on accommodating them.

The majority of projects have been initiated at the locals behest. The people of Bung and Gudel have despaired for many years at the number of trekkers that trek from Jiri and Lukla (Rais are regular sellers at Namche's Saturday market and many work in the Khumbu too). They simply didn't know how to attract trekkers, then once they did come, they didn't know how to look after them. This is changing.

The people of Bung and Cheskam have several ambitious ideas. One is to promote the Panch Pokhari region as an eco-tourism area. Another is to construct a trail from the Mera La down the Hunku/Hongu Khola to Bung. This would give climbers an alternative entry or exit (it would also partly relieve the environmental impact that climbing groups are having on the Tagnag area).

❏ **Where your park fee goes**

The park is taking an innovative approach to the conservation of one of the richest almost untouched ecosystems in the eastern Himalaya. Local people are involved as guardians, decision-makers and ultimately as beneficiaries of the rich biological and cultural heritage of the Makalu-Barun area.

Tourists have yet to discover the region in large numbers. Some of the negative tourism impacts evident in Nepal's more popular trekking regions – litter, pollution, deforestation, inflation and deterioration of cultural and social values – are just beginning to appear. Anticipating increasing growth in tourism the strategy of the Makalu-Barun project is to minimalise and mitigate problems as they occur. Unlike other national parks, regulations are not enforced by Nepal's army. Instead MBNPCA helps provide the infrastructure, support and investment capital to carry out imaginative and comprehensive remedies to complex problems. Essentially instead of the usual top down approach Makalu-Barun is working bottom up.

The area has been divided into three basic zones: a nature preserve where nobody is allowed to visit except for scientific research, a multiple use protected area which is the rest of the park including the tourism regions, and a few special sites and trails of cultural and historic importance.

(Adapted from a report by **Wendy Brewer-Lama**)

Facilities for the trekker

ACCOMMODATION AND FOOD

Our travels in Solu-Khumbu depended on Sherpa hospitality. When we arrived at a village where we wanted to spend the night, we would yell up at the window of any convenient house and ask to spend the night there. Permission was invariably given, whereupon we went upstairs to the main room, cooked our meal on the family fire, and went to sleep on whatever flat surface was available, usually the wooden floor. The host typically gave us any extra pillows lying around. We paid for food but, from Junbesi east, not for firewood. James Fisher in the 1970s.

The development of lodges

The hill peoples of Nepal have traditionally provided food and accommodation for the many traders passing through their villages on the trade routes that cross the country. These small family-run establishments were nothing like hotels in the Western sense of the word. Guests were charged for food but not for their lodging, which was very basic. Not so long ago these teahouses were providing the same level of facilities for the first foreign trekkers: little more than dal bhat and a hard bed. As the flow of trekkers grew it was soon realised that these foreigners were prepared to pay more for better accommodation and a choice of food.

Development was slow at first. In 1985 Kenja, Junbesi, Kharikhola and Monjo were the only places below Namche that had proper lodges. In the 1990s, however, many new lodges have been built and teahouses upgraded. Double rooms have replaced dormitories, and showers and toilets have been built. Extensive menus are provided for meals according to Western tastes. (Nepalis have just two main meals a day, both comprising dal bhat). Chimneys have now been installed in many places, and smoky lodges are rare. Lodges are now run as businesses, very different from the old teahouses with their hosts eager for news of the world beyond the village.

Nepal now offers surprisingly well-developed mountain lodge systems in the Solu Khumbu, Annapurna and Langtang areas. This is, however, a developing country that is still one of the world's poorest so although the lodges may be not be as grand as those you might find in the European Alps neither are the prices. Each lodge is, for the most part, owned and managed by a single family. Supplies are purchased or grown locally where possible but most things are carried in by porters.

Hygiene

Eating in well established lodges is now probably safer than eating a cooked meal on an organised group trek. The concept of washing hands, basic cleanliness and boiling water has been learnt from courses in Kathmandu as well as at the insistence of trekkers. Kitchens may lack stainless steel sinks and running water but they are, nevertheless, cleaned frequently. The style of cooking (frying or boiling) renders much of the food safe and salads are not to be found. Hot drinks are safe but local drinks such as *chang* are not always so hygienically prepared.

Lodges on the main routes

Food A typical lodge in this area offers an extensive menu (vegetarian except in and around Namche) based on noodles, rice, flour, potatoes, eggs and the sparing use of vegetables. Breakfast offerings include muesli, a variety of porridges, pancakes and bread with jam or eggs. Most meal choices are carbohydrate-heavy: exactly what trekkers require. Apple pie, chocolate cake, pizza and toasted cheese and garlic sandwiches have found their way onto the menus of some resourceful lodge owners. All serve tea, coffee, hot chocolate, hot lemon and Coke. Bottled beer can also be found along with *chang* (local beer), the respected Khukri rum and infamous *rakshi*. Porters and guides can locate this fire-water quicker than an Aussie can sniff out a beer!

Bathroom facilities These are not so developed but a primitive hot shower or a bucket of water are usually available. Toilets are usually just a hole in the ground to be squatted over. No spotlessly-white antiseptic auto-flush toilets here, so watch your ankles. The rural Nepalese have land that needs fertilising so before foreign trekkers took to the mountains there was no need for toilets.

Lodgings Sleeping arrangements vary. Older lodges have dormitories while most newer or larger places often boast simple double rooms with thin partitions that will not insulate you from a snoring neighbour. Ear plugs can be helpful. Beds in the newer lodges have reasonably thick foam mattresses

---

❑ Choosing a lodge

Most trekkers tend to head either for the biggest and best-looking lodge or for the one where other trekkers are staying. Lodge-owners are well aware of this and will sometimes try very hard to attract the first trekkers arriving in the village, occasionally even trying to seat them outside (on seats provided for this very purpose) in order to attract more. Overcrowding can be a problem in the most popular lodges. At dinner there may be 15 trekkers ordering eight different dishes, all to be cooked on two fires, although most lodges do seem to cope remarkably well.

Look around at a few places before deciding where to stay. Except at the height of the season, you may find an empty lodge that is equally good as the one the other trekkers are crowding into. It's also worth trying out some of the smaller lodges and teashops, at least occasionally. This can be a rewarding cultural experience that gives you a better chance to see how the family lives. Expansion and competition with the big lodges is beyond the means of many of these small lodge-owners, their money going to support relatives and pay school fees.

but in simple lodges the mattress is barely thick enough to disguise the knots in the wood below. It's covered by a single clean sheet and there's a pillow that can be of granite consistency. Down jackets make great pillows.

There is virtually no chance of getting bedbugs or fleas if you use your own sleeping sheet and sleeping bag, especially since most lodges wash the sheets and air the mattresses frequently. Hotel blankets and quilts, however, having often been used by porters, can contain unwanted bed companions. Unless you expect star-quality facilities, you may be pleasantly surprised and happy with both the food and accommodation along the main trekking routes.

Simple lodges

The lodges in Lobuche, Gorak Shep, half the lodges in Chukhung and Gokyo, and lodges in out-of-the-way places above Namche are all simple lodges. These are basic places where there may only be a couple of dormitories (occasionally rather cold) and the menus are less extensive although the food is usually good. There's little privacy in these lodges but with the friendliness of the owners and warm gear they're quite satisfactory.

Lodges now remain open all the year round, even at Gokyo, Lobuche (but not Gorak Shep) and Chukhung, so trekking options are no longer restricted during winter and the monsoon. They also never seem to suffer the problem of being full to the extent that trekkers are stranded without a bed. There always seems to be space somewhere; you'll never be turned away. There are, however, a few particularly busy places (Tengboche and Lobuche especially) that during October-November are filled almost to bursting. Sometimes this is because people on a group trek inconsiderately decide a lodge is more attractive and warmer than their tents. The national park has been reluctant to allow the building of new lodges or the expansion of old ones in this area. Elsewhere, supply-and-demand laws seem to work well.

Off the main routes

In general, wherever there is a village, accommodation can be found. There may not be a lodge as such but people will often invite you to stay. If this does not happen try asking around (this is not considered rude by the Nepalis) and something will turn up. Conditions can be extremely basic

---

❏ **A plea to group members**

Please make voluble complaints to trek leaders and trekking company directors if any of the environmental recommendations noted in this section are not carried out. The entire group's unburnable litter must be taken out right to the end of the trek. Kerosene must be provided by the company not just for the trekkers but for porters' use also. They may not use any firewood either in the national park or en route to Mera Peak. The police of the area are lackadaisical and although the park staff have authority there are no penalties for contravening park rules. The trekking companies and sirdars do not yet care, seemingly motivated only by personal gain.

however – very different from the lodges on the main trekking routes. In strongly Hindu areas, your presence may be considered as *jutho* (polluting) so you may have to eat alone and perhaps even sleep on the porch.

Wilderness areas and base camps offer no shelter other than the occasional overhanging rock. You should also be aware that on detailed maps the dots marked in *kharkas* (high-altitude pastures) are usually just roofless stone buildings occupied only in the summer. Even then they are often unable to offer food or shelter.

SHOPS, BANKS AND POST OFFICES

Most lodges also run a small shop offering bottled drinks, three or four types of biscuits, chocolate, Mars Bars and some sweets. Often tins of fruit or fish can be found, along with noodles, coffee, drinking chocolate, tea, muesli, porridge, milk powder, jam and cheap batteries.

Namche Shops are well stocked and sell film (slide and print), batteries of all sizes including camera batteries, torches, socks, postcards, Swiss chocolate and Tibetan souvenirs. There's also a wide range of new and used mountaineering equipment for rent and for sale.

Camping food If you're not choosy it's quite possible to assemble enough for a few nights' camping from the better shops in almost any village. The diet may be monotonous but it is light and cheap. In Namche there's a strange variety of expedition dried foods, usually little cheaper than in the West. Lobuche, Pheriche, Chukhung and Gokyo always have an interesting cheaper selection. Many of the locals are involved with expeditions and in little villages the weirdest collections of left-over expedition food can sometimes be found.

Banks and post offices There are banks for foreign exchange at Namche (reliable), Salleri and Khandbari. Post offices are also found in these three places, plus Junbesi. All are closed on Saturdays.

Minimum impact trekking

Take nothing but pictures, leave nothing but footprints (Motto of the Sierra Club)

It is undeniable that trekking has had a significant impact on the environment, the culture and the economy of the Solu Khumbu, with effects both negative and positive. The opinions of experts as to the extent of the damaging effects of trekking on this region vary. Awareness of the problems has been raised, however, and solutions are being effected far more rapidly than elsewhere in Nepal.

It was most fortunate for the people of the Solu Khumbu that the trekking industry started just as the vital trade links with Tibet were being severed by the Chinese. The industry has now developed into the single most important force in the economy and the Khumbu has become the richest area in rural Nepal. Many schools, hospitals and bridges, the obvious benefits of development, have been built.

The negative effects are also obvious. For most Nepalis, firewood is the only source of energy, indeed more than 90% of Nepal's energy is derived from this source. This has led to severe deforestation in parts of the country which in turn has led to soil erosion. Trekkers contribute to this problem by placing greater demands on the fuel supply. The amount of wood burnt by the average lodge in just one day to supply trekkers with apple pies and hot showers would keep a Nepalese family fed for up to two weeks. Litter, never a problem before packaged goods arrived in the Nepal, is now an eyesore, especially glass beer bottles and plastic mineral water bottles. Less apparent but probably even more important, are the negative effects of trekking tourism on the culture of the area. Impressionable younger Nepalis mistakenly develop a Utopian image of the West and lose confidence and pride in their own culture.

Awareness of the problem is the first step, and there are a number of simple, practical measures that trekkers can and should take in order to lessen their impact on a fragile land.

ENVIRONMENTAL CONCERNS

Pack it in, pack it out
In national parks in the West, visitors are encouraged to take out all their litter (and indeed anything they bring into the park with them) when they leave. However, in Nepal the situation is not so straightforward since many of the national parks contain villages and much of what you consume is purchased locally.

Litter
The most worrying and obvious litter problems in the Khumbu and Hinku (Mera Peak area) are directly related to the activities of trekking groups. Tinned food and bottled sauces are served at every meal. The members may be careful with their litter, putting it in the bins set up in the camp but what happens to this rubbish? Sometimes it is burnt, the leftovers sitting in the embers. Sometimes it is buried in the toilet, covered by little more than an inch of dirt. It may be dumped at the nearest village or simply left in the snow. The problem goes virtually unnoticed by group members because the kitchen crew are the last to leave a camp or lunch spot. Despite constant clean-up campaigns, litter left by groups is now considered by the park management to be a serious local problem. Park rules specifically state that all rubbish generated by trekking groups must now be packed out and not dumped in village garbage pits which were dug for the needs of the villagers.

The problem of litter generated by individual trekkers is not so serious. There is little non-burnable litter that is not recycled, apart from some glass bottles and plastic mineral water bottles (which are both a definite problem). Flour, sugar and rice come in sacks, the cardboard from egg-boxes is reused, oil comes in tins that are prized for roofing and very little tinned food is on menus. Most lodges now burn the burnables and the park staff have dug rubbish pits at many strategic sites and instructed the local people in their use (although one hopes this is not a permanent solution).

● **Don't use mineral water** Since mineral water is sold in non-returnable, non-biodegradable plastic bottles and is now widely available in Nepal the empty bottles are becoming a serious litter problem. Use iodine to purify water (see p235) instead of buying mineral water; you can then also be sure that the water really is safe.

● **Put litter in bins** There is absolutely no excuse for dropping any litter along the trails. Yet many trekkers are guilty of this, even if only for the odd sweet wrapper. However, one piece of paper, multiplied several thousand times becomes a significant problem. Tissues, film cartons and biscuit wrappers are all easily stuffed into a backpack pocket for disposal in a bin at a lodge. You could also help by picking up a few bits of the litter generated by other people.

● **Set an example** The concept of litter is a relatively new one for the Nepalis. In the past almost everything that was discarded was biodegradable so not a threat to the environment. Take-away meals have always been served on sal leaves which do not become a problem when thrown away beside the trail. Trekkers can help here by example.
Dispose of excess packaging before arrival. Today virtually everything comes wrapped in multiple, sometime unnecessary layers. Expeditions, especially, will find it more environmentally sound and more economic to plan packaging thoughtfully.

Other pollution
● **Use the toilet facilities provided** Most lodges have toilets which individual trekkers should use. Group trekkers should ensure that the toilets that are dug in their camps are of a sufficient depth and are properly filled in when the campsite is left. Trekking organisations have been criticised for not doing this. With the large number of groups there are now so many holes that finding a new space to put a toilet tent can be a problem. This is particularly acute in Tengboche and Gokyo. Toilet blocks specifically for the use of trekking groups are now being constructed throughout the Khumbu.

● **Bury or burn used toilet paper** Nepalis use the 'water method' rather than toilet paper so all the pink streamers beside the track are generated by trekkers. Used toilet paper is easily burnt or put in the bin provided for the purpose. It should not be dropped into the toilet since villages often use human waste, as well as cow dung, as fertiliser on the fields, mixing it with leaves. Tampons must be wrapped and put in rubbish bins.

● **Don't pollute water sources** In the West the provision of clean drinking water has reduced the incidence of diarrhoea-related diseases so that they are now negligible. Nepal still has a long way to go but efforts are being made to provide villages with water from uncontaminated sources. If bathing in streams don't use soap or shampoo. Do not defecate close to the trail or a stream. If there is no toilet ensure you are at least 20 metres away from any water source, bury your waste and used toilet paper.

Fuel conservation

The total consumption of firewood by trekkers may be less than 0.1% of all the firewood consumed each year in Nepal but its effect is highly concentrated in a narrow ribbon along the main trails. Not only is wood used directly by lodges but also by all the porters who carry supplies for the markets. It is true that these porters would, like other Nepalis, use firewood anyway but in their villages away from these busy main trails. Depletion of the remaining forest cover compounds the already serious erosion problems.

For villages on the Jiri to Namche trail there is no instant solution. Kerosene has to be imported and is not entirely practical for lodge use. The micro-hydroelectric schemes cannot, so far, generate enough electricity for cooking and the establishment of an extensive national electricity grid is beyond the means of Nepal. Tree replanting is well established and is showing returns.

There is some good news, however: Namche now has the most advanced hydroelectric system in rural Nepal, a 600kw medium-size hydro scheme. The lodges and the local people of Namche and the surrounding villages are adapting to cooking on electricity. Electric cookers are being adopted because they are cheaper to run than wood-fired stoves. One hopes that this admirable project will serve as a pilot scheme for others.

● **Help conserve firewood** To help in a small way do not make open fires, use iodine to purify water instead of getting it boiled, co-ordinate meal times and limit hot showers to lodges where the water is heated in back boilers or solar panels.

Trekking companies deserve the harshest possible criticism for contravening park rules by allowing their porters to cook on open fires, although they do use kerosene for meals for the trekkers and main crew. If you're trekking with a group and see fires being lit for cooking you should make a complaint in the strongest terms.

Accelerated erosion

Erosion is a natural phenomenon that creates river deltas and shapes mountains. In some parts of the world, however, it may occur at an accelerated rate that has serious consequences. The Himalaya are a young range of mountains which are still in the process of formation and erosion has always been considerable here. In the last few decades the problem has been exacerbated by rapid deforestation. The natural ground cover is being stripped away for firewood or animal fodder allowing rain to erode the essential topsoil. The problem is very serious: Nepal's forests are disappearing at the rate of 3% per year. One hectare of cleared forest loses around 50 tons of soil annually and approximately 400,000 hectares are cleared each year in Nepal.

● **Don't damage plants and stick to the trails** In the alpine areas, above the tree line, plants battle to survive in a harsh environment. Trekkers can have a negative effect on these areas. Big boots and yak hooves disturb the topsoil and sliding down a slope can leave scars that never heal.

CULTURAL CONSIDERATIONS

There is precious little in civilisation to appeal to a yeti. Sir Edmund Hillary

One of the great attractions of Nepal for the first visitors was the fact that the cultures of the many different peoples living here had evolved independently of Western 'civilisation'. Day-to-day life for most people had remained virtually unchanged. Sudden outside influence, however, has brought profound cultural change, particularly in the areas popular with tourists.

Whilst trees can be replanted in areas that have been deforested and mountains can be climbed leaving scarcely a trace of the climb, it is impossible not to leave some impression of your country and culture while visiting a foreign country and interacting with its people. The media is another major purveyor of images of the West, particularly through the cinema, where a fantasy world of exaggerated wealth and violence is portrayed. In Nepal, the effects of these cross-cultural exchanges may well be far more serious and damaging than environmental concerns.

There is no denying that the West is a technologically advanced society but its superiority over less 'developed' cultures does not, necessarily, extend beyond this. A visit to a country like Nepal can be a very rewarding experience, especially if you have not travelled much outside the West. Many things are done differently here but this does not make the methods any less valid and in some cases they may be better. The Nepalese way of solving problems, for example, is to avoid confrontation which starkly contrasts with the head-on 'Rambo' style of the West. The incidence of murder, theft and rape (outside the family) in Nepal is negligible in comparison to most nations, although it is rising with contact with the outside world.

● **Dress decently** Dress standards are important despite the fact that they are overlooked by many trekkers. Whilst men may go around without a shirt in the West, this is considered indecent in Nepal. Women should not wear shorts or sleeveless tops. See p42 for further information.

● **Respect people's right to privacy** Ask people before you take their photograph and be considerate when looking for subjects. Some older people believe that if you photograph them their lifespan may be reduced.

● **Don't flaunt your wealth** By Nepali standards, even the poorest foreign trekker is unimaginably wealthy. Nepalis often ask how much you earn
– qualify your answer by giving them some examples of the cost of living in
your country. Don't leave valuables lying around as this is further evidence
that you have so much money you can easily afford to replace them.

● **Respect religious customs** Pass to the left of mani-walls and chortens. Prayer wheels should be turned clockwise. Remove your boots before
entering a gompa and leave a donation; there's often a metal box provided.

● **Respect traditions** There are a number of other customs and traditions
that you should take care to respect. Not doing so is insulting to your hosts.
The left hand, used for washing after defecating, is not considered clean so
you should never touch anyone with it, offer them anything with it or eat
with it. The head is considered the most sacred part of the body and you
should never touch anyone on it. Avoid pointing the soles of your feet at a
person's head. If you're sitting with your legs out-stretched and a Nepali
needs to pass, he or she will never step over you. Move out of the way.

● **Encourage pride in Nepali culture** Express an interest in what people are doing and try to explain that not everything is as rosy in the West as
the Nepalis might believe. In restaurants don't consistently shy away from
Nepalese food. Local people are being taught by insidious example that
packaged sweets, biscuits, noodles and chocolate are more desirable than
local equivalents but in most cases they are actually less nutritious.

ECONOMIC IMPACT

The initial effect of independent trekkers using local lodges was a sudden
increase in prices for many commodities along the major trekking routes.
The villagers, naturally enough, sought the best prices for their produce and
the highest bidders were the trekkers. In the short term this created a problem because villagers were more willing to sell scarce commodities to
trekkers. It should, however, also be considered as a stage in the long development process: demand encourages production where previously there was
no advantage in producing more. If the commodity is not available locally
and it must be carried in by a porter, this creates work in areas where there
may be few employment opportunities.

Teahouse trekking stimulates the local economy. Money from individual
trekkers enters the local economy via the shops and lodges but it can have an
effect on the whole area. Porters carry in the additional goods, new buildings
may need to be constructed requiring local resources and labour, staff are
required at the lodges and local producers have a new market. Collectively
these provide more jobs and can lead to a higher standard of living, not just
among lodge-owners. This is immediately obvious from visiting areas frequented by trekkers and comparing them with villages without this stimulus.
Namche probably has the highest per capita income in Nepal, ahead even of
Kathmandu. It's often stressed that little of the money stays in the lodge-

owners' pockets. This may be true but there are many others who benefit.

The economic impact of trekking groups is somewhat different. The main beneficiaries are the government (in the form of taxes) and the trekking company directors (profits). The secondary beneficiaries are the employees, who are rarely local people so their earnings do not stay in the area. In fact, locals receive virtually nothing. Camping fees are Rs5 per tent and since the bulk of provisions are carried in, little food is purchased locally. Only firewood is used, and rubbish left.

● **Don't bargain for food & lodging** These prices are fixed.

● **Don't give to beggars** Some trekkers, embarrassed at the disparity in material wealth between their country and Nepal, have given money to beggars and sweets and pens to children. They may have thought that they were helping but the opposite is probably true. As well as fostering an unhealthy dependency attitude, begging can in some places be more profitable than earning money by portering or working in the fields. Giving sweets to children not only encourages them to see Westerners (and hence the West) as bringers of all good things but also leads to tooth decay, until recently quite rare in Nepal. On the trail you may encounter teenagers asking for funds for their school. It's hard to judge how genuine these claims are but you don't *have* to give anything. You'll be shown a book with amounts donated; if the sums are unrealistically large, the solicitation probably isn't genuine.

❏ **THE MINIMUM IMPACT CODE**

Developed by environmental groups in Nepal affiliated with the King Mahendra Trust for Nature Conservation, the Minimum Impact Code requests trekkers to:

● **Conserve firewood** Be self-sufficient in your fuel supply and make sure your trekking staff uses kerosene and has enough warm clothing. Make no open fires. Limit hot showers. If possible stay at lodges that use kerosene or fuel efficient wood stoves and space heaters.

● **Stop pollution** Dispose of all trash properly. Paper products, cigarette butts, toilet paper, food scraps etc should be burned or buried. Bottles, plastics and other non-biodegradable items should be packed out or deposited in rubbish pits if available. Use the toilet facilities provided. If none exist, make sure you are 20 metres away from any water source and carry a small shovel to bury wastes. Don't use soap or shampoo in any stream or hot spring. Supervise trekking staff to make sure they cover toilet pits and dispose of garbage properly.

● **Be a guest** Do not damage, disturb or remove any plants, animals, animal products or religious artifacts. Respect Nepali customs in your dress and behaviour. Women should not wear shorts or revealing blouses and men should always wear a shirt. Avoid outward displays of physical affection. Ask permission to take photographs and respect people's right to privacy. Begging is a negative interaction that was started by well-meaning tourists – please do not give anything to beggars. Don't barter for food and lodging. Encourage young Nepalis to be proud of their culture.

Above all, remember that your vacation has a great impact on the natural environment and the people who live off its resources. By assisting in these small ways, you will help the land and people of Nepal enormously.'

PART 5: ROUTE GUIDE AND MAPS

Using this guide

Routes and itineraries
The routes described here are not broken up into a rigid day-by-day schedule. Instead all the possible stopping points are listed, leaving it for you to decide how far you want to walk each day. Be as flexible as possible when planning your itinerary and don't always try to stay at the biggest and best lodges. Often the most memorable interactions with local people occur in places not frequented by large numbers of trekkers. Sample itineraries are given in Appendix A, p223. Main route sections are as follows:

> Jiri to Namche p129 (overview map p21)
> Trekking from Lukla p146
> Namche p155
> To Lobuche and Kala Pattar p164
> To Gokyo p178
> The Tsho La/Cho La p186
> Khumbu side trips and pass-hopping p188
> Starting from Phaplu p193
> Salpa-Arun to the Khumbu p195
> Starting from Bhojpur p210
> Rowaling p212

Scale
The maps are drawn to a scale of roughly 1:100,000 (one centimetre is equivalent to one kilometre). For this third edition the maps on the Salpa-Arun route have been redrawn at 1:100,000. The maps of the Rolwaling Valley are still at 1:250,000. Features have been stylised so that roads, rivers and villages appear larger (easier to read) than on a true topographic map.

Limited space has dictated that only the main geographical features required for route-finding – major ridges, rivers and streams – can be shown. To work out which mountain you are admiring, a detailed colour topographic map is invaluable.

Route finding
Unlike many tracks in developed countries the trails in Nepal are unmarked. Paths lead off the main route to grazing areas, firewood collecting areas and water sources. The main trail, however, is usually wider and runs in a consistent direction, so generally it is easy enough to follow. If you think you have inadvertently taken the wrong path look carefully at the size of it – on

a main path you don't usually brush against branches and undergrowth. Is it still heading in the right direction? If you must climb to the village and the path has been contouring for a while, don't be afraid to turn back. Occasionally trails divide and rejoin a little while later. This has been marked on the trail maps in this book.

The paths across glaciers and other difficult terrain are usually littered with stone cairns (stone men). The majority mark the correct route but a few merely show that it is possible to climb a point. Occasionally cairns are toppled by snow, wind or animals. If you are sure that you are on the correct path, don't hesitate to rebuild these guides or add new ones. Locals take pride in the art of constructing ones that are surprisingly well balanced and in just the right spot so that they are visible from afar.

Walking times

The hills render measured distances in miles or kilometres virtually meaningless; walking times are far more useful. These are given along the side of the maps, with arrows indicating the villages they refer to. While I have tried to be consistent as to the times quoted, inevitably there is a high degree of variation. The walking times on the trail maps give a wide spread. Hiking briskly and steadily with few stops should approximate the lesser time while ambling along admiring the scenery and spotting wildlife should approximate the longer time. This is also the *group* pace.

The times are not meant to performance-orientate you: fast walkers could easily come in under the lesser times. The maps are really only intended to be a guide to help lunchtime and end of the day decision-making: eg if it is half past three and you are wondering how far away the next lodge is and whether to stay or to go on.

The group pace is sedate with plenty of time for relaxation. Porters carry 30-35kg on group treks so the length of the trekking day is limited by this. Time must also be allowed for the kitchen crew who are the last to leave camp after cleaning up and must then race ahead to prepare the next meal. The need for adequate shelter for porters effectively prevents camping in unfrequented wild spots unless groups are well prepared. Groups may walk short days in order to stop in a camping place that is a traditional night stop. So the days are generally easy and lunch stops sometimes last half the afternoon. For people who are not used to exercise the pace is good but anyone who keeps fit by regularly playing sport will find the pace leisurely after the first few days.

Individual trekkers tend to cover more distance in a day than groups. Once at Namche, the pace is dictated solely by the altitude gains and so involves rest days and half-day walks only.

When taking **day trips** uphill you can assume that the return will take you half to two thirds of the time. Don't forget to allow time for relaxing and exploring too. On a fine day there is no more satisfying place to bask in the sun than atop a glorious viewpoint.

Altitudes

These are given in metres on the maps and in the text they're also quoted in feet. Altitudes are approximate and rounded for villages since there are very few truly flat bits of ground. Don't get too worried about the sometimes huge differences in altitudes between some villages. Trekking in Nepal involves crossing mammoth ridges all the time. Simply go at a pace that suits, stop frequently and you'll soon get used to walking uphill and downhill. There is in fact one absolutely flat stretch near Tumlingtar but, strangely, instead of being pleasant it's hell. You seem to be getting nowhere, the ground is hard and it actually seems tough walking. Main ridges and mountains are shown as **thick lines** on the trail maps that follow.

Facilities

Facilities available along the trail are indicated by symbols on the trail maps. **Large lodges** 🔼 are the bigger and better establishments that will have a comprehensive menu and double rooms. **Simple lodges/teahouses** 🔼 may not have a separate dining room and may have only one dormitory but they're certainly more homely than the fancy places. Some are in locations where trekkers rarely stay, stopping at them only for tea or a meal. **Tea shacks** ▽ are the simplest places. In the lower country they are often just a few bamboo mats over a wooden frame and generally don't look too hygienic. In the most basic there are no beds, only room on the floor.

If there's just one lodge or teahouse it'll be shown as an **outline**, a few will be shown **half blacked-in** and if there are many lodges or teahouses they'll be shown with a **black symbol**. For larger villages there is a village plan. This shows the names and locations of the lodges, with the words lodge, hotel, restaurant and guesthouse omitted. New lodges are being built all the time so don't be surprised if you find places not on the maps.

Place names

Most of the Sherpa villages have both a Nepali name and the traditional Sherpa name. A few even have a name exclusively used by trekkers. All the familiar names of a village are mentioned with the one most commonly used by trekkers and guides repeated in the text.

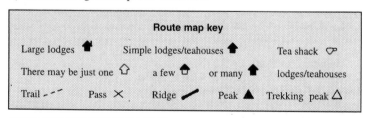

Route map key

Large lodges 🔼	Simple lodges/teahouses 🔼	Tea shack ▽
There may be just one 🔼	a few 🔼 or many 🔼	lodges/teahouses
Trail ╌╌ Pass ✕	Ridge ╱ Peak ▲	Trekking peak △

(Opposite) From Namche to Dingboche and Thuklha, Ama Dablam dominates the skyline. It is seen here from near Pangboche after some winter snow. Yaks are commonly used to carry group equipment above Namche.

Jiri to Namche

INTRODUCTION

Jiri to Namche takes most people seven to nine pleasant days walking, usually including a rest day at Junbesi and a shorter easy day or two. If you have more time and energy there are plenty of opportunities for side trips exploring little-visited villages and gompas. Several alpine valleys are also worth more thorough exploration by well-equipped parties. For the extremely fit in a hurry, walking from Jiri to Namche in four days is possible – just. There are good lodges along the main route and since these are usually only a few hours apart it's no longer necessary to plan a detailed itinerary as suggested by some guidebooks. Simply follow your instincts and the advice of other trekkers rather than sticking to a rigid schedule.

The walk is strenuous, following a route that goes against the grain of the land; all the rivers and ridges flow north to south and the trail runs west to east. Following the standard route (not including side trips) by the time you reach Namche you will have climbed up almost exactly the height of Mt Everest, 8848m/29,028ft, and the corresponding descents to Namche total the height of Ama Dablam, 6828m/22,402ft. Since you have trekked the majority of the time between 2000 and 3000m this means you are well acclimatised to around 3000m and unlikely to feel the altitude at Namche. However higher up you should take it just as cautiously as everyone else.

Leaving Jiri there is an introductory hill, then three higher major ridges: an unnamed 2700m/8858ft pass, the Lamjura Pass 3530m/11,581ft and Trakshindo Pass 3071m/10,075ft. Once across the Dudh Kosi (river), the trail climbs high up the valley sides skirting steep rock faces before descending to recross the river several times before the final hill to Namche.

Services – Jiri to Lukla

There are a surprising number of medical facilities. Phaplu has a bush hospital and there is usually a good Nepali doctor at Kenja and at Kharikhola. Between Jiri and Namche there are no banks. Jiri has an unreliable and busy phone and Phaplu has a telephone system, then there is Lukla. It is likely that telephones will be introduced to more villages soon: the Nepal Telecommunications Company has promised to put a telephone in each village development committee (a set of villages totalling around 3000 people) by the new millennium.

Kathmandu to Jiri

This part of the journey is made by bus (see p91), taxi or air. Budget travellers take the public bus while groups usually organise a private bus or take taxis. Asian Airlines can drop a small group (but not individuals) at Jiri while en route to Lukla or Phaplu. There was, at the time of writing, no regular tourist bus service but one can only hope that a mini-Tata (a class of medium-sized buses) service will start. The extra speed, comfort and safety would be appreciated by wealthier locals and trekkers alike.

Hiring a car and driver is the most comfortable alternative but you can go by bus for a fraction of the cost. From the old bus station in the centre of Kathmandu the first departure for Jiri is at around 5.30am. Thieves are now working this route intensively so **take great care of your luggage**. These people are no mere opportunists, they are professionals – many trekkers have lost things from side-pockets, and occasionally a whole rucksack goes missing. It's best to try to take

---

(Opposite) Top: Junbesi at the end of the monsoon season. **Bottom:** On the trail between Lukla and Namche there are still large areas of forest remaining.

your rucksack inside the bus; the ticket office is helpful and will often give you front seats or even a seat for your rucksack as well but other passengers may object to this. Most buses have a dusty boot at the back that can be locked. If you're in a group ensure that all the packs are stowed together on the roof and at the first chance for passengers to ride on the roof, go up and keep a close eye on them. There are also occasional pick-pockets at the bus station. Their favourite trick is to watch where you put the change after buying your ticket then hurry you onto the bus while their hand delves into your pocket. The police have been unhelpful in all cases.

The first part of this 10 to 12 (and occasionally up to 16) hour bus journey is to Lamosangu (78km, five hours) along the Chinese-constructed Arniko Rajmarg or Kodari Highway that runs to the Tibetan border and Lhasa. Leaving Kathmandu you pass through the lower part of **Bhaktapur** where, until the early 1960s, the trek to Everest began.

There is a steep climb out of the Kathmandu Valley and from **Dhulikhel**, at the crest of the hill, there are views on a clear day of the Himalaya from Manaslu to Everest. The road drops to **Dolalghat** (*ghat* means 'bridge') and crosses the Indrawati River. The Chinese road had progressed this far by 1967 so the first commercial treks to the Khumbu started from here.

After crossing the Sun Kosi ('Gold River'), the bus follows the river to **Lamosangu** ('Long Bridge') stopping by the scruffy stalls by the bridge for dal bhaat. One only needs to have a quick look around and sniff the air to realise that hygiene is not even marginal but there are biscuits, chocolate and soft drinks available.

From the bridge it's a further 110km to Jiri, marked by kilometre posts that start at 0km from the Lamosangu bridge. This road was part of a programme of Swiss aid as a model to demonstrate building techniques for mountain roads using appropriate technology. Rather than

employing expensive machinery it was decided to maximise the use of local labour. Rocks were broken with hammers and a lot of sweat, and all the wire netting was woven by hand, providing a vast amount of work. In addition to wages, food was sold in set quantities at subsidised prices to reduce the local impact of the hungry workforce. The only heavy machinery used was a road roller. The result is a Swiss-quality road that will probably last longer with less maintenance than any other road in Nepal. Unfortunately the technique and attention to detail hasn't been duplicated for the rest of Nepal's rural hill roads.

From Lamosangu it can be pleasant to ride on the roof of the bus (theoretically illegal) but take a jacket or windcheater. At the top of the first major ridge is **Muldi** where there may be another stop before continuing to **Charikot** (km54) where trekkers are sometimes requested to register. The turn-off to the left here leads to **Dolakha**, a few kilometres away (see p220). On a cloudless day the monumental twin-headed Gauri Sankar stands out for the next half hour. The high peak slightly right is Menglutse in Tibet.

The descent to the Tamba Kosi ('Copper River') is steep. At the bridge the driver takes a break for a cup of tea or two. If you are on the roof it's a good idea to start putting on warm clothes because it is still several hours and 38km to Jiri. The plantations you pass are a Swiss reforestation programme. After another pass the gradual descent to Jiri begins and at a stop at **Kot**; you might have to register at the police checkpost. **Jiri** is 10 minutes further on.

Note that in winter it's not unknown for a snowfall or sheet ice to block a high section of the road, which means a couple of extra days walking.

JIRI (1935m/6348ft)

Jiri nestles in a fertile valley and beyond the ugly materialism of the road it's a prosperous and tidy village. The people are mainly of the Jirel caste who originate, so the legend goes, from a Sherpa

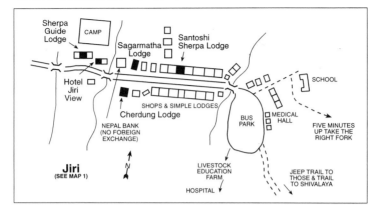

Sherpa Guide Lodge
CAMP
Sagarmatha Lodge
Santoshi Sherpa Lodge
Hotel Jiri View
SCHOOL
SHOPS & SIMPLE LODGES
Cherdung Lodge
NEPAL BANK (NO FOREIGN EXCHANGE)
BUS PARK
MEDICAL HALL
FIVE MINUTES UP TAKE THE RIGHT FORK
Jiri
(SEE MAP 1)
N
LIVESTOCK EDUCATION FARM
JEEP TRAIL TO THOSE & TRAIL TO SHIVALAYA
HOSPITAL

mother and a Sunuwar father. There are also some Sherpas and with the road (which linked Jiri in 1984) came the merchant castes, mainly Newars.

There are many *lodges* but only a few that trekkers frequent. Most are four storeys high but look the same height as the three-storeyed buildings and inside the low doorways are headbangingly obvious.

Electricity comes from Lamosangu, from the Chinese hydro project there. The fact that it costs something means that the farmers cannot afford it so it's used mainly by the local businesses and lodges. Since fire-wood (for cooking) is still cheap, apart from a couple of refrigerators and a hot water cylinder, electricity is used only for lighting.

With Jiri being the beginning or the end of a trek most people are anxious to be on their way and there is little to hold you here other than to inspect the various Swiss projects. Don't expect peaceful lie-ins in the morning. You'll be woken at the crack of dawn by a cacophony of bus horns announcing the departures to Kathmandu. If you do have more time the hill above Jiri (at least a day's walk up) offers stunning Himalayan views.

Planning the first day's trek

Groups generally stay at Shivalaya for the first night. This is only half a day's walk

from Jiri but the first morning is busy with the porters and their loads being sorted out. The short, easy day is also ideal for gently accustoming the legs to the rigours of trekking. The facilities at Shivalaya are quite good so less fit independent trekkers may also consider spending the night here. The next accommodation is in two simple *lodges* up the hill at Sangbadanda.

Fit walkers can comfortably make the numerous lodges at Deorali. Reaching Bhandar is possible but your legs will suffer the following day.

JIRI TO SHIVALAYA
STANDARD ROUTE [MAP 1, p132]

Each time this guide has been brought out the trail leaving Jiri has changed about a month later. Since there is a jeep road under construction no doubt this will happen again! Apologies to everyone. My advice is simply to follow porters. I guess they will head along the jeep road and leave the road at an unmarked junction. If the road has been extended to Those, jeeps or buses may even continue there.

Assuming you are following the standard route via Chitre:

Chitre An hour out of Jiri is Chitre, a shanty of primitive *tea-shacks*. The surrounding area looks horribly bare with goats having eaten all the vegetation and the people look decidedly poor. This is probably one of the most impoverished-looking areas on the whole route, although throughout Nepal there are many places similar to it. Around a bend lurks an unwelcome surprise – it's still a little way to the top of the small pass.

Small pass (2400m/7874ft) At the crest are a couple more *tea-shacks* and some new vistas. The path heads down; it's easy to follow and in about 10 minutes you pass a primary school. Around here is the usual spot for groups to have lunch. Another five minutes along the trail brings you to Mali.

Mali First there's a simple *teahouse*, then three *lodges* that look reasonable, one with a small shop in it. The facilities are basic and with it being so close to Jiri few trekkers ever stay here.

Leaving Mali the trail leads down, and down is the word. One hour later cross a small stream, then past a couple of buildings is the long suspension bridge over the Khimti Khola to Shivalaya.

JIRI TO SHIVALAYA (THE THOSE ALTERNATIVE) [Map 1]

This pleasant detour goes via Those, a bazaar town on the old route that was used before the road reached Jiri. There is still one simple *lodge* left in Those but walking to Shivalaya in a day is no problem. The new jeep road will change the route to Those, hopefully making the trail easier to follow. Until the road is finished at the end of the jeep road head up to a small pass on a surprisingly small trail then meet the old main trekking route from Lamosangu. This traverses in forest around the next ridge. After this it drops to Kattike and descends further to the Khimti Khola. Upstream a suspension bridge crosses to Those. Don't be afraid to ask the way.

Those This village was the centre of an ancient iron mining and manufacturing industry that began to decline during the 1940s when Indian iron became readily available. Farming implements forged here were traded as far away as Tibet and this business was one of the first sources

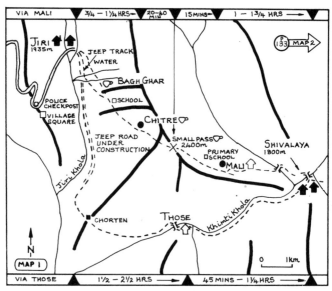

VIA MALI   ¾ — 1¼ HRS   20–40 MIN   15 MINS   1 — 1¾ HRS

JIRI 1935m

JEEP TRACK

WATER

BAGH GHAR

SCHOOL

POLICE CHECKPOST

VILLAGE SQUARE

CHITRE

JEEP ROAD UNDER CONSTRUCTION

SMALL PASS 2400m

PRIMARY SCHOOL

MALI

SHIVALAYA 1800m

Jiri Khola

CHORTEN

THOSE

Khimti Khola

N

MAP 1

133 MAP 2

0   1km

VIA THOSE   1½ — 2½ HRS   45 MINS — 1¼ HRS

of wealth for Namche. A few iron products, especially steel roosters, are still made here and it is worth the slight diversion. Shivalaya is a little over an hour upstream from Those.

Shivalaya (1800m/5905ft) Resting on the east bank of the khola, Shivalaya ('Shiva's home or temple') is not much more than a hamlet of eight or nine *lodges*. They are all modest but pleasant. The settlement has an air of being new, and it is: the original Shivalaya was slightly downstream. When the road reached Jiri the main trekking route changed, so the villagers moved too.

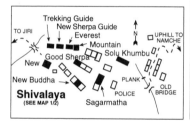

SHIVALAYA TO BHANDAR [MAP 2]
The trail out of Shivalaya is steep from the first step, and will get the sweat flowing. The gradient relents only after the next village.

> ❑ **Side trip to Thodung**
> For the energetic this route is worth the extra effort, providing you don't get lost. The views are good, especially on a clear morning when Gauri Sankar sparkles in the distance. In Thodung (3090m/10,137ft) there's one lodge set in the forest. The cheese factory here follows processes introduced by the Swiss, using similar technology to that in the small factories in the Alps. The idea was first introduced in the Langtang area after an FAO (United Nations Food and Agriculture Organisation) study. Now there are many similar government-run factories and the trekking route passes close to three more en route to Namche.

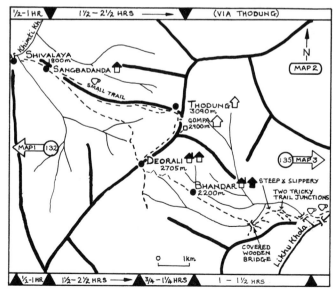

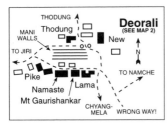

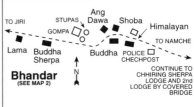

Sangbadanda This is a mainly Sherpa settlement and has a couple of simple *lodges* with shops.

Two minutes west is an important junction and a choice: the upper/left path leads to Thodung (see below); the right-hand trail is the slightly more direct and lower route to Deorali, about a couple of hours away depending on your hill speeds.

Deorali (2705m/8875ft) This means 'pass' in Nepali so this is a common village name. The actual village (see above) is slightly south where the water supply is better so again this is just a group of *lodges*. They are set in two neat rows divided by a set of mani walls, the first real sign of Buddhist Sherpa country. You should pass to the left of a mani wall or a wall of prayer wheels.

From some rocks immediately above the lodges there are superb views into the distance on a clear day; you can see much of the route ahead. Below, the hillside stretches down where the twin chortens of Bhandar are clearly visible. Take the left fork a couple of minutes below the pass; the descent is initially steep.

Bhandar (2200m/7218ft) The Sherpa name for this area is Chyangma. Immediately above the chortens is a small gompa and below, a group of four *lodges*. The two main ones are *Ang Dawa Lodge* and *Buddha Lodge* but the others are also good.

A few of the lodges boast environmentally-friendly features that have become common in the better trekkers' lodges along the route. 'Green' showers are provided by running pipes through the cooking fire, then into a hot-water tank which is sometimes connected directly to the shower-room. This produces essentially free hot water, using energy that would otherwise go straight up the chimney. It's a simple though effective system that has taken off not because of the green revolution but because there are numerous advantages for the lodge owners (the only way change can be introduced in an economy that generates virtually no surplus cash). Lodge owners are asked to cook a variety of meals, sometimes in huge quantities, and trekkers also request hot water for washing. Heating water takes a long time so an instant source of hot water is invaluable. The system is cheap enough for the lodges to afford but beyond the reach of ordinary villagers.

From the chortens the descent is gentle with about seven simple *lodges* or *teahouses* evenly spaced a few minutes apart down the hill. Past these is a flattish field with several houses around it, a regular camping spot for groups for their second night out of Jiri.

BHANDAR TO JUNBESI [MAPS 2-4]

From Bhandar to the covered wooden bridge, the trail is fairly easy to follow. Turn sharp left after crossing the bridge and keep left for a few minutes, dropping down to a group of buildings, a two-storey house and another with the second storey level with the track, reached in a few more minutes. Immediately after them are some stone steps. Follow these, **not** the trail that continues straight ahead. There's a similar trap at the next few houses: follow the path that sometimes

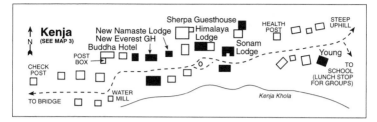

resembles a stream descending to the left. Once across the next wooden bridge there are a few **teahouses** and a house by an obvious T junction; turn left here and follow the Likhu Khola to Kenja.

Kenja (1640m/5380ft) This is a thriving 'lodge' town with a few good hotels and no bad ones. It's a mixed village, mainly Sherpa with some Chhetri (a caste immediately below the Brahmins). Kenja is slightly unusual in this respect because, apart from Jubing, the trek from Bhandar to the Khumbu is through exclusively Sherpa country. The mix here can be attributed to tourism. Once Kenja was nothing more than a couple of houses but people from up and down the valley were attracted by the rumours of fantastic wealth possible by setting up a lodge. By 1984 there were a couple of lodges and five houses but this has now grown to 10 **lodges**.

In mid-1989 Kenja was linked to an electricity supply as part of a Japanese aid project. There are nine small generators

and when they're all working (rarely) this generates 55kw which is enough power to provide electricity for cooking. Firewood is starting to become expensive but very few can afford the enormous cost of a stove. However, it was pleasing that the lodge owners I spoke to thought it entirely possible that if the project works well enough lodge owners would begin cooking with electricity. Electricity would probably be a cheaper option than firewood in the near future. Stereos have already arrived here and one has to wonder how long it will be before there are video nights in Kenja.

In October you might see something that looks like a prickly pear dangling from leafy creepers. The local name is *iskus* and it must be cooked to be edible and tastes like a slightly sweet potato. The side trail to Pike Peak (pronounced 'pee-kay'), the home of the benevolent spirit for this area, starts from the bridge over the Kenja Khola. The trail goes up the ridge to the south, then skirts the peak to a ridge heading north. It finally drops

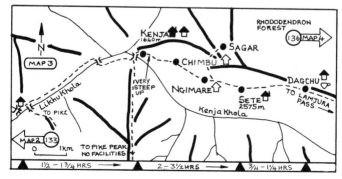

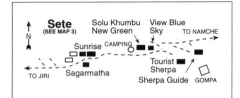

to the main trail after the Lamjura Pass but this is an incredibly long route with no facilities along the way.

Leaving Kenja From Kenja it's an altitude gain of 1900m to the top of the Lamjura Pass and for this reason many people recommend staying in Sete to break the climb. If you're reasonably fit, however, climbing over the pass in a single (tough) day from Kenja is quite possible. If you don't make it over the top there are some *lodges* where you can stay en route.

Sete (2575m/8448ft) This friendly Sherpa settlement (see map above) is in

two parts. First there are two *lodges*, one very spartan, then five minutes further on another five minutes further on another three lodges with a few camping places.

Sete is not a big village, with almost as many lodges as houses but it does have a small gompa.

Dagchu When you've got your breath back, it's around an hour from Sete to Dagchu, a recent village of six rather simple *lodges* atop the ridge. Out of the forested areas there are some good views. To the south-east (right) you can see the twin tops of Pike Peak, home of the local benevolent spirit.

The trail to the pass continues up the ridge. Ignore all trails that lead off it. From some parts you can see the pass, well to the left of the ridge.

Goyem Another half an hour up brings you to Goyem with two groups of *teahouses/lodges* about five minutes apart. Apple juice, cider and apple brandy are

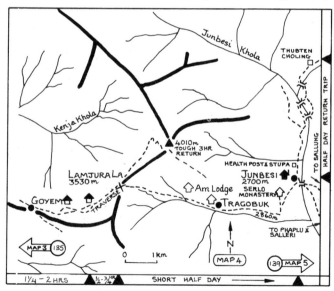

all available here but the water supply is not clean so take particular care to purify water for drinking. A minute out of Goyem is an important junction: continue up on the ridge through forest on a somewhat scrappy trail avoiding the good trail that begins contouring on the south side of the ridge. That is the direct, steep and rarely-used route to Salleri. The forest here is magnificent. Demand for firewood, however, grows with each new lodge built – a negative impact of the teahouse style of trekking. In spring the rhododendrons put on quite a show with whole hillsides covered in blossoms that from late February spread upwards reaching the crest of the pass by the end of April. The air is heady with their scent and with that of the many other flowering trees and shrubs. Soon the trail becomes clearer and you reach a few *tea-shacks*. This is the point where the trail starts contouring to the north of the ridge. There are several junctions but each trail rejoins the main route a few minutes later. The last *teahouse* before the pass, usually has little water to spare but rarely closes since porters like to stop here for tea. The obviously-recent deforestation of the rhododendron trees just above is a horrifying sight.

Passing a few mani walls, it's around half an hour to the top of the pass. Unless the weather is perfect this section can be very cold and windy, and even in October snow can fall with the patches shielded by the sun not melting for several days. In winter there may be quite a bit of snow lying around making the track muddy and even icy – real down-jacket weather. The difference to the temperature that altitude makes is really driven home to you as you head up this pass.

Lamjura La (3530m/11,581ft) The prayer flags and chortens mark the gateway to the Solu (sometimes called Shorong) Sherpa area. It's common to suffer some altitude sickness, especially if you stay up here for a while to admire the view. This does not mean that you will not make it to the top of Kala Pattar, it's

just a warning that ascending too fast has its consequences. You are in fact higher than Namche, where several nights are spent acclimatising.

It's possible to climb the hill to the north of the pass. At first there is no trail but head along the ridge slightly on the western side and soon a small but definite path begins. This contours under the peak before finally doubling back with a stiff climb to the summit. It is a very strenuous climb and even if you felt perfectly well on the pass, the extra 500m gain in altitude is often enough to induce a headache.

Heading down from the pass, there are many paths weaving through the forest but luckily they all head to the same place: a few well-spaced restaurants an hour below the pass. Occasionally you may see monkeys in the forest here.

Tragobuk/Taktok (2860m/9383ft) A new gompa was being built in 1997. It is beside the trail and so hard to miss. It is customary to leave a donation when visiting a gompa; Rs20-100 is appropriate.

❏ **Asking directions**

There's a certain art to asking the way on Nepal's trails. Naturally polite, the Nepalis don't like to cause offence by answering 'no' to a question like 'Is this the way to Namche?' So an affirmative reply to this question is just as likely to mean, 'Yes, I understand the question but I don't know the answer,' as 'Yes, it's the way to Namche'. You can try re-phrasing the question as: 'Which path is for Namche?' but rather than admitting they don't know, a Nepali may just take a guess at the answer. The solution is to ask again in a different way, and ask more than one person. If you ask the way at a junction and then walk away down the wrong trail locals will usually shout after you that you're going the wrong way.

Continue straight through the long village and at junctions avoid trails that descend; these go to Salleri and not Junbesi. The scenic trail stays fairly high and rounds a major ridge and a large rock, with views of Junbesi and its distinctive yellow-roofed gompa. Take a look at the trail options immediately across the river from Junbesi while here.

A few minutes later at a sign-posted junction a trail leads off to **Serlo Monastery** where it is possible for a few people to stay.

Junbesi (2700m/8858ft)

This is one of the most pleasant Sherpa villages en route to Namche and it boasts some particularly good family-run *lodges* offering delicious fresh bread, pizzas, apple juice and cider.

Although Salleri is the district head-quarters, Junbesi has a primary school, high school and a **health post**. The high school has a particularly good reputation, largely due to the dedication of the head-master. The health post has extension workers who are supposed to roam the surrounding hillsides offering vaccinations and health education programmes.

School education in Junbesi became available in 1964 when Sir Edmund Hillary helped construct a school house. It was quickly expanded and in 1972 a middle school was added. Both were run by the Himalayan Trust until 1975 when Nepal nationalised the primary and middle schools. In 1983, a high school was created with Himalayan Trust assistance and now the three schools (under one roof) muster nearly 300 pupils. High schools in Nepal are still privately-run, supported by student fees. In a country where the majority of the population has no money to spend on education it takes hard work and dedication to attend a high school. The costs (Rs2000-3000 for a year, including fees, books, bed and board) may not seem much but a village family, if they have any money at all, will need it to buy necessities and a little food around the lean time before harvest. Most of the pupils are boys and school fees, whether earned by father or son, will come from portering to Namche, low-paid agricultural work or, with luck, a job as a porter-guide or sherpa for a group, where a month or two's work will pay for a year's schooling. For the even luckier

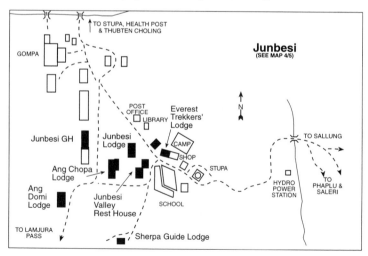

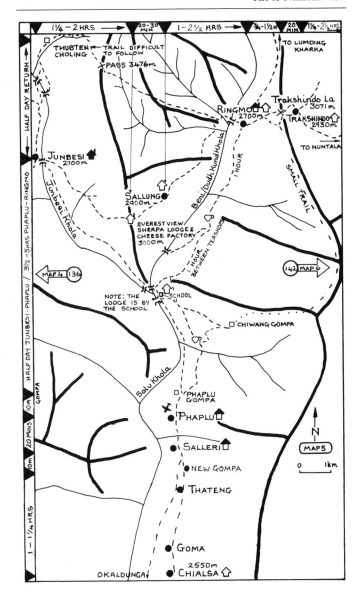

few the Himalayan Trust offers three scholarships a year for the high school.

Development on a pleasant scale is evident everywhere in Junbesi. Agriculture is diversifying and a few lodges provide the majority of their vegetable requirements from their own gardens. The brandies, wines, ciders and jams are made with local fruit, as are the apple pies. Soybeans, wheat, corn, beans, potatoes and highly-prized barley are the traditional crops. However, the altitude and problems with irrigation prevent the growing of rice which must be carried in from Jiri. There's a small hydro-electric scheme that provides lighting (with the odd hiccup).

In the centre of Junbesi is a **police check post** (often unmanned). Make sure you register here since it's for your own safety. If you go missing they'll have some idea of where to start searching.

A half-day trip to Thubten Choling

This is an active Buddhist monastery/ nunnery with about 50 monks and over 200 nuns. Many are Tibetan; some are very recent arrivals. The murals were painted around 1970, a few years after the monastery was founded. The walk up is pleasant and, although it is little more than an hour away from Junbesi, with the friendly monks and beauty of the area do not count on being back for an early lunch. From the monastery there's an **alternative route to Ringmo** over a 3476m/ 11,404ft pass. Unless you are confident about your route-finding ability, it is better to hire a lad from Junbesi who has been over before.

Other gompas Around Junbesi are a scattering of gompas perched atop hills, good alternatives to visiting Thubten Choling. Rumbak, to the south above the track to Salleri, takes one and a half hours one way. Take something to eat and drink with you.

JUNBESI TO KHARIKHOLA [MAPS 5-6]
Leaving Junbesi The Junbesi Khola is crossed on a wooden bridge and from the

other side, looking slightly downstream, you can see the hydro-electric plant. Note that after crossing the Junbesi Khola the main track divides twice. In each case take the upper/left path which should be signposted. The lower paths head to Phaplu and Salleri, a good half-day's walk away. The section around this huge ridge is one of the most pleasant walks so far. Although the trail climbs in places, it's not steep. The track is set high above the valley floor, at first through open forest. Later the view extends across the valley to picturesque villages surrounded by terraces and divided by sparse woodland.

Everest View Sherpa Lodge (3100m/10,170ft) This is an 'Everest View' lodge from which you can actually see Everest, the first point on the trek from Jiri where this is possible. Expanded in 1992 to provide dining with a view, it's perched on the end of a long grazing ridge that runs up to Numbur. Naks (female yaks) are milked in the summer and autumn months and the rich milk is used to make just under 1000kg of pure nak cheese (although everyone wrongly refers to it as yak cheese) every year. The lodge owner manages the production using old Swiss methods. Delicious curd is often available too.

Early morning is generally the best time to spot Everest. If there's a single cloud in the sky a corollary of Murphy's Law says it will obscure Everest first, and it does. For the energetic even better views can be had by climbing part of the ridge behind.

Sallung/Solung (2980m/9777ft)
This hamlet also boasts magnificent views including a fraction of Everest and down the valley to the Phaplu airstrip. Once it had four *lodges* but they seem to be in decline, although it is still possible to stay. These and the Everest View Lodge are convenient places to stay if you visited Thubten Choling monastery in the morning and had a late lunch in Junbesi. Leaving Sallung, the clear trail wanders gently downwards. After a few gullies

you round another ridge for a change of view, the amazing knife-edge ridge of Karyolung whose ridge extends down to Ringmo and the Trakshindo La, the next pass.

The trail winds around ridges and streams to the old suspension bridge across the Beni/Dudh Kund Khola, whose waters originate from the glaciers in the impressive basin formed by Karyolung (6511m/ 21,361ft), Khatang (6853m/ 22,483ft) and Numbur (6959m/22,831ft). The twin peaks of Numbur and Khatang are the Shorong Yul Lha, where the Sherpa god for the Shorong area resides. It's possible to camp at the high grazing areas below their glaciers and stunning mountain faces; but this is virtually never attempted by trekkers.

Ringmo (2700m/8858ft) From the suspension bridge the trail climbs, steeply at first, to Ringmo and a major trail junction by the recently-built stupa. The south/right-hand trail heads to Phaplu and Salleri on a beautiful, wide path (see p193). Straight on is the route to the pass, Trakshindo La.

Ringmo is a spread-out settlement set among apple orchards and famous for all things apple. Try their apple pie, apple cake, apple juice, apple cider, and/or their pink apple brandy. Apples, peaches and apricots are cultivated to such an extent that half the crop has to be made into delicious cider and fire-water brandies. This is also the main source of fruit for the famous Namche apple pies.

At the top of Ringmo are two 50-metre mani walls. After correctly passing to the left of both do **not** continue straight on unless you're going to Lumding Kharka. The correct route (often signposted) is to the right. This is the beginning of the ascent to the Trakshindo La.

Side route to Lumding Kharka The path that continues straight ahead from the Ringmo mani wall leads to high grazing pastures below Numbur and several isolated high routes into the Dudh Kosi. There are no lodges or even villages until the Dudh Kosi, a two- to four-day walk away (depending on which route you take). The Lumding La route offers some good and unusual views of Everest, Lhotse and Makalu. Interestingly it was used extensively by Tibetans who, because many yaks had died at Kharikhola in 1959, preferred this high route until the early 1970s. It was also the alternative route if the bridge across the Dudh Kosi below Jubing had been washed out. This was why the 1952 Swiss Everest Expedition was forced to use it. Two porters died of the cold which led to the Swiss providing the suspension bridge that now spans the Dudh Kosi.

Following the main route Immediately right after the Ringmo mani walls, the trail divides after a few minutes at a well-signposted junction. The right fork goes to the Ringmo cheese factory and lodge (often closed in winter), at least ten minutes up (not the advertised five). The cheese and garlic sandwiches are potent enough to keep even the yaks away from you! The left/straight fork continues directly to the pass, less than an hour away.

Trakshindo La (3071m/10,075ft) The pass, marked by a white stupa, divides the Solu (Shorong)

Ringmo
(SEE MAP 5)

TO LUMDING KHARKA
MANI WALLS
TO NAMCHE
Quiet View
MANI WALL
Apple House
Sherpa Guide
NEW SCHOOL
Himalayan Sherpa
TO JUNBESI
New
New
Centre Sherpa
TO PHAPLU & SALLERI
N

and the Pharak Sherpa areas. There's only a simple *teahouse* and a few tea-shacks where porters stop for a welcome glass of tea. It's less than half an hour down to the gompa at Trakshindo on wide stone steps (or what's left of them).

Trakshindo (2930m/9612ft) There are two large but simple *lodges* and the shell of a house that serves as a kitchen-cum-dining room for groups. If you arrive in cloudy weather and stay here be sure to have a look outside upon waking: the views are stunning. Trekking peak fans will enjoy the impressive pyramid of Kusum Kangguru. In the coldest winter

months you may wake up to snow here and ice on the trail. The **gompa**, established in 1946 by the Tengboche Lama, can be visited and is usually open sometime early in the morning or around sunset. For a group of people the monk will often open up specially and you should leave a donation.

Nuntala is visible from the gompa, and when leaving the path contours around immediately below the gompa fence and past a house or two before descending. The route down continues to contour in and out of gullies with a steep descent or two. You pass some camping spots popular with porters heading for Namche.

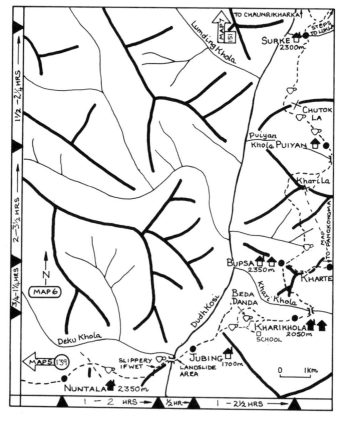

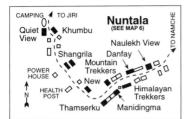

Nuntala/Manidingma (2350m/7710ft)

Primarily a Sherpa village with a few Rai inhabitants, Nuntala (see above) is pleasantly situated in a large valley. The bushes around and below the village are tea bushes. The views are better at the pass or gompa but the snowy tip of Karyolung can still just be seen, above a ridge to the north.

The wide paved street is lined with inns. Development here has been rapid since the first real lodge started operating around 1983. Environmentally-friendly water heating systems were installed in the fireplaces of some lodges in 1988 and electricity first lit the street lamps in July 1991. This mini hydro-electric scheme was set up privately by Pasang Sherpa, one of the many lodge owners, using a bank loan. The 'power house' is easily identified by the water pipe used to power the generator. If it's open take a look inside; Western concepts of a power station are of huge buildings and complex machinery but this system would fit in a Paris bathroom. It's all been well thought

❑ The Dudh Kosi

The origin of this river is intimately tied to where you are heading; the Khumbu. Dudh is the Nepali word for milk and 'milky river' is an apt name for it. The colour is caused by powdered rock, a product of the massive forces involved as glaciers grind their way down valleys. Although rock is heavier than water the turbulence doesn't give the finely divided silt a chance to settle.

out for the needs of the village. By switching belts during the day the turbine is used to drive a circular saw or a flour milling machine. It had to be carried up here because an airlift by helicopter would have virtually doubled the total cost.

Leaving Nuntala there's a steep descent of at least a couple of hours to the suspension bridge across the Dudh Kosi. Early in the morning it can be slippery with dew. There's a couple of simple *teahouses* five minutes before the bridge but little else on the way.

Jubing (1700m/5577ft)

Half an hour uphill from the bridge, this is the only non-Sherpa village past Sete. It's a pretty Rai village, especially attractive in winter when the Khumbu appears brown and dry. Here plants thrive in the tropical warmth of the low altitude with flowers

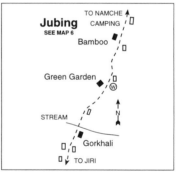

and vegetables growing year round. It is a rice-growing area, although the higher reaches of the village can support only millet and maize, the monsoon crops, and wheat plus barley in the winter. There are four *lodges*, each spaced a few minutes apart. Being warm year-round it's a good place to do a batch of washing – or at least a sock rinse.

Around 10 minutes out of Jubing is a small but distinct trail junction. Continue upwards, **don't** take the path that cuts left through paddies and can be seen contouring around the next ridge. Another 10 minutes up the hill is a group of three double-storeyed houses and another trail divide. Both forks head for Khari-khola, the left path is slightly longer in distance but not in time and is a little more gentle on the legs. The right fork is the 'Nepalese way' (the shortest distance no mat-

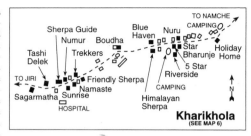

ter how steep) and is always used by porters. It heads over a small pass which offers good views up the valley. Khumbui Yul Lha is prominent, and with a map it is easy to figure out roughly where Namche, Khumjung and Khunde are, although they cannot actually be seen. The high snow and rock peak in the distance is Gyachung Kang (7922m/25,990ft), not Cho Oyu as guides will tell you.

Kharikhola/Khati Thenga (2050m/6726ft)
This is a large spread-out village with houses dotted among the countless terraces. Among the Sherpas are a few Magars, there are thriving businesses, a boarding school and it's an agriculturally-productive area though not nearly as productive as Jubing. Not only is it at a higher altitude (and so significantly cooler) but it also gets less sun, the terraces being north facing. Despite higher-yield crops, with the rapidly rising population there can be food shortages in the weeks leading up to the harvest. This is an especially difficult time for villagers as there is little trade from trekkers in the summer.

Kharikhola is developing into a focal point for the surrounding villages. This was started with the founding by Hillary and the Himalayan Trust of a school and health post. The school grew rapidly, developing into a high school with an excellent reputation that has drawn pupils from villages several days' walk away. Now tailors and merchants have set up shop. Electricity arrived in 1989, a private scheme organised by one of the lodge owners. In 1997 a foreign-funded **health-post** staffed by a Nepali doctor was added

to the list of facilities. The many *lodges* strung out along the main path for several kilometres are basically in three groups. Some are very tidy and freshly painted but all are smaller and more homely compared to the Junbesi or Namche lodges. Groups often camp in the noisy centre of town, or by the lodge on the outskirts closest to the khola.

If you spend the night make an early start next day, leaving well before the sun actually reaches Kharikhola or the going gets hot and sticky. The chorten at Bupsa can be seen from Kharikhola but once over the small bridge there are several false crests that can be rather demoralising on the slog up to Bupsa.

BUPSA TO SURKE   [MAP 6, p142]

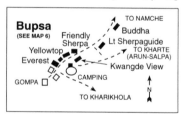

Bupsa/Gompa Danda/Bumshing (2350m/7710ft)
Perched on top of the ridge, this is a very welcome refreshment stop after the long climb.

There are three *teahouses* in a cluster and, a few minutes further on, a couple more well-spaced *lodges*. Below, along the ridge, is a small gompa you may be invited to visit, donations expected, of course.

Route to Salpa-Arun, Tumlingtar and Hille Take the trail straight up the ridge behind the lodges in Bupsa (see p210).

Route to Namche

The trail between Kharikhola and Chourikharka was considerably altered in the early 1980s, levelling several small climbs. Despite the quicker trail, porters haven't changed the stopping places so for groups this day is easier than it once was. Old maps still mark the original route which climbed to Kharte, above Bupsa.

There's another trail that goes directly from Kharikhola to Surke but it's dangerous and therefore not recommended. It stays much closer to the Dudh Kosi and was used mainly by porters wanting to make a quick return down valley. Considered too steep for laden porters, it was never used for the journey up-river. Trekkers were never encouraged to go this way and now, since it has been neglected, it is really dangerous, involving some tricky traverses where the track has fallen away.

Khari La The hills are not over yet: the trail continues steeply up, cutting into valleys and rounding ridges to the Khari La. From here, at 2850m/9350ft, Khumbui Yul Lha and Gyachang Kang are visible. This is not really a pass, the real Khari La being a little above on the route of the old trail.

Puiyan/Paiya/Chutok (2780m/9121ft)

The surrounding area was once heavily forested but many trees were cut down to make charcoal. This practice was banned in 1992 to try to save the remaining forests lining the Dudh Kosi here.

Chutok La The new route passes 200m below the actual Chutok La, at 2780m/9121ft, but the views of Khumbui Yul Lha and Gyachung Kang are still good, though better just around the corner. The steep rock peak is Gonglha, above Lukla and the bigger mountain is Kusum Kangguru. Part of Lukla airstrip can also be seen, but this is hard to recognise: it's no use looking for a stretch of level ground.

Surke/Surkie/Bua (2300m/7546ft)

Local legend says that this area was once a lake and this would account for the fertile soil. Bua, the Sherpa name for the hamlet, means 'damp', no doubt from the lack of sun, but in fact it's a pleasant enough place. Just around the corner from Surke are the first good views of Nupla (5885m/19,308ft) which forms part of the spectacular Kongde ridge that rears up above the Bhote Kosi by Namche.

Route to Lukla About 10 minutes out of Surke by a mani are some stone steps

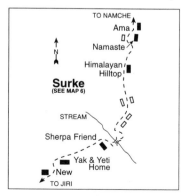

heading up; these lead to Lukla in about an hour. Although the trail starts off well-defined it breaks up into many confusing paths. You need to cross a bridge en route. If in doubt stay on main trails but going left at intersections usually works except around a carved mani rock. There are tracks up both sides of the runway. Note that it's not necessary to visit Lukla; if you wish to do so in order to confirm an air ticket this can be done only a few days in advance. Note also that opening hours are very limited (see Lukla below).

Direct route to Namche This continues straight ahead from the mani wall out of Surke. A little further on is an impressive waterfall, so high and close that it defies most camera lenses, although over the bridge and up the hill there's a more complete view. The trail traverses some impressively steep hillside. In the past, in tough country like this, the trails tended to be precarious and narrow but to cater for tourists this has been blasted out to a safe width. Stone steps and a few cunningly-constructed stone shelters herald Mushe, still a few minutes away.

Mushe/Nangbug This is a pleasant place with a few *lodges*; since it is overshadowed by Lukla few people stay here. Many vegetables are grown in the area especially for the hotels in Lukla and Namche.

Chourikharka/Dungde (2760m/9055ft)
Meaning 'yak-herding area', Chourikharka is often mis-spelt Chaunikharka, although if you listen hard to a local person saying the name, the quietest of 'n's can often be heard. Dungde, the Sherpa name, means *dingma* or flat farming area: a more accurate name now. The village begins at the top of the short steep climb to the kani and has three well-spaced *lodges*.

Route from Chourikharka to Lukla
Thankfully Lukla is not visible from here but there are numerous small trails up. First head for the school, then from there

a path leads up to join the main trail. The Hillary school was constructed in 1964 and has expanded to provide education to the final grade 10. There is also a **health post** founded by the Himalayan Trust. Alternatively walk to Chaplung and take the main trail.

Direct route to Namche If you're bypassing Lukla, the route description continues on p150.

Trekking from Lukla

INTRODUCTION
For the majority of trekkers and expeditions, this is where the Everest trail now begins. Surprisingly though, Lukla was not built with tourists in mind. The intention of Sir Edmund Hillary and his friends when they constructed the airstrip in 1964 was to make it easier to bring building supplies in for the ever-growing number of projects they were undertaking. To this very day Hillary regrets that it was ever built, and (unfairly) blames himself for volume of trekkers now arriving (assaulting, he thinks) the Khumbu. Undoubtedly the Lukla airstrip has made access easier, and so, too, has the increasing standard of the lodges. Now the Khumbu isn't the exclusive domain of mountaineers and tough trekkers, instead it is enjoyed by a surprisingly broad spectrum of people.

With a bump, you step out of a time capsule back into rural Nepal. It is no longer a huge leap back in time, instead the Time Lords have jumbled the modern world with the ancient in a confusing mess. Bottled beer is drunk alongside *rakshi*, the most basic of spirits and Mars Bars sit along side *chirpee*, a dried cheese as old as yak herding itself. From now on the only wheels are prayer wheels. It can take a few days to discover your trekking legs and settle into the rhythm of the days. It can even take a while before you begin to look around with a true appreciation of the surroundings, which is a pity, because the trail to Namche sits in a magnificent gorge (beginning a day's walk to the south). The cultural side of the villages is fascinating and shouldn't be forgotten in the race to see Everest.

Services in the Khumbu

Namche has a bank and a moneychanger. If you are stuck the occasional lodge-owner will change US$ cash at less than favourable rates. Visa and other plastics are **not** accepted anywhere. Namche and Lukla have simple post offices. The Western-staffed Khunde bush hospital is open year-round and during the peak trekking seasons Western doctors staff a clinic at Pheriche. Lukla has a healthpost with a capable health assistant who can contact Khunde if needed. There are public phones at Lukla, Namche and Khumjung. In emergencies there are two-way radios at the National Park HQ in Choi Gang, the army post at Dole, the Pheriche clinic, and telephones at Lukla, Khunde, Syangboche, Namche and Thame. The Pyramid at Lobuche has a US$13 a minute phone/fax and larger expeditions usually have a satellite phone too.

LUKLA (2850m/9350ft)

Lukla means sheep corral, which is all it was before the airstrip was built. Now it's more like a tourist pen operated by a mish-mash of peoples: many Sherpas but also Rais, Brahmins and Chhetris. The sole industry is tourism but with four to ten flights a day during the busy season, it's now quite a large industry.

The Syangboche airport began to change this during 1994-6, with many people choosing to exit Khumbu from there, but its rising popularity was abruptly stopped by a Ministry of Tourism decision in late 1996 (see p161).

For the children of the local people, Lukla boasts one of the few schools in the area that was not initiated by the Himalayan Trust. It's only a primary school so the middle and high school children must go to Chourikharka or to boarding school in Kathmandu.

Lukla now has a three-phase 15kw electricity system but charges are high so only the lodges can afford to be connected. Demand from the lodges outstrips supply although it's not used for cooking.

❏ Lukla airstrip

The airstrip was constructed by local Sherpas with Hillary's supervision. It took a month and cost US$2650. Being quite short, it could safely handle planes with only about 8 passengers but it's subsequently been extended several times.

It's a tricky place to land a plane because everything is down to the judgment of the pilot with no radio beacons for guidance. He appears to aim into the lower end of the runway, pulling up at the last minute. This looks rather alarming from the passenger compartment as you dive into the mountains, then onto the runway hurtling towards the rock wall at the end of the airstrip. The landing is rough and bouncy since little is done to maintain the airstrip. Not surprisingly there've been some accidents. The last was in July 1991 when a plane came in for a heavy landing and the undercarriage snapped but nobody was seriously injured.

Helicopters, rather than landing vertically, use the same approach as the planes, coming in at speed and lifting the nose up at the last minute. They rely on downdraft to stop them not only against the runway but often also against the rock wall at the end of the runway. The reason they take off and land along the runway is that it's easier than landing vertically.

Taking off by plane is no less exciting. With the propellers on fine pitch and the brakes locked the pilot pushes the throttles to maximum, only releasing the brakes as the locked wheels begin to slide. With a glorious rush the plane bounces into the air.

❑ Mountain madness

'A number of lodge-owners laugh at this phenomenon. We at Khunde Hospital cry over it. Some of our patients with serious AMS have been so goal-orientated that their trek, instead of being the experience of a lifetime, has turned into the journey from hell, with the one objective of seeing Everest close up over-riding all else. The Khumbu has so much more to offer than Everest. If your only focus is to see Everest, why not take a scenic flight instead?

We see too many cases of severe altitude sickness. Many people arrive close to death, and none of them would have got so dangerously sick if they had followed altitude advice and guidelines. For example, a trekker arrived dying from HACE. He was from Iceland and in his early twenties. From Monjo he had climbed to Gokyo in three days and had attempted Gokyo Ri. He said he knew there were warnings about altitude sickness, his English was excellent, but 'whoever reads them?' He did live to tell his story.

Our sickest patient who lived was a lowland porter. He was in a coma for five days. The Nepalese, especially Sherpas, have the completely untrue belief that Nepalese don't suffer from altitude sickness; they consider it a foreigners' disease. Yet lowland porters are just as susceptible as foreigners, if not more so because of the load they carry. Make sure your sirdar is aware of this and watch the porters carefully. Porters often ask for aspirin: many never drink enough fluids, but this is also a sign that they may indeed be suffering AMS'.

Sue Heydon, Khunde Hospital

This would require a supply of about 50kw more, necessitating the building of a small dam. There's enough electricity, however, to power a few stereos in some lodges – a gentle re-introduction to the 'real' world after a long trek. It is planned to link Lukla to KBC's (Khumbu Bijuli Co) Thame generating system in the next couple of years.

Lodges

There's a wide variety of *lodges*. The most expensive and luxurious is the *Sagarmatha Resort* where rooms with attached bathroom cost around US$20/£13.50 a night. At the other end of the market are basic *lodges* for the porters and guides hanging around for another job and, of course, there's everything in between. The large number of lodges is due to the long queues that used to form in the mad rush for a flight out in the height of the season. Despite the numerous comfortable places to stay here, many trekking companies still provide accommodation in tents and members who want a bed in a lodge must pay for it.

Services

Airlines RNAC and the other relevant airlines all have offices in Lukla. RNAC's office is open for reconfirmation only between 3pm and 4pm. These are the hours quoted by most other offices, but in practice tickets can usually be reconfirmed or bought at any time. When the Russian helicopters operate commercial flights they run as many flights as needed, so tickets can be surprisingly easy to come by. If flights return to fixed wing planes only, and mainly by Lumbini and RNAC, obtaining tickets during any season will be considerably more challenging. Talk with your lodge-owner if you have problems.

Other services Since national park rules prohibit trekking companies from using firewood a **kerosene depot** has been opened here. There's also a **health-post**, set up with French aid and supported by the Himalayan Trust when other funds aren't forth-coming. Lukla, as of January 1998, had eight **telephones**, including one busy public call office

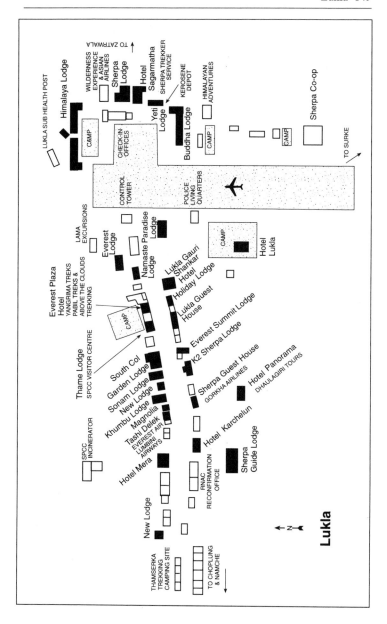

Lukla

(PCO), handy for making a reservation at your Kathmandu hotel if you are on the way out. There's no bank.

Avoiding altitude sickness

All the scheduled flights arrive before lunch so it's quite possible to have a snack, then hit the trail and stay at Phakding or Monjo for the first night. Nevertheless some sensible planning is required to lessen the risk of altitude sickness occurring later. Already at Lukla there is only 70% of the oxygen compared to sea level. Altitude-specialist doctors recommend taking a minimum of two to three nights to reach 3000m/9843ft. Since Lukla is at 2850m/9350ft you are already close to that altitude limit and Namche, at 3450m/11,319ft, is well above it. Yet most trekkers who fly in trek to Namche in just over a day. These people are twice as likely to experience troublesome AMS, and form the majority of serious cases. The reasonable rates of ascent from Namche are widely publicised but this recommendation for the days below Namche has been totally ignored. Caution at this point will undoubtedly lessen the impact of problems experienced later. Diamox may also help: see p239.

There are many people in the trekking industry who would consider the above advice over-cautious. However two American studies found that 9-12% of people who ascend directly to 2800m (Lukla: 2850m) suffer noticeable AMS, admittedly usually non-life-threatening but definitely uncomfortable. The AMS tended to resolve itself in two to three days staying at the same altitude. Arriving directly at 3860m caused AMS in 84% of people.

LUKLA TO NAMCHE [MAP 7]

This is a trekkers highway with *teashops* and *lodges* lining the route. Other than while ascending the hill to Namche lodges are never more than half an hour apart. Although it is a busy and often rushed hike up, focusing on the surroundings brings rewards. There are several gompas en route and many smaller lodges where you can sit around the kitchen fire and chat with the owner.

Chaplung/Chablung/Lomdza (2660m/8727ft)

Here the trail from Lukla meets the main trail from Jiri and Salpa-Arun. The turn-off, if you're coming down from Namche, is after Ama Dablam guesthouse taking the stairs up.

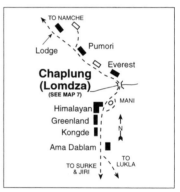

Thado Kosi Here an elegant bridge crosses the Kusum Khola. The tables outside the *lodges* offer impressive views of Kusum Kangguru. This mountain is revered by local people; its name means the 'White (or Pure) Mountain House of the Three Gods'.

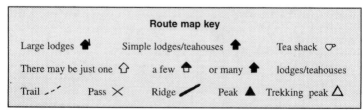

Route map key

Large lodges 🏠	Simple lodges/teahouses 🏠	Tea shack ☕
There may be just one ⌂	a few 🏠 or many 🏠	lodges/teahouses
Trail --- Pass ✕	Ridge ╱	Peak ▲ Trekking peak △

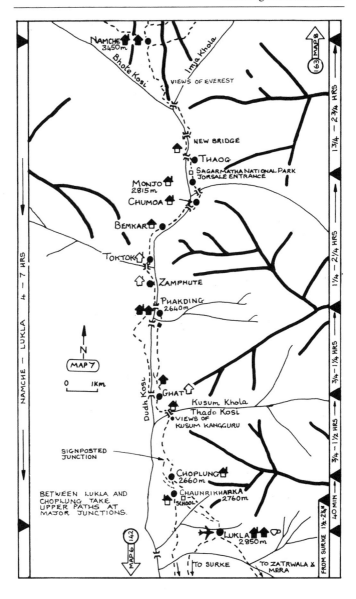

NAMCHE — LUKLA   4 – 7 HRS

NAMCHE
3450m

Bhote Kosi

Imja Khola

VIEWS OF EVEREST

1¾ – 2¾ HRS

NEW BRIDGE

THAOG

Sagarmatha National Park
Jorsale Entrance

MONJO
2815m

CHUMOA

BEMKAR

TOKTOK

ZAMPHUTE

PHAKDING
2640m

1¼ – 2¼ HRS

N

MAP 7

0   1Km

Dudh Kosi

GHAT

Kusum Khola
Thado Kosi
VIEWS OF
KUSUM KANGGURU

¾ – 1¼ HRS

¾ – 1½ HRS

SIGNPOSTED
JUNCTION

CHOPLUNG
2660m

CHAUNRIKHARKA
2760m
SCHOOL

40 MIN

BETWEEN LUKLA AND
CHOPLUNG TAKE
UPPER PATHS AT
MAJOR JUNCTIONS.

MAP 6 142

LUKLA
2850m

TO SURKE

TO ZATRWALA &
MERA

FROM SURKE 1½-2¾V

63 MAP 8

Ghat/Nynyung This is the next settlement, just around the corner. Ghat means 'bridge' in Nepali and the bridge here was once important because it was one of the alternatives to the bridge at Jubing that was often washed away. With the advent of steel-cabled suspension bridges it has lost its importance. The route to Namche does not cross the bridge but instead follows a trail lined with *lodges* a few minutes apart. Few trekkers stay here but there are some friendly lodge-owners, even if the lodges aren't so fancy. It is often possible to have a look in the gompa at the top end of town.

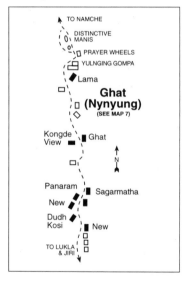

Phakding/Ramding 2640m/8661ft

A short half day's walk from Lukla, Phakding is the first overnight spot for groups who've flown in to Lukla. Since it's also the normal overnight stop for groups from Jiri, in the high season sirdars often send one of the crew to race ahead and reserve their favourite spot. There are other suitable villages to camp at (Zamphute, Chumoa, Monjo or Ghat) but porters and most trekking companies

don't like to change their routine. The large numbers of people stopping here accounts for the extraordinary number of *lodges* at Phakding. If you arrive with time to spare there is a gompa on the west side of the river, half to three-quarters of an hour up the hill.

At Phakding a long, rough suspension bridge with an interesting history crosses the Dudh Kosi. By the *Alpine Club Lodge* is a short suspension bridge which was meant to replace an insecure wooden bridge further up; but the wooden bridge continued to be more popular because the route to the short suspension bridge bypassed many lodges and involved a stiff climb. So eventually a second (long) suspension bridge was constructed to replace the wooden bridge. This suspension bridge that in recent years had rather more character than a few trekkers cared for will be superseded

sometime in 1998. Just beyond Phakding the river bank has been ravaged by erosion, the area by-passed by a high detour.

Toktok and Bemkar Between Phakding and Monjo, a leisurely couple of hours' walk, are many simple *teahouses* and small shops and the odd proper lodge. From Toktok the sheer face of Thamserku comes into view to the northeast. Bemkar has a developing set of *lodges* beginning above the waterfall pool.

Chumoa is a town that has moved with the times. Old Chumoa lies just south of the long 1997 cable bridge so, to catch the trekking business, a couple of *lodges* (one quite simple) have moved north to join the ageing *Chumoa Lodge Hatago*. This was one of the first high standard lodges between Lamosangu (before the days of the road to Jiri) and Namche and was really a place to be looked forward to after the basic places on the long walk in.

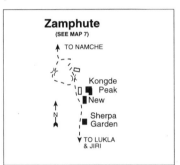

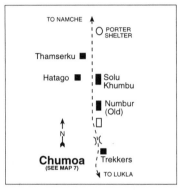

Monjo (2815m/9235ft) There are a handful more *lodges* here and a few simple inns and tea-shacks. Signs welcoming donations herald a monastery situated a hundred metres or so off the main trail. A minute later you reach the gateway to Sagarmatha National Park.

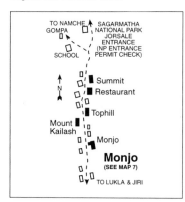

Sagarmatha National Park (Jorsale)
At the guarded entrance to the park your national park permit will be checked. If you don't already have a permit you can get one here. The fee as of January 1998 was Rs650, but don't be surprised if this is raised to Rs1000 since ACAP now sets the charges. Jorsale is also the true beginning of the Khumbu.

From this point on no firewood is allowed to be cut so all groups must use kerosene for themselves and also for the porters. Implied also is the universal 'Pack it in, pack it out' national park principle, a rule that most trekking companies flagrantly flaunt. The rules for rubbish are that whoever provides the goods or supplies should dispose of whatever rubbish they generate. This means that groups should pack out their rubbish, or at the very least dispose of it properly, but many don't. For individual trekkers the locals, who also get the benefits of business, are responsible for disposal of the rubbish. In practice this is a surprisingly small quantity of rubbish since egg cartons and sacks

for rice are recycled, empty noodle and biscuit packets are burnt. Glass bottles, however, are a problem. The national park tried banning them but it was found that they didn't have the legal authority to impose its.

Rubbish is better managed in the Khumbu than anywhere else in Nepal. There are two rubbish removal projects, one organised by the national park and the other by the Sagarmatha Pollution Control Committee. In fact the locals have seen the tourism benefits in keeping their villages tidy and free of rubbish and generally do a good job although the trails between villages aren't always so clean, nor is the entrance to Namche. Groups and porters are by far the worst offenders when it comes to rubbish.

Leaving the park entrance the path drops steeply to the long suspension bridge, built in 1995, across the Dudh Kosi. In the past yaks have taken the higher trail that stays on the east bank.

In September 1977 a huge avalanche peeled off Ama Dablam into a glacial lake. Not surprisingly the lake burst and sent a great wave of water down the valley. A number of bridges which were normally unaffected by monsoon floods were wiped out, as well as some sections of the trail. It has taken a long time, but finally the washed out bridges have virtually all been replaced. The next calamity is less than eagerly awaited.

❏ **Timbore**
Beside the trail between Lukla and Namche you might notice a bush with large thorns similar in shape to rose thorns. In September this bears red berries, from which a black seed emerges as the berry dries. The flesh (rather than the seed) is crushed to make the spice timbore.

The spice has a sharp distinctive taste and numbs the tongue and gums so it is widely used for toothache.

Bridge over the Dudh Kosi Some boulder hopping and a couple of short climbs bring you to this long Swiss-built suspension bridge constructed in 1989 across the Dudh Kosi, the gateway to the Khumbu. Apparently designed with catastrophes in mind, it is indestructibly high above the river. After the steep concrete steps the path is broad and pleasant, having been widened and tidied up to lessen erosion. It is still quite a hill – especially hard on the legs if you flew in to Lukla – and the rapid gain in altitude may induce a headache. The halfway point is marked by a pile of rubble that was once a tea-shack (and hopefully will be rebuilt). From the ridge extending to the rear, now a bit of a toilet, are views of Everest, Lhotse and Nuptse. As you near Namche, with occasional views of the town ahead and above, you reach a collection of lodges for porters followed by a junction. The proper entrance to the town is via the lower path through a kani and up past the spring but local shopkeepers prefer that you take the upper route along the trail that resembles a small stream and sometimes a rubbish pit to pass their wares.

NAMCHE/NAUCHE (3450m/11,319ft)
Welcome to the Namche bowl, the Zermatt of the Khumbu. This thriving village has grown up around a magnificent spring, the only water supply. Since all routes upwards pass through here and it's an essential acclimatisation stop, facilities are well-developed and the village bustles with trekkers most of the year.

Called Nauche by all Sherpas and Naboche by Tibetans, the village is more widely known as Namche, a century-old Nepali mispronunciation. It's also long been referred to as Namche Bazaar, inaccurate since at the time all trading was conducted in private homes; the weekly market started only in 1965. The Sherpa name, Nauche, is in fact only a short form of an older name, thought to be Nakmuche or Nakuche, meaning 'big dark forest', unfortunately now an inappropriate name. However the couple of walled off areas on the hillside above the village are remedying this. Slowly but surely a forests of pine are growing.

Acclimatisation
It is important for all trekkers to spend at least **two nights acclimatising** here, and if fresh from Lukla spending three nights in Namche may be advisable, especially if you have spent only one night on the trail between arriving at Lukla and coming to Namche. Even if you do adhere to this advice, however, it's not unusual to suffer mild altitude sickness at Namche and some people have trouble sleeping. If AMS symptoms do occur or are worse on the second night then staying three nights or taking Diamox is a good policy; you will only invite further trouble higher up if your body is not given a chance to cope adequately here. A sound alternative is to spend the third night at Phunki Tenga which is slightly lower and may give your body a chance to recuperate. The fact that the next night will be spent 600m higher should not matter if you have already spent two nights at Namche. See p239 for more information on Diamox and AMS.

If you have plenty of time, an extra night's stop in Thame or Khumjung/Khunde would be rewarding and further aid acclimatisation. Since these villages are at an equivalent altitude to Tengboche they are also excellent alternatives to spending two nights there.

Note that it is possible, although rare, to develop serious altitude sickness here: several trekkers have even died in Namche.

Lodges
In and around Namche there are about 20 lodges. The most popular are the group in the centre of town simply because of their location, but all the lodges are good and a number are run by locally renowned sirdars and high altitude climbers.

As is common further up there is a two-tier pricing system. The bed charge is nominal if you eat breakfast and dinner at the lodge. If, however, you are in a group with your own cook or wish to eat at other lodge restaurants then the bed charges climb to cover this loss. The menus tend to be extensive and one of the Namche specialities is yak steaks. Sufficiently tenderised and with a fried egg on top, they are delicious. With the installation of electric ovens new varieties of cakes and pies are appearing on menus.

Services

Although Namche feels important it isn't the district headquarters: that is to the south at Salleri. However, with a customs post, the National Park headquarters, an army post and other facilities for trekkers there are still rather too many government officials.

The **bank** is useful but it's dark and cold as death with dusty leather-bound ledgers and untidy piles of papers everywhere. It's open for changing money from 10am to around 2.30pm but closed on Saturday. Beside it is a **money changer**, usually open from 7.30am to around 5pm, with a variable break for lunch. The **post office**, open from 10am to 4pm, daily except Saturday, is really just a filing cabinet and a box. For your own safety you should register at the **police checkpost**, which is up the hill.

Namche-Syangboche-Khumjung-Khunde now have a small but good **telephone system**. In Namche the telephone office is open 7am-12pm then 1-7pm. It is possible to send faxes. It has moved frequently and is due to move again so ask your lodge owner for its location.

Namche boasts the only modern **dental clinic** out of Nepal's cities. It was initiated by Brian Hollander and funded by the American Himalayan Foundation and money raised by the 1991 Everest Marathon. It's run by Nawang Doka (a Namche Sherpani) and Mingma Nur who both trained for three years in Canada. It's usually filled with local people: they treat roughly 70 patients a month and are obviously doing a good job repairing the damage caused by the candy-culture, for which trekkers are partly to blame. Charges for foreign patients begin from US$20. Visitors are welcome but running costs are high; donations are appreciated. The clinic sells logo T-shirts and also basic medicines, which can save a trip to Khunde.

There is a **healthpost** in Namche but there is no doctor, indeed, often no staff at all. The reason is partly the hospital at Khunde, an amazing facility, especially for being in the middle of nowhere. See p162 for more details.

Namche now produces its own mineral water. The seals don't always look professional but lodge-owners are honest about these things.

Hermann Helmers Bakery and the companion *Namche Bakery* are the latest additions to the Khumbu's already superior facilities. Try the pizza or apple strudel. With 24-hour electricity several places offer cappuccino too.

The Saturday market

At this popular weekly gathering, Sherpas meet friends, catch up with the gossip, and of course trade supplies. Surprisingly, this famous market does not date back centuries but only to 1965 when it was started by an army officer to cater for the increasing number of civil servants the village was attracting. Tough, sheepskin-clad Tibetans sell tsampa, dried meat and perhaps a few souvenirs, while throngs of lowland porters offer food and goods arduously carried up to Namche. Most things originate from the road-head at Jiri, but there are also suntalas and rice from the Hinku, vegetables from Solu and eggs from Salleri. Lodge owners from up valley can often be seen with wads of rupees collecting yak-loads of goods; others by-pass the market by employing their own porters.

Being one of the tourist highlights, the market determines many group schedules. Crowds gather early in the morning and thin out by late morning when all the trails out of Namche become busy. Sherpas from the closer villages drive yaks home, groups trek up to Tengboche and several hundred unburdened porters race down to warmer climes having delivered or sold their goods.

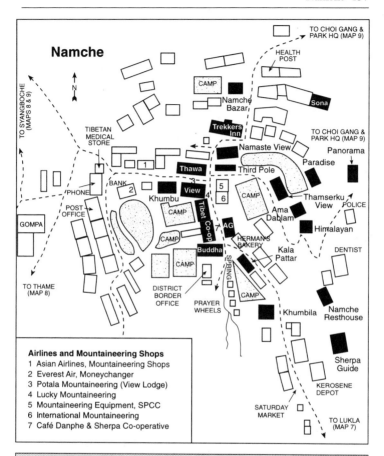

Namche

TO SYANGBOCHE (MAPS 8 & 9)

TO CHOI GANG & PARK HQ (MAP 9)

HEALTH POST

CAMP

Namche Bazar

Sona

Trekkers Inn

TIBETAN MEDICAL STORE

Namaste View

TO CHOI GANG & PARK HQ (MAP 9)

Panorama

Thawa

Third Pole

Paradise

1

BANK

2

View

3

Khumbu

4

5
6

CAMP

Thamserku View

POLICE

PHONE

POST OFFICE

Tibet Co-op

Ama Dablam

AG

Himalayan

GOMPA

CAMP

CAMP

7

HERMANS BAKERY

Kala Pattar

DENTIST

Buddha

TO THAME (MAP 8)

CAMP

SPRING

DISTRICT BORDER OFFICE

PRAYER WHEELS

CAMP

Khumbila

Namche Resthouse

Sherpa Guide

KEROSENE DEPOT

SATURDAY MARKET

TO LUKLA (MAP 7)

Airlines and Mountaineering Shops
1 Asian Airlines, Mountaineering Shops
2 Everest Air, Moneychanger
3 Potala Mountaineering (View Lodge)
4 Lucky Mountaineering
5 Mountaineering Equipment, SPCC
6 International Mountaineering
7 Café Danphe & Sherpa Co-operative

❏ Traders from the beginning

Although the Saturday market was started only relatively recently, the Sherpas have long been traders, acting as middlemen between the Tibetans and the Rais. Traditionally Rais bartered maize, millet, buffalo skins and rice for Tibetan rock salt and wool. A wide variety of other goods were also traded. Iron farm implements forged in Those were prized in Tibet until cheap Indian steel became available. Solu supplied butter, stored in stomachs, for the thousands of butter-burning candles in the massive Tibetan monastic institutions, and a special soot used for making ink for the Buddhist printing centre of Shigatse.

This trade flourished until the Chinese invaded Tibet in 1959. For the Sherpas tourism conveniently filled the gap and is now more significant for them than trade with Tibet ever was.

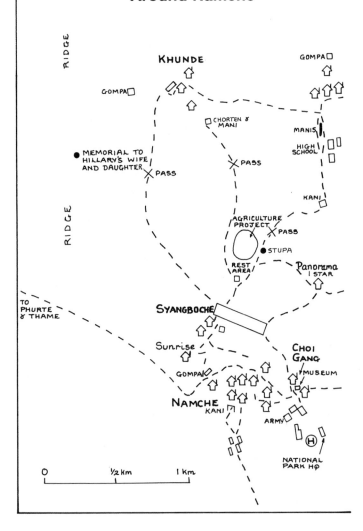

Around Namche

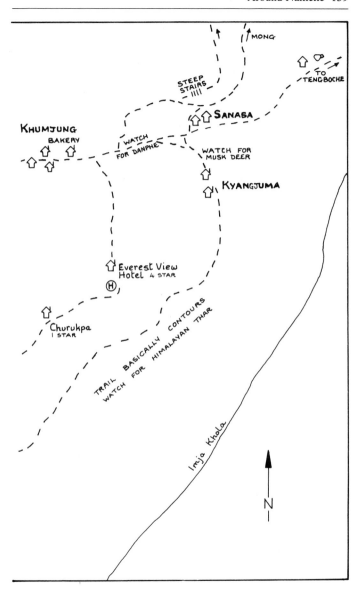

MONG

TO
TENGBOCHE

STEEP
STAIRS
||||

SANASA

KHUMJUNG
BAKERY

WATCH
FOR DANPHE

WATCH FOR
MUSK DEER

KYANGJUMA

Everest View
Hotel 4 STAR

Ⓗ

Churukpa
1 STAR

TRAIL BASICALLY CONTOURS
WATCH FOR HIMALAYAN THAR

Imja Khola

N

AROUND NAMCHE [MAP p158-9]

There are several possible day trips. Visits to the picturesque Khumjung and Khunde villages can be combined with the pleasant walk to the Everest View Hotel. A longer scenic trek is to Thame, with its gompa on the hill and the hydro-electric power station below. Closer and well worth visiting is the National Park Headquarters at Choi Gang. This is also easily visited the morning that you leave for Tengboche but note that the Park Headquarters are closed on Saturdays. Less strenuous is the trek to Namche Gompa which is better visited early in the morning or late afternoon; it is, of course, open for tourists most of the day. A donation is expected. Other equally popular activities are clothes washing, apple pie feasting, chocolate bingeing and chang sampling.

Choi Gang and the National Park Headquarters

With *choi* (or *cho/tsho*) meaning lake and *gang* meaning hill dropping into a valley or flats, the name commemorates the fact that there was once a lake here. Nepali speakers have mistransliterated the name as Chorken or Chorkang, which in Nepalese translates to 'thieves' den'.

Long ago it was the main trading area before Namche and Thame took over. Deserted until the 1970s, it's now the Sagarmatha National Park Headquarters.

Information Centre Built with New Zealand aid, the main building houses modest displays on the history and points of interest in the park. It's open from 8am to 4pm daily except Saturdays and public holidays.

There are superb views from the helicopter landing pad behind the information centre. Previously this was a favourite camping spot offering from-the-tent views of Everest, the Nuptse-Lhotse wall, Tengboche and Ama Dablam. Even the addition of a toilet in the foreground cannot detract from the magnificent views. With binoculars, considerable segments of the route to Dingboche can be seen.

While walking up also note the pine trees surrounding the park building. These were planted in 1976 but are still small. Whereas in New Zealand, for example, commercial pine matures in 25 years, here it will be a hundred years before the trees look healthily large.

The Sherpa Cultural Centre, beside the Hotel Sherwi Khangba, is also well worth visiting; entry is approx Rs50.

Lodges Several companies have bases at Choi Gang and there are four or five pleasant hotels. The latest addition is a huge traditional style building with double rooms and dormitories, the *Hotel Sherwi Khangba* (Sherpa's Old House). The concept is a little different from most other lodges – it has a library, evening slide shows and educational plus historical photos. It's an ideal place for groups to book, but marginally more expensive than normal Namche lodges.

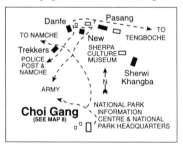

Danfe Pasang
TO NAMCHE
Trekkers
POLICE
POST &
NAMCHE
ARMY
New
SHERPA
CULTURE
MUSEUM
TO
TENGBOCHE
Sherwi
Khangba
N
NATIONAL PARK
INFORMATION
CENTRE & NATIONAL
PARK HEADQUARTERS
Choi Gang
(SEE MAP 8)

(Opposite) Many villages in the Everest region are built around a *gompa* (Tibetan Buddhist monastery). The interior of the temple at Pangboche Gompa is shown. Built 450 years ago it's the oldest in the region; and it housed a curious relic, said to be the scalp of the Yeti, but this was stolen in 1991.

❏ The Syangboche saga

From 1995 the new private helicopter companies began offering commercial flights to and from Syangboche, often flying cargo in and trekkers out. The region developed rapidly with a handful of scattered hotels catering for the increasing number of flights. Then in 1996 Lukla and Phakding (an area collectively called Pharak) lodge owners went on strike, blocking the runway just before the main trekking season. They complained that they were losing business and demanded that commercial flights to Lukla be banned. Their arguments were flawed and driven only by shameless and short-sighted greed but, almost unbelievably, the government bowed to their demands. In addition to trekkers losing a valuable service, the people of the Khumbu also lost out, for many of them and their children enjoyed the new-found convenience. Their chance to retaliate came soon: The Khumbu Bijuli Company (KBC electricity company), whose recent medium-scale project has worked so well, was approached by Pharak to provide high-quality electricity for them. The KBC is managed by mainly Namche people who immediately stopped negotiations, asking that Syangboche flights be resumed, which of course, they weren't. Then in mid-1997 the situation escalated when the forestry management committees of Pharak people decided that they would no longer allow firewood to be sold to Namche (although this doesn't affect wood used for building, since this is regulated by a government forestry officer). One hopes that Pharak will see sense (and it will be to their benefit) rather than let the situation escalate further, with unpredictable results. The only winner was the national park who had lobbied unsuccessfully for helicopters to be banned to reduce noise pollution. At present only small helicopters, rescues and cargo flights are allowed.

If you have flown here without coming from altitude you are likely to suffer some altitude sickness, even if you descend to Namche to stay there. Don't forget there can be a delay of a day or so before you feel the full effects of the altitude. Descent to Phunki Tenga (3250m/10,633ft), although at a lower altitude, is not as safe as Namche since to escape from there requires climbing. It would be foolish not to stay at least three nights at Namche and a night at Phunki Tenga before attempting to trek higher. If you experience troublesome altitude sickness you may have to descend below Namche.

Syangboche (3900m/12,795ft)

Directly above Namche, although out of view, is Syangboche. The short airstrip here is capable of taking only the small single-engined Pilatus Porter planes and helicopters.

The Everest View Hotel This is an upmarket hotel for the rich to fly into and view Everest in absolute comfort. Luckily the views are excellent even from the beds because with the dangerously rapid gain in altitude this is where many people spend their time. Additional oxygen is provided and there are now also two small pressurised rooms to aid acclimatisation. When this 12-room hotel was first built there were teething problems and it

(**Opposite**) **Top:** Monks' quarters at Thame Gompa. **Bottom:** The popular Buddhist prayer chant *Om Mani Padme Hum* is carved onto thousands of flat stones and slates that are known as mani stones (see p108). As with any Buddhist shrine or monument, keep to the left when passing a wall of mani stones.

was closed for several years. It is now open year-round and sometimes even full during the high season, mainly with Japanese on package tours. The cost is around US$200/£135 a night. The hotel is pleasantly designed, a low key affair that provides welcome employment for the locals, who never cease to be amazed by the outrageous costs. One job is the transportation of water from Khumjung, when the hotel supply runs out.

Khumjung (3790m/12,434ft)
This is a picturesque village with many beautiful houses. Until recently the direct impact of tourism was low with few trekkers staying here. With the addition of a handful of new *lodges* and the bakery groups and individuals more frequently sample the various delights. Khumjung has always looked wealthy because virtually every family has some involvement with the trekking industry. All bar four of the lodges from Dole to Gokyo are owned by Khumjung people.

Khumjung's **gompa** is at the top end of town amid a pleasant stand of protected trees. It was established around 1831AD. The other major building is the school on the flats. This was the first built by Hillary and friends. It has subsequently been expanded several times and is now a large high school.

There are a growing number of *lodges* here. At the far end of town on the route to Sanasa are grand views of Kangtaiga, Thamserku and Ama Dablam.

Leaving Khumjung The track to the Everest View Hotel begins by the chorten at the end of town and heads up the hill. The trails to Sanasa and Gokyo are initially the same, dividing by a house a few minutes down from the stupa.

Khunde/Khumte (3840m/12,598ft)
Although Khunde virtually adjoins Khumjung the two villages are actually quite separate communities. The Khunde villagers have traditionally been associated with the Pangboche Gompa, while people from Khumjung go to Thame,

despite the fact they have their own gompa. The village name is invariably pronounced Khunde or Kunde but originally it was Khumte: *Te* is upper, so upper Khum, while *jung* is lower flats. *Khum* means Khumbu and Khumjung is considered the middle of the Khumbu.

Khunde is well-known for its excellent **hospital**. Built in 1966 as a Himalayan Trust project, it's staffed by a volunteer doctor from New Zealand or Canada. It offers exceptional services for a 'bush' hospital: there's even an X-ray machine. It's also one of the few places in rural Nepal where contraception and pregnancy testing are readily and reliably available. Most patients are local people who have developed a great respect for the hospital. Patients are asked to pay according to their means – from a few rupees for a destitute porter to US$25 (or rupee equivalent) for a foreign trekker. You are most welcome to have a look around. Often tours are run at around 2pm, but this very much depends on how busy everyone is. Donations are appreciated. It's open from 9am to 5pm (closed on Saturdays except for emergencies).

NAMCHE TO THAME   [MAP 8]
Thame is a pleasant village with a beautiful gompa and is about three hours' walk from Namche. Since it's 350m higher than Namche, groups often stay the night here as part of an acclimatisation programme before trekking to Gokyo – a sensible idea. Even a day-trip, however, can help acclimatisation.

Leaving Namche If planning to stay at Thame the latest you can leave Namche is about 2pm, walking at an ordinary pace. Head up to the gompa and continue traversing up on the same trail which rounds the ridge enclosing Namche. Soon you come to a forest, a favourite area for local women to collect *soluk* (leaves and vegetation that are mixed with dung and used to make fertiliser), singing as they work. It's also a good region to spot pheasant, especially the danphe, the colourful national bird of Nepal.

Phurte is the first village you come to and it has a forestry nursery funded by the Himalayan Trust. The fields between Samde and Phurte are known as *gunsas*; they are owned by villages at higher altitudes and used by them to provide crops earlier in the season. The gunsas here belong to Thame Cho residents but several sons with their families have moved down here permanently, establishing a small village.

Between Phurte and Thamo, visible high above the main track is a gompa. This is **Laudo**, a small monastic establishment built around 1970 as an arm of Kopan Monastery (near Bodhnath in Kathmandu). Laudo Monastery is often used by foreign meditation groups.

Thamo/Thammu/Dramo The offices of the Khumbu Bijuli Company who manage the Thame hydro-electric scheme are here. The remains of the previous project can be seen on the opposite bank of the river, destroyed just before completion in 1985 when a glacial lake burst. The wall of water engulfed many bridges

and washed away farmland. The Himalaya is a young mountain range so sudden natural occurrences like this are frequent.

Scenic (normal) route Immediately after the last houses of the village, climb the stone stairs on a track that slightly doubles back on itself. This climbs by a stream to the Khari Gompa, then crosses it. The trail continues to climb until suddenly dropping slightly to cross the Nangpo Tsangpo. A steel suspension bridge straddles a roaring tight gorge then the trail winds up and along to Thame.

To Thame via the powerhouse Continue straight ahead and across a temporary bridge to the Austrian hydro-electric project. See p164.

Thame (3800m/12,467ft) Thame is part of the group of villages called Thame Cho – Thame Og (lower), Thame Teng (upper) and Yulajung – and is an area noted for its potatoes. These villages have traditional trading links with Tibet so when the Nangpa La is crossable Tibetans

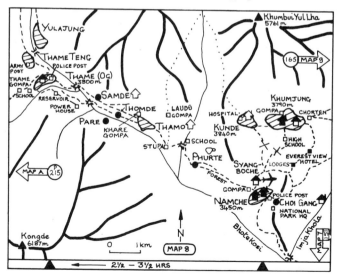

❑ **Thame hydro-electric project**
This Austrian project provides power for Thame Cho, Namche, Khumjung, Khunde and the villages in between. The 630kw output provides enough power for village lighting and for all the lodges to cook on, a welcome attempt to counter the tourism-related problem of firewood-use. There is also enough power to pump water in Namche so that water no longer has to be laboriously carted up from the spring, however the community has yet to get its act together and organise a system. The generators are housed in a traditionally decorated building below Thame. The two small turbines are fed by a pool, near Thame village, which collects glacier runoff from up the valley. A 600mm diameter pipe, one km long, drops 200m to provide the head. A Sherpa technician was trained in Austria to maintain the plant.

camp here and in Thame Teng. It is also home to a surprising number of Everest summiteers including Apa Sherpa who in autumn 1997 climbed the mountain for the eighth time.

Thame Gompa Thame has two gompas, the most frequently visited being a 15-minute walk up the track that begins on the ridge to the north and heads west. It was established on the advice of Lama Sangwa Dorje, fifth reincarnate Lama of Rongphu/Rongbuk, who played an important part in the spiritual history of the Khumbu. The gompa was established around 325 years ago and it's said that some of the books here are over 300 years old. Recently the gompa has been partially rebuilt but using the original materials. The interior has been preserved as it was. The result is stunning.

To Lobuche and Kala Pattar

In this galaxy, which included a host of unnamed peaks, neither the lesser or the greater seemed designed for the use of climbers. – HW Tilman Nepal Himalaya.

NAMCHE TO TENGBOCHE [MAP 9]
Leaving for Tengboche The trail that traverses from Choi Gang to Kyangjuma

is wide and set high above the river. It's a beautiful walk except on Saturdays after the market when it's crowded with groups of trekkers and yak caravans that kick up dust. Tengboche is consequently also worth avoiding on Saturday nights.

Kyangjuma (3600m/11,811ft) This is the first set of *teahouses* you come to, about 1-1½ hours from the National Park HQ. There are a couple of good *lodges* with friendly owners. They also boast a decadent panorama.

Here and at Sanasa Tibetan souvenirs line the path. The trekking groups often stop here to buy things and their porters look on first in amazement at the prices paid and then in horror as they realise the extra weight they'll be expected to carry.

Route to Gokyo or Pangboche via Phortse Across the stream past Kyangjuma and just before Sanasa is a small junction. The upper trail climbs in a couple of minutes to the main trail from Khumjung to Mong (see p178).

Sanasa (3600m/11,811ft) is five minutes beyond Kyangjuma. There's another couple of *teahouses* and more Tibetan souvenirs. Often, Himalayan thar (goats) and pheasants may be seen just out of Sanasa but it takes keen eyes to spot them. Around the ridge are the simple *teahouses* of Tashinga. There is also a forestry nursery established by the Canadian Sir Edmund Hillary

Foundation. Here descent to the suspension bridge across the Dudh Kosi begins. There are a few **teashacks** suitable for lunch along the way.

Phunki/Phongi Tenga (3250m/10,663ft)

Either side of the beautifully situated old suspension bridge is a simple *lodge*. If the altitude at Namche was troubling you this is the lowest place north of Namche to stay the night. The lodge before the bridge is a better choice. In the evening look out for musk deer drinking from the stream.

The walk up the hill to Tengboche is pleasant, if sometimes hot. You pass through a blend of forest and shrub on a wide trail with many shortcuts leading from it. It's also one of the better places for spotting pheasant, thar and deer. They seem quite undisturbed by all the noise of passing trekkers.

The end of the climb is heralded by a kani, an arched entrance with ceiling paintings of deities and forms of Buddha. Its function is to cleanse people of the many feared spirits before entering the sacred area.

Tengboche/Thyangboche (3860m/12,664ft)

True we were awakened at 4am by the din of horns and the clash of cymbals, but we were not expected to rouse out for prayer or meditation, or indeed do anything beyond reach out for a wooden jorum thoughtfully left in readiness. In this, of course, lurked what we called 'lama's milk', which was raksi flavoured with cloves. HW Tilman 1950.

You may still be wakened here by the clash of cymbals. And a snort of lamas's milk might still be in order. During the cold winter months most Sherpas will down a shot of raksi before breakfast, sometimes even the Sherpas that profess to avoiding the demon stuff. They firmly believe in its warming properties.

Tengboche is a cultural and religious centre for the people of the Khumbu region. It is unique in that all the other gompas of the region are associated with a village but Tengboche isn't. The newly-reconstructed gompa is famous as the setting for the Mani Rimdu dance festival in late October or early November. It is a

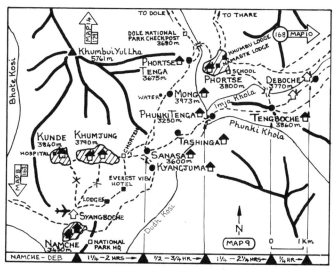

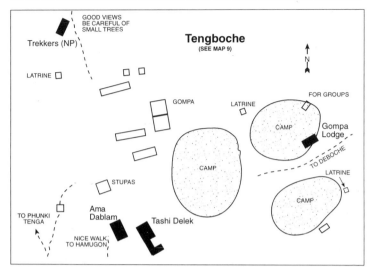

favoured overnight stop for all trekkers heading to Kala Pattar. Being an acclimatisation stop, some trekkers, groups included, stay two nights so in the high season it is very busy. If it snows groups often abandon their tents and unfairly take over the *lodges*. Good alternatives to a second night here are Pangboche, Phortse, Khumjung or Deboche.

Behind the Trekkers Lodge is a ridge pointing to Khumbui Yul Lha that affords superb views. Look especially for the spectacular high trail from Pangboche to Phortse on the opposite side of the valley.

Rubbish and human waste are big problems at Tengboche. Each group used to put up a toilet (tent) leaving hundreds of unsightly half-filled holes. Toilet blocks constructed by the park to solve this problem are now becoming dilapidated but all groups should use them. Your trekking crew might need a hint and porters instructed to use this facility. There are also rubbish bins provided.

Lodges

There are only four lodges: the *Tashi Delek Lodge*, the *Ama Dablam Lodge* above, the *Gompa Lodge* below and the

Trekkers Lodge on the ridge behind the monastery buildings. Three of them are owned by the gompa and are rented out, providing further income for the gompa.

Tengboche Gompa

This justly famous gompa is spectacularly situated under the mighty Kangtaiga ('horse saddle') and Thamserku ('golden door') mountains, in a commanding position with superb views up and down the surrounding valleys. You can see the Everest View Hotel and the National Park HQ down the valley, perhaps now more easily spotted at night. With these as markers it's easy to work out where hidden Namche and Khumjung are, and the path that brought you up here.

The gompa serves as a spiritual and occasional social centre for the people of the region. The majority of the other buildings belong to the monastery. Boys are sent here from all over the Khumbu to study Buddhism. For the period of study they must remain celibate but they may (and most do) get married when they have graduated.

Although the area has long been considered revered ground, the gompa was established only in 1916 by Lama Gulu at the request of the Abbot of Rongbuk. In 1934 a disastrous earthquake struck the area, causing considerable damage to the gompa. Lama Gulu died of shock.

Rebuilt and headed by the present lama, Nawang Tenzing Zangbu, the gompa's move into the 20th century was not an auspicious one. Less than a year after electricity was installed, on 19 January 1989, a heater overturned burning the magnificent gompa to the ground. Not all was lost since some of what could be removed, including the priceless book collection, was rescued. The construction of the grand new gompa was considerably aided by the American Himalayan foundation (set up by Sir Ed) and donations from wealthy locals. The library has now been put on micro-film, and the hydroelectric system has been revived. The gompa is often flood-lit at night to great effect.

Sherpa Cultural Centre
This was started by Frances Klatzel and a number of Sherpas who have taken an active interest in the preservation of their culture for future generations. It's not intended as a dusty museum, more an archive for the storage of important documents and a place for Sherpas to meet and learn more about their culture.

Excursions from Tengboche
The forests above and below Tengboche are protected and are still considered to be owned by the monastery. It is pleasant to wander through the trees and there is a reasonable chance of seeing deer and pheasant. The rhododendrons are spectacular in April.

For a longer half-day trip, the rock peak above Tengboche, often called Hamugon, offers better views of the awesome Thamserku-Kangtaiga glacier. It's an easy but breathless scramble to the top of the first peak. The higher peak requires some more committing scrambling. Listen to your body though, while ascending.

TENGBOCHE TO PHERICHE & DINGBOCHE [MAP 10, p168]
Leaving Tengboche The route passes the water tap then takes the gully between the fields where groups camp.

Deboche (3770m/12,369ft) Down
through pleasant forest on a trail that is icy long after snowfall is a series of four or five *lodges*.

Deboche is five minutes further on and there are superb views of Khumbui Yul Lha which looks formidable from here. Behind a barrier of trees is a nunnery with approximately 12 nuns. You are welcome to have a look round the gompa, which dates from 1925. The atmosphere is quite different from Tengboche.

After passing a few other hamlets you cross a spectacular little gorge on a short suspension bridge. This is the junction for the trail to Phortse (see p185). Follow the main trail for Pangboche.

About 20 minutes later the trail passes through a cleft in some rocks, with a mani wall virtually in the middle. Just after, the trail divides and is usually signposted, the upper trail heads to Upper Pangboche and the gompa, while the lower path takes a more gentle route through the fields to Lower Pangboche.

Pangboche (4000m/13,123ft) This
used to be the highest permanently occupied village until trekkers created a demand in winter for accommodation higher up the valley. Once few trekkers stayed here but now both the upper and lower villages are popular places to stay. Consequently there are quite a number of new *lodges* in this pleasant village. Coming down the valley from Pheriche/Dingboche the turn-off to Upper Pangboche is by a small chorten, where the river widens and the first fields of Lower Pangboche can be seen. From Lower Pangboche there's another trail which starts from the corner of Namaste Lodge and winds up to the gompa. In **Pangboche Te Lim** (the upper village)

the houses are clustered round the old gompa and there are five *lodges* here. The surrounding juniper trees have long been protected and are now very large. Legend has it that they were created by Lama Sangwa Dorje who tossed a handful of his hair into the air and it took root as juniper. Once the whole valley would have been thickly forested with trees this size.

The monastery is believed to have been founded around 1667 which makes it the oldest Sherpa gompa in the Khumbu. Many trekkers take the opportunity to have a look around; the lama (the 14th re-incarnate) or his wife are usually close by. It is customary to leave a donation. This gompa was home to one of the Khumbu's famous yeti scalps until it was stolen in mysterious circumstances in 1991.

The lower village, **Pangboche Wa Lim** (3840m/12,598ft) was once just (big) grass fields, which is what the name 'Pangboche' means. There's now a small

settlement here with at least six *lodges* on the edge of the lower fields. Potatoes, radishes and a few vegetables are grown and there is often an abundance of wild mushrooms. Firewood collection in Pangboche is still well organised. Dead wood is collected from the opposite side of the valley from selected spots and when the supply thins another part of the forest is used. Yak dung, a valuable fertiliser, is now also used as fuel, something that started with the arrival of trekkers.

Route from Pangboche to Phortse
The most direct route is a high and wild trail that begins from near the gompa. From the top of the gompa take the trail that contours west to two white chortens 100m above *Tashi Lodge* and begin contouring. The path crosses fields and a stream. Once a little way out of Pangboche it is a large well-used trail. It takes a couple of hours to reach Phortse.

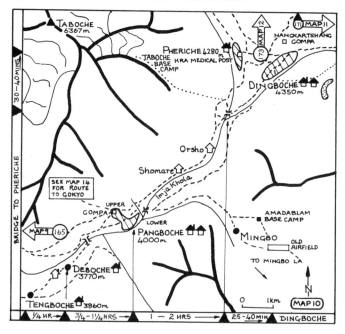

❑ Pheriche or Dingboche?

The villages are 45 minutes apart, separated by a ridge. Both have lodges and are at roughly the same altitude so it depends on your plans for the important acclimatisation day as to where you stay. If the climb to Nangkartshang Peak (or Gompa) appeals, or you plan simply to relax it really does not matter where you stay. If planning a day trip to Chukhung then it is more convenient to sleep at Dingboche. There's a trail to Lobuche from either village, and they are of equal distance.

Route from Pangboche to Pheriche and Dingboche There are several small chhusas (yak herding areas) en route. The first you come to is **Shomare**, owned by the villagers of Pangboche and used for growing potatoes. There are at least three small *teahouses* here. **Orsho/Warsho** is the next kharka and it also has a single *teahouse-cum-lodge*. Both are occasionally closed.

For Mingbo and Ama Dablam Base Camp See p191.

Route to Pheriche The track to Pheriche turns off perhaps five minutes out of Orsho. The trail veers left and climbs up to a small pass before descending on a wide trail to the bridge. The turnoff to Pheriche takes 30-40 minutes. Despite its being marked on even the most recent maps, there is no trail immediately after the bridge to Dingboche.

Pheriche (4280m/14,042ft)
There are five *lodges*, most recently rebuilt bigger, better and warmer, and a few houses spaced along the track that runs through the village. The lodge shops can be a good place to replenish camping supplies. Pheriche can get quite crowded during the high seasons.

Himalayan Rescue Association Medical Post This was built in 1976 by the Tokyo Medical College for research purposes. Now it's staffed by two or three Western volunteer doctors who are available for consultations and who also give daily lectures on altitude sickness that are well worth attending. Recently lectures have been given every few days in Dingboche as well; look for a notice in the middle of the village. The Pheriche post opens only during peak trekking seasons (October to mid-December and March to May), when the donations and consultation fees can cover the running costs. It is an extraordinary service, please don't take it for granted. They carry out numerous rescues (surprisingly survivors often forget to donate) and consultations. One of the most unusual was a yak that required a band-aid.

Route to Dingboche From Orsho follow the straight trail that drops to a *teashop* then the bridge across the Lobuche Khola. Dingboche is still a hill and 30-40 minutes away from the bridge.

❑ The Garden of Eden

This was one of the 1977-vintage lodges in Pheriche: a pit dug into the ground, the excess dirt made into a wall around it. A plastic sheet was the 1.5 metre high roof. People slept on turf around the edge. At night we put cardboard boxes in the open windows but it was still a fridge. After several days we made the mistake of asking the Sherpani how she made the chang. She explained that after the rice was first boiled she spread the mixture out on a blanket, then put another on top and slept on it for three days while it fermented, then it was thrown in a pot and water added for the final fermentation.   Russell (Australia)

❑ **Dingboche, Pheriche and Lobuche – AMS advice**
Previously the HRA recommended trekkers stay a minimum of two nights in Dingboche or Pheriche before moving on to Lobuche. However even this relatively cautious approach meant that many people would suffer altitude sickness at Lobuche. Now that it is possible to stay at Thuklha the best advice is to spend one (or two) nights at Dingboche/Pheriche then a night at Thuklha then stay at Lobuche. Breaking the 600m jump in altitude into two 300m gains will considerably lessen the occurence of mild altitude sickness. Gradual ascent is the safest!

Note that if you have slept at Chukhung (or Dzongla) without problems you should be able to trek directly to Lobuche rather than stopping en route.

Dingboche (4350m/14,271ft)

The houses of this summer village are dotted about the fields, on land owned by people from Pangboche and Khunde. As Dingboche has become more popular than Pheriche, so too have the *lodges* grown. The lodges are in three groups.

From Dingboche you can make the half-day trips described below or head to Chukhung. If you suffered mild AMS on the first night here it may be a better idea to rest here or if you really suffered, trek slightly lower during the day. The bridge across the Lobuche Khola is the closest point that's easy to reach. Often this small drop in altitude can make a difference.

Day trips from Pheriche/Dingboche

● **Half-day to Nangkartshang Peak** For the amount of effort involved, this excursion from Pheriche or Dingboche offers some of the best views in this region – a perfect scenic lunch spot.

From Pheriche the path zigzags up directly behind the HRA building on the track heading to Dingboche. Some time before the steep descent, continue up the ridge past a stupa.

From Dingboche any track heading up to the ridge will do. Then, from the stupa is a small trail that follows the ridge up, and up, and up. The top is marked by prayer flags and you are brought up short by a sudden drop. The views here are magnificent with Numbur, Chukhung, Makalu and Ama Dablam visible. There are several origins given for the name Ama Dablam (Amai Dablang). One says that it refers to the necklace of turquoise

or coral usually worn by married women. With a little imagination it's possible to visualise shoulders and a head, and the pendulous lump of blue ice (a glacier) is roughly in the right spot for a necklace.

The gompa is usually locked and the trail to it is difficult to follow. Nearby are some meditation caves.

● **Half-day to the Ama Dablam lakes** Among the moraine below Ama Dablam are two lakes at 4700m. Sometimes there's a bridge across the Imja Khola at the base of Dingboche and a track to Duroo, a small yersa. The alternative is to cross the creek at the top of Dingboche and climb the steep hillside, or head upriver to Shangtso where there is usually a bridge and hook back on the trail heading up. The lakes are also a great place for lunch.

● **Half-day to Taboche Base Camp** Opposite Pheriche is stunning Taboche. Atop the broad ridge are a couple of small rock peaks that can be climbed, or a hidden higher valley to explore. Cross the bridge to Pangboche and from Tsuro Teng follow small steep trails up. It is quite a grunt up there. Don't forget to take lunch.

TO & AROUND CHUKHUNG [MAP 11]

To Chukhung By the top lodges in Dingboche the track continues between the hill and the upper fences and is easy to follow through the low scrub. **Bibre** is above the main trail but below, beside the path, is a solitary one-roomed house where people from Dingboche sell cups of tea as well as biscuits and chocolate during the trekking seasons. From here

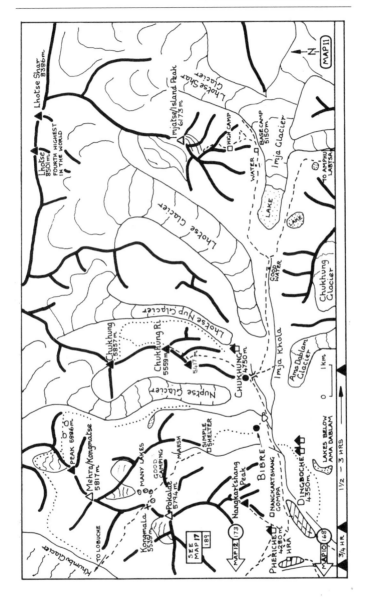

Imjatse/Island Peak looks awesome, a triangle of almost sheer rock and incredibly steep snow faces, steep enough to bring a lump to climbers' throats. Yet strangely at Chukhung its magnificence fades. Chukhung is perhaps 20-25 minutes beyond Bibre but, until you are almost on top of it, it remains invisible.

Chukhung 4750m/15,584ft

This is traditionally a Pangboche herding station (or *phu*) used as a base to graze the rich and extensive grasslands of the valley. It's nestled between two streams, which is what the name means. Viewed from above it is also surrounded by glaciers and their debris. The views here are fantastic, even from the base of the valley, and they get even better the higher you explore. Looking down valley, Numbur, Khatang and Karyolung rise majestically above Kongde while Taboche (Tagouche/ Tawouche literally means 'horse's head' but can be loosely translated as 'big ego') and Tsholatse ('Lake-pass Peak') are closer to the right. Ama Dablam is quite something to see from here and the fluted snow wall above Chukhung Glacier is stunning, especially at sunset.

With the number of trekkers and climbers passing through, the *lodges* at Chukhung have developed from the simple teahouses they once were. Now at least one lodge remains open throughout the year. The phu makes a good base to explore the huge valley system with its many 'small' peaks that can be fun to climb. Once the lodges here stocked enough equipment for trekkers to hire to climb Island Peak. Now they don't.

Half-day trip to Chukhung Ri (5559m/18,238ft)
This is an understandably popular excursion from Chukhung, involving an ascent of a ridge similar to Kala Pattar. The top cannot be seen from Chukhung but the paths are obvious scars ascending the side of the big pile of grass and dirt. At the saddle there's a choice: a lower peak (5417m/ 17,772ft) to the south or a trickier ascent on rock to the high peak (5559m/

18,238ft). The views are staggering from both with Makalu dominating amongst a ring of mountains. It is possible to do this as a day-trip from Dingboche but the altitude, for the unacclimatised (rather than the time), creates a problem.

Chukhung Tse (5857m/19,216ft)
This is the peak north of Chukhung Ri (5559m/18,238ft) and is the highest hill in the Khumbu commonly scrambled by trekkers. The ridge between Chukhung Ri and Chukhung Tse is tricky to traverse in its entirety; take particular care on some short exposed moves and don't attempt if wet or snowy. The safer route is a steep gully scramble on the east side directly to the summit. The ablation valley to the east provides access and/or exit. It is possible but strenuous to ascend both Chukhung Ri and Tse in a day, good preparation for Imjatse/Island Peak or the Amphu Labtsa. An axe, stick or ski pole would be handy. Views are stunning and include Chomo Lonzo (north of Makalu) and Gauri Sankar.

Other routes: **Island Peak and the base camp** see p227; **Amphu Labtsa** see p190; **Kongma La** see p189; **Pokalde and Kongma Tse** see p233; **Peak 5886m** see p190.

PHERICHE & DINGBOCHE TO LOBUCHE [MAP 12]
Route from Pheriche to Thuklha
Leaving Pheriche, the trail meanders up the open valley, beautiful when the weather's fine but muddy if snow or rain has fallen. It then cuts up a small but obvious valley. A smaller trail then branches off to the left and heads directly to the bridge over a few slippery boulders, while the main path heads up to join the trail directly from Dingboche just a minute before the bridge to Thuklha.

Route from Dingboche to Thuklha
Climb the ridge behind Dingboche on one of the many trails to the higher plain. There are then several paths to follow, all leading to the bridge across to Thuklha.

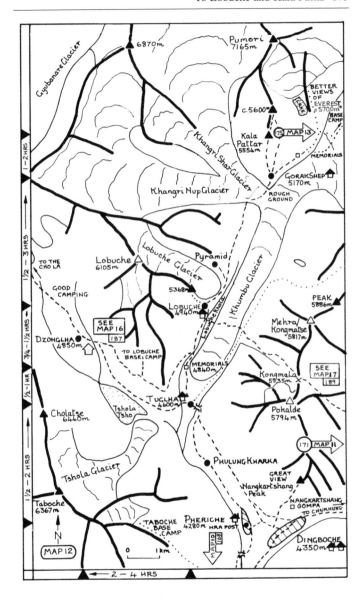

Gyubanare Glacier

6870m

Pumori
7165m

BETTER
VIEWS
OF
EVEREST
≥5700m

LAKE

c.5600m

BASE
CAMP

Khangri Shar Glacier

Kala
Pattar
5554m

175 MAP 13

MEMORIALS

GORAKSHEP
5170m

Khangri Nup Glacier

ROUGH
GROUND

TO THE
CHO LA

Lobuche Glacier

Pyramid

Lobuche
6105m

GOOD
CAMPING

5368m

Khumbu Glacier

PEAK
5886m

Lobuche
4940m

SEE
MAP 16
187

Mehra/
Kongmatse
5817m

Lobuche Khola

DZONGLHA
4850m

TO LOBUCHE
BASE CAMP

MEMORIALS
4840m

SEE
MAP 17
189

Kongmala
5535m

Cholatse
6440m

Tshola
Tsho

TUGLHA
4600m

Pokalde
5794m

171 MAP 11

Tshola Glacier

PHULUNG KHARKA

GREAT
VIEW
Nangkartshang
Peak

NANGKARTSHANG
GOMPA
TO CHUKHUNG

Taboche
6367m

N

MAP 12

TABOCHE
BASE
CAMP

0   1 km

PHERICHE
4280m HRA POST

MAP 10
188

DINGBOCHE
4350m

2 – 4 HRS

1 – 2 HRS

1/2 – 3 HRS

3/4 – 1 1/2 HRS

1/2 – 1 HR

1/2 – 2 HRS

Thuklha/Tuglha/Duglha
(4600m/15,092ft) Ram's Corral (uncastrated male sheep) is the translation. Tourist Corral is perhaps a better name now. The three *lodges* here primarily used to make lunch for trekkers on the way up. Once poky and smoky, now at least one of the lodges has some double rooms. Now it is possible to stay overnight in relative comfort and break the 600m gain in altitude between Dingboche or Pheriche and Lobuche.

The hill immediately beyond Thuklha is tough, especially if your pack is heavy. At the crest (4840m/15,879ft) are more than 20 memorials for Sherpas and a few foreign climbers who tragically didn't make it down again. From here the trail climbs gently and it's just over an hour to Lobuche. At this altitude, even in October there's ice on the streams; by December they may be frozen over.

Lobuche (4940m/16,207ft)
Lobuche is set on the slopes of a pleasant ablation valley which, possibly because of the altitude, is very little explored off the path to Gorak Shep. It has long had four *lodges*, but 1997-98 has seen some overdue changes. There is a large new lodge with double rooms. Prices hadn't been fixed at the time of writing, but it won't be a cheap place. The other addition is the 8000m Inn (see below).

Groups have a wide area to camp in but more often than not members decide that the lodges are rather more attractive than their cold tents and move in. This may then create accommodation problems for individual trekkers. Nights here from October are invariably below 0°C and January temperatures are sometimes lower than -20°C/-3°F. Once the sun strikes Lobuche mornings are pleasant.

Supplies Lobuche is on the return route to Namche from Everest Base Camp so many expeditions sell off their surplus food to the lodges here. There's often an abundance of foreign delicacies, chocolate, energy snacks and dehydrated foods for sale.

Pyramid and 8000m Inn The Pyramid was built in 1990 for research purposes, and until now, the Italians requested not to be mentioned in this guide. In 1997 the facilities were expanded to include better accommodation for researchers, and also when not full, some rooms for trekkers. Costs are likely to be in the region of US$10 per person, with food on top. There is an inside toilet, but this is only usable during the warm season, and even a real shower. The Pyramid and the 8000m Inn's first priority is high altitude research. The Pyramid has emergency facilities for trekkers, Nepalis and expeditions. This includes a satellite phone and fax (for emergency only, US$13 a minute), a radio for helicopter rescue, a portable altitude chamber gamow bag and an oxygen concentrator.

The environment Lobuche is in a sensitive alpine region. Please ensure that the water supply is kept clean and ensure your group's kitchen crew clean up after themselves properly, and don't just chuck it in the stream. The toilets are far too close to the water supply but at present nobody is interested in rectifying this. There is far too much toilet paper beside the Gorak Shep trail, all dropped by trekkers. Just because you might be trekking in the early morning when it is dark doesn't mean toilet paper remains invisible. Toilet paper can be put under a rock or in a plastic bag and tucked under a flap or in a side pocket. If you got to the toilet make sure you are at least 10m off the trail and at least 30m from the stream.

Short excursions The small moraine towards Nuptse offers scenic sunset views if clouds have not rolled up the valley too far. The moraine immediately north of the phu is a stiff climb that's a little longer than it first looks but it also offers a few surprises: the Lobuche Glacier is close and spectacular. The grassy slopes behind Lobuche are also worth the climb. The sure-footed and energetic can attempt the three rock pinnacles, each harder than the last.

LOBUCHE TO KALA PATTAR [MAP 13]
To Gorak Shep and Kala Pattar

Early in the season when it's still not really cold many groups leave Lobuche well before dawn to reach the top of Kala Pattar for sunrise. This is a rare and usually rewarding experience (once you've got over the shock of the early start). By December, however, the low night temperatures make starting with the sun a more reasonable proposition. If the weather has been stable Kala Pattar and the surrounding mountains usually display themselves at their absolute best for much, if not the entire day. Afternoon or evening cloud sweeping up the valley from lower down and **no** high cloud or clouds hanging around lesser peaks is a good sign. High cloud means the weather is harder to to predict. Use the previous afternoon (ie when you arrived at Lobuche) and lodge-owners' advice. In the spring season during a patch where cloud forms regularly around or before lunchtime a dawn start is advisable.

Some days a vicious cold wind picks up around 10 or 11am on the top while other days there is little more than a breeze on top for the whole day. Always take your warmest clothes (including a down jacket if you have one), wind-proof clothing and a bag big enough to put it all in for the walk up. In winter, especially in snow, try to avoid getting your boots wet and beware of frostbite.

If the previous day was hopelessly cloudy don't despair. It could dawn perfectly fine the next day (but might not also). Being so far up a high valley system Kala Pattar is an unusually fine place and probably has one of the better weather records in Nepal.

Even during the monsoon a day or two's patience will usually be rewarded with a stunning panorama.

Having two days set aside rather than one can give you some peace of mind. Note that the majority of groups only allow a single day for Kala Pattar. Planning for two would be much better!

The walk to Gorak Shep takes only about one and a half hours for the fit and fast, or up to three hours for the less fit. Kala Pattar is one to two hours above

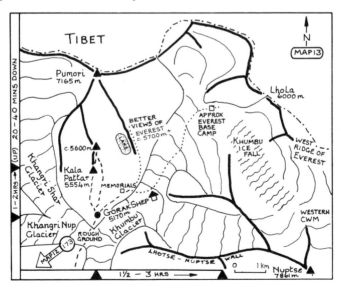

Gorak Shep. Even for the slow, the round trip should take less than eight hours. Look out for furball Pikas, on the trail up and down.

From Lobuche the path is clear and pleasant at first, gently leading up the ablation valley. Then it climbs, twisting and turning, to thread its way onto the rough moraine of the Khangri Glacier. Here it's important not to lose the main track. The rough walking ends suddenly: the trail virtually falls into Gorak Shep.

Gorak Shep (5170m/16,962ft)

There are three simple (dorms only) *lodges* with abundant supplies of biscuits and tea, in addition to menus that include the most expensive Coke in Nepal. The lodge-owners are friendly but if you intend staying here you must be confident that you won't suffer altitude problems and you need a very warm sleeping bag. On a November night the temperature **inside** a lodge could plummet as low as -20°C/-3°F. Even in September the inside temperature can drop below 0°C/-32°F. The lodges are usually closed during January and February.

It pays to be well acclimatised before staying at Gorak Shep. A few people cope with two nights Dingboche/Pheriche, one at Lobuche then one at Gorak Shep but many still have problems. A better plan is Dingboche, Thuklha, Lobuche then Gorak Shep. If you have previously stayed two nights at Chukhung or Gokyo then Dzonglha you are in a better position to go direct to Gorak Shep and bypass Lobuche. You'd be stupid to go directly from Dingboche/Pheriche to Gorak Shep.

Ascending Kala Pattar

Kala Pattar, which means 'Black Rock' in Hindi, is the most popular viewpoint in the area for Everest and the Khumbu Icefall. The first foreign ascent was in 1950 by Tilman and Oscar Houston (father of the doctor, Charlie, AMS specialist) who rated it a 'subsidiary feature' without the extensive view of climbing access to Everest they sought. However, surrounded by stupendous set of faces,

peaks and glaciers, it offers a breath-taking arc of views. Stop and look for the two trails up Kala Pattar before crossing the sand. The one that zigzags straight up leads to the slightly lower and easier peak at 5554m/18,222ft while the trail that traverses around gives the option of ascending this easier peak or the more northern peak (5600m/18,373ft). In snow use the longer but less steep route. Between where the two trails begin is a small spring with delicious water.

Other points of interest
Two Glacier Rock 5529m/18,140ft
Less imposing but virtually as high is the hill marked 5529m on the National Geographic Everest map and 5527m on the Khumbu Himal map. The 360° panorama is not as impressive but you can see more of Everest. Pick up a trail of sorts at the northern-eastern end of Gorak Shep and head for the square cairn on the skyline. Over the other side is rough moraine and a small ridge, behind which, near the lake, is a flat spot often used as Pumori Base Camp. Pick up a rough trail somewhere around here than climbs to the eastern side of a minor rock spur (really a big lump of rock). A small trail leads to where the rock meets Pumori and a way up onto the spur.

Pumori advance base camp For a better view of the Khumbu Icefall you can climb another of Pumori's spurs. Pick up a faint trail at Pumori base camp (the lake mentioned above) then pass by the Two Glacier Rock, continuing a little north. Pick up, if you aren't already on, a small trail that soon begins climbing. The going gets steep and exposed but higher up you will come across a few tents/places for tents at an altitude of around 5700+m, Pumori advanced base camp. From here it is obvious that to get any higher takes some rope and perhaps a fair amount of stupidity. Don't attempt these view points in anything other than perfect snow-free conditions. Pumori was named by Mallory (in 1921) and this Tibetan name means 'Daughter Peak'.

More memorials Close to Gorak Shep are some more memorials to mountaineers who died on Everest, in particular Rob Hall's and others who died on Everest in 1996. To reach them walk the length of the Gorak Shep flats and continue a little further in the same direction. They are on the obvious minor ridge.

Everest Base Camp

While this walk can be interesting, there are no views of Mt Everest and it's not a popular excursion for trekkers. During the climbing season (August, September and early October, then mid-March, April and into early May) there are frequently yaks and sherpas on the trails. During winter the trails can sometimes be hard to find or follow unless there's a trail through the snow. Groups often take a guide from one of the lodges at Gorak Shep. To visit Kala Pattar plus the Base Camp in a single day is extremely tough – beyond most people. If you're going to visit one or the other, then Kala Pattar is the better choice.

There are in fact usually two trails to the base camp which both change year by year, depending on conditions. Both trails are very rough and easy to lose. Usually the most obvious path is the yak route which at the end of the Gorak Shep flats usually plunges down the loose and sometimes dangerous moraine wall before heading towards the middle of the glacier. The quicker trail is the trail for people which usually follows the top of the moraine past the Gorak Shep flats for a considerable distance before dropping onto the glacier. The route sometimes seems roundabout since there may be crevasses to avoid. Some expeditions

don't mind the occasional visitor (especially when from their home country) while others prefer no distractions. It takes between 1½ and 3 hours each way.

HEADING DOWN

From Lobuche most trekkers reach Pangboche, Deboche or Tengboche in a day. Groups tend to make for Deboche or Tengboche (making it more crowded). It's possible to reach Namche in a tough single day – the Everest marathon is from Gorak Shep to Thamo and Namche.

Alternatively, after climbing Kala Pattar some trekkers head down immediately. Reaching Pheriche or Dingboche takes only a few hours from Lobuche, but can be a tough end to a day. If you have been suffering the altitude descending the short distance to Thuklha may offer relief.

Coming down the valley from Pheriche/Dingboche the turn off to Upper Pangboche and the gompa is by a small chorten, where the river widens and the first fields of Pangboche can be seen. Through Lower Pangboche there are many junctions; don't be afraid to ask.

A good alternative to the standard Tengboche route down is to go via Phortse and Mong – see p178. Trekkers with more time can walk to Chukhung easily in a day via Dingboche or the Kongma La (see p189). To Gokyo via the Tsho La is covered on p187.

Namche to Lukla takes a day for the fit although many groups break this up – Namche to Phakding, Phakding to Lukla. This then gives time for a special dinner and party in Lukla. From 1994 until late 1996 you could fly out of Syangboche, saving a hard day's walk. Flying from Syangboche is no longer possible.

❏ **Porters and AMS**
Many people trek with a porter. Nepalis, especially sherpas, believe that altitude sickness is only a foreigners' disease. It isn't, and lowland Nepalese are just as susceptible as foreigners, as a British trekker found out. His porter became very sick at Lobuche. He had probably been suffering altitude sickness for a while but either didn't know what it was or didn't tell anyone. As soon as the trekker realised what was up, he helped him down but the porter died on the trail. The trekker will doubtless suffer regrets for the rest of his life.   **Sue Heydon**

To Gokyo

From Dole up the majority of the lodges are run by Khumjung people. In years past most trekkers would stay two nights only at Gokyo. Now lodge owners comment that most stay three nights or more.

Acclimatisation

Planning a sensible acclimatisation programme is essential if you're heading directly to Gokyo. The helicopter rescue pilots call it 'Death Valley' because many people go up too fast, unaware of the consequences. This is partly because the walking days are short, tempting trekkers to go on past their acclimatisation limits. The other reason serious AMS often results in death here is that there isn't the backup of medical facilities that the Lobuche and Chukhung routes have with the Pyramid and Pheriche HRA clinic.

The minimum acclimatisation programme is two nights at Namche, one at Phortse Tenga (or Thame, Khumjung, Khunde, Tengboche or Phortse), a night at Dole then a night at either Machermo or Pangka. You can still get AMS following this (and many people do) so allowing an extra day would be the most sensible approach. Groups should allow one extra day or take Diamox. A longer but rewarding itinerary would be Namche, Namche, Tengboche, Phortse, Dole, Machermo/Luza/Pangka, Gokyo. See Appendix A for sample itineraries.

The route

The first section out of Namche is a high open traverse; its highest point at almost 4000m/13,123ft. The trail then drops abruptly through forest almost to the level of the river before climbing again. You may see deer and pheasant in this area. The countryside opens out offering great vistas of mountains on both sides of the deep valley and back to the stunning mountain wall above Tengboche. The climb up to the ablation valley beside the Ngozumpa Glacier leads you into a different world of azure lakes and golden alpine pastures beneath sparkling mountains overlooking Nepal's longest glacier.

Facilities

Phortse used to be the last permanently inhabited village with only high *kharkas* higher up the valley. Now strategically-placed lodges stay open during the monsoon, even in the depths of winter to cater for trekkers. Now at least one lodge in each place between Dole and Gokyo has double rooms and all lodges still have a dormitory.

NAMCHE TO GOKYO [MAPS 14-15]

Route from Namche to Khumjung/Sanasa see p164.

Route from Khumjung This beautiful village is a sensible place to spend the night at the start of the Gokyo trek. By a house with a blue roof a few minutes after the large chorten at the end of the village is a junction. Straight ahead is for Sanasa. Taking the left path you can continue directly to Mong. A little further along a path heads steeply up. This leads up to a hair-raisingly steep stone staircase, the classic route. Alternatively, contour and head up the newer less steep stone stairs.

Route from Sanasa From Sanasa it's little more than 100m along the trail to Kyangjuma (ie towards Namche) to a small junction beside a rock. This trail climbs in a few minutes to the main trail from Khumjung to Mong. Turn right for the gentle stairs, or left then right a moment later for the classic route. Once through the rocks the trails cross the golden hillside gradually gaining height to a point overlooking Tengboche. Close to Mong is a small stream, in dry times the only water supply for an hour in either direction.

Mong/Mohang (3973m/13,035ft) is marked by a chorten and is in effect a

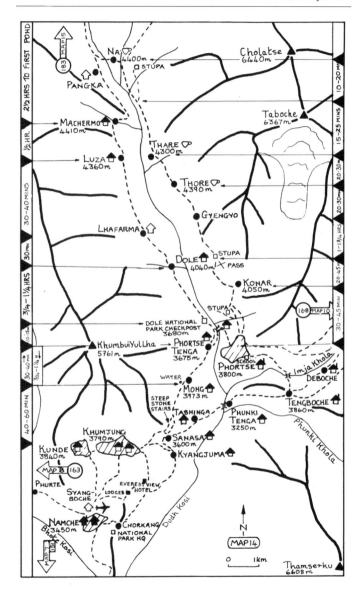

2½ HRS TO FIRST POND

183 MAP15

NA 4400m
□ STUPA

PANGKA

Cholatse 6440m

MACHERMO 4410m

THARE 4300m

Taboche 6367m

LUZA 4360m

THORE 4390m

GYENGYO

LHAFARMA

DOLE 4040m
□ STUPA
PASS

KONAR 4050m

STUPA

168 MAP10

DOLE NATIONAL PARK CHECKPOST 3680m

KhumbuiYulLha 5761m

PHORTSE TENGA 3675m

SCHOOL
PHORTSE 3800m

Imja Khola

DEBOCHE

WATER

MONG 3973m

TENGBOCHE 3860m

STEEP STONE STAIRS

TASHINGA

PHUNKI TENGA 3250m

Phunki Khola

KHUMJUNG 3790m

SANASA 3600m

KUNDE 3840m

MAP 8 163

KYANGJUMA

PHURTE

EVEREST VIEW HOTEL

SYANGBOCHE

LODGES

Dudh Kosi

NAMCHE 3450m

Bhote Kosi

CHORKANG
□ NATIONAL PARK HQ

MAP 7 161

N

MAP 14

0   1km

Thamserku 6608m

10-20 MIN
15-25 MINS
20-30 MIN
20-30 MIN
1-1¾ HRS
20-45 MIN
30-45 MIN
½ HR.
30-40 MINS
30 MIN
¾-1½ HRS
10-15 MIN
30-40 MIN
3¼-1¾
40-60 MIN

small pass. It is known to all Sherpas as the birth place of Lama Sangwa Dorje. In 1985 there were no lodges up here. Now, villagers from Khumjung and Tashinga have established some simple *lodges*.

The track to Phortse Tenga is rather steep but with great views over to Phortse and the spectacular river gorge below, including an inaccessible natural rock-bridge.

Phortse Tenga/Phortse Drangka (3675m/12,057ft) *Tenga* means bridge but if heading to Gokyo you no longer need to descend to the river: a more direct trail contours from inside the grounds of the *Phortse Tanga Lodge* and the *Himalayan Lodge*.

Once a dirty place, these two lodges have now cleaned up their act, although they are still simple, without double rooms. *Drangka* means river in Sherpa, and if you follow the main trail, passing the Himalaya Lodge and camping area, this is where you will end up. For the village of Phortse and the routes to it see p185.

Dole National Park Check Post (3680m/12,073ft) The staff here, stuck in this horribly cold and miserable spot, may want to see your receipt for the National Park entrance fee. A minute further on is an army post. They're here supposedly to protect the wildlife (especially the valuable musk deer) and the forests. The village of Dole is about an hour further on, up the long hill, through an area where you're likely to see colourful pheasant and shy deer. In rain or snow this trail can be slippery.

Dole (4040m/13,254ft) The name means 'many stones' but despite this it's a pleasant kharka with four *lodges*. Here the yaks and naks are brought up in mid-June to graze and fertilise the soil with their dung, producing a rich crop of hay. If you arrive with time on your hands there are a couple of exploration possibilities. Following the valley formed by the stream leads relatively gently up to a

large grassy area in less than an hour. Alternatively follow the ridge from Himalayan Lodge up a steep trail to a rocky viewpoint, in an hour or so.

After Dole the trail continues to climb, then flattens to a pleasant traverse with broad vistas.

Lhafarma/Lhapharma (4300m/14,108ft) has one pleasant *lodge*. The mountain views both up, down and across the valley are extensive. While walking the fragrant smell comes from the small rhododendron plants. There are two types, that look similar but only one, *sunpati*, is burnt at offerings.

Luza (4360m/14,304ft) is an hour or so from Dole and has several pleasant *lodges*. If you're feeling the altitude staying here rather than Machermo and spending the next night at Pangka or Machermo is a good idea. When leaving, immediately after crossing the stream continue up through the fields rather than taking the left trail.

Machermo (4410m/14,468ft) This is a relaxing spot with good views, especially of some little-known mountains. There's a big new *lodge* (in season: double rooms Rs250 or more) and a few smaller hotels. Since Lhafarma, Luza and Machermo are so close together and at a similar altitude it doesn't matter which one you stay at.

Most people head directly from here to Gokyo but if acclimatisation is causing a problem it might be wiser to stay another night at Luza or Machermo. Alternatives are **Na** (4400m/ 14,436ft, see p185) and explore the area, or rest at Pangka.

Pangka (4480m/14,698ft) This kharka has a chequered history. Two lodges opened in 1994. Then in 1995 one was hit by an avalanche during a massive unseasonal snow storm. On the night of 8 November 1995 more than 40 people, including 13 members of a Japanese trekking group, were killed in an avalanche here. Now there are two simple

lodges, both built further away from the slopes above so that the same accident shouldn't re-occur.

There are trails around both sides of the fields. They rejoin and briefly drop out of the kharka then climb close to the Dudh Kosi. There are some more magnificent views and then the path leads to where the high moraine of the Ngozumpa Glacier meets rock walls. Follow the rock wall on a good trail, crossing the wooden bridge over a stream that comes from the first pond. To the right (east) is a milky stream, the beginnings of the Dudh Kosi. **Do not** attempt to cross this. A cold night, especially in winter, freezes the spray and sometimes even freezes the stream, diverting it onto the path which becomes treacherously slippery.

Longponga (first pond/lake) A sudden change of scenery introduces the first pond; it's really too small to be called a lake. It has taken until this third edition for me to find out definitively that this first pond is called Longponga.

Taujung (second lake) Groups occasionally camp in this tranquil place (4720m/15,485ft).

Gokyo (4750m/15,584ft)

On the shores of the third lake is the Gokyo kharka. The lodge facilities have really developed in the last couple of years, spurred on by the *Gokyo Resort*, a modified leftover of the film room built for the 1991 'Balloon Across Everest' expedition, and the fact that trekkers tend to stay here longer than previously. Although Gokyo has several shops they are simpler than the expedition-stocked lodges of Lobuche and Pheriche; finding a variety of camping food is not so easy.

The view from Gokyo Ri is only one of the many reasons for visiting Gokyo. Relaxing on the lodge patios or their sun rooms overlooking the picturesque lake is considered reward enough by some but it's the potential for far-ranging exploration that sets it apart from Lobuche. Climbing to the top of the Renjo/Henjo

La is exhilarating and walking up to the fifth lake and beyond can only be described as 'out of this world'. Many of the peaks around here require some steepish scrambling or bouldering. Recognise your limits and take account of the weather; wet rocks are slippery when damp – otherwise enjoy!

With everyone heading off exploring at all hours of the morning don't expect to sleep in undisturbed. At the same time plan ahead if you are leaving early: the kitchen may not be open so stock up the evening before on boiled eggs and chapatis or plenty of biscuits and chocolate.

Leaving, the **Na-Phortse alternative** is covered on p185.

Gokyo Ri (5340m/17,519ft) A stiff

one and a half to three hour climb on an obvious track brings you to this viewpoint. The panorama stretches well into the distance, a blend of glaciers and grass, rock, snow and ice. Sunsets can be unforgettable here, as can be the descent afterwards, if you forgot to bring your torch/flashlight.

Henjo/Renjo La (5417m/17,772ft)

The trek to the top of this pass can be a pleasant short day walk. In addition to some breathtaking new vistas, you end up in real alpine territory and pass beside a white glacier. Being so close to the mountains above the lake is exhilarating. Although it looks much further from Gokyo, it's only two to three hours to the top. A reasonable sense of balance and adventure is required as there are a few steep sections.

Begin by crossing the stream at the head of the lake, then follow the trail that contours, skirting the lake. At the head flats the views of Everest, Lhotse and, later, Makalu are interesting and quite photogenic. Cross the flats and stay to the right. There are some cairns once the rock scrambling begins but no real paths. The idea is to gain altitude up small stream gullies, eventually crossing the main stream that issues from high above. At the first crest the view is quite unexpected and looks substantially different from the view from Gokyo. Again, stay to the right on the flat area. From here note the position of the pass above (it's marked by at least 10 large cairns) and pick your own route up. It's best to ascend following cairns over glacier-rounded slabs to the top of these then skirt south a short distance at a point that looks as if it could be tricky, to find the dusty steep track up. Alternatively, walk alongside the glacier on rough rock and later there is a steep loose scree slope to the dusty track. For the route over the other side see p191.

Donag (the fourth lake, 4870m/ 15,977ft) A track leads up the valley but a more scenic way is to follow the crest of the moraine as far as possible. In about an hour you reach the fourth lake. This is large and beautiful, flanked on one side by sheer cliffs. The most exciting features, however, are the Nameless Fangs.

The Nameless Fangs (5800m/ 19,029ft) It's well worth scrambling up to have a closer look at these tooth-like towers, and the views are fantastic. The climb can be made in a day-trip from Gokyo but with the altitude this is a trip for the fit and acclimatised only. The route up steepens over large boulders, getting quite tricky. It looks as if there is no way on but it's possible to climb over the boulders to the point where you reach a drop to the next tooth, at around 5600m.

The views are simply incredible – the wall between Cho Oyu and Gyachung Kang defies description from this distance and the web of glaciers is fascinat-

ing. There's also the most extensive view of Everest you'll get anywhere in the Khumbu (without resorting to serious mountaineering). You can see part of the Geneva Spur (but not the Hillary Step), the South Col, the stunning Lhotse face and Nuptse. To the north is the famous North Ridge and the First, Second and Third Steps where Mallory and Irvine went missing. The perspective from this point, although not as close as from Kala Pattar, is more realistic than elsewhere.

Ngozumpa (the fifth lake, 4990m/ 16,371ft) This jewel is about one and a half to three hours from Gokyo. Climbing the moraine, the pile of dirt to the east, to overlook the Ngozumpa Glacier also offers a 'scoundrel's view' of Everest that is more extensive than from both Gokyo Ri and Kala Pattar. It's called a scoundrel's view (the local name is Thoknag) because no climbing is involved to reach this 5000m/16,404ft point. There is a tarn (small lake) there and a few dirty, rotten scoundrels have even camped there. Look out for furball pikas beside the trail.

Ngozumpa-tse (Knobby View) (5553m) Another stunning viewpoint, better even than Nameless Fangs. It is also more satisfying in that you can make the actual summit. I rate this as possibly the best viewpoint in the whole Khumbu. The only route that can be recommended is the spur that begins close to the fifth lake. Initially the ridge is steep but it soon eases off. Closer to the top is a steep boulder field (pick your route carefully).

❏ **The Nup La 5985m**

Viewing the icefall that leads to this pass from the peaks above Gokyo, one has to wonder why this was ever named, and whether it has ever been crossed. The name means West Pass, and was named by early explorers to Everest who also named Lhotse, which means south peak, ie south of Everest. Amazingly enough, the Nup La has been crossed, by none other than Edmund Hillary and George Lowe, who, frustrated that the Chinese invasion of Tibet had stopped mountaineering attempts from the north, resolved to visit Everest's north base camp anyway. They also returned by the same route, without getting caught by the Tibetans or Chinese, which was better than Eric Shipton fared – see p98.

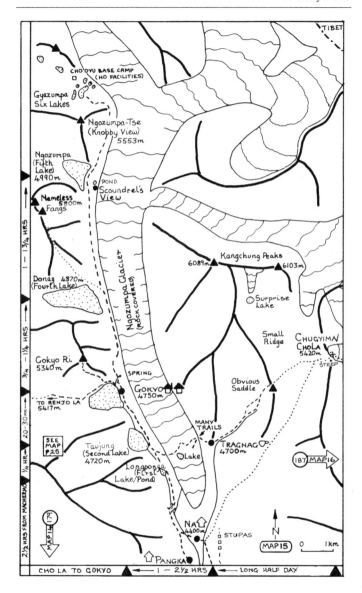

TIBET

CHO OYU BASE CAMP
(NO FACILITIES)

Gyazumpa
Six Lakes

Ngozumpa-Tse
(Knobby View)
5553m

Ngozumpa
(Fifth
Lake)
4990m

POND

Scoundrel's
View

Nameless
5800m
Fangs

Ngozumpa Glacier
(ROCK COVERED)

Kangchung Peaks

6089m   6103m

Donag 4870m
(Fourth Lake)

Surprise
Lake

Small
Ridge

CHUGYIMA
CHOLA
5420m

Gokyo Ri
5340m

STEEP

SPRING

Obvious
Saddle

GOKYO
4750m

TO RENJO LA
5417m

MANY
TRAILS

SEE
MAP
P.25

Taujung
(Second Lake)
4720m

TRAGNAG
4700m

187 MAP 16

Longponga
(First
Lake/Pond)

Lake

MAP 14 179

NA
4400m

STUPAS

N

MAP 15   0   1 km

PANGKA

2½ HRS FROM MACHERMO   ¼ HR — 20-30 m — ¾ — 1¼ HRS — 1¾ HRS

CHO LA TO GOKYO ← 1 – 2½ HRS ← LONG HALF DAY

Once on the main ridge and at the top of what looked like the summit from below is a surprise, the real top is a couple of knobs away, although the false summit will be satisfying enough for most trekkers. The real summit requires some bouldering over steeper ground on the eastern side. From the real summit you overlook Gyazumpa (six lakes) and the exploration possibilities unfold below. With the Cho Oyu-Gyachung Kang wall to the north, the lakes under your toes, glaciers, snow and ice everywhere, this is as alpine a scene as it gets without climbing a major peak.

It is possible to descend due east but this is dangerous. The terrain is very steep, there are a couple of places where you can be bluffed out, and there is a very real rockfall danger. In summary, don't descend on this route. Ascending here would be even trickier, and it isn't obvious.

Gyazumpa/six lakes/Cho Oyu Base Camp The scenery up here is so spectacular it's overwhelming. It's a half-day trek from Gokyo but well worth camping/bivvying here so that you can have more time to appreciate the region. North-east of the flat lakes area it is possible to climb several minor summits, only one of which is marked on the Schneider map. For going where you shouldn't, there is a steepish (technical) ice route to the Sumna Glacier. Despite being labelled Cho Oyu base camp, very few expeditions have used this base camp. All that remains are a couple of shelters and some Russian rubbish. As you might notice, from here, Cho Oyu presents a formidable challenge. The standard route is from the Tibetan side, accessible from just over the other side of the Nangpa La. Cho Oyu is considered one of the least difficult 8000m mountains, if climbing on the standard route from the north-west.

Pass 5443m (17,857ft) Between Gyazumpa and Ngozumpa is a minor pass, marked as 5443m on the Schneider map.

The glacier to the north has an even set of crescent crevasses so stay on the edge or on the rock. It is a bit of a scramble to the top but descent down the other side is pleasant, passing a small lake that begs to be camped by.

Pass 5493m (Ngozumpa) West of the Ngozumpa, the fifth lake, is a pass that has long been known to Sherpas – in contrast the pass 5486m, west of Donag, is unknown to them and requires a rope, if it is passable at all. Conditions have changed since it was regularly used and now the east face is steeper than it used to be. The difficulties are less on the west side. It's difficult to say whether or not it is still easily crossable.

The Tsho La is covered on p186.

TO/FROM PHORTSE [MAP 14: p179] Route from Na to Phortse The quickest route down from Gokyo is via Dole and Machermo. However, rather than back-tracking, there's an alternative trail on the east valley wall directly to Phortse via Na. Note that during the monsoon often there is no bridge between Pangka and Na. So the only way to take this route is to cross the Ngozumpa glacier to Tagnag and descend from there.

Na/Nala (4400m/14,436ft) The tourist world of lycra and thermo-nuclear protection for your eyes has all but passed this place by. There are only two basic places where it's possible to stay and eat.

Leaving Na Aim for the small bridge. The trail is so faint that it can't be seen from the opposite side of the valley but it is there and it becomes clearer.

At **Thare (4300m/14,107ft)** tea and bikkies are served during the high season from the single simple *lodge* here. **Thore (4390m/14,403ft)** also boasts a quaint lone *teahouse* that is occasionally open. Joining the duo is a *teahouse* with a few beds at **Gyengyo**. I have arrived during January and February snow storms, a monsoon downpour, as well as during the normal trekking seasons, to find at least one of these places open. They are all run by women from Phortse who speak little English or Nepali. A short climb leads to the chorten at 4278m/14,035ft with magnificent views.

Konar (4050m/13,287ft) is deserted during the trekking season but with the increasing number of trekkers using this side of the valley expect a lodge here sometime. In summer it's a large hay-growing area. Around the corner all of the trails leads to Phortse.

Phortse (3800m/12,467ft) Pronounced 'Phurtse' by the locals, *phurte* means 'flight', and it's supposed to have gained its name when the Khumbu saint, Lama Sangwa Dorje, landed here after a trance-induced flight. Apparently it was here that he attained enlightenment. It's a picturesque village, magnificently-situated and defended by steep hillsides. The area is famous for its buckwheat but potatoes are also grown in large numbers.

The forests to the south-west and the north are protected by a ban on wood cutting that was made over one hundred years ago by the lama who lived in the forest. In other areas, notably Namche, Khumjung and Khunde, when the government took over control of the forests and redefined the areas that could be cut, the pattern of use changed quickly. Here, the old lama's edict seems to have proved more effective. It is also a shelter for innumerable danphe, other pheasants and deer. Late afternoon is good spotting time: only the blind would miss seeing a variety of wildlife: and they would be likely to trip over them. Phortse is reputed to be one of the most conservative villages in the Khumbu and previously suffered a lack of reasonable lodges. Now *Namaste* and *Phortse* guesthouses in the centre, their names written on the roof, have filled this gap. There are several other simple but pleasant *lodges* at the top of the village and another on the way to the two bigger lodges. Phortse is also home to a number of Everest summiteers, including Panuru (Phortse Guesthouse).

Phortse to Na From the *Khumbu Lodge* at the top of the village head north (left) on a path that follows the walls but stays above the fields. There's another trail that starts from the middle level of the village but it's harder to follow. If in doubt take upper trails.

Phortse to Phortse Tenga The trail starts behind the mani walls at the lower northern part of the village. It's a wide but sometimes slippery track passing through forest where there's a good chance of spotting pheasant. It continues down until you reach the wooden bridge. Close by is a protected stand of trees that is set aside exclusively for bridge repair.

Immediately after the bridge is a junction. Slightly to the right a path leads up to the main trail to the **Dole Checkpost** (p180). The route to the left goes to some reasonable camping spots and Phortse Tenga (p180).

Phortse to Pangboche or Tengboche Walking without watching where you're going could be hazardous on this trail. If you're scared of heights and not happy walking along trails with steep drops beside them avoid this route.

The track starts from the top of the village on a gentle gradient with excellent views of Tengboche.

For the **gentle route to Deboche/ Tengboche**, the turn-off for the bridge that crosses the gorge is immediately after the first small rock cleft. The path heads down steeply before continuing at a more gentle rate of descent. It's not always obvious, sometimes little more than an imaginary trail, and divides many times but it is not easy to become totally lost. Once close to the bridge the path heads up 100m or so to climb over bluffs below, crosses a stream, then drops to join the main Pangboche-Tengboche trail immediately above the bridge.

For Pangboche, at the first rock cleft continue straight on the main trail as it winds and climbs in and out of bluffs. It finishes in Upper Pangboche.

For Tengboche, direct from the

southern corner of the village a trail drops to a small bridge for the steep climb to Tengboche.

From the bridge above Tengboche to Phortse The old path skirting around the bluffs immediately west of the bridge is now disused, for obvious reasons. You must now climb up about 100m on goat tracks until you reach a point where it's easy to cross the little creek to your left. Follow the tiny trail on the other side down to the fields. Work your way across, taking the upper paths where possible until you reach the main Pangboche-Phortse trail.

CHUGIMA LA / TSHO LA / CHO LA
[MAP 16]
Safety
Although the crossing of the Chugima La (5420m/17,782ft) has become popular, it does cross a glacier which could be dangerous. Note the general information on glaciers (see p227). If it has snowed recently either avoid the pass or take great care descending/ascending the smooth slabs on the Gokyo side of the pass and the steep section on the Dzonglha side. If it has snowed heavily or the weather is unstable avoid the pass altogether.

The rock approaches are steep and exposed but present no real problems in good conditions. However the glacier is sometimes icy and treacherously slippery. Porters are never provided with crampons, instead they tie thick string around their shoes at the ball of the foot. This concentrates the load at that point and provides more grip, a handy trick that everybody without crampons should adopt on ice. String can usually be found at Lobuche and Gokyo, as well as on either side of the pass, where it has been discarded.

Crossing between Gokyo and Lobuche in one day is tough; it's much more pleasant to break it up. Now that there are lodges in Dzonglha and Tragnag there are possibilities to suit everyone. Fit trekkers should, in good conditions, be able to make Dzonglha from Gokyo or vice versa, or Tragnag from Lobuche. Groups and trekkers taking it easy break Gokyo to Lobuche up into three days. Note that Dzonglha to Gorak Shep is a relatively easy day, and if you stayed at Gokyo for a few days, Gorak Shep's altitude shouldn't be a problem. For people equipped to sleep outside there are good camping spots between Dzonglha and the pass, and on the Gokyo side there is a huge area worthy of exploration.

Route from Lobuche
Follow the track towards Thuklha but do not continue across the creek: stay on the right (west) side. After a flat area there's an obvious track that contours up around the huge spur to another flat area about an hour away. Up this broad gully is the route to Lobuche Peak Base Camp. Continue straight ahead for the route to the Cho La, climbing to the top of the ridge and then dropping down to an area with many streams. After crossing the biggest of them on a stone bridge the path heads gently up a tiny valley to hidden Dzonglha.

Dzonglha (4850m/15,912ft) This is a summer yak herding station on the left, or south, side of the miniature valley. There are two new *lodges* here, convenient for trekkers crossing the Chugima La. In the quiet seasons ask at Thuklha (where the sister of one of the owners also runs a lodge), Lobuche or Gorak Shep to check that at least one of the lodges is open. If camping, there are suitable watered spots from here up to the beginning of the steep climb.

The approach There are two routes up the pass but one is disused now. After the broad valley the path crosses the main stream, which can sometimes be tricky, then climbs a ridge on the southern side on a clear path. At the rockface the trail virtually disappears. Head right or north and climb up big boulders and slabs staying close to the wall on your left (west). There are a few cairns to look out for and eventually a heavily cairned flattish area is reached. The route continues to climb still staying close to the rock wall which is now to your south since the trail has taken a 90° turn.

If you have crampons head for the glacier as soon as you can see a way onto it, otherwise continue up to where the rock meets an almost flat snowy area. From here the tip of Everest is just visible and down-valley Baruntse begins to look formidable. Little of this wild mountain is normally visible.

Care is necessary as you pass the bergschrund, the gap between the glacier and the rock. It's partly filled with rocks and sometimes crossed by unsafe snow bridges. There's no path here and the route passes within a metre or two of it.

The glacier Stay to the very southern edge of the glacier. Never cross to the middle. Sometimes the footprints stay high on the south bank and at other times they drop down a little. It's very important to keep a good look out for crevass-

es, although they do not often occur on this side of the glacier. The highest point of the pass is at the far end of the snow/ice.

CHUGIMA LA/TSHO LA TO GOKYO
[MAP 15: p183]

Down to Tragnag Before continuing down, have a look at the route possibilities in the valley below. The main valley descends gently to the south to Charchung and Tshom Teng while the route to Gokyo crosses a couple of ridges via a shallow saddle with a large boulder with a cairn on top, the correct route. This saddle is apparently called Tar-Kure or perhaps Targula, meaning like a horse's back.

The descent is via rounded rock ledges which are wide but often slippery. Staying on a track, or sometimes even finding one, is hard. Stay close to the southern rock wall. There are several vague trails and plenty of cairns around/over the rocky ridge to a camping

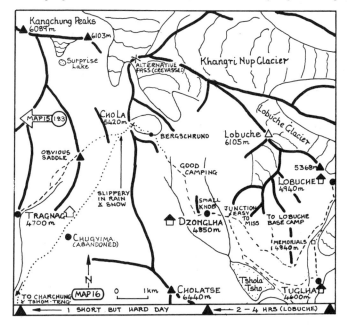

place occasionally used by groups. Once over the shallow saddle it's down, down, down, mainly on the north side of the khola, although the path always looks better on the side that you are not on.

Tragnag (4700m/15,420ft) This collection of yak sheds has grown in the last couple of years to include two real *lodges* which are normally open while the Chugima La is passable. Gokyo is still an hour or two from here over rough ground.

Crossing the Ngozumpa Glacier
Just north, around the corner, is a prominent cairn on the crest of the moraine which you should head for. Scan the glacier and look for signs of the most direct route. The path across is well used but not always obvious and there are older paths further down (glaciers move!). Don't attempt to cross in thick cloud. The walking is tough for tired feet but after climbing the moraine on the opposite side you drop somewhere around the Second Lake.

Route from Gokyo to Lobuche
If you're beginning from Gokyo, start early. From just below the Second Lake look for the trail over the moraine in a small notch. It is essential to find exactly where it begins. Alternatively, descend the moraine where possible and safe from somewhere off the bank of the second lake, onto a small path below that heads south to meet the main trail. You should be able to see the path climbing the moraine on the opposite side to Tragnag. From Tragnag ascend the valley initially on the north side. After 30-40 minutes head up a smaller valley on the left, marked by a couple of cairns. After 15-20 minutes recross the main stream, leaving it behind, and head up to a minor saddle, another 12-20 minutes away. There are new views, including the Cho La, the snowy saddle, which looks formidable from here. Descend, crossing streams, and traverse to a camping area sometimes used by groups. From here the rough rock begins. There are several rough cairned paths that lead to a flat area with a pond

above it. Pick up a trail ascending a debris cone to the southern rock wall.

This ascends moderately steeply and the trail is quite exposed. In deep snow this can be impossible or at minimum highly dangerous. Thirty minutes to 1¼ hours up you reach the glacier and many cairns. Stay high on the southern side. Once you reach the rocks descend on difficult slopes to a set of cairns. Continue down on difficult ground, staying close to the rock wall. At the ridge a clear path descends to the open valley.

Once across the pass itself, the walking in the valley is pleasant.

Dzonglha If you have reached Dzonglha and are contemplating continuing, Thuklha is about an hour away but involves a descent that would be tricky in half-light. Alternatively, about 2 hours of hard walking will bring you to Lobuche.

Khumbu side trips and pass-hopping

Some of these routes are distinctly adventurous so come mentally prepared. On one route, a couple of days from anywhere and on dicey ground, a sherpa employed by some trekkers said, 'I know a shortcut – did you bring a ladder?' They decided to turn back!

Khumbu to Makalu
Crossing between the Everest region and Makalu Base Camp is a route that requires serious planning (see the 1988 National Geographic Mount Everest map) and mountaineering experience. The route is via Sherpani Col (6146m/20,164ft) or East Col (6183m/20,285ft) over the large, almost flat, snow field to West Col (6143m/20,154ft) which drops down a glacier to the 5200m/17,060ft head of the Hongu Basin. There are several ways out of this. You can go over the Mingbo La (5866m/19,245ft), or over the

Amphu Labtsa (5780m/18,963ft) with its steep (or vertical, if your route-finding isn't spot-on) descent and couple of big open crevasses at the base. The third option is down the Hongu valley to Mera La and one more pass to Lukla. These routes should only be attempted by well-equipped, seasoned mountaineers. The survival rate among the inexperienced does not make nice reading.

Makalu Base Camp

A brief discussion of this route was included in the first and second editions. In this edition it has been cut in favour of more space for the Salpa-Arun trek. Information is available on the Internet at: webfoot.co.nz/nepal-treks/info_ma kalu_bc.html.

THE KONGMA LA   [MAP 17]

Meaning Pass of the Snowcock, the Kongma La (5535m/18,159ft) provides an interesting high route between Chukhung and Lobuche. It takes a tough day to walk and is longer than the lower route via Dingboche. If free of snow, it's

a non-technical pass. It requires only a little confidence and steady feet for the last short section to the crest. A walking-stick may be handy. It's more pleasant to do in the Chukhung-Lobuche direction because the walk up is on grass, leaving the rock-hopping and loose scree for the descent. It's really worth camping by the high lakes or even slightly above the pass itself (views in both directions) for the stunning sunset and sunrise.

Route from Chukhung to Lobuche

Contour and cross the large stream issuing from the ablation valley just west of the Nuptse Glacier. Then there's a long climb up the huge grassy ridge. There is no trail, instead aim for the point where the high, sharp rocky spur peters out into the grass. Pick up the track on the western side of this ridge at a high kharka which has some rock shelters and a water source. There are several ways up and the main track from here is easy to lose. It stays above the marshy/icy grass flats, then heads left (north-west), parallel to some bluffs where you may see

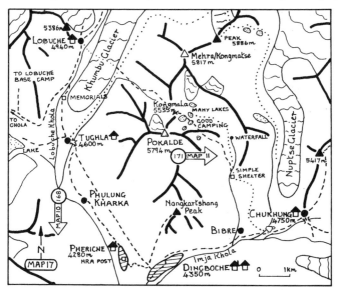

Himalayan thar nimbly cavorting over the sheer rock faces. The track then curves and ascends right to round a big knob of rock (on the right side of it).

The lakes After a couple of climbs and short descents, the lakes are the next stage with the highest being the most beautiful. The sun arrives around here wonderfully early in the morning which makes up for the night temperatures (usually well below 0°C). Even when the lakes are frozen there's a tiny spring by one of the smaller ones.

The Kongma La The track to the pass goes to the right (north) of the highest lake to start the diagonal traverse of the steep face. The pass itself is littered with cairns up each ridge, and 50m to the north up the ridge is a small ledge perfect for a single tent. Bring a block of ice up from the lake as there's no water.

The route down drops only a little while heading right (almost due north) for a long way before beginning a slide down scree. From the ablation valley, crossing the Khumbu Glacier takes another tiring hour before Lobuche appears.

Route from Lobuche to Chukhung

To locate the trail across the glacier from the Lobuche side, head downstream about 200m to a large rock right beside the stream. Perpendicular to the stream at this point there are a couple of tracks on the moraine that head for a small notch. Once across the glacier, take care not to lose the path heading up to the pass.

PEAK 5886m (19,311ft) [MAP 17: p189]

This peak is marked as 5880m on the Schneider map; the lakes below are unmarked. Accessed via the short north summit ridge from east or west sides, it could also be used as a possible glacier pass-hop. There is the odd hole and step in the ice, and a sling plus 10m cord would aid retreat off the scenic lunch spot. Since there are lakes on either side, camping here is easy. A good nose to follow and steady feet are required.

AMPHU LABTSA (5787m/18,986ft) [MAP 11: p171]

The Amphu Labtsa is a tough and dangerous pass, nothing akin to the Tsho La or Thorong La (Annapurna area). It's a mountaineering proposition that leads into some particularly isolated country. You need a climbing-experienced guide who has crossed the passes many times, good equipment and a rope. Each year several porters get frost-bite and ill-prepared trekkers have died here.

The pass is well concealed, visible only as you near it or from Imjatse/Island Peak Base Camp. It's best attempted early in the morning to lessen the danger of avalanche and rockfall. This means camping below at Amphu, a short half-day's walk from Chukhung. This grass/stone area gets very little sun making it one of the coldest parts of the entire valley and it also lacks water. The nearest easily accessible water is a clear spring just west of where the trail joins the Imjatse/Island Peak Base Camp path. Other possible sources are two small lakes above the faint trail and there's also glacier runoff or ice.

Routes to the top of the pass

There are two routes each with a subroute or two. From both sides both routes look sheer but on the way up the route unravels. For the snow/ice route beginning in Amphu, head up the glacier and across the big crevasses to the avalanche-smoothed diagonal gully – the route up. It is possible to stay mainly on rock for the first part even if at first this does not appear to be the case. Then there is a short exposed traverse before the final petit basin to the crest. If you're coming over from the Hongu it's difficult to reach the top of the pass in the correct spot and many lengths of rope testify to the number of parties that decided it was easier to simply abseil down a vertical wall than attempt to find the easiest crossing point. From a distance look for the two low spots. In the centre is a small notch that is slightly higher – the pass.

If snow-free, the higher **rock route** (5900m/19,357ft) is an alternative. Pick up the trail on the way up. One steep section often requires a short rope pitch. From the summit there is a tricky rock trail down. Sometimes it is possible to descend partly on the glacier beside, staying near the rock.

To Mera

Along the shore of the larger lake of Panch Pokhari is a small trail that descends to the other lakes. The trail crosses briefly to east bank of the Hunku/Hongu Khola to skirt the lake marked 5004m on the *Shorong Hinku* map. Otherwise the trail remains on the west bank. See p230 for the Mera La.

MINGBO VALLEY   [MAP 10: p168]

Just above and opposite Pangboche, the Mingbo Valley is an infrequently explored but spectacular valley. Reaching a satisfying distance into it requires an overnight camp and perhaps some acclimatisation.

Leaving Pangboche descend to the bridge, then follow the trail accurately marked on the National Geographic and *Khumbu Himal* maps to the stream just before Mingbo. Here a trail branches off to roughly follow the stream to Ama Dablam Base Camp. The path straight ahead leads to Mingbo with its *goths* which are usually locked. Over the ridge from the Base Camp or 10 minutes north of Mingbo is the outline of the old Mingbo airstrip which was used to ferry supplies to the Tibetan refugees leaving Tibet after China invaded. A glance at the approach will reveal why it is disused now. It was another 'Hillary job'. Several small paths continue up the valley and the keen can scramble to 5700m on the larger of Ama Dablam's southern ridges.

Mingbo La (5800m/19,029ft)

Groups occasionally use this pass rather than the more standard Amphu Labtsa after climbing Mera (p229). The approach from the Hinku Valley up the Hunku/Hongu Nup Glacier is straightfor-

ward although crevassed. Conditions on the Mingbo side vary: sometimes the fluted face drops off at perhaps 60° and requires at least two pitches to reach the glacier proper, sometimes it is tamer, and occasionally it is virtually impassable.

From the pass look for the small trail on the ridge descending from Ama Dablam. Once off the glacier you will have to cross some rough terrain and climb up to this.

THE BHOTE VALLEY

The Bhote Valley (see p25) is closed to trekkers above Thame since it is close to the Chinese border. Foreigners wandering into China this way are simply deposited in jail until Beijing can be contacted. The valley, because it is closed, has generated some special allure but in fact it is very similar to the other main valleys. There are no lodges and no year-round occupied villages above Thame Teng.

With the new trekking regulations (in theory) opening up all of Nepal to specially organised trekking groups, there may soon be tours to the Nangpa La, the trading pass on the Tibetan border. Other areas that would undoubtedly be interesting to explore are Panbug-Na (as marked on the Schneider map) and perhaps the Sumna Glacier.

From the Renjo/Henjo La

From Gokyo to the top of the Renjo/Henjo La (5417m/17,772ft) is described as a day trip from Gokyo. On the Bhote Valley side the descent isn't easy. With snow or ice it could be quite dangerous. The pass itself is long. You can descend in two places to head left (south) along smoothed, slightly exposed slabs close to the bluffs above. Beware of yetis throwing stones down. Then, when you can, head for the lake aiming to go around it on the northern shore. The overflow stream leads to another lake area where there's a *phu* (herding station) with a good small rock shelter. From this point your route depends on your destination. For Thame continue to another *phu* where there's a real track down.

To Nangpa La

Despite the fact that yaks are used for the crossing of this pass into Tibet, it is no ordinary trek. It's tough, even for yaks, judging from the number of carcasses along the track. The trek from Gorak Shep to Everest Base Camp is a trifle compared to the slog over the Nangpa Glacier.

There's shelter and a spring at **Lunag/Lonak** (5070m/16,634ft), the only roofed buildings in either direction for a long way. From here the ground begins to get rougher and water can be hard to find. The scenery also becomes wild. At **Dzasampa** the ablation valley ends and it's time to cross into the middle of the glacier. Conditions are quite variable and it's not difficult to turn an ankle on the rocks which look firmly fixed to the slopes of verglas (glass-ice) but aren't. As you work your way up, concentrating on finding a safe route, the surrounding mountains begin taking on mythical shapes. The rubble gives way to a smooth white glacier with contouring hair-line cracks every 10m or so. Crevasses have, on occasion, swallowed a yak or even a person. The pass is marked in true Tibetan fashion and the view of the purple-brown hills is enough to inspire any explorer. The nights up here are even colder than at the Six Lakes/Cho Oyu BC area.

KYAJO

The Himalaya and Tibet have many legends about mythical valleys accessible only to flying lamas. This is the real thing, a hidden valley that is an absolute delight to explore. The ability to fly at least for short sections would be appreciated: the routes in and out of this valley are adventurous even in the best of conditions. In poor visibility it is easy to lose the trail while in snow the thin trail in and out would be lethal. Yaks do occasionally graze up here but that says a lot about how tough yaks are rather than the quality of the trail. They are the sort of trails that unless you are standing directly on them you would have difficulty believing there is a trail at all.

Without climbing gear take three to four days food otherwise take supplies for at least five days; seven would be better. Increase your chances of success by camping as high as possible.

From Laudo Gompa Continue directly up the ridge. This turns into more of a steep valley that passes between some rock faces. Then head right (at about 4200m) under one rock face on a more distinct trail and follow this up. From around 4300m the small trail begins traversing in and out of ridges to a minor pass at 4525m from where the route becomes more obvious, although it is still small and little used and there is little or no water along this stretch. The consolation is it's on the sunny side of the valley.

Finally traverse and descend to the valley floor at 4450m. Here the valley reveals its glacial heritage; impossibly sheer sides with a crystal creek meandering through. Looking back it feels as if you are looking over at the edge of the world.

The rock wall at the valley head looks formidable but a steep gully does lead to the next flat step. Not much lingers here except snow and ice. Ahead is the last step, topped by a glacier.

Exit via Khunde If you thought the trail in was fun you'll be happy to know the surprises don't end. A couple of short sections of this route follow little more than your imagination. If coming from Khunde you might want to use a rope but heading up you can escape without – just– if you have steady nerves.

(Opposite) Gorak Shep (see p176) in late January. There are several tracks leading up Kala Pattar, the Black Rock. The mountain behind is Pumori.
(Overleaf) The spectacular view from the top of Island Peak (Imja Tse, see p227).

If you are wondering if there is a trail down the valley; at first it looks like it might go, but later it is obvious that there is no way down without a rope.

The route drops under bluffs then climbs a short slippery gully at around 4230m, which is sometimes icy. It looks as if a ledge above this might go but it is even more difficult. These sections are the reason this trail is now barely used.

Traverse around then head up on a real trail up to a pass, 4410m, with views of the civilised world below. Pass by the new water supply tank and piping.

PHAPLU TO RINGMO [MAP 5, p139]
Beginning a trek from Phaplu is a great way to experience the middle-hills Sherpa culture. The main difference is that flying in rather than beginning from Jiri saves all but one hill and two days.

Phaplu
The short runway describes a gentle 'U' shape, a real 'Hillary job'. It was constructed to help build the Himalayan Trust hospital here. The hospital, now government-run, sits a few minutes' walk below the runway.

Phaplu is the airport that services Salleri, the district headquarters of the Solu-Khumbu district. It has a collection of dal bhaat hotels, houses and offices that could more properly be described as mansions and some shops that even stock chocolate. RNAC and the helicopter companies have offices here. It has a strange atmosphere with the large buildings and a rubbish dump in the middle of it all. There is a string of *bhattis*, simple hotels where you can stay. The biggest and most comfortable hotel is the *Hotel del Sherpa*. It is set slightly off the main trail through a *kani*. Ornate dragons guard the main door. Apparently it boasts a sauna but when I visited the hotel there wasn't a soul around.

Leaving north The main trail passes beside the airport. At the Phaplu Gompa the lower trail leads to Junbesi while the higher one leads to Chiwang Gompa.

Chiwang Gompa On the path up it is common to see langur monkeys, squirrels and deer. The gompa is particularly old, being originally built at the time of Lama Sangwa Dorje, and is of an interesting design. Although there is no real lodge, monks will generally invite you into stay with them, and expect a donation for the service. There is also a good camping place a little below the gompa.

Salleri
This is the hustling, bustling district headquarters of the Solu-Khumbu Jila (or district). It has a strange atmosphere, lackadaisical almost to the point of being unfriendly. They aren't used to trekkers but there are several Nepali-style *lodges* and restaurants. The path running through town has been widened with the expectation that the Okaldunga road will be extended to here. It is many years off though.

The Pemba Thuben Choeling gompa, slightly south of Salleri is worth a visit. In part it is funded by the Himalayan Trust and was only completed in 1998.

Route from Phaplu to Ringmo
From Phaplu you can either walk directly to Ringmo or make a very worthwhile detour to Junbesi. For Ringmo, take the wide trail beginning just above the end of the airstrip. There are a couple of basic places en route that could provide lunch, some snacks and even a simple bed. For Junbesi, head north and down to the valley floor. Follow the valley to cross the suspension bridge. This leads to the trail on the northern bank of the Junbesi Khola.

(Opposite) On the summit ridge of Island Peak (Imja Tse). Ama Dablam (top left) takes on a different shape from the familiar view of it you see from the trekking routes.

Route from Ringmo to Phaplu

The junction for the path to Phaplu is obvious at Ringmo but don't believe local assurances that Phaplu is only a couple of hours away. It'll take more than three hours and probably almost five.

The trail is well constructed and passes though some pleasant forest. An hour or so out of Ringmo another path branches off the main trail. This descends to the river and the bridges below to join the track from Junbesi to Phaplu. However, it's better to continue along the main trail, the branch that contours leading to Phaplu without any serious climbs. After many more bends the airstrip at Phaplu comes into view.

To/from Bung direct

Although little used by trekkers, the direct trail between Bung and Salleri is a main local route. Between the two is the Dudh Kosi, which must be descended to, and a high ridge close to Salleri, which must be crossed. It is normally a two-day walk.

From Bung Near the Makalu-Barun National Park and Conservation area post ask for the trail to Sotang. From there keep asking for Salleri.

Slightly above the main trail leading through Salleri is a parallel trail.

Chialsa

This is commonly called a Tibetan refugee camp, implying a temporary nature. Now it is perhaps better called a sanctuary. Although the people are distinctly Tibetan they have adapted and more or less integrated with the surrounding region. For the trekker with energy or time and a desire to learn a little more on Tibet it is well worth a visit. The people are friendly, although not much English is spoken. Ask for the hotel or restaurant. The *hotel* is simple and only has one double room. The food is whatever you can think of that they can make: momos, thukpa (Tibetan soup), fried and boiled potatoes, sukuti (fried dried meat), roti, tsampa and the inevitable Tibetan salt-butter tea.

❏ Tibetans in Nepal

Beginning in 1949 the Chinese built a road to Lhasa so as to 'peacefully liberate' Tibet. This peaceful liberation and the Great Leap Forward, the Cultural Revolution, resulted in the deaths of around one million Tibetans, perhaps a quarter of the population. In 1959 the Dalai Lama, Tibet's leader escaped to India and the consequent fighting set off an exodus of Tibetans. It was estimated by the International Red Cross (IRC) that between 7000 and 10,000 fled over the Nangpa La alone. The IRC set up 10 transit camps throughout Nepal but still many Tibetans died of hunger and disease. In 1961, using thinly veiled threats, China forced Nepal to expel the IRC. The Swiss Red Cross stepped in buying 40 acres of land in Chialsa for the Nepal Red Cross. Tibetans scattered throughout Solu-Khumbu trekked there to establish new, hopefully temporary, lives. During the 1960s and 1970s over 1000 Tibetans lived there. SATA helped with agricultural and handicraft programmes. Carpet-weaving, established in 1961, boomed but by the late 1970s some workers migrated to Kathmandu and set up business there. With intense competition from imitators in the Kathmandu Valley, Chialsa's carpet sales declined to next to nothing by the 1990s. Though high-quality carpets are still made here, to make up for the loss of income five orchards have been planted. After selling in the surrounding area the surplus will be dried, and what is left after that will no doubt be made into brandy!

In 1989 the Nepalese Government stopped allowing Tibetans to seek refugee status in Nepal, although existing Tibetans may remain. Chialsa has been expanded to 100 acres and around 250 Tibetans still live here.

There's an extensive mountain panorama from the top of the ridge, an hour or so up. Apparently even Everest is visible. For less breath-taking views visit the gompa that is ringed by flags. This gompa is one of four that the Dalai Lama commissioned to face Tibet. The others are in India: Zanskar, Ladakh, Bumdila and Deurali-Gangtok (Sikkim).

Heading south Okaldunga is around 36km away, a long day's walk for locals, but two days for loaded porters and trekkers. A road from the Terai to Okaldunga is under construction and will perhaps be completed by the time you read this. Once the new Eastern highway out of Kathmandu is finished as well, this could provide an alternative trekking route to Jiri and the Salpa-Arun. Those that hope that this route might involve no hill-climbing may be disappointed: there is still a 3000m ridge to cross between Okaldunga and Salleri.

Salpa-Arun to the Khumbu

INTRODUCTION

Nowhere in Nepal are the differences between ethnic groups so striking as on the walk between the Khumbu and the Arun Kosi. Although the Sherpa and Rai peoples are both of Mongolian stock and speak Tibeto-Burmese languages, the fact that they live at different altitudes influences many areas of their lives. The Sherpas inhabit the higher regions, growing potatoes and barley or wheat, and have herds of cattle. Throughout the year they wear heavy dark woollen clothing. In contrast the ancient Rai people occupy land at a lower level growing rice, millet and maize. It's warm enough for cotton clothes and they often harvest two crops a year in the frost-free climate.

With more trekkers walking into the Khumbu this way, this section has been

substantially expanded for this edition; I trekked the route no less than three times and Suzanne Behrenfeld, who worked in the region for 18 months, added substantial input. The trail maps have been completely redrawn to approximately 1:100,000, the same scale as the rest of the trail maps. For the Hille-Tumlingtar section the map remains at 1:250,000.

Since **rafting trips** on the Sun Kosi end roughly where the Arun and the Sun Kosi merge it's worth considering doing a trip (see p30) before beginning this trek.

The route

Less experienced trekkers planning to walk in and out (rather than fly from Lukla) should still consider walking in from Jiri then out to Tumlingtar/Hille/Basantpur. The reason is the Salpa-Arun route is tougher than the Jiri to Namche section – the hills are steeper and the lodges are spaced further apart. Being fitter and more used to the trekking lifestyle definitely makes the going easier.

The whole route is surprisingly sparsely populated so some planning is required, at the very least at the beginning of the day, to work out where you can eat

❑ **The first trekkers**
The first foreign visitors to the Khumbu were Tilman, Oscar Houston and his wife, Dr Charles Houston and a couple of other companions. This was perhaps the first true trek undertaken in Nepal; it was purely for pleasure, rather than science and mountaineering. They trekked from Dharan to the Khumbu and back during November 1950. Their trek in via Salpa-Arun was considerably more pleasant than the Everest reconnaissance of 1951, lead by Eric Shipton, who trekked in during the monsoon. His party had great difficulty in recruiting porters, had to avoid villages struck by bubonic plague, suffered leeches, and were even attacked by hornets.

lunch then stay. Virtually every lodge there is, as of October 1997, is mentioned in this section.

When beginning in the Arun valley the hills to be climbed are initially more challenging than when coming in from Jiri. The first pass you come to is, in fact, the highest pass on the route. Tumlingtar to Namche involves somewhere around 10,000 vertical metres of ascent (and 7000m of descents).

The most sensible place to begin this trek is from Tumlingtar airport. Other possibilities are Hille, Basantpur or Bhojpur (p211). In late 1991 the Hille road was extended to Basantpur giving a choice of two routes to Tumlingtar, of roughly equal length. From Hille the track immediately drops to the Arun Kosi and follows it up, while from Basantpur you traverse a ridge, with a chance to visit historic Chainpur, then drop to Tumlingtar. At present Hille and Basantpur are a rough long drive from Kathmandu. Eventually the new East-West highway from Kathmandu will shorten this trip by something like 10 hours.

From the flats of Tumlingtar the trail crosses the mighty Arun river then climbs over a spur to follow the Irkhuwa Khola up to Phedi (which means bottom of the hill). From here it is a long climb to the top of the first pass, the Salpa Bhanjyang (3349m/10,987ft), the highest pass en route. The Surkie La (3085m/10,121ft) then the Satu La (3173m/10,410ft) follow in quick succession. Between them, of course, are deep valleys. The route joins the main Dudh Kosi trekking highway from Jiri between Puiyan and Kharikhola.

The route description below follows the trail in the Hille/Tumlingtar to Lukla direction. At the end of each section there are notes for trekkers walking in the opposite direction (Lukla to Tumlingtar/ Hille), marked '▲'.

Timing

The amount of time required for this walk varies considerably. Namche to Hille/Basantpur can take 10 to 12 days. Walking in, with the usual initial lack of fitness, may even add another day. Flying to/from Tumlingtar reduces this by two days, or by a day via Bhojpur.

There are no places en route that warrant a full day's stop, although this is no reason not to spend a day or two relaxing on the way, or have some short walking days.

On the way out the fit and hill-hardened could reduce Namche to Hille to five and a half tough days.

❏ The Salpa-Arun Conservation Project

This was created in the spring of 1997; a joint effort between the lodge owners from Pangum to Kartiki Ghat and the Makalu-Barun Conservation Area. It is an attempt to maintain the uniqueness of this off -the-beaten-track route through conservation education for both locals and tourists, promoting sustainable tourism practices.

An increase in trekkers in the area (700 registered in 1996, up from 350 in 1995) prompted desire for assistance with development. Every lodge owner along this route met for a one day Appreciative Planning and Action (APA) meeting in Bung to work together in guiding their future. A lodge management committee was developed which than organised a seven day lodge management training with technical assistance coming from the MBNP and Kathmandu. During this week, the lodge owners learned about first aid, hygiene, housekeeping, conservation, lodge-style cooking and English skills. The participants also took great interest in discussing and defining development and created a game plan to help maintain cultural integrity and improve conservation practices for this trek. These new skills will take time to refine, and don't be afraid to offer suggestions. It will be interesting to track the developments.

Facilities

Between the Arun and the Dudh Kosi there's a scattering of *lodges*, and family homes masquerading as lodges, that offer food and a bed. These have sprung up only relatively recently and their varied standards add to the pleasure of trekking along this route. Do not expect apple pie or pizza here. In fact, don't expect even a menu, just a share of what the family is eating. The lodge owners along this route have decided not to provide menus due to lack of resources and variety. If price is a concern, ask before ordering. Many people seem to expect rock bottom local rates rather than prices that actually reflect the true costs of running a small lodge. Although at a lower elevation than the Sagarmatha National Park, most products are portered in so prices remain somewhat high. The majority of lodges have at least a dormitory and simple double rooms are becoming more common.

The Arun Valley itself still has few facilities specifically for trekkers. Instead there are many bhattis and tea shops catering for the multitude of porters that transport goods up and down the valley. Often, families curious about foreigners will invite trekkers to stay. Sleeping out on the banks of the river under the stars is another possibility. There are a number of stone shelters, mainly used by porters who cannot afford to pay for accommodation, so **camping** is an alternative. You can also pitch a tent outside most lodges.

During peak seasons the lodges are modestly stocked with supplies for trekkers: muesli, porridge, packet soups etc. Trekking off season some lodges may be closed and you might find little more than biscuits in the way of supplies.

Biratnagar

Nepal's second largest city is an air hub and trading centre for the east. The majority of trekkers sensibly manage to avoid it, as I have, hence the short description. The airport is well out of town, the bus station is in the centre of town and hotels are scattered randomly. There are frequent night buses to Kathmandu.

HILLE TO TUMLINGTAR [MAP 18, p199]
Hille (1850m/6069ft)

The mass of shops, the dust and throngs of porters are all typical of villages that have been turned into ugly towns overnight with the arrival of a road.

If you've travelled non-stop from Kathmandu, you'll probably arrive mid-afternoon and feel the worse for wear. There are a few *lodges* scattered along the road, nothing special but they're OK.

The start of the main trail to the Arun is not particularly obvious. It begins at the top end of town, descending west on a path lined with dirty tea shops before opening out towards Pakribas. Ask directions frequently or follow a heavily laden porter. This is a major staging point for the goods heading up valley so there are numerous shops competing for the same market and the flow of porters is almost continuous. The goods are destined for villages scattered over a wide area and some are even traded across the border with Tibet. If you are feeling the heat it might be worthwhile hiring a porter (ask around at the lodges) for the stretch to Tumlingtar.

Early starts in this hot low country are the way to go, hopefully leaving the hot midday for a siesta and swimming.

▲ First impressions of this town may not be pleasing although after the peace of a few weeks' trekking, any town is liable to induce some form of culture-shock.

The last bus down leaves about 2pm and usually goes as far as Dharan. If you've missed the 4pm Dharan to Kathmandu bus, head for Itahari where many buses stop on the way to Kathmandu. An alternative is to go to the pleasant hill-town of Dhankuta, which the main road by-passes, and spend the night there.

Pakribas On occasions the road has been motorable to here. The town is ugly but there are some simple **restaurants** and **hotels** where it is possible to stay. As with all roads into the hills it take a while to walk out of their influence. If the weather is clear, the views of Makalu and the surrounding peaks are inspiring.

The British Pakribas Agricultural Research and Development Project is modestly famous throughout Nepal. It is largely as a result of their work that the concept of kitchen gardens growing vegetables and herbs has been established. Much of their work is also developing new high yield and disease-resistant crop strains.

Mangmaya (250m/746ft)   At the Mangmaya Khola and the small village beside the bridge the trail meets the Arun. There are a few simple bhattis here where trekkers occasionally stay. From here it's a long day's walk to Tumlingtar.

With several of the tributaries of the Arun you have the option of crossing on the suspension bridge or, if the stream is low, wading across.

▲ If you stay here begin in the cool early morning for the long hill climb. Across the bridge take the trail to the left, although it's not very obvious, which leads up the hill; the trail to the right does not go to Hille. Now the route climbs out of the hot valley, through many villages where you can get hot and cold drinks. The path divides and rejoins many times on the way up. After gaining a ridge the trail levels off as it nears Pakribas.

Along the Arun Kosi   The trail mainly follows the river, taking several shortcuts when it is low. The Sabbhaya Khola is a delightful spot for a siesta and swim. The water is refreshing and usually crystal clear. Ascend to the Tumlingtar plain.

Basantpur to Tumlingtar

For information on the first part of this route see the Web site (address p50).

Chainpur   Chainpur is famous throughout Nepal for the brass pots, pans and dishes that are made here. The brass comes from Singapore (and has done for the last 70 or so years) and is worked by skilled crafts' people. Since brass is valuable and not the lightest material to transport every effort is made to recycle old and dented objects. Some are salvaged from villages up to five days' walk away.

Tumlingtar (515m/1700ft)

Arriving here from Kathmandu is like stepping back in time. The runway is grass-covered with a simple fence to keep the cows and goats out. The hotels are virtually the only buildings around so getting lost is difficult. The majority of the hotels are grouped along the main track and there are a couple more slightly north-east by the pits dug for the manufacture of mud bricks. They mainly cater to the locals arriving and leaving by plane, although a couple can do pancakes for foreigners that want them. Cold beer is cheaper than in Thamel. Tumlingtar has a phone system – all local numbers start 029 69. *Hotel Makalu* is 057 and *Hotel Kanchenjunga* 120.

On a clear day mountains rise surreally out of the heat haze. Chamalang is the left-most peak and Makalu is the right-most peak, often with a tell-tale cloud spinning off it, jet stream turbulence.

Most flights arrive mid- to late afternoon. If you arrive early you could walk south for a swim, begin trekking or wander up the main track to the east to a modestly higher plain and wander around the scattered houses.

▲ If you're not flying out there's no compelling reason to stay the night here. From here until the approach to Hille, the trail has few hills, at least no major climbs.

If you are flying, find out what time the airline office opens and book or reconfirm your flight. For RNAC flights note that there are two seats reserved for government officials that, if unused, can only be booked the evening before, or the same day as the flight. There are flights to Kathmandu and to Biratnagar. Tumlingtar is one of the few rural airstrips long enough to handle an Avro (a twin-engined 48 seater).

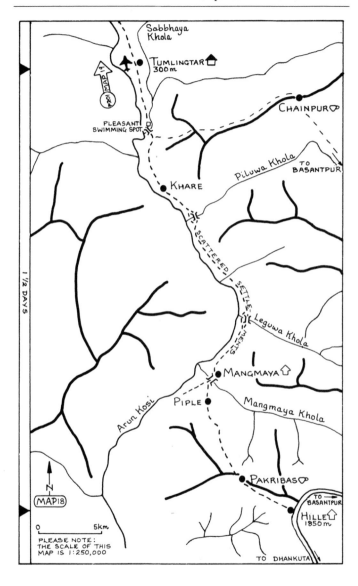

TUMLINGTAR TO BALAWA BESI [MAP 19]

Assuming you are staying the night at Tumlingtar, Chewa Besi is the place for lunch although the quick may make Kartiki Ghat. There are several choices for where to stay. The first village after the spur is Mardura, then there is Charlissay, where women commonly invite you in. Reaching Gothe Bazaar (pronounced Goatay) is for those keen to put in a harder day.

If you flew in and made it to Kartiki Ghat or Balawa Besi that evening then the next day aiming for Dobani, or for the fit, Tallo Phedi, is realistic.

Leaving Tumlingtar Beat the heat by starting early. The main path heads north from the hotels and passes to the left, or west, side of the brick pits. Follow the electricity poles. The track is straight, passing the occasional house and shop. After an hour the trail drops close to the river bank and uses every opportunity to follow the shore. At Kartiki Ghat a suspension bridge crosses the Arun, a short half-day's walk from Tumlingtar. Sometimes a small bridge tax is collected. There are plenty of simple restaurants and it is possible to find a rough bed although Balawa Besi with its one lodge is only a few minutes away.

The Dingla alternative The standard trekking route (as described) is the shortest trail. In fact the main trail detours via Dingla, a bazaar. Although it is a main route, Dingla to the Salpa trail, see p212, isn't straightforward trekking.

Balawa Besi

This is a bridge across a sparkling khola plus a few houses and a simple *lodge*.

Leaving, cross the sturdy frame bridge and head right past the **teashacks** and homes then head left climbing up and up. At first the trail is clear but approaching the top of the spur there are trails everywhere. I doubt I have taken the same one twice. Locals point the way but few speak English. It is a 600m climb.

Heading down and traversing from the top of the spur repeatedly ask the locals for the track to Phedi and Salpa Bhanjyang. It is probable that the trail from Balawa Besi to Gothe Bazaar will be considerably improved and hence easier to follow if a UK trail improvement project goes ahead. In fact the plan is considerably more ambitious; it is possible that they improve the trail all the way to Phedi.

BALAWA BESI TO TENDOR [MAP 20, p202-3]

Mardura/Marduwa From the top of the spur Mardura is approximately 20 minutes beyond. Follow the most worn track (ask too!) through terraced fields. Between Mardura and Charlissay basically contour around a small bowl.

Charlissay is the name of a Chhetri caste that lived in these areas generations ago. It is said that they now live in the Kathmandu Valley. Villagers, usually older women invite you to stay.

From here the main trail is around 20-25 minutes away. Contour and cross a small ravine. Once out of this head for two large pipal trees with a chautara and rejoin a larger clear trail here.

▲ If you continue to stay on the main trail after the pipal trees this leads to Dingla and an alternative route to Tumlingtar. This route requires more climbing than the shortcut round the ridge.

From the pipal trees Descend through dense semi-tropical forest to the Irkhuwa Khola. A few minutes along the bank is a **teashack**, *Tabutar*. Between here and Gothe Bazar the trail and point where it crosses the Irkhuwa Khola changes regularly – ask!

Gothe Bazaar (775m/2550ft) After crossing the Irkhuwa and climbing a small hill you reach the delightful settlement of Gothe. There are two *lodges*. The people here are Rai and Gurung (who come from the Pokhara region).

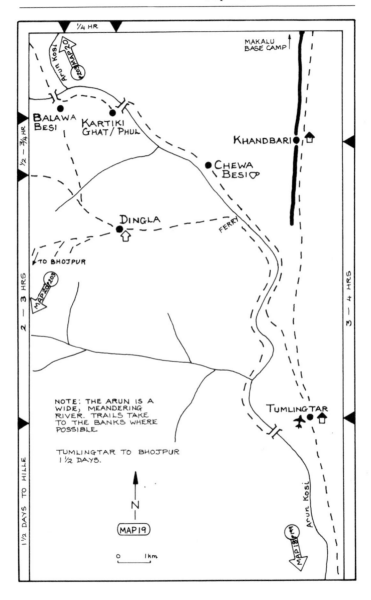

¼ HR

Arun Kosi

P20 MAP 20

MAKALU
BASE CAMP

BALAWA
BESI

KARTIKI
GHAT/ PHUL

KHANDBARI

CHEWA
BESI

DINGLA

FERRY

TO BHOJPUR

MAP20 P203

NOTE: THE ARUN IS A
WIDE, MEANDERING
RIVER. TRAILS TAKE
TO THE BANKS WHERE
POSSIBLE.

TUMLINGTAR

TUMLINGTAR TO BHOJPUR
1 ½ DAYS.

N

MAP19

0   1 km.

½ – ¾ HR

2 – 3 HRS

1 ½ DAYS TO HILLE

3 – 4 HRS

Arun Kosi

MAP18 P144

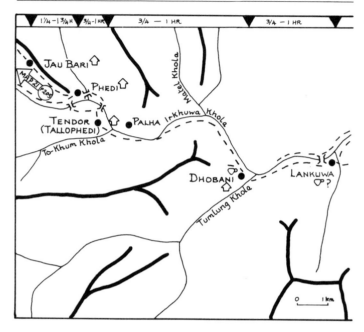

Lankuwa (875m/2870ft) The people here have aspirations of starting a lodge but it is difficult to see this happening. Tea may be available.

Dobani/Doban (975m/3200ft) At the confluence of two rivers is a small cluster of buildings including a small *lodge*. Around this region paper is made by hand (see opposite p224) for the Kathmandu market. Here and at Tallo Phedi you can watch the process and buy some of the finished product.

Leaving Dobani, the track divides: take the immediate right turn, the slightly smaller path. The potential for getting temporarily lost around this area is high. This trail roughly stays above the Irkhuwa Khola for a while.

Look out for cardamom (*elaichi*) plants in small fields in the cool shaded forest. In early October they are distinctive for having a red fleshy-flower at the

base of a 1-1.5 metre stem with well-spaced leaves around 30cm long. By the end of October the stem withers and all that's left is the thick red flower with mainly white seeds. The plants are used for soil conservation and as an income generator, the seeds being sold in Kathmandu. Among other things it is added to tea to produce the distinctive Kashmiri brew.

Tendor/Tallo Phedi (1400m/4600ft) Don't confuse Tallo Phedi (lower bottom of the hill) with Phedi (merely bottom of the hill). There is a **paper factory**, shop-cum-café and a single new Rai *lodge*. Leaving, descend into the gully. At the next village Tendor, there is a choice of two trails. One climbs the ridge to Chole then contours and descends to the suspension bridge. The other, more usual, route stays low by the river to **Phedi**, which is just around the corner.

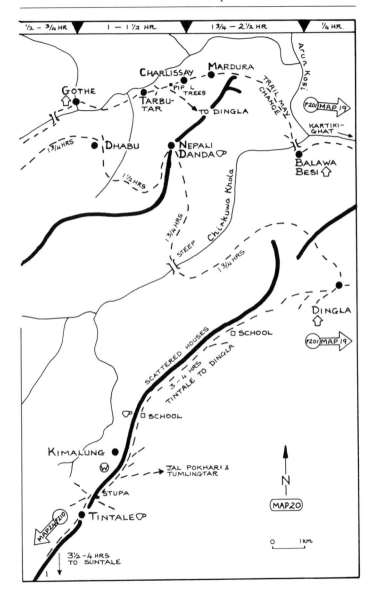

½ – ¾ HR.   1 — 1½ HR.   1¾ – 2½ HR   ¼ HR.

Arun Kosi

CHARLISSAY   MARDURA

GOTHE

PIP L
TREES

TARBU-
TAR

TO DINGLA

TRAIL MAY
CHANGE

P201 MAP 19

KARTIKI-
GHAT

1¾ HRS   DHABU   NEPALI
DANDA

BALAWA
BESI

1½ HRS

1¾ HRS

STEEP   Chi-+kuwa Khola

1¾ HRS

DINGLA

SCATTERED HOUSES   SCHOOL

3 - 4 HRS
TINTALE TO DINGLA

P201 MAP 19

SCHOOL

KIMALUNG

JAL POKHARI &
TUMLINGTAR

N

STUPA

MAP 20

MAP 21 P210   TINTALE

0   1 KM

3½ – 4 HRS
TO SUNTALE

Phedi 1700m/5575ft Virtually at the confluence of two rivers, Phedi boasts three simple *lodges*, the lowest houses of the village. Trekking up through the village, if in doubt take two lefts and follow the steps. By this stage of the trek you have already gained 1400m, perhaps barely noticing it. But from here the real climb begins – with the killer stone steps. At the same time as cursing the never-ending steps one has to wonder who built them. Was it a labour of love, was it for money, or for penance, and how old are they? It's a very tough day from Phedi to Sanam so an early start is required. It's not a bad idea to see if you can find a porter to help for this stretch, especially if you are not so fit.

Jau Bari/Thulofokte (2300m/7550ft) The trail is relentlessly steep, brutal at the end of the day, to this spread out small settlement. There are three scattered *lodges*.

▲ Prepare to fall off the end of the world!

JAU BARI TO SANAM   [MAP 21]
Gurase (2920m/9580ft) After cresting the sharp ridge there is a flattish area with a pond and a stone shelter. The trail to Gurase (pronounced Gurasé) stays on the south side of the main ridge. The trail up the ridge goes to Salpa Pokhari. Gurase is about 20 minutes past the pond.

This is a rhododendron region, *laligurans* or *laliguras* in Nepali. There are a couple of buildings, both *lodges* although only one is generally open year-round.

▲ The thin track runs though untidy grazing land to pass by a pond with a stone shelter, then climbs to the crest of the obvious razorback ridge and descends steeply.

Salpa Bhanjyang (3349m/10,987ft) A weathered chorten graces the top of the pass. Slightly better views can be had by climbing south for a short distance. The pass also marks the boundary of the Bhojpur district, which you have been in

since Kartiki Ghat or Bhojpur. You are now entering a Sherpa region.

The path down soon follows a stream and passes a few old mani walls. At the main valley, well down, the track to Sanam is on the north bank of the Lidung Khola. There's a camping place here. Later, where the trail emerges from the forest is Orkobug/Whaka, a *teashack* is developing. The trail mainly traverses to Sanam, which is well above this river and around 40 minutes away.

The top part of the pass receives snow during the winter and the locals may wait several days after a fall before crossing. If the track is covered by snow, the route can be slippery and challenging to follow.

▲ Going down the other side is easy. Follow the stone track that curves left, and continue roughly in the same direction, eventually to Gurase.

Side trip to Salpa Pokhari (3460m/11,350ft) This trail begins on the right side of the large boulder, to the north of the chorten on the pass. Traverse northeast, gradually ascending for 30 minutes and walk through a flat open area. A large stupa marks the start of the holy area.

Side trip to Silingchuk (4156m/13,630ft) A difficult scramble on narrow, steep, almost non-existent trails. Don't attempt this climb in winter with snow lying around. There are no possible camping spots on or near the top. Locals swear there is a route from Silingchuk to Sanam and Gudel but the only way to find this would be to take a local guide.

Sanam (2650m/8700ft)
'Land of the Sky' is the Sherpa translation of Sanam. The locals are keen for trekkers' business and all the houses there seem to be turning themselves into *lodges* or *homestays*. Some even have double rooms.

The gompa is also being renovated. Delicious dairy products are often available here.

▲ In reverse The pass is a half day's walk from Sanam and is not at the obvious head of the valley but up a small valley to the right or south. Note that in dry conditions the Lidung Khola is often the last source of water until well over the pass.

SANAM TO NAJING DINGMA [MAP 22, p207]

Tiu/Duire (2600m/8500ft) Means mare and .commemorates the fact that once someone was silly enough to bring one up here. There are a couple of simple *lodges*, one with an attached small shop.

Nimtsola/Gompa The monastery here gives tutelage to a number of boys from the surrounding villages. As of 1997 there was only a single *teashop* but the people are friendly, offering tea and food.

Gudel (1950m/6400ft) The main trail leads to a mani (visible from afar) on the ridge that overlooks the large Rai village of Gudel. As well as Gudel and Bung the panorama includes the Naulekh Mountains (which hide Mera) and, for keen eyes, the Chambaling (Boksom) Gompa. Look for Gudel's new *lodge*, one of the largest buildings in the core of the village beside the main trail. CARE International has a local **healthpost** here.

Leaving Gudel From Gudel you can see the trail from the bridge zigzagging up to Bung. Follow the stream on a mainly stone path for a while. Then the trail veers right (north) away from the stream, and down towards a beautiful waterfall before cutting back south-west to the bridge that crosses the Hongu Khola at about 1280m/4200ft. Bung begins approximately 10 minutes up. The *Dudh Kosi* Schneider maps mark the trails in and out of Gudel inaccurately.

Note the large stream north of Bung: for several hours the trail above Bung stays approximately parallel to this but about half to one km away.

▲ Gudel to Sanam Climb on one of several trails to the mani walls above Gudel on the spur to the south. From here the wide trail climbs gently but steadily, hugging the steep valley wall. Once the

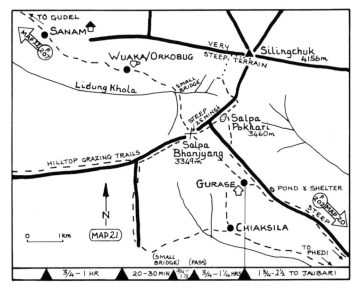

mani walls are out of sight, you come to a major junction and for a change you must follow the trail that contours, not climbs. At the next two major junctions however, take the upper trails.

Bung

Meaning beautiful flower in Rai, this is the largest (Kulung) Rai village of the region and is spread over a large hillside. There are now at least two *lodges* close to the bottom of the village (1420m/4650ft) then there is a second cluster around the Makalu-Barun Conservation Area Bung sector headquarters (1800m/5900ft).

This region is known for its *tungba,* an alcoholic brew served in a tall wooden vessel and drunk using a bamboo straw. Boiling water is poured over fermented millet to make this warming drink. If there's a really big celebration it's served in a barrel, everybody using their own straw. The more mature the millet, the smoother the taste with a special vintage (rarely served to tourists) being about a year old.

Makalu-Barun National Park
Bung sector checkpost A few people seem to resent paying the entry fee here. If you have a look around the centre and discover what has been and is being done in the region, you will quickly realise that your fee is a mere drop in the bucket; tens of millions of rupees have been spent (wisely). In 1996, trekkers paid a little under half a million rupees, of which Rs175,000 ended up here. Of direct benefit to the trekker has been the lodge management courses that have provided improved lodges from Kartiki Ghat to Shubuche. See p114 for more information on the park and conservation area.

To Phaplu The trail starts at the MBN-PCA sector office. The path to Sotang contours and is easy to follow. See p194.

Cheskam   Locals here are keen to attract trekkers to their large Rai village although it is somewhat off the usual route. There is one small *lodge* run by

Sherpas. Bung to Cheskam takes at least two hours, perhaps a short half day at a slower pace. The trail from Bung starts at the MBNPCA sector office. It is also possible to trek from Gudel and from a little below the Surkie La.

▲ **In reverse**   From Bung it's a short day's walk to Sanam or one very long and tough day to Ghorashey. It's possible to camp after Sanam but not on top of the pass since there is no water there. Leaving Bung, there is a maze of paths, hopefully sign-posted. After some clumps of bamboo there are many tracks and slips but most lead to the suspension bridge Take the left fork after crossing the bridge for the steep ascent to Gudel.

Khiraunle-Chambaling Gompa
After an initial steep ascent out of Bung the trail eases to a continuous gently ascending traverse. It's easy to get lost as there are numerous trails, but all lead close to Chambaling Gompa (several hours away) and its distinctive ring of large trees. The main trail is perhaps half a kilometre above this. The friendly owners of a small new *lodge* close to the gompa are intent on creating a new trail that passes through a school then on to the gompa and their lodge. It isn't necessary to take this new trail; the lodge is only five minutes off the main trail higher up, and is of course, also signposted. However, once the new path is finished it may prove marginally quicker. The gompa is being rebuilt and you are welcome to look around.

Surkie/Sipki La (3085m/10,121ft)
Above the gompa on a ridge are some chortens followed by some mani walls before entering a beautiful mainly rhododendron forest. At a *teashack* there is a major trail junction: go up for the pass. This is an uneventful pass although you can see Khatang and Numbur, collectively called Shorong Yul La, the holy mountains of the region around Junbesi. The descent is initially quite steep (and icy in winter) through bamboo groves.

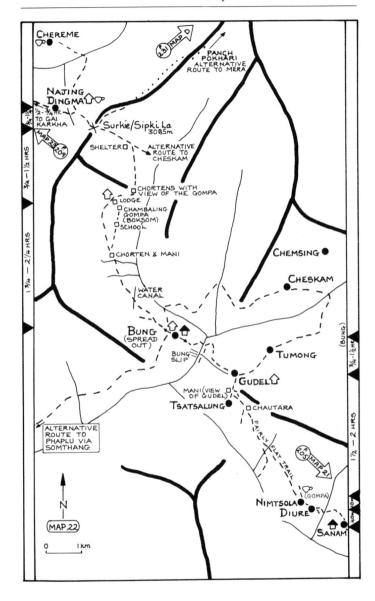

CHEREME

NATING
DINGMA

½-¾ HR
TO GAI
KARKHA

MAP 23 P.209

¾ – 1½ HRS

1 ¾ – 2¼ HRS

PANCH
POKHARI
ALTERNATIVE
ROUTE TO MERA

MAP D p.231

Surkie/Sipki La
3085m

SHELTER

ALTERNATIVE
ROUTE TO
CHESKAM

CHORTENS WITH
VIEW OF THE GOMPA

LODGE

CHAMBALING
GOMPA
(BOKSOM)

SCHOOL

CHORTEN & MANI

CHEMSING

CHESKAM

WATER
CANAL

BUNG
(SPREAD
OUT)

BUNG
SLIP

TUMONG

(BUNG)

¾ – 1½ HR

GUDEL

MANI (VIEW
OF GUDEL)

TSATSALUNG

CHAUTARA

ALTERNATIVE
ROUTE TO
PHAPLU VIA
SOMTHANG

FAIRLY FLAT TRAIL

MAP 21 p.205

1½ – 2 HRS

HR p.107

NIMTSOLA

DIURE

(GOMPA)

SANAM

N

MAP 22

0   1 km

Najing/Naji Dingma is on a flat grassy knoll at 2650m/8694ft. Here, among the few houses are two *teahouses* and a small shop. These are run by people, often kids, from the Sherpa village of Cheram (Chereme on the *Shorong/Hinku* Schneider map).

Although most trekkers take the shorter Gai Kharka route to Shubuche it is possible to go via **Cheram**. Cheram is a worthwhile side trip as the locals are hospitable and the new gompa (which serves as both a religious and community centre) radiates the commitment of locals meeting and working together to make life better. The gompa has partly been funded by MBNPCA as part of their cultural preservation policies. Continuing problems with crop production is forcing the people of Cheram to look for for alternative income generating activities. They are now seeking support in constructing a through trail for trekkers to Mera Peak and a 6kw hydro-electric project in the hope of producing rhododendron and juniper perfume, nettle fabric, handmade paper and incense. You can stay in Cheram, although there are no real lodges. People from Najing Dingma can show you the way.

GAI KHARKA TO PUIYAN [MAP 23]
Gai Kharka means cow pasture, but now the area is under cultivation. Apart from a new water tap there are no facilities for trekkers. It is easy to lose the way. At first stay right on trails then once well down, a path leads across a small stream then

❏ Allo
Nettle fibre,*allo,* was once the main source for cloth. A few items, such as vests, are still main from allo-but weaving has greatly decreased owing to the the ready availability of cotton clothes. Weaving classes are being offered by the Makalu-Barun Conservation Area as an income-generating activity and to help preserve this part of the Rai heritage.

heads up – but three metres after crossing the stream another trail, only visible when you're almost upon it, heads down. Take this down a minor ridge. In all it takes approximately 15 minutes to descend through Gai Kharka.

Bridge over Inkhuwa/Inukhu/Hinku Khola (1850m/6069ft) A MBNPCA sign marks the border of the conservation area. The bridge was built in 1993 by the Himalayan Trust with money provided by Canada International development Association (CIDA). It is an impressive height above the river, and even more impressive are the hills on the western side. This is one brutal, unrelentingly steep hill.

Shubuche/Shiboche The fields begin as the hill relents in gradient but it is still perhaps half an hour to the main *lodge* of Shubuche. This lodge is occasionally closed: either temporarily while the family work the fields, or sometimes completely closed while the family goes shopping. One other family sometimes offers to put up trekkers. There are great views of the Inkhu Valley and the peaks of Mera.

▲ In the opposite direction The trail continues straight to the end of the ridge, crossing a fence or two then drops off (literally), turning slightly south. It's a very steep, knee-jerking descent.

Satu/Pangum La (3173m/ 10,410ft) Ahead on the far side of the valley you may just be able to make out the trail heading up to the Trakshindo La on the Jiri route. Looking behind you across the valley it's possible to see Najing Dingma, about two-thirds of the way up the previous ridge.

Pangkongma/Pangum (2850m/9350ft) The village has a wonderfully-located 1970 Hillary school and a gompa. There are two *lodges* and being close to the main Jiri route they use the menu system.

Leaving Pick up the trail at the parallel mani walls just below the lodges and head north-west. Bupsa can be seen on the ridge slightly north and Kharikhola below on the southern wall of the valley. At first the trail is straightforward but further on are several junctions that can be confusing. Ask directions for Bupsa, Kharikhola or Puiyan.

▲ From the main trail to Pangkongma
The main Namche to Kharikhola trail can be left at Puiyan, Bupsa (possibly the best option) or Kharikhola. It is about half a day's walk to Pangkongma (sometimes called Pangum) from these places. At the

beginning of Pangkongma after two approximately parallel mani walls walk to the left and head up to a group of houses and lodges.

If you're very fit you may be able to reach Najing Dingma from Bupsa in a day, or make Bung from Pangkongma or Shubuche. For most people, from Pangkongma or Shubuche to Najing Dingma is a long day. Carry lunch and snacks.

Route from Puiyan
Ten minutes north of Puiyan is a big boulder that makes an attractive view-point. From here the several trails south of

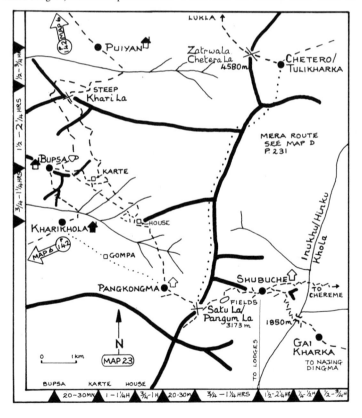

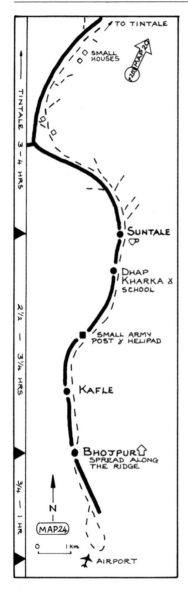

Puiyan are visible. You can also see the rocky gully that the main Namche trail traverses. Just visible above is a trail which can be reached by a short scramble up the rocks and a slip to the path. This is part of the old route between Puiyan and Kharikhola, via Kharte. The present direct trail to Bupsa was constructed in the early 1980s. Head over the ridge and the **Khari La (3081m/ 10,108ft)** and down to the distinctive two-storey white house (a couple of hours in total). Five minutes below is the main trail leading to Pangkongma, heading up the valley.

Route from Bupsa
Go straight up the ridge behind the *Solu Khumbu Trekkers' Lodge* on a mainly mud trail. At the mani wall further up, just before the two-storey white house, turn right and contour or drop to the main trails ahead and below. The Bupsa-Pangkongma trail is narrow but well-used and contours with some real ups and downs. A couple of days before the Namche Saturday market the trail is crowded with heavily-laden porters heading for the bazaar.

Route from Kharikhola
The locals recommend going via Bupsa, although there is a direct trail from Kharikhola after the maze of fields. Pass by a gompa on the way.

BHOJPUR TO SALPA BHANJYANG
[MAPS 24, 20: p202-3, 21: p205]
This is tourist-free Nepal. Since there aren't the trekkers lodges this route to Salpa Bhanjyang is better attempted with a Nepali-speaking guide or by the most adventurous of trekkers. Occasionally groups begin from here. The advantages of a Bhojpur beginning over Tumlingtar are that this mainly ridge route is cooler during the Arun's steamy months of October and April-May.

There are RNAC passenger flights from Biratnagar and Kathmandu. Helicopters operate irregular cargo flights only from Biratnagar.

Bhojpur airport

The short runway is nestled amid paddies. You are dumped rather suddenly into rural Nepal. It is a pretty region and reasonably developed. Bhojpur is approximately ³/₄ hour's walk. There are several trails, all easy enough to lose so follow locals. Bhojpur is at an angle of approximately 25 degrees east from the direction in which the plane lands.

Bhojpur

Among Nepalis Bhojpur is famous for *khukri* (Gurkha army knives) and *suntala*, Nepali oranges. The bazaar stretches along a ridge and is almost big enough to lose your way in. There are a few ***restaurants*** (called hotels) where it is possible to stay but be warned the accommodation is less than basic, grungy even. They aren't the least bit set up for teahouse trekkers. Dal bhaat is the staple but samosas, momos, noodles and omelettes are also available.

The white-washed shops stock a surprising array of goods to soak up salaried workers' wages. The bazaar is pleasantly busy with goldsmiths working gold, barbers shaving and cutting and blacksmiths hammering out khukris. Goats cavort around and roosters crow. There's electricity here so stereos and electric heaters are on sale. There is also a telephone system and occasional TV aerials and satellite dishes can be seen. The large field hosts football games and a surprising range of other sports such as tai-kwondo and volleyball. Because it is a district headquarters (one of 75 in the country) there is a full set of government offices, a district court, district police headquarters and even a prison.

Bhojpur is also an education centre with several boarding schools and a college offering two year commerce and arts courses.

Saturday market Saturday morning features the *hat* or *hati*, an open market. A fascinating mélange of mainly foodstuff sellers, some of whom have walked a day or two to get here. This is the only place

where vegetables and meat are sold. Bazaar merchants and porters sell sweets, biscuits and snacks. *Sakaar*, raw sugar, comes from Chainpur. A surprising variety of dals, rices, spices, black pepper, chillis, salt, eggs (both duck and chicken) feature. You can even buy whole tobacco leaves to make your own.

Route from Bhojpur

At the top of the main bazaar veer right up a steep stone staircase through the rest of ribbon Bhojpur. Houses turn redwashed with tile or thatched roofs as the trail climbs more or less along the ridge.

Kafle has a school and a community forestry plantation opposite and a couple of shops that can make dal bhaat. Terraces dotted with trees extend farther than the eye can see. Occasional prayer flags reveal that this is a Tamang region.

Half an hour past Kafle is a well worn short cut going right while the main stone-paved trail continues ahead. If you are lucky Kanchenjunga rears on the horizon at the beginning of a large pine plantation that the locals are proud of.

Dhap Kharka, which you pass, has a Japanese-financed school, hence the unusual architecture.

Suntale This is the first real village after leaving Bhojpur. It appears around the corner as views of the ridge extend into the distance. There are some ***dal bhaat restaurants*** and it is possible to find rough places to stay. If the atmosphere is clear to the north is Makalu; the long white summit ridge slightly left is Chamalang. Slightly further left part of the Lhotse-Nuptse ridge is visible. You may even just see the tip of Everest. To the east is the huge Kanchenjunga massif.

Tintale This is also a Sherpa village. Meals are available but expect to sleep on the kitchen floor if staying. Until this point the ridge has been more or less level but now it begins falling off. Parts of the trail are wide and deeply incised. There are magnificent views of Makalu along here. Across the Arun river valley the flat area is Tumlingtar and along the ridge you can pick out Khandbari.

Dingla This is a bustling bazaar village nestled in a saddle. Unlike ribbon Bhojpur it is a rough circle of houses, shops and simple restaurants. There are several simple places to stay. *Suntala* are usually available. Dingla also features a Saturday market. The village's claim to fame is that the first public school in Nepal was founded here in approximately 1876. The Ranas established the school for their children after their visit to Europe. It is only in the last 15 years that schooling has become widely available in Nepal and considered a right rather than a privilege.

Leaving, the trail gently drops and contours but isn't straightforward to follow. At a water pipe, chautara and small cattle shelter take a left turn. If you go straight, the stone steps take you to a bridge across the Arun. Mountains tantalise in the distance.

Nepali Danda is recognisable by the solar panels for the telephone (which occasionally rings). Not a lot happens here on the ridge top but food is available. Head west along the northern side of the ridge. Eventually descend to the river at Lankuwa where the trail meets the more usual route in from Tumlingtar. The description continues on p200.

There's also a regular trail between Dobani and Bhojpur. From Dobani it passes through Kuda Kaule, Khartham Cha, and Kimalung before joining the trail mentioned above at Tintale. Taking a local guide would be wise.

Rolwaling

INTRODUCTION

Rolwaling means 'the furrow left by the plough', an appropriate name for this steep-walled valley. It's a rugged yet beautiful area inhabited by friendly Sherpas. Unlike their Khumbu cousins, they form a single isolated community with just one main village. Above the inhabited area the valley divides into several little explored glaciated valleys dominated by formidable 6000m/19,685ft peaks. The highest mountain in the area is the holy Gauri Sankar, an ice-castle that can be admired even from Kathmandu.

Permits
Despite the dotted line marking the route on many trekking maps, the Tashi Labtsa (5755m/18,881ft) is a mountaineering challenge not a teahouse trekking route. It's far more dangerous than the Kongma La, Tsho La or Annapurna's Thorong La. Officially only groups who have a permit to climb the trekking peaks Ramdung-Go (5930m/19,455ft) or Parcharmo (6273m/20,580ft) can trek in the Rolwaling valley and, for safety reasons, it's unlikely that this valley will be opened to individuals.

Safety
It would be insane to try to cross the Tashi Labtsa by yourself. Several climbers have disappeared while alone in this area. Crevasses are a real danger and there are some areas in the icefall that may need an

---

❑ **Tsampa**
The process of making tsampa (barley flour) is quite complex. Dark high-altitude barley is dried in the sun, then mixed with white barley. The grains are soaked in water and dried three times before being stored for a few days. Next the barley is roasted in sand. The grain explodes like popcorn and is ground up into a light fluffy flour. It can be eaten dry and washed down with *chang*, mixed with *solja* (salt-butter tea) to make a thick porridge or rolled into a doughy ball to be chewed. For trekkers, ordinary tea is used for tsampa porridge, rather than *solja*.

abseil. From Thame or Beding you will need at least three days' food and should carry reserves for two more days, plus enough fuel to melt snow or ice for water. For small parties ice-axes and crampons are needed by all, plus a rope with a few ice-screws and slings and gear for a short abseil. Conditions have changed considerably on the glaciers in Nepal: as recently as 1972 yaks could cross this pass.

There is one section of the route that could quite possibly change making traversing around the Tsho Rolpa even more challenging than it already is, if the lake isn't frozen. You **must** consult someone who has crossed the pass that season to find out the exact situation.

Route planning and acclimatisation
The Rolwaling valley is a destination in its own right but most trekkers combine it with a visit to the Khumbu. Commercial trekking groups usually approach the valley from Dolakha or Barabise, attempt the trekking peak Ramdung-Go for acclimatisation, then cross the Tashi Labtsa. For proper acclimatisation 12 nights should be spent between Simigoan (2000m/6562ft) and the first night above 5000m/16,404ft. Since the highest village (Beding) is at 3700m/12,139ft this means many days camping. Independent trekkers will find crossing from the Khumbu to the Rolwaling makes more sense logistically than the other way around. From Thame (suitably acclimatised) it is possible to reach Dolakha/Barabise in just under a week and taking eight to nine days would be quite leisurely. Extra time will allow exploration of the valleys that head the Rolwaling and the wall of mountains to the south.

There are two route possibilities for starting (or finishing) the trek (see Map B: p219; Map C: p221). Dolakha (near Charikot) is a few kilometres off the Jiri road and the walk to Simigoan takes two to four days following the Tamba Kosi. Barabise is on the Arniko Highway and from here to Simigoan takes four to six days. Between Simigoan and Beding there is also a choice of routes.

Note that the route is described crossing the pass from Thame to the Rolwaling and on to the roadheads at Dolakha/Charikot and Barabise. Information relevant to travelling in the reverse direction is also given, marked by '▲'.

Facilities
Since it's usually groups with tents that pass through here, there's no organised system of lodges but finding basic food and a place to stay at villages en route isn't difficult. However, there are a number of nights where camping is unavoidable and camping supplies are far more difficult to find than in the Khumbu. Don't expect them to stock things like noodles, muesli and milk powder, except perhaps in Beding. It's best to carry in all you need and it's worth considering employing porters unless you're approaching from the Khumbu.

ROLWALING VALLEY [MAP A: p215]
Leaving Thame The trail leaves from the little *lodge* beside Thame Gompa (visible from Thame village). Take the upper tracks at each of the main junctions and you pass several small *chhusa,* deserted except during summer.

Tengpo (4350m/14,271ft) is a couple of hours from the gompa. This large *chhusa* has a number of minuscule two-storey houses. It's overlooked by the spectacular south faces of Teng Kangboche. There's ample spring water year round and plenty of places to camp. If, however, your party is well acclimatised then it's a better idea to camp closer to the pass.

The track continues but is smaller now. Looking back there's an unusual view of Ama Dablam with the fluted cirque and glacier of the Mingbo La clearly visible and with Makalu almost hidden behind Ama Dablam. There are good camping areas around the point from where the views of Ama Dablam start to disappear. Further up, the track stays above the valley base and heads to the black rock spur (north-western side of the valley), where there are more camping places but these lack water after a spell of dry weather. Over and slightly down the other side of the moraine (the route does not follow the valley by the black rock ridge) there are several more rocky sites.

To the north is an icefall and to the left of this are several rough moraine ridges. Partially ascend one and head up, keeping to the left of the icefall. There should be a rough track to follow. Above are another two groups of campsites called **Ngole/Mgole** (5100m/16,732ft) with windy and very cold overhanging rock shelters.

▲ **Crossing in the reverse direction** Note that when coming down from the pass to these camps you must keep to the left and avoid descending to the obvious and large valley floor.

Crossing the Tashi Labtsa/Tesi Lapcha (5755m/18,881ft)

Access to the pass involves passing areas of frequent rockfall so an early morning start is best. In the early morning the rocks may still be frozen in place but as the sun hits them they expand, loosen and come thundering down. On a winter's day things might be stable but on a warm October afternoon it's like Russian roulette. It's said by the Sherpas that Lama Sange Dorje crossed this pass and the name Tashi Labtsa bestows a certain protection on travellers.

Onto the glacier There are two obvious routes. You can head left, down and under an icefall close to a large avalanche cone from Parcharmo. However, the quicker and more popular route is simply to stay on moraine-covered ice and head up the ice valley. This could also be totally snow covered. Once up here the lay of the land becomes clearer. To the left, almost on Parcharmo's flanks, is a small diagonal icefall that fails to meet the smooth, white, almost flat glacier below. The upper part meets a rock wall that stretches from the right of the glacier to

above you. Make for the point where the icefall and the wall meet, which involves an ascent of the steep unstable scree slope below the wall. Beware of heavy rockfall here. Sometimes stepping onto the icefall is easier. Groups often use a rope here although with crampons and good glacier conditions it may not be necessary.

Alternatively right of the small icefall is a large avalanche cone which leads to a rock shelf that runs between it and the top of the small icefall. Consult locals as to which route might be easier and safer.

From above the small icefall the going is easier and it's a simple plod to the top of the pass. Crevasses are not normally a problem but if there has been a lot of snow recently then use a rope. Parcharmo's snow bulges rise to the left and you should watch out for falling rocks from Tengi Ragi Tau (6940m/22,769ft) to the right. Just before the pass is Tashi Phuk (Tashi's Cave), a few daringly placed camping spots sheltered by a slightly overhanging rock wall. These make a good base for an attempt on Parcharmo.

The pass (5755m/18,881ft) New vistas unfold at the pass which is a small flat rock rib running out from Tengi Ragi Tau/Kangi Tau marked by cairns and a few prayer flags.

The descent is steeper than the ascent and requires care – there are several crevasses and a bergschrund. Head directly down, to where the glacier flattens out and meets the white Drolambao Glacier, divided by a line of moraine rubble. Once down stay close to, or on, the nearest medial moraine. Most groups camp somewhere around here (Tolungbawe Nang) but if you're making good time then you may be able to reach the next camp. Don't cross to the far side of the glacier – the route marked on the *Rolwaling Himal* Schneider map is the 1950s route, now out of use, considered too dangerous and impractical.

From this point several routes have been used. Some trekkers have crossed the Drolambao Glacier before it starts to

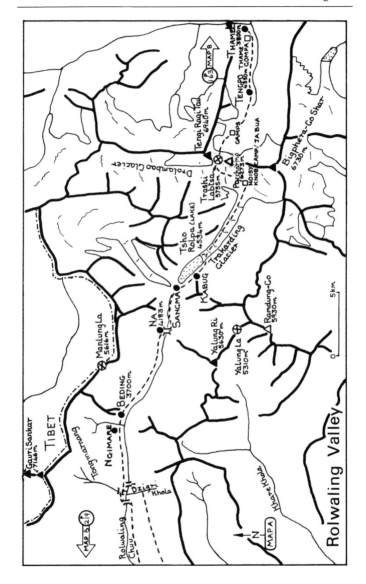

break up (and off!), then descended against the wall of Dragkar-Go but this requires some abseils and appears to descend a very dicey ramp. On my explorations, after descending some distance, I could not find a practical way down that did not need several ropes. Much better is to continue following the moraine, then cross over the broken ice to the left to another line of moraine debris formed by a glacier entering from Bigphera-Go Shar. This begins under a distinctive striped rock face. It leads, sometimes easily, sometimes hazardously, off the glacier/icefall onto solid rock. Conditions vary tremendously just here and at times it may require an abseil of up to 25m. Below, perhaps slightly to the right, is a massive lump of rock with obvious camping spots perched on top of it.

Dza Bua / Dzenasa / Noisy Knob Camp (5000m/16,404ft)
To reach this camp, either drop to an obvious wide rock ledge below or bear right and drop into it further along. Then drop down the small diagonal gully within view of Noisy Knob. Depending on conditions and your skill, a rope may be necessary here. The camp is a classic, perched almost under the falling seracs and above the Trakarding Glacier. A warm night will surround you with the roar of avalanches, the crash-tinkle of seracs and continual groans of the glacier ghosts.

▲ Crossing in the reverse direction
This camp is situated on the large blunt knob of rock clearly visible projecting at the far end of the Drolambao Icefall, dividing it and the next icefall. It's shown on the *Rolwaling Himal* Schneider map. The route up the knob is from the Bigphera-Go Shar side.

The Trakarding Glacier
Continuing, the most frequently used route is on the north side where there's a definite track but moving down on the south side is equally feasible. You could perhaps even head for the ablation valley early. If on the north side then once

you're well down, the glacier cairns lead to the south side, while a vague path continues. Don't follow this path unless the lake is frozen. You must cross to the south to traverse around the lake. The old northern route is extremely dangerous. Some of the steep moraines extend to sheer rock faces and are shelled with a virtually continuous hail of stones and rocks.

Once on the south side of the glacier, climb up on a rough track, eventually reaching the steep crumbling moraine (groups use a rope down here). With binoculars you will be able to spot a large cairn well above. There's grass and a big flat dust bowl with a track across it here. Then it's up again to avoid the huge bowling alley that drops into the side of the lake.

At the top, walk south-west a little before crossing among the boulders. The descent is steep but with great views of the Tsho Rolpa (4550m/14,927ft) and the mountains towering above it. This section of the trail is getting more and more precarious each year. It is possible that the hillside might fall away making this route impassable.

Down the ablation valley is **Kabug** with its small cave, water and pleasant camping spot. **Sangma** and the areas below the lake are also pleasant camping areas, especially for a day or overnight trip up to Bombok (or higher) beside the Ripimo Shar Glacier. The bridge below Sangma is sometimes dismantled for winter.

Na (4183m/13,724ft)
After a few hours of pleasant walking down the valley, cross the bridge to Na. This is a large *chhusa*, a summer village set under an incredible wall of mountains on the sunny northern side of the valley. It's deserted soon after the potatoes have been harvested, the fields left for the yaks and naks to pick over and add their dose of fertiliser.

It's a short half day's walk above the north bank to Beding, still with the spectacular Chobutse/Tsoboje (6689m/21,945ft) rising behind. The forests en route are striking for the size of the trees, even in areas that get very little sun. This is how the area around Namche, and even as high as Dingboche, must once have looked. As Beding becomes visible it is framed against one of the twin peaks of Gauri Sankar (7146m/23,445ft), or Jomo Tseringma as the Sherpas call it.

Beding (3700m/12,139ft)

Beding is a picturesque cluster of buildings centred around the gompa, with a well-kept stupa in the river bed. Although it's the only real village in the upper Rolwaling Valley, it's not permanently occupied. During the coldest winter months the entire population huddles down in the *gunsas* (Gyabrug to Nyimare). In the summer, some villagers move up to cultivate potatoes at Na and others roam higher with their grazing yaks.

The people seem to manage their village well without outside interference or government offices but there's no health post. There is a school, opened in 1972 by Hillary and bridges erected with Japanese aid. The way of life here has changed less than for the Khumbu Sherpas in recent years. Trade with Tibet has been replaced with trekking-related jobs here too but since only groups pass through, there are no trekking lodges. (Nevertheless almost every resident will more than willingly put a few people up in local style.) Locals find employment as sirdars, cooks and especially as high-altitude sherpas on expeditions. Lots of Everest summiteers live here. Lowland porters sometimes quit en masse on the Tashi Labtsa so there's often portering work for local people. The Rolwaling Sherpas are not as poor as Sherpas in non-tourist areas and the relative wealth has manifested itself in the modernisation of many houses, expanding them to Khumbu proportions.

Trading with Tibet has virtually faded out now that Indian iodised salt is so cheaply available. Previously salt, tsampa, yaks and naks, dried meat and Chinese manufactured goods were traded. The route was over the Manlung La

(5616m/18,425ft) which is reached up the impossible-looking slabs a little to the north of Beding. The glaciated pass affords amazing views of the mountain known to the Sherpas as Jomo Garu (7181m/23,559ft). This beautiful peak is more commonly known as Menlungtse, the name Shipton gave it in 1951.

Routes to Simigoan There are two routes: the direct lower winter route via Gyalche (a short day's walk down but tough coming up), or the high scenic Daldung La route (for which it's best to allow two days). Snow in winter virtually precludes using the high route because the track is mostly in shaded areas where the snow is slow to melt. In addition, except in the early part of the season, this route is uninhabited until Simigoan.

To the Dzigri Khola, the boundary of the high Rolwaling Valley, both routes follow the same trail. The path is sunny and pleasant, always on the northern side, sometimes through forest, and, lower, sometimes in stunted bamboo. Prayer flags mark the wooden bridge (3200m/10,499ft).

The low route The trail, narrower now, continues on the north bank to cross the Tongmarnang, the stream with a view up Gauri Sankar's stunning face. A little further down, the trail crosses to the south bank and starts its long roller-coaster ride to Simigoan. There are infrequent small campsites and perhaps one *teashack*. The trail is different from what is marked on the *Rolwaling Himal* Schneider map but is wide, well-used and easy to follow. It leads directly into Simigaon Gompa rather than heading via Shakpa.

▲ Trekking in the reverse direction The high route is especially rewarding on the way in, with stunning views of Gauri Sankar and perhaps even a glimpse of Menlungtse. It's also an introduction to altitude, and a rather harsh one for many people but relief should come when crossing the Rolwaling Chhu. For this reason it is preferable to stay at Shakpa

(2650m/8694ft), rather than Simigoan, and it reduces the climb the next day over the Daldung La (3976m/13,044ft).

SIMIGOAN TO DOLAKHA/CHARIKOT [MAP B: p219]
Simigoan (2000m/6562ft)

This is a large agricultural village, spread way down the hillside: Sherpa in the higher parts and Tamang in the lower section. There are a couple of *campsites* (where it is also possible to stay inside and get a meal) but signs giving directions for them are only along the route coming up to Simigoan. Camping by the gompa offers superb views (but rubbish left by groups is a problem here).

Leaving Simigoan descend through the village, pass the small police check post with its tiny sign in English and continue down. At the edge of a flattish cultivated area is a junction almost overlooking cliffs. It's worth asking someone around here to check that you're on the correct trail. Go right (north) here on what may look like the slightly less used trail. This descends steeply, writhing down a gully to the suspension bridge across the Bhote Kosi at 1520m/4987ft.

On the west bank, the trail to the north leads to Lamabagar/Chhogsham and the police post controlling traffic to Tibet. The trail to the south leads (in just a minute) to Chetchet and a *teashack*. The route down follows the impressive Bhote Kosi (Tibetan River) with the path, in places, held together by concrete. Further along the valley, the Bhote Kosi becomes the Tamba Kosi (Copper River). The tide marks on the river rocks show the height of the torrent that rages through during the monsoon. For this reason there's a second higher route to Gongar, used when the river is at its most dangerous, which branches up half an hour below Chetchet. Around here the waterfalls and the gorge are particularly impressive.

Gongar (1400m/4593ft)

This is just a small village but *lodging* is available. Around the corner, a few hun-

dred metres upstream, is the new bridge across the Gongar Khola. On the main part of the far bank the trail divides: the lower path passing a large house just below is for Charikot, and the upper path goes to Barabise (see trail description on p220).

The trail roughly follows the river, sometimes traversing and sometimes with short climbs to avoid bluffs. Jagat is approximately the half-way point to the old suspension bridge at Manthale. Here, particularly on the east bank, are some shops and frequently fruit, usually *suntala* (mandarin oranges) can be found. The valley starts to widen out although en route to Suri Dhoban there are still some narrow traverses that preclude the use of animals instead of porters.

Suri Dhoban / Dhovan (1020m/ 3346ft) has *teashacks* and *bhattis* and is
a normal overnight stopping place or lunch spot for Rolwaling Sherpas heading to or from Kathmandu. Across the fine suspension bridge up-valley is one of the trails for the route over the Yalung La, up the Khare Khola. The route down passes a post office little bigger than a postage stamp. The trail continues more or less along the river bank and after a cluster of houses crosses to the west bank on a suspension bridge. At the Sangawa Khola is a small but often busy village with a *bhatti* or two. The trail that zigzags up the hill goes to Laduk and is heavily used. Take the suspension bridge across the Sangawa Khola instead and continue south.

Singi Ghat/Piguti On the west bank of
the river, this trading town even has a bank (no foreign exchange department) and a few Nepalese-style *lodges*. The trail continues south, staying on the west bank of the river (not marked on the Schneider map). A little before Bong Khola is a reasonable camping place.

Bong / Bongu Khola / Malepu (880m/ 2887ft) An hour further is a sec-
ond large trading village with *hotels* and shops. It's a regular overnight stop since,

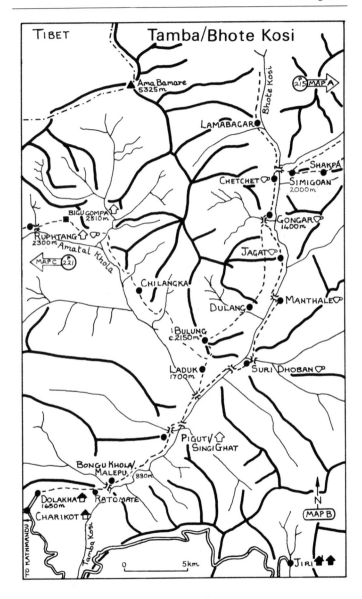

TIBET

Tamba/Bhote Kosi

Ama Bamare
5325m

Bhote Kosi

215 MAP A

LAMABAGAR

SHAKPA

CHETCHET

SIMIGOAN
2000m

BIGU GOMPA
2510m

GONGAR
1400m

RUPHTANG
2300m Amatal Khola

JAGAT

MAP C 221

CHILANGKA

MANTHALE

DULANG

BULUNG
c.2150m

SURI DHOBAN

LADUK
1700m

PIGUTI/
SINGI GHAT

BONGU KHOLA/
MALEPU 880m

DOLAKHA
1650m RATOMATE

CHARIKOT

TO KATHMANDU

Tamba Kosi

N

MAP B

0   5km

JIRI

with tired legs, the climb to Dolakha and Charikot can be soul-destroying in the afternoon sun. The path widens (it's more like a road here) and runs through fine forests for a short time.

Ratomate Continue for 1½ -2¼ hours to the hamlet of Ratomate (red mud) where the climb actually begins. The *accommodation* and *restaurants* are simple but it is possible to stay. By the khola is a camping place and across the bridge the haul up to Dolakha begins.

The ridge is tough and unrelenting for the climb of almost 800m. Count on a two hour haul. There are several paths leading off to villages but the trail heading up is usually the correct one and the volume of traffic into the town means you're unlikely to get lost.

Dolakha (1650m/5413ft)
This is a beautiful and historic town with a few stupas and some flagstone-paved streets. Once it was a main town on the trading route from Tibet to the Indian plains and it still has a Saturday market. Becoming a roadhead has increased prosperity here but not ravaged the town, except by the bus station, as has happened elsewhere. There are at least three **buses** a day to Kathmandu – at 6am, 8am and 10am.

Dolakha, sometimes also called Charikot, and the new Charikot further up the ridge share the title of headquarters for the Dolakha District, which stretches from here to the Tibetan border. Consequently there are a number of government departments. The latest addition is a modern **hospital** funded by Korea. The view alone is worth the visit.

▲ **Starting at Dolakha** If the bus you were on was heading to Jiri you'll be dropped off at Charikot. Depending on the time, you can either start trekking along the 3.5km dirt road to Dolakha, or stay in Charikot. Both have simple Nepali-style *lodges* and great views of the dominant Gauri Sankar and Menlungtse slightly to the east.

At the group pace, Simigoan is about four days' walk away, or a quicker two to three days. Returning in a hurry, two days is plenty of time. For the first expeditions, walking from Kathmandu to the Khumbu or Rolwaling, Dolakha was six days into the trek.

Charikot If you arrived too late for the last bus out of Dolakha walk up the road to Charikot and catch one of the buses passing through from Jiri. The last one leaves Charikot at approximately 2pm. The atmosphere here is quite different from Dolakha. It is a relatively new town and has grown rapidly. There are a few *hotels* and *restaurants* that look fancier than they really are.

GONGAR TO BARABISE
[MAP B: p219; MAP C: p221]
This is one of the classic routes which has been superseded by the Jiri road. As a route into the Rolwaling, it still has advantages because it offers a degree of helpful acclimatisation. It's also little changed since the early days of trekking and is very much a route suited to the expedition approach or to individual trekkers happy to eat dal bhaat and learn some Nepali. Simigoan to Barabise is a pleasant four-day walk including perhaps a half day rest at Bigu Gompa. It could be shortened to two-and-a-bit days by strong legs in a hurry.

Routes There are several possible routes from the Bhote/Tamba Kosi to Bigu Gompa and on to Barabise. See the *Lapchi Kang* Schneider map. The route described here leaves the Bhote/Tamba Kosi after crossing the Gongar Khola on a good trail that is not marked on the Schneider map.

Leaving Gongar Take the upper of the equal-sized paths, heading up and around on the south bank of the Gongar Khola. Shortly after a stupa is a small but interesting Hindu shrine. Although virtually nothing is marked on the Schneider map this is a well-populated, mainly Tamang area. The trail passes through several villages during the several hours to Dulang (1900m/6234ft). Around here, since there are so many small trails, it pays to repeatedly ask the way. Ask for Bigu or Bigu Gompa, otherwise villagers tend to direct you to Laduk and the slightly shorter route out to Charikot.

Bulung (2150m/7054ft)

This sprawling village is a few hours further on. You may meet the pleasant high school teacher or some of the friendly children, many of whom are more interested in practising their English than in the usual begging. Bulung has some **shops** but since few visitors pass through they are not obvious. You'll need to ask a villager where they are and, if you need accommodation, asking around will soon turn something up. On leaving the village there are superb views of Gauri Sankar.

All the main trails lead to **Laduk** (1700m/5577ft) which, once out of Bulung and around the major ridge, is visible below. Stay high on the terraces and look for the large high school that sits

above Laduk. The main trail continues directly from the school and is the one that contours and descends slightly. Laduk is a large centre with many shops. The porters prefer to walk here from Charikot rather than Barabise since the Tamba Kosi route is considered shorter.

Continue contouring and descend, then drop to the Thuran Khola. After climbing steeply, head around the ridge on an easy-to-follow trail.

Chilangka (1900m/6234ft) This little village spreads above and below the main trail with little to offer except a shop beside the path. Contour, staying fairly high, and cross the Jorong Khola on a log bridge. Then head up and out onto the hillside and a pretty forest. Contour to **Loding/Lading (1800m/5904ft)** and after it reaches a prominent view-point. Look for Bigu Gompa: a mass of prayer flags. The best route from here is to wander upstream along the east bank of the Kothale Khola and cross on a major suspension bridge although there are some temporary bridges.

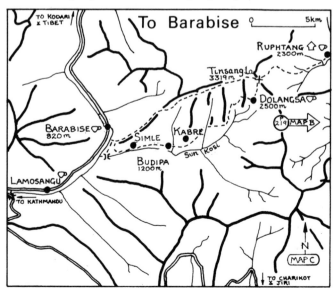

Numerous trails lead through the villages stacked up the hillside so ask for the gompa, sometimes also called Tashi Gompa. It is also possible to by-pass the gompa, although it's one of the main reasons for taking this route, by dropping to Amatal and continuing up the valley on the south bank of the Amatal Khola.

Bigu Gompa (2510m/8235ft)

This nunnery is impressively-located amid prayer flags and huge juniper trees at the top of the village. The gompa is an island of Buddhism in the surrounding Hindu area. Many of the nuns are Tibetan refugees and some are very recent arrivals. There are some beautiful paintings in the gompa and the setting is very pleasant. It's possible to stay at the tidy, smoke-free *guest house*. Below, in Bigu village there's a **paper factory** that sells its products in Kathmandu.

Leaving the gompa, it's a fairly gentle descent passing through an area ravaged by forest fires, to the distinctive roofed bridge across a tributary. There are many water-driven flour mills above and this heralds **Rupthang (2300m/7546ft)**. It boasts a *teahouse* just up from the bridge and more *teashacks* a little further on. These are the last facilities en route to the pass, still a 1000m/3281ft haul away.

The Tinsang La (3319m/10,889ft)

The sometimes eroded and elusive trail stays on the north bank of the Amatal Khola. In the kharkas and forests of tall firs maintaining your sense of direction may not be easy. Just before the crest of the Tinsang La is beautiful flat pasture used for grazing in summer, and dotted with roofless huts in the fall and winter. It's a good place to camp with a reasonably good water supply.

The panorama here stretches from Gauri Sankar (7146m/23,445ft) and the closer rock cone of Jomo Bamare (5927m/19,445ft) on the Tibetan border to Numbur (6959m/ 22,831ft) in the east, the Yul Lha (holy mountain) of Shorong.

Unlike the gentle ascent, the route down to Dolangsa seems unrelentingly steep though it takes only an hour or less.

Dolangsa (2500m/8202ft)

This is an extensive village resting on a large flat area. There are a few *bhattis* and *teashacks* above and below the gompa. Winter here is a time of crafts: knitting and weaving bamboo mats and dokos.

There are numerous ways down to Barabise but most widely used is the route on the northern side of the Sun Kosi via Budipa. Once across a few streams, down a ridge and across another stream you come to the village of Kabre. Stay on the large well-defined trail on the north bank and cross a large tributary to Budipa.

Budipa (1200m/3937ft)
There are some *teahouses* and shops in this village. You can stay either here or in Simle, the next village, so as to avoid having to spend the night in Barabise. The trail from Budipa contours above the river and around a sharp ridge before descending into Barabise, and the mess of modern civilisation.

Barabise (820m/2690ft)

Big, dirty and crowded, Barabise is a trading post for many Chinese goods that have found their way over from Tibet via the Arniko Highway or been smuggled in along the older trading routes.

▲ **Starting from Barabise** Route-finding for the first few hours is difficult so it's a very good idea to hire a local porter. As well as acting as a guide, he (or she) will enable you to start with a light load in a hot area with a 2400m/7874ft climb to the Tinsang La. Note that if you camp just below this pass (a few days later) you're likely to feel the altitude as a result of the rapid ascent. By the time you reach Bigu Gompa, however, all symptoms should have cleared.

APPENDIX A: ITINERARIES

The preceding trail guide was deliberately not written on a 'Day 1, Day 2' basis to encourage trekkers to travel at their own pace and not stop all in the same places. Some guidelines are, however, necessary for overall planning. Overnight stops are given in the tables below.

ACCLIMATISATION PLANNER

Awareness of the time taken for your body to acclimatise is the key to planning itineraries in this region. Although the process of acclimatisation begins even at altitudes as low as Kathmandu (1400m), planning only becomes important if heading above 3000m. The usually ignored medical recommendation is that a minimum of two to three days (and better four to five days) should be taken to reach 3000m or 10,000ft, followed by a daily altitude gain of 300m or 1000ft with a rest day every 900m or 3000ft, as shown on the table below.

Some people acclimatise slower than others but you should find that your body will tolerate deviations of plus or minus approximately 300m from these figures. Larger deviations may bring on symptoms. For example, if after Night 8 at 4200m/13,779ft you spend Night 9 at 5000m, this may cause some symptoms, although often a night later. Spending Night 8 at 4800m/15,748ft, however, is much less likely to bring on mild AMS especially if you stay a further night there to synchronise with the table again.

Night	00	below 2000m/6562ft	Night	07	3900m/12,795ft
	01	2-3000m/6562-9842ft		08	4200m/13,779ft
	02	2-3000m/6562-9842ft		09	4500m/14,764ft
	03	3000m/9842ft		10	4800m/15,748ft
	04	3300m/10,827ft		11	4800m/15,748ft
	05	3600m/11,811ft		12	5100m/16,732ft
	06	3900m/12,795ft		13	5400m/17,716ft

GETTING TO NAMCHE

	Jiri (sedate*)	Jiri (rapid)	Phaplu (medium)	Tumlingtar (sedate/medium)
01	Ktm-Jiri (bus)	Ktm-Jiri (bus)	Ktm-Phaplu§ (plane)	Ktm-Tum (plane)
02	Shivalaya	Bhandar	Jubing	Balawa
03	Bhandar	Sete (short day)	Surke	Phedi
04	Sete	Junbesi/Sallung	Monjo	Sanam (long day)
05	Junbesi	Kharikhola	Namche	Bung
06	Junbesi(rest)	Chourikharka	Najing	Dingma
07	Nuntala	Namche		Pangkongma
08	Kharikhola			Surke
09	Puiyan			Monjo
10	Phakding			Namche
11	Namche			

* or group pace   § overnight at Ringmo

Note that it's possible to get from Jiri to Namche in four days but only if you are extremely fit. To walk from Kathmandu to Tumlingtar takes three to four days. For Tumlingtar to Namche, whether you are fast or slow, allow 10 days.

LUKLA TO NAMCHE

The table below shows the safe rate of ascent if you have flown from Kathmandu (1400m) to Lukla (2850m). The recommended maximum altitude for each day (as laid down by AMS specialists) is indicated. Ascending above Namche in four days, which is the schedule followed by most trekking companies, has been shown to cause troublesome mild AMS in about 50% of trekkers.

	Altitude guideline*	Itinerary 1	Itinerary 2	Unwise option
01	2-3000m	Phakding/Monjo 2650m	Lukla 2850m	Phakding/Monjo
02	2-3000m	Namche 3450m	Phakding/Monjo	Namche
03	3000m	Namche	Namche	Namche
04	3300m	Namche	Namche	(higher)
05	3600m	(higher)	(higher)	

NAMCHE TO LOBUCHE/GOKYO

For acclimatisation, you should spend two nights at Namche (or three if you flew to Lukla), two nights at Tengboche or similar altitude and two nights at Dingboche or Pheriche, before reaching Lobuche and attempting Kala Pattar. Note that an alternative to spending three nights at Namche is to spend just two nights there and an extra night at somewhere near Lukla.

Studies have shown that spending one night at Phakding, two nights at Namche, one at Tengboche, and two nights at Dingboche before reaching Lobuche causes mild AMS in about 50% of trekkers.

	Altitude guideline*	Itinerary 1	Itinerary 2	Itinerary 3
00	(additional night at Namche for people who flew to Lukla)			
01	3000m	Namche 3450m	Namche	Namche
02	3300m	Namche	Namche	Namche
03	3600m	Tengboche 3860m/Khumjung 3790m		Namche**/Khumjung
04	3900m	Tengboche/Pangboche	Pheriche 4280m	Phortse/Phortse T
05	3900m	Dingboche/Pheriche	Pheriche	Dole 4040m
06	4200m	Dingboche/Pheriche	Duglha 4600m	Machermo§ 4410m
07	4500m	Lobuche 4940m	Lobuche	Gokyo 4750m
08	(day)	up Kala Pattar	◄┘	up Gokyo Ri
08	4800m	Lobuche		Gokyo
09	(down)	Tengboche/Namche		Phortse T/Namche
10	(down)	Lukla		Lukla

This acclimatisation plan seems to work quite well for most people but obviously the more time spent acclimatising, the better you will feel. Conversely if you cut out just one of the nights listed above the risk of minor altitude sickness greatly increases.

* The altitude guideline shows the fastest recommended rate of ascent.
** or Thame
§ or Pangka

(Opposite) A number of small-scale paper-making operations are found on the Salpa-Arun trek. The *lokto* plant is used, the heartwood boiled, smashed to a pulp and mixed with water so that the pulp is evenly distributed. A wooden-framed piece of mesh is then dipped into the mixture and set in the sun to dry for a day.

GRAND TOUR – NAMCHE TO CHUKHUNG, LOBUCHE & GOKYO

	Itinerary 1 (long)	Itinerary 2 (short)	Itinerary 3 (reverse)
00	(additional night at Namche for people who flew to Lukla)		
01	Namche	Namche	Namche
02	Namche	Namche	Namche
03	Tengboche/Khumjung	Tengboche/Khumjung	Namche/Khumjung/Thame
04	Pangboche/Tengboche	Pangboche/Tengboche	Phortse/Phortse T
05	Dingboche	Dingboche	Dole
06	Dingboche Chukhung Ri	Dingboche ▼	Machermo/Pangka ▼
07	Chukhung ▼	Lobuche Kala Pattar	Gokyo Gokyo Ri
08	Dingboche/Duglha	Lobuche	Gokyo
09	Lobuche Kala Pattar	Pangboche/Phortse ▼	Gokyo Gokyo area
10	Lobuche	Machermo/Gokyo	Gokyo
11	Pangboche/Tsho La	Gokyo	Phortse/Cho La
12	Machermo/Gokyo	Gokyo	Pheriche/Dingboche
13	Gokyo Around Gokyo	Phortse/Dole ▼	Lobuche Kala Pattar
14	Gokyo	Namche/Monjo/Phakding	Lobuche
15	Phortse/Dole	Namche/Lukla	Tengboche
16	Namche		Namche/Monjo/Phakding
17	Namche		Namche/Lukla
18	Lukla		

RETURN – NAMCHE TO JIRI OR TO THE ARUN

	Itinerary 1 (medium)	Itinerary 2 (rapid)	Itinerary 3 (sedate)	Itinerary 4 (rapid)
00	Namche	Namche	Namche	Namche
01	Surke	Puiyan	Surke	Puiyan
02	Nuntala	Trakshindo	Pangum	Shubuche
03	Junbesi	Tragdobuk	Najing Dingma	Bung
04	Kenja	Bhandar	Bung	Salpa/Thulofokte
05	Shivalaya	Jiri	Sanam	Balawa Besi
06	Jiri		Phedi	Past Tumlingtar
07			Balawa Besi	Hille
08			Tumlingtar	
09			Arun Riverbank	
10			Hille	

BHOJPUR START

00	Kathmandu	05	Phedi	10	Puiyan
01	Bhojpur	06	Gurase	11	Lukla/ Chaurikharka
02	Suntale	07	Sanam	12	Monjo
03	Dingla	08	Bung	13	Namche
04	Lankuwa	09	Shubuche		

(Opposite) Sunsets in the high Himalaya are often spectacular. **Bottom**: Chamalang.

APPENDIX B: TREKKING PEAKS

INTRODUCTION

The Nepal Mountaineering Association (NMA) has classified 18 peaks in Nepal as 'trekking peaks', a misleading name because all involve climbing. Ranging from 5650-6500m (18,537-21,325ft) some are, however, appropriate heights to combine within a trekking programme.

Permits and costs

The procedure for obtaining a permit is streamlined in comparison to the months of planning required for expedition peaks. It's therefore possible to arrive in Kathmandu, organise a trekking peak trip from scratch and be on the trail in just under a week. At present the rules are biased towards larger groups because the fee is a flat rate – the same for one person as for ten. The noticeboards at the HRA, KEEP Trekkers' Information Centre and the Kathmandu Guest House are the best places to advertise for partners in Kathmandu.

The 18 peaks are divided into two categories: 12 'A' group peaks above 6000m/19,685ft and 6 'B' group peaks below 6000m/19,685ft. 'A' group permits cost US$300/£200 and 'B' group US$150/£90. An NMA-registered sirdar must accompany the group for the entire trek and if you wish he can act as guide, rather than overseer. This is to ensure that every climbing trip is organised as a fully guided group trek, involving porters (who must all be insured) and tents, and costing at least US$20/£13.50 per person per day. Some trekking companies are willing to waive this rule.

Equipment and safety

If climbing in a trekking company group headed by a climbing guide, then harnesses and ropes will be used on every one of the peaks below, whether for crevasse danger or steep slopes. If climbing without a guide, recognising your personal limits is important. Some of these peaks are 'easy' but what this really means is that to be safe you don't need a sackful of karabiners, ice-screws, snow-stakes and rock racks – just a partner, rope, a few bits of protection, experience using this gear and an overriding urge to die of senility.

Routes described below cover the least difficult way up some of the main trekking peaks in the region. For proficient technical alpinists none of the routes is particularly challenging **under good conditions**. For safety-conscious amateurs they have potential to provide satisfaction and experience without excessive danger.

Itinerary planning

Heading straight up to high altitude for the first time, even if following the recommended guidelines, is usually a shock to everyone's system. The effort required for walking, let alone climbing, uphill at 5000m is much greater than you might think. By far the best approach to climbing trekking peaks or the very high passes is to warm up first by heading high, say to Kala Pattar or Gokyo, then down, sleeping a night or two much lower, eg at Namche. Although this advice is not yet scientifically proven, HRA doctors and many climbers will attest to how much easier the next slog to high altitude is.

Glacier preparation

Everyone on the rope should always carry prussik loops/jumars and be familiar with their use. If you fall in a crevasse and do the job properly, knocking yourself out, then rescue, particularly by only one partner is an arduous, sometimes impossible, business requiring a pulley system and some gear. Crevasses can be completely invisible, especially in spring. Practise rescue moves and reacting quickly before entering dangerous territory.

Avalanche danger

Just as the Himalayan mountains are the largest in the world so too are some of the avalanches. They should be treated with similar respect. Debris cones are a telltale sign that avalanches are frequent. Try to avoid going within 300m (or less) of these. One of the most dangerous times for avalanches is late winter if there is a massive dump of snow. Parts of Island Peak Base Camp can be hit in these conditions.

Glaciers for the uninitiated

When falling snow doesn't melt quickly enough, it accumulates, consolidates and is compressed to ice. Its weight forces it slowly downhill, literally bulldozing its way down to a warmer area where it melts.

The **neve** is the glacier's accumulation area, (the Western Cwm below Everest, for example) where snow falls in avalanches from the steep walls to the basin below and is squashed to ice. Next, as it moves down, it bends and catches on the valley walls, the uneven pressures forming cracks or **crevasses**. In the Himalaya these may be hundreds of metres deep, and in Greenland and Antarctica more than a kilometre. When snow falls, rather than fill the bottom of the crevasse, it often sticks to the top of the sides forming **cornices**. Instead it can cover the crack, sometimes with a snow bridge little stronger than a playing card.

Sometimes the ice drops down a steep slope and completely breaks up into a mess of building-sized blocks of ice, known as **seracs**. The infamous icefall above Everest Base Camp is a good example. Here the danger is not so much the huge cracks but of being squashed flat by them as they fall. The Drolambao Icefall on the Tashi Labtsa route is particularly risky.

The big glaciers shovel rocks up on themselves, especially where they meet another glacier. These rocks appear to be held in gravity-defying poses – that is until you put your weight on one whereupon it shoots away. Rocks tend to protect and extend the life of a glacier.

Technical climbing

Although some of the peaks are regularly climbed by groups many of the peaks are delightful technical mountaineering propositions. For an introduction see APA's *Insight Guide to Nepal*, and for more detailed information there's Bill O'Connor's *The Trekking Peaks of Nepal*.

IMJATSE/ISLAND PEAK (6173m/20,252ft)

The name was coined by Shipton, who thought this peak looked like 'an island in a sea of ice'. Finding a route to the top could be a challenge in itself were it not for the fact that as many as 25 people a day reach the summit during the busy season, October to November. This does not, however, detract from the fact that it's a hard climb that many people fail to complete, either because of a badly-planned acclimatisation itinerary, or because they set off too late in the morning or the winds become too strong. Often in spring, deep snow makes even reaching the Base Camp difficult.

Suggested itinerary

Before attempting this peak it's essential to include an acclimatisation trip (eg to Lobuche and Kala Pattar or any of the other Chukhung valley peaks). The table on the next page shows the absolute minimum number of days required to allow for relatively safe acclimatisation for most climbers. Night stops are shown.

Day No	Altitude guideline	Overnight stop
Fly to Lukla		
01	2-3000m	Phakding 2650m/Monjo/Lukla 2850m
02	2-3000m	Namche 3450m/Monjo
03	3000m	Namche
04	3000m	Namche
05	3300m	Tengboche 3860m/Khumjung 3790m
06	3900m	Tengboche/Pangboche 4000m
07	3900m	Dingboche 4350m/Pheriche 4280m
08	4200m	Dingboche/Pheriche
09	4500m	Lobuche 4940m
10	4800m	Lobuche
11	4800m	Chukhung 4750m
12	5100m	Base Camp 5150m
13	(day)	Climb Imjatse, return to Base Camp
14		(extra day for safety)
15		Pangboche
16		Namche
17		Lukla

Chukhung to Base Camp (5150m/16,896ft)

This walk takes a short afternoon on the well-defined track, accurately marked on the 1988 National Geographic map. The long thin base camp area is a real cesspit despite being cleaned up occasionally. Other problems here include the frequent howling winds and a lack of water in December and January, with only a trickle available a 10-minute walk above the camp near a couple of cairns on the rock fan south and above the Base Camp. As well as this it's not safe to leave a tent unattended, not so much because things will be stolen (although this is starting to happen) but because of the birds. They seem to enjoy ripping through even the toughest tents so leave them packed up and, with all your other gear, well covered with rocks or leave someone to mind the camp. The high camp suffers from this problem as well, and so does the 8000m South Col on Everest.

The route up

As early a start as possible is best: before dawn or at dawn at the latest. It can be a long day and the wind sometimes arrives just before lunch. With an early start, quick parties may then return to Chukhung the same day. From the high camp, leaving just as the sun hits may be sufficient.

A trail heads clearly up the hill and then branches into direct and zigzag yak routes up to the high camp which is a series of tent platforms in several groups. From the high camp beside the steep stream, ascend the dry gully immediately to the left of the stream. After about a 50m ascent (measured vertically), cross the gully with the (frozen) stream in it and traverse, continuing around to the right. It's important here to find the correct route. Do not continue ascending the more obvious route or you'll come to a tricky white rock wall that is difficult to solo. Beware, also, of many misplaced cairns, some in the oddest of places. You should traverse around and continue ascending on black and brown rock to reach a further gully that steepens, bringing you onto the spur which shortly leads to the glacier. There is a convenient spot to put on crampons but take care where you sit – it's amazing where some people have the audacity to shit. Well-acclimatised groups sometimes set up a camp just on the snow. From here there should be a nice cramponned track threading through the maze of gaping holes and crossing snow bridges to the flat, but still lightly crevassed, glacier above. If there's no clear track, route-finding can be difficult and possibly fatal without a rope. Head up the smooth, sometimes crevassed glacier and look for a line of weakness where the snow extends to the summit ridge. Beware of the bergschrund. The two general routes are either straight up (120-200m of fixed rope) or a diagonal traverse away from the summit. Groups always fix a rope although careful crampon and axe work alone may be enough in good conditions. The summit ridge presents the last surprise often with strong winds and in bad conditions a rope is necessary. Even with good snow many people will feel far happier with a fixed rope (250m).

The north ridge

Lots talk about it but few ever do it. Firm snow would make it a nice proposition with a rope and a few screws, stakes and a piton. Getting on/off the ablation valley by the Lhotse Shar Glacier can be tricky.

MERA (6476m/21,246ft)

Mera is one of the most popular of the trekking peaks and, despite being considered little more than a walk to the summit, it is also one of the most dangerous. It's often attempted by people who have flown in to Lukla and not given themselves adequate time to acclimatise. Several people each year pay for their lack of awareness (or their foolhardiness) with their lives. The following is a dangerous acclimatisation planner as followed by many groups. Don't book on such a trek!

Dangerous itinerary (see overleaf for recommended itinerary)

Day No	Altitude guideline	Overnight stop
Fly to Lukla		
01	2-3000m	Lukla
02	2-3000m	Chutanga 3050m
03	3000m	High camp 4200m
04	3300m	Tuli Kharka 4300m
05	3600m	Tashing Ongma 3600m
06	3900m	Tangnag 4350m
07	3900m	Tangnag 4350m
08	4200m	Khare 5000m
09	4500m	Mera La 5400m
10	4800m	High Camp 5800m
11	4800m	High Camp 5800m
12	5100m	Head out, three to five days

The ignorance of the trekking companies that sell expeditions based on the above is hard to believe but many groups approximately follow this itinerary. Typically, out of a group of 10 members two to four might make the summit, perhaps eight or nine will feel sick and two or three mightn't even make the Mera La. In most groups at least one person will get ataxia and without immediate descent death is only a day or so away.

There are many itinerary options that provide better acclimatisation. If time is at a premium then consider visiting Namche first or flying in to Phaplu and taking the alternative Pangkongma route. While superior to the shortest itineraries these still bring you to altitude at a rate that is slightly too quick for some people (a course of Diamox may help). With more time why not walk in from Jiri (the crew need only join you at Lukla) or for more adventure, try the Arun route via the Surkie La and Panch Pokhari. For better preparation first trek to Kala Pattar then over the Amphu Labtsa. There are many more variations, the only limits are time and your imagination.

Recommended itinerary

Day No	Altitude guideline	Overnight stop	
		Fly to Lukla	Fly to Phaplu
01	2-3000m	Phakding 2650m	Phaplu
02	2-3000m	Namche 3450m	Ringmo 2700m
03	3000m	Namche 3450m	Nuntala 2350m
04	3300m	Lukla 2850m	Kharikhola 2050m
05	3600m	Chutanga 3050m	Pangkongma 2850m easy day
06	3900m	Tuli Kharka 4300m	Tuli Kharka 4300m
07	3900m	Tashing Ongma 3600m	
08	4200m	Tangnag 4350m	
09	4500m	Tangnag 4350m	
10	4800m	Khare 5000m	
11	4800m	Mera La 5400m/Khare 5000m	
12	5100m	High Camp 5800m/Mera La 5400m	
13	5400m	High Camp 5800m/Mera La 5400m	

The Hinku and Hongu/Hunku areas are particularly isolated so groups planning to go faster than the recommended acclimatisation rate **must** carry a Gamow bag and should have trained Western medical personnel with them who have altitude experience.

To Mera over the Chetera La/Zatrwala La (4580m/15,026ft)

Note that the Chilli La/Zatr Teng (4943m/16,217ft) is infrequently used, being steeper and higher and impractical for loaded porters. Some place names on the *Shorong/Hinku* Schneider map are incorrectly placed according to locals: Gondishung is often referred to as Orshela, Dupishung is Gondishung, Lungsamba is Dupishung and Lungsamba is the name for the whole region, not a single place name.

The first camping place is often Chutanga. Although only three hours out of Lukla it's a sensible choice for the purposes of acclimatisation. The second camp (or the first if the group is acclimatised) is at 4200m/13,780ft where there's the last reliable water source until well down the double pass. This area can be entirely snow-covered in March-April. The trail traverses steep terrain but is straightforward if snow-free. In snow, however, a handline for porters in a couple of spots may be advisable.

Chetero/Tuli Kharka camp (4300m/14,107ft) is marked by a huge boulder that offers fine weather shelter for porters. Beyond the views open up spectacularly. Half an hour on is another camping place, part of the same kharka. The exposed trail is usually cairned although it descends several streams. The next possible camp, but more often a lunch stop, is the Tashing Dingma clearing. Tashing Ongma is the more usual camp. The trail (in October, the expressway) alongside the Hinku Khola is small but clear. At first, views here on either side are not very inspiring – rough, barren country, but ahead is the awesome Peak 43 (6769m/22,208ft) a real eye-catching pyramid and also a sacred mountain. Then the west face of Mera comes into view, sheer and horrible, but climbed once via a buttress by a Japanese expedition.

Tangnag (4350m/14,271ft) is a summer grazing area with the simplest lodges and shops beginning to develop. An acclimatisation day is essential here and a visit to the Sabal Tsho or the cairn (5271m) on the flanks of Kusum Kangguru can be rewarding, if the views are not already enough. It's a slog to **Khare 5025m/16,486ft**, a regular camping spot, where another acclimatisation day or short trekking day is necessary. For the energetic there are plenty of exploring possibilities. Alternative camping spots are Dig Kharka or near the snout of the Hinku Nup Glacier. There are two trails on the western side of this glacier, a higher one (for the lake) and a lower trail that both lead around to near the Kangtaiga Glacier. Conditions on the climb to the Mera La 5415m/17,766ft are variable. When the glacier is dry and the crevasses open, it presents few problems but in new snow a rope (at the very least for the leaders) is essential. A camp may be made either on top of the savagely-windy pass, or slightly the other side, but even with a slow ascent it's likely you'll suffer the effects of altitude.

Mera Peak

The standard route up is through a potentially dangerous crevassed area – note that the *Shorong/Hinku* Schneider map does not mark crevassed areas – to the top of the rock band, marked by a large cairn. Here it's possible to establish a high camp either in the snow or on the rock at 5800m. From here the views are outstanding, with Everest, Makalu, Cho Oyu and more piercing the skyline.

Mera has two peaks. The easier one attempted by most groups, is accessed by taking a higher line to the eastern 6461m/21,197ft peak, with its steep last 20ms or so. The true 6476m/21,246ft summit can either be reached by a drop and traverse, beyond many people by this stage, or by initially taking a more westerly lower line out of the high camp for a steep haul to the true summit. Note that both of these routes are crevassed.

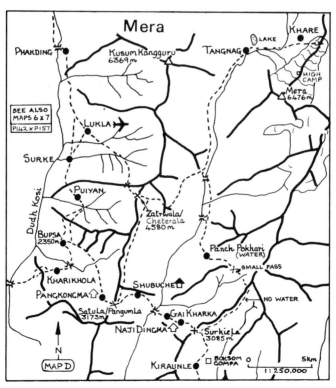

Approaching Mera from the Surkie La

There are two routes to the Surkie La: from Hille/Tumlingtar via the Arun Kosi, or via Bupsa from Jiri or Phaplu. The trail junction, a little east of the Surkie La, is by a crumbling mani wall and soon leads on to the high and pleasant ridge, passing through pastures. A couple are suitable for camping if water is still available. The holy lakes of Panch Pokhri, where there is a Hindu shrine, also offer good camping but they would be a rapid ascent from the Surkie La to do in one day. Route-finding out of the lakes area is a little tricky. The trail now contours in and out of numerous gullies where, if the monsoon runoff has dried up, there is no water until the Mojang Khola/Drangka and quite a descent to the Hinku Khola. You can cross the bridge to Tashing Ongma or go up the valley to Mosom Kharka, where there's another bridge and a camping area. The trail then crosses the Hinku on temporary bridges, joining the regular route from Lukla.

Approaching Mera from the Pangkongma La

This is an alternative to the standard route over the Zatrwala if coming from Jiri or Phaplu or even from Lukla. Although the route from Lukla is longer, it would give useful acclimatisation time. The route to the Pangkongma La is covered on p208, then, just east of the pass is a trail that follows the ridge. This route is used occasionally but it is not always obvious. It joins the Lukla-Chetero La/Zatrwala approach around Chetero/Tuli Kharka.

After Mera

Some groups backtrack or head to Lukla for a quick exit. The more daring head east down the Mera La then north to reach the Khumbu via the Mingbo La (5866m/ 19,245ft), see p191, or into the Chukhung Valley via the Amphu Labsta 5787m/ 18986ft. The trail is unmarked on the *Shorong/Hinku* map but descends from just before point 4919 near the lake and joins the valley floor roughly where the 270 45' line intersects the Hunku Khola. Note that the logistics of getting fully-laden porters over the Amphu Labtsa early on in the expedition are difficult. It's easier later in the trip when the majority of the supplies have been consumed and packs are lighter.

LOBUCHE (6105m/20,029ft)

This is the hardest of the trekking peaks that ordinary commercial groups attempt and while many clients attain the worthwhile false summit, very few make the real summit.

Lobuche Base Camp

There are two routes to Base Camp. If you're coming down from Lobuche, where the track to Tuglha crosses the creek stay instead on the west bank. From the first flat area, that valley ascends to the Base Camp area via a short rope pitch. To reach Base Camp without using a rope continue around the huge spur between Tshola Tsho and Tuglha and at the large, roughly flat, area a cairned track heads up the valley. The Base Camp is pleasant with lots of snow for water.

The climb

Good conditions and a dawn or pre-dawn start are essential. The average angle for the entire climb is not steep but there are some areas of messy seracs that require two axes, front pointing and belaying. The ridge route is sometimes easier. Many people stop at the top of the ridge thinking this is the false summit. It isn't; continue on the knife-edged ridge (groups fix a rope) to the false summit.

PARCHARMO (6273m/20,580ft)

There is some confusion over the height of Parcharmo. The height given on the Schneider maps is 6273m, the Nepal Mountaineering Association state the height to be 6187m/20,298ft and surveyors on the first expeditions calculated it to be 6318m/20,700ft. However it's over the magic numbers 6000m and 20,000ft.

There's a reasonable view of the least difficult route up as you approach Parcharmo and from the Tashi Labtsa but a cursory glance here may lead you to under-estimate the difficulties. Although of modest angle, the access to the ridge is crevassed and, further up, seracs tower. Basic equipment should include a rope with a few stakes and screws, and two axes (at least for the leader).

POKALDE/DOLMA RI (5794m/19,009ft)

When snow-free and with clear weather, the top of Pokalde is a great place to have lunch. Although below 6000m or 20,000ft, the view is reward enough for a few hours' scrambling.

There's a splendid base camp by the lakes below the Kongma La. From here, there are two easy routes up, with a traverse quite possible. Novices, however, may well feel more secure with a real rope and harness backed by slings and perhaps a simple rock rack. The east ridge, high up, has a step a few metres high that the simplest of gear would make safe: a friend to push or catch you, and a 3m sling or 5m cord. An ice-axe or something to jam in a crack might also be useful.

The north ridge runs directly up from the Kongma La and is a little more haz-ardous. There are some exposed moves, requiring steady feet and nerves, that prudent climbers would not solo. Infinitely safer would be to take 10m of cord, a sling harness, a couple of slings and a tool or two.

If there's no snow lying around then both routes are solid rock, but beside a sec-tion of the north ridge is an ice/snow slope that is convenient to climb with crampons and axe. If there is snow, conditions are infinitely more variable, requiring a real rope.

OTHER TREKKING PEAKS IN THE REGION

Kongma Tse (5817m/19,084ft)
Once called Mehra, this can be climbed from either the east side or from the south. The south route from the superb camping spot below the Kongma La goes up beside the glacier, at times on slippery rocks, then continues on steep rock to the summit ridge. A rope (plus limited gear) is widely considered necessary.

Ramdung-Go (5930m/19,455ft)
This is usually climbed from the north and combined with a crossing of the Tashi Labtsa. The southern approach is long, difficult to follow and crevassed but otherwise isn't technical.

Kongde (6187m/20,298ft)
This peak is seldom attempted. It's more of a climbing than a scrambling peak and requires a stocked rock rack and bivvy gear.

Kusum Kangguru (6369m/20,895ft)
Rarely climbed, its razor ridges provide challenge for the serious and well-prepared.

Kangchung Shar (pyramid) 6103m/20,023ft and Kangchung Nup (6089m)
The twin peaks of Kangchung are eye-catching from all the high points around the Gokyo region, sticking up like islands from the surroundings. The Sherpa name means 'small mountain'. The Schneider map marks a pass between the peaks and approach-ing from the south is fairly straightforward up an icefall. The north side, however, is impossible, not a pass at all.

The eastern Kangchung (Shar) is, if viewed from Knobby View, a steep pyramid. Camping on the col will give the best chance of success. The angle of the snow on the face changes season to season, perhaps depending on wind loading. However, expect the steepest pitch to be around 60 degrees, and an average of 40 or so degrees. I met a climber who had soloed it, but on closer inspection, he was game.

The west (Nup) peak is best attempted from a rock saddle south-west of Surprise Lake. This rock ridge meets the snow summit ridge and in good conditions is a fairly straightforward climb, possible to solo by the game. These peaks would make excellent trekking peaks, so in the forlorn hope that the trekking peak list will be expanded they are included in this description. The whole area is fun to explore.

Changri Lho (6189m) and unnamed pass (5690m)

Slightly north of the Tso La is another pass. It is considerably higher, but except for variable conditions for the last 10m, is quite straightforward. The approaches are gentle although crevassed. From the Gokyo side gain access to the glacier by skirting under the Kangchung Shar peak. On the Dzonglha side the route is lightly cairned to the glacier. From the pass itself it is possible to ascend Changri Nup (unnamed on the Schneider map). The ridge is a series of seracs and under most conditions requires some ice-climbing gear.

APPENDIX C: HEALTH

STAYING HEALTHY WHILE TREKKING

In the developed countries, we take for granted clean drinking water, hygienically packaged food and comprehensive sewage systems, none of which exist in the villages of Nepal. New arrivals to Asia will be lucky to escape a visit to Nepal without some form of upset stomach, although in many cases this is quite mild and soon clears up of its own accord. It seems to make little difference whether you trek with an expensive group package or independently, staying in lodges. Most group cooks working for the bigger agencies have completed a basic hygiene course. Their assistants, however, usually have not and the conditions under which food is prepared are far from perfect. Some lodge owners have attended basic hygiene courses, their working conditions are better and they attempt less adventurous dishes. Lodge hygiene, however, has improved significantly in the last few years.

DIET

The food you will eat in the mountains is nutritious and healthy. The diet is carbohydrate-weighted, exactly what is needed, with protein coming mainly from eggs, nuts, beans and dal. Walking every day, breathing harder and the cold at higher altitudes all mean that you'll burn far more calories than normal. Don't be afraid to eat as much as you like! A vitamin tablet every few days will do no harm (women may want to take an iron supplement too). Snack frequently to avoid hypoglycaemia (getting dangerously low on energy).

WATER PURIFICATION

All water from taps, streams and rivers in Nepal (even at high altitudes) is contaminated to some degree and should not be considered safe to drink without purification. Only spring water and water made from clean snow is safe without being treated. There are several methods of purifying water but, first, it helps to know who your enemies are. The most difficult to kill of the various pathogens are the cysts that cause giardia and amoebic dysentery; even one or two can cause the disease. These can survive in very cold water for several months and can even survive when the water freezes. High concentrations of chemicals are required to penetrate their protective shell. They are, however, killed immediately by bringing water to the boil. Bacteria and viruses are less resilient. Larger numbers are needed before infection occurs and they are destroyed by very low concentrations of chemicals.

Boiling
Water that has been brought to the boil, even at 5000m/16,404ft, is safe to drink. It need only be pasteurised (heating to 75°C/162°F), not sterilised (boiling for 10 minutes). At 5800m/19,000ft water boils at around 81°C/177°F so hot drinks, like tea, coffee and hot lemon etc, are all safe.

Iodine-based methods
● **Iodine tablets** The active ingredient is tetraglycine hydroperiodide. If the water is very cold allow 30 minutes rather than the usual 10; if it is cloudy double the dose (ie two tablets per litre). These tablets are convenient and easy to use but are not generally available in Kathmandu. The two brand names are: Potable Aqua and Coghlan's Drinking Water Tablets.
● **Polar Pure** This method relies on dissolving a small amount of iodine directly in water. It is very effective and cheap. The iodine crystals come in a glass bottle with a filter to prevent the crystals from falling out of the bottle. There's a temperature sensitive strip on the side to determine the dose needed.
● **Betadine/Povidone** This method uses a non-iodine based molecule to bind free iodine. For a 10% solution use eight drops per litre of water. If the water is 20°C wait 15 minutes before drinking; if very cold, one hour.
● **Lugol's Iodine Solution** Unless purchased in the West, the solutions come in different concentrations that are often not indicated on the bottle. The solution could be 2%, 4% or 8%. In addition, the free iodine (the active ingredient) is dissolved in potassium iodide so the total amount of iodine consumed is much higher than necessary. However, if you have no choice, it's definitely better than nothing. For 2% solution use five drops per litre of water and leave for 15 minutes before drinking. If the water is very cold, or cloudy, then it should be left 30 minutes or 10 drops should be used.
Note that iodine solutions are messy, so put the bottle in several plastic bags, and the iodine (except Betadine) should be kept only in a glass bottle.

Chlorine based methods
● **Sierra Water Purifier** This uses super-chlorination, a high dose of chlorine that is later neutralised by adding hydrogen peroxide. It's very effective.
● **Chlorine based tablets** (Steritabs, Puritabs) If used alone, they aren't effective against giardia. However if used with a fine filter (to remove the giardia), half a tablet is adequate. Note that standard Micropur tablets are not effective for trekking.

Water filters
There is quite a variety on the market and some now include an iodine resin. Follow the manufacturer's instructions carefully, especially with regard to cleaning and maintenance. The drawbacks with filters are their size, weight and cost.

Using bottled water
This can be obtained along the trail at some points, but only very rarely above Namche. Because it must be carried in, its price rises dramatically. The leftover bottles are also unsightly and difficult to dispose of. Using purifying methods is a far better solution. Boiled water is available in the lodges but it requires valuable firewood.

AMS – ACUTE MOUNTAIN SICKNESS

Commonly called altitude sickness, AMS can affect all trekkers in Lukla and above. It's caused by going up too high too fast and can be fatal if the warning signals are ignored. Your body needs time to adjust to the smaller quantity of oxygen that is present in the air at altitude. At 5500m/18,044ft, the air pressure is approximately half that at sea level, so there is half the amount of oxygen (and nitrogen) in it (see table below). For treks below an altitude of about 2400m/7874ft, AMS is not normally a problem. See also p148, p170, p177.

Barometric pressure table

Altitude	mmHG	Pressure	O₂ sat	Altitude	mmHG	Pressure	O₂ sat
Sea level	760	100%	99%	5000m/16,404ft	404	53%	80%
1000m/3281ft	670	88%		5500m/18,044ft	380	50% *	
2500m/8202ft	554	73%		6000m/19,685ft	356	47%	75%
3000m/9843ft	520	68%	93%	7000m/22,966ft	314	41%	
3500m/11,483ft	489	64%		8000m/26,247ft	277	36%	
4000m/13,123ft	460	60%	88%	8848m/29,028ft	249	33% **	
4500m/14,764ft	431	57%		* (Kala Pattar) ** (Everest)			

Mean oxygen saturation levels (O₂ sat) are also reduced at altitude – see table above. Altitude sickness is preventable. Go up slowly, giving your body enough time to adjust. The 'safe' rates of ascent for 95% of trekkers involve spending two to three nights between 2000m/6562ft and 3000m/c10,000ft before going higher. From 3000m you should sleep at an average of 300m/c1000ft higher each night with a rest day every 900m/c3000ft. These rates are marked on the sample itineraries on p223. Be aware of the symptoms and only ascend if you are symptom-free. Note that when trekking to altitude the idea is to stay ahead of trouble, this is what is normally termed acclimatising. This is different from adapting to the altitude, the process of gaining strength, as required by high altitude climbers. Also note that the altitudes attained while trekking in the Khumbu are more extreme than virtually anywhere else, perhaps requiring a different approach than, for example, skiing at 3000m in Colorado.

NORMAL SYMPTOMS

Don't expect to feel perfect at altitudes of more than 3000m. These are the normal altitude symptoms that you should expect but **not** worry about. Every trekker will experience some or all of these, no matter how slowly they ascend.

● Periods of sleeplessness
● The need for more sleep than normal, often 10 hours or more
● Occasional loss of appetite
● Vivid, wild dreams when you are at around 2500-3800m in altitude
● Unexpected momentary shortness of breath, day and night
● Periodic breathing that wakes you occasionally – consider taking Diamox
● The need to catch your breath frequently while trekking, especially above 4000m
● Runny nose
● Increased urination – many trekkers have to go once during the night (a good sign that your body is acclimatising). Others may need to go more frequently.

❑ The Himalayan mountaineer's trick

Many people struggle with acclimatising for 5000m and wonder how 8000m mountaineers do it. One of the tricks they use to acclimatise to extreme altitudes is to force themselves to drink vast amounts of fluids, especially water. This is so often ignored by trekkers.

MILD AMS SYMPTOMS – NEVER GO HIGHER!

You need have only one of the following symptoms to be getting altitude sickness, not necessarily all of them.

Mild symptoms

● **Headaches** are very common among trekkers. A headache is usually frontal, all over or all-round pressure, and often comes on during the evening and nearly always worsens during the night. Raising your head and shoulders while trying to sleep sometimes offers partial relief. A bad headache may be relieved by taking Diamox (best) or a painkiller: aspirin (which shouldn't be mixed with Diamox), paracetamol, Ibuprofen (Aduil) or acetamenophen (Tylenol). Never take sleeping tablets. Headaches arise from many causes (dehydration, for example) but if you develop one assume it is from the altitude.

● **Nausea** can occur without other symptoms but usually develops with a bad headache. Try Diamox but this may make you retch. If you are better in the morning take a rest day; if you still feel bad descend.

● **Dizziness (mild)** If this occurs while walking, stop out of the sun and have a rest and a drink. Stay at the closest teahouse.

● **Appetite-loss,** or generally feeling bad, is common at altitude after too rapid an ascent.

● **Dry raspy cough** This may sometimes be painful.

In other words, anything other than diarrhoea or a sore throat could be altitude sickness and you should assume that it is. If, for example, your headache is due to dehydration ascending further is not dangerous but if it's due to AMS the consequences could be serious. You cannot tell the difference so caution is the safest course. Don't try to deceive yourself and accept that your body needs more time to adapt. The basic AMS rule is: **Never go higher with mild symptoms.**

What to do about mild AMS symptoms

There are two basic choices: the natural way and the Diamox way.

● **The natural way** If you find mild symptoms developing while walking, stop and relax (with your head out of the sun) and drink some fluids. If the symptoms do not go away completely then stay at the same altitude. If your symptoms get worse, go down. Even a small loss of elevation (100-300m/328-984ft) can make a big difference to how you feel and how you sleep. You should descend to the last place where you felt fine. If symptoms develop at night then, unless they rapidly get worse, wait them out and see how you feel in the morning. If the symptoms have not gone after breakfast then have a rest day or descend. If they have gone, you should still consider having a rest day or at least only an easy day's walking. Continued ascent is likely to bring back the symptoms.

Note that there can be a time lag between arriving at altitude and the onset of symptoms. In fact, statistically it is just as common to suffer mild symptoms on the second night at a set altitude as on the first night.

● **The Diamox way** If mild symptoms develop while walking, stop and have a rest, drink some fluids and take 125-250mg Diamox. Diamox generally takes one to four hours to begin alleviating symptoms. Drink more water and consider staying close by. If symptoms develop in the evening take 125-250mg Diamox and drink plenty of fluids. Be prepared to make many toilet journeys or obtain a pee bottle. If symptoms partially go away but are still annoying it is safe to take another 250mg six to eight hours later. Provided symptoms did go away seriously consider staying at the same altitude. If you still have some symptoms go down. Strongly consider taking 125-250mg of

Diamox every 12 hours until you begin descending in sleeping altitude (in a few people the good that Diamox has done can be reversed, leaving you roughly where you started).

Altitude sickness must be reacted to when symptoms are mild: going higher will definitely make it worse. You trek to enjoy, not to feel sick.

SERIOUS AMS SYMPTOMS – IMMEDIATE DESCENT!

● **Persistent, severe headache**
● **Persistent vomiting**
● **Ataxia** – loss of co-ordination, an inability to walk in a straight line, making the sufferer look drunk.
● **Losing consciousness** – inability to stay awake or understand instructions.
● **Liquid sounds in the lungs**
● **Very persistent, sometimes watery, cough**
● **Difficulty breathing**
● **Rapid breathing or feeling breathless at rest**
● **Coughing blood, pink phlegm or lots of clear fluid**
● **Severe lethargy**
● **Marked blueness of face and lips**
● **High resting heartbeat – over 130 beats per minute**
● **Mild symptoms rapidly getting worse**

Ataxia is the single most important sign for recognising the progression of AMS from mild to serious. This is easily tested by trying to walk in a straight line, heel to toe and should be compared with somebody who has no symptoms. Twenty-four hours after the onset of ataxia a coma is possible, followed by death, unless you descend.
Take note of the second basic AMS rule: **Immediate and fast descent with serious symptoms.**

If the patient is conscious give 250mg Diamox and make a note of the time. If you are at or above Lobuche head to the Pyramid. If at Chukhung or higher head to the Pheriche HRA post, if open, otherwise head for Deboche, to the Rhododendron lodge where there is a Gamow bag. Note that the doctors are frequently called out to sick people. Normally their first action is to get them back to the clinic where there is light and equipment. So if you are considering calling a doctor out, it may be wiser to begin descending towards the clinic first. If at Gokyo, head down to Phortse Tenga, but note that there is no Gamow bag there. If far away from expert care consider carefully which type of AMS – HACE or HAPE (see below) – and give the appropriate drugs. The patient must be taken as far down as possible, even if it is the middle of the night. He or she must be supported by several people or carried by a porter since the condition may get worse before getting better. Later the patient must rest and see a doctor. People with serious symptoms may not be able to think for themselves and may say they feel OK. They are not.

Medical conditions at altitude
● **High Altitude Cerebral Edema (HACE)** This is a build-up of fluid around the brain. It causes the first four symptoms on the mild and severe lists above. HACE can occur in 12 hours but normally takes one to three days. At the first sign of ataxia begin descent. If the condition has developed doctors usually give 8mg of dexamethadrone first dose then 4mg six hourly, Diamox* (250mg) every 12 hours and 2-4l/min oxygen**. A Gamow bag*** will be used if available. See p239-240 for explanations.
● **High Altitude Pulmonary Edema (HAPE)** This is an accumulation of fluid in the lungs and can be serious. It is responsible for all the other mild and serious symptoms.

Immediate descent is vital and Diamox (250mg) may be given every 12 hours, Nifed orally (10mg, every eight hours) and 2-4l/min oxygen. A Gamow Bag should be used if available. Before much was known about AMS, HAPE was often mis-diagnosed as pneumonia and since treatment was antibiotics rather than descent, most people died.
● **Periodic breathing** Less oxygen in the blood affects the body's breathing mechanism. While at rest or sleeping your body seems to feel the need to breathe less and less, to the point where suddenly you require some deep breaths to recover. This cycle can be a few breaths long, in which after a couple of breaths you miss a breath completely. Alternatively it may be a gradual cycle over a few minutes, appearing as if your breathing rate simply goes up and down regularly. It is experienced by most trekkers at Namche, although many people are unaware of it while asleep. At 5000m/16,404ft virtually all trekkers experience periodic breathing, although it is troublesome for only a few. Studies have so far found no direct link to AMS.
● **Swelling of the hands, feet, face and lower abdomen** An HRA study showed that about 18% of trekkers experience some swelling, usually minor and women are more susceptible. It is not a cause for concern unless the swelling is severe, so continued ascent is OK. Rings should be removed.
● **Altitude immune suppression** At base camp altitudes, cuts and infections heal very slowly but the reasons for this are not known. For serious infections, especially bronchitis, descent to Namche level is recommended.
● **High Altitude Flatulence Emission (HAFE)** This is commonly known as HAF (High Altitude Farts). The cure – let it rip! You're not a balloon that needs blowing up.

* **Diamox (Acetazolamide)** This is a mild diuretic (leads to increased urination) that acidifies the blood to stimulate breathing. Generally it was not recommended to take it as a prophylactic (ie to prevent AMS before you have symptoms) unless you ascend rapidly, unavoidably (eg flying to a high altitude, Lhasa, for example, or on a rescue mission), or unless you have experienced undue altitude problems previously. However thinking on this may be changing. It is a sulfa drug derivative and people allergic to this class of drugs should not take Diamox (sulfa allergy is very rare). The side effects are increased urination and tingling sensations in the lips, fingers or toes but these symptoms are not an indication to stop the drug. It can ruin the taste of beer and soft drinks. It should not be used at the same time as aspirin.

The recommendations are to carry Diamox and consider using it if you experience mild but annoying symptoms, especially periodic breathing if it continually wakes you up. The dosage is 125-250mg every 12 hours until you descend in sleeping altitude. Diamox actually goes to the root of the problem: so if you feel better, you are better. It does not simply hide the problem. However this does not mean that you can ascend at a faster rate than normal, or ignore altitude sickness symptoms since it is quite possible to still develop AMS while taking Diamox. The further away you are from medical care, the sooner you should consider beginning Diamox, if you are experiencing problems. Note that it used to be recommended that you needed to start taking the drug

---

❏ **What happens if you ascend too quickly?**
One Kathmandu trekking company followed this dangerous schedule:
Night stops at: Kathmandu, Namche, Tengboche, Dingboche, Lobuche, the HRA Pheriche clinic. Upon reaching Lobuche the group immediately turned back. Three out of the 12 had cerebral odema that would have killed them if it hadn't been for the HRA doctors, and two still had to be evacuated by helicopter. The rest came down with moderate AMS but felt better at the Pheriche clinic (most were given Diamox). Nobody made it up Kala Pattar.

before ascending for it to be most effective. This has, however, now been found not to be necessary.

**Oxygen Supplementary O_2 does not immediately reverse all the symptoms but it does help significantly. Descent in conjunction with O_2 is more effective.

***Gamow Bag This is the latest device to assist with severe AMS. Basically, it's a plastic tube into which the patient is zipped. A foot pump is used to raise the pressure inside the bag simulating a lower altitude.

The acclimatisation process

When you move to a higher altitude your body quickly realises that there is less oxygen available and its first reaction is to get you to hyperventilate (breathe more). More oxygen (O_2) is inhaled but more carbon dioxide (CO_2) is breathed out and with the O_2-CO_2 balance upset the pH of the blood is altered. Your body determines how deeply to breathe by the pH level (mainly the dissolved CO_2 in your blood). If you exercise hard at sea level, your muscles produce large amounts of CO_2 so you breathe hard and fast. While resting, your body is using little energy so little CO_2 is produced. When this balance is upset your body may believe that it needs to breathe less than it really does. Over several days it tries to correct this imbalance by disposing of bicarbonate (carbon dioxide in water) in the urine. (Since it's not very soluble you need to drink plenty). Diamox assists by allowing the kidneys to do this more efficiently thereby enhancing many people's ability to acclimatise. In addition, after a day or two, the body moves some fluid out of the blood thus increasing the haemoglobin concentration. After four to five days more new red blood cells are released than normal.

Rates of acclimatisation

Individual rates of acclimatisation are dependent on how fast your body reacts to compensate for the altered pH level of the blood. For slow starters Diamox can provide a kick-start but for people already adapting well its effect is minimal. Even Sherpas who live in Kathmandu occasionally get AMS upon returning to the Khumbu. Studies have shown that people who live at moderate altitudes (1000m-2000m/3281ft-6562ft) are acclimatised to those altitudes. They are much less susceptible to AMS when ascending to around 3000m/9842ft (ie going to Namche). However the benefits decrease once higher and they should follow the same acclimatisation programme as others.

Trekkers who fly from sea level to Kathmandu and then almost immediately fly to Lukla are more likely to suffer AMS than people who have spent a few days in Kathmandu (1400m/4593ft) on the way. Unfortunately it is usually these people who are in a hurry to go higher. This is why group trekkers are initially more susceptible to troublesome AMS than individual trekkers who often walk from Jiri or spend time in Kathmandu first.

❏ If Mild AMS doesn't go away

If mild AMS symptoms continue, descending for a few hours may be more beneficial than staying at the same altitude. The following case is a good example. A climber bound for Island Peak experienced mild AMS in Pheriche (4280m/14,042ft) and wisely decided not to go higher. Three days later he had improved and continued to Chukhung (4750m/15,584ft), even though he was not 100%. Here, his mild AMS returned and he was advised to go down to Dingboche (4350m/14,271ft) for the rest of the day. On arrival, he immediately felt better, had lunch and for good measure spent the rest of the day by the bridge below Dingboche. He returned to Chukhung late that day, had the best sleep since Lukla and suffered no problems the next night at the Base Camp (5150m/16,896ft).

Effects of long-term exposure to altitude

If you stay at altitude for several weeks there are more changes: your muscles' mito-chondria (the energy converters in the muscle) multiply, a denser network of capillar-ies develop and your maximum work rate increases slowly with these changes. Expeditions have run medical programmes with some interesting results. Climbers who experience periodic breathing (the majority) at base camp never shake it off and have great difficulty maintaining their normal body weight. Muscles will strengthen and stamina is increased but not the muscle bulk. Interestingly Sherpas who have always lived at altitude, never experience periodic breathing and can actually put on weight with enough food.

How long does acclimatisation last?

It varies, but if you were at altitude for a month or more your improved work rates could continue for weeks so you'd still feel fit upon returning to altitude. You could not, however, ascend faster than normal if you return to sea level for a few days since you'd be susceptible to HAPE.

If you have been up to 5000m/16,404ft and then go down to 3500m/11,483ft for a few days, returning rapidly to 5000m/16,404ft should cause no problems. Thus, hav-ing been to Lobuche and Kala Pattar, then rested for two days in Namche, you should be able to ascend to Gokyo or a trekking peak quickly.

Sleeping at altitude

Many people have trouble sleeping in a new environment, especially if it changes every day. Altitude adds to the problems. Apart from the condition known as periodic breathing (see above), the decrease of oxygen means that some trekkers experience very wild dreams. This often happens at Namche, on the way up.

Appetite

Altitude causes some people to lose an interest in food but you should try to eat as much as you can since your energy consumption, even at rest, is significantly higher than normal. Your body needs to generate heat to combat the constant cold, especial-ly while sleeping. Very energetic trekkers, no matter how much they eat, will often be unable to replace the huge quantities of energy used.

The pill and fertility

The theoretical risk of a blood clot while on the pill is higher at altitude but no stud-ies have been undertaken to see if there is actual risk. However no problems have been reported at the medium altitude ski resorts in the US. It is important to keep hydrated. Prolonged periods at altitude do reduce men's fertility, although this returns to normal after a few weeks.

Retinal haemorrhages

A study conducted in the Khumbu found that 30-35% of trekkers at 5000m suffered retinal haemorrhages. Upon descent these cured themselves rapidly.

Acclimatising for 8000m peak expeditions

Most groups heading to Tibet for Shishapangma, Cho Oyu and Everest plan an accli-matisation trek/climb in Nepal, usually in the Khumbu. During the monsoon an alter-native region is Ladakh, especially the Nimaling Valley (4700m+) and the surround-ing 6000m peaks.

● **Oxygen saturation meters (O_2 sat)** With the arrival of some relatively cheap bat-tery-powered models some trekking companies now carry them. Oxygen saturation levels vary with altitude (see the table on p235) and vary from individual to individ-ual; values plus or minus approx 5% are still within the normal range. O_2 saturation values also vary enormously between resting and exercising. Normally only resting rates are meaningful. A low O_2 sat is an indication that HAPE may be developing, or has developed. However it gives no indication of HACE; somebody can be dying of HACE and still have an O_2 sat in the high 80s.

DIARRHOEA

This is a very common problem in developing countries, especially Nepal, and few trekkers escape without some (usually mild) form of diarrhoea. Ideally you should visit a doctor for a stool test if it doesn't clear up in a few days. While trekking, however, this is usually impossible so some self-diagnosis may be necessary.

Many people over-react and start taking medication at the first loose stool. Diarrhoea will not normally kill you so urgent treatment is neither necessary nor always recommended. It's better to wait a few days and see if it goes away on its own. Unless the diarrhoea is particularly severe (eg as with food poisoning) there is no need to stop trekking. Just drink lots of water and listen to your body; if you feel hungry, eat, and if you don't then take soup and light foods. If the diarrhoea is still troublesome after a few days and you are fairly sure what type it is you may want to treat it. Note that this isn't, however, absolutely necessary.

Travellers'/bacterial diarrhoea
Hitting many new arrivals to Asia, it's caused by eating food that contains strains of bacteria different to those that your body is used to. The onset is often accompanied by or even preceded by a fever and/or chills and nausea, followed by fairly sudden, frequent, watery diarrhoea and often cramps.

Treatment There are several methods of treatment. First, it's worth waiting to see if your body can fight it off on its own. Tough Nepalese bacteria, however, may need stronger measures. Most effective is to begin a short course of **Norfloxacin**, available under the name of Normaflox in Nepal. There are two dosage regimes. Recently a single 800mg has been advocated; if the diarrhoea hasn't cleared 12 hours later begin the normal course. This is 400mg, every 12 hours, for three days. Alternatively the more expensive Cipro can be used. Similarly, a one-off dose of 1000mg (ie 1gm) or 500mg every 12 hours for three days if the first dose doesn't clear it in 12 hours. An often recommended drug is Bactrim/Bactrim DS or Septra but as there are now resistant strains these are not nearly as effective.

Mild food poisoning
This comes on suddenly and severely, with vomiting and diarrhoea, about four to eight hours after eating contaminated food. Luckily, it usually lasts less than 24 hours and recovery is quick, although you may feel weakened. There are no drugs that can help – the body just has to eject all the contaminated food and rid itself of the poison. Rest and drink plenty of fluids. Oral rehydration solutions are helpful.

Giardia
Common in Nepal, giardia is caught from infected water, especially in Kathmandu, and from high mountain streams near areas where yaks graze. It generally takes seven to 10 days to develop and does not come on suddenly. The classic symptoms are sulphurous (rotten egg) smelling farts and burps. Additional symptoms that make it easier to distinguish from other types of diarrhoea include a rumbling upset stomach, bloating and cramps. There is usually no fever, chills or nausea. Giardia can also be virtually symptomless; just a slightly upset stomach with occasional soft stools or even constipation. Some forms may go away on their own after several weeks but treatment is usually required.

Treatment There's a choice of two drugs. **Tiniba** can be bought at all Nepalese pharmacies without a prescription. The name of the active chemical is Tinidazole. The dose is two grams, ie four x 500 mg, taken all at once. It's better taken in the evening because the usual side effects (nausea and a strong metallic taste in the mouth) may be slept off. Do not mix with alcohol. This dose is about 90% effective but, if you feel positive that you have giardia, the same dose may be repeated 24 hours later.

Alternatively **Flagyl/Metronidazole** may be used. The dose is 250mg, three times a day for five to seven days. This should also not be mixed with alcohol.

Amoebic dysentery
The onset of amoebic dysentery may be sudden and severely weakening – sometimes to the point where the sufferer is barely able to leave the toilet. However, it usually starts slowly, a mild diarrhoea that comes and goes, something that can almost, but not quite, be ignored. This is when it is most dangerous because although the symptoms can eventually clear up, your system is still infected and being slowly damaged. If you suspect you might have amoebic dysentery have a stool test when you return to Kathmandu. Only 1% or less of all diarrhoea cases are caused by amoebic dysentery.

Cyclospora
Any diarrhoea that doesn't clear up with the above drugs could be cyclospora. Luckily it is rare. You should consult a doctor in Nepal. The cure is cotrimoxazole.

OTHER HEALTH PROBLEMS
Dehydration
Trekkers lose large quantities of water, not just through sweating but by breathing harder at altitude. Water vapour is exhaled with each breath and the thinner air means more breaths are required. If the fluids lost are not replaced dehydration will result, making you feel lethargic and sometimes resulting in a headache. The symptoms are similar to AMS so the easiest way to avoid confusion is to always keep hydrated.

A happy mountaineer always pees clear! If your urine is a deep yellow or orange colour you are not drinking enough. Even if you are not feeling thirsty you should still try to drink more. This can include any liquids (soups and tea but not alcohol) and as much water as possible. Many people find that with supper they often drink more than a litre of water, catching up on what they should have drunk during the day.

Hypoglycaemia
Especially after prolonged bouts of exercise, the body can quickly run out of energy. The solution is to snack frequently and stop often.

The Khumbu cough
Few trekkers manage to escape this one. The extra amounts of cold dry air that you need to breathe in at altitude irritate your bronchi (windpipes). Your body reacts to this as it would to an infection like flu, producing large quantities of phlegm, a mild cough and a runny nose. Since there is, in fact, no infection it's pointless taking antibiotics but throat lozenges help so take plenty along.

Bronchitis
This is also an inflammation of the bronchi but it's caused by an infection. Differentiating between this and the Khumbu cough is difficult but it may be accompanied by a fever and an even more productive cough. Since it can be a viral or a bacterial infection, taking antibiotics will not always help and is not particularly recommended. It's best to get some rest or return to a lower altitude, eg Namche, and see a doctor.

Snow blindness

This is sunburn of the cornea, a painful affliction that feels like hot sand in your eyes. Porters often get snow blindness. It is entirely preventable by wearing sunglasses that block UV light. This precaution is most important not just in snowy areas but also at altitude since the concentration of UV light increases with altitude.

If you lose your sunglasses, make yourself two cardboard eye-shields shaped like glasses with two narrow slits for vision. These are surprisingly effective at cutting down UV.

Frostbite

When flesh freezes the results are very serious. Amputation may be necessary. Frostbite occurs usually in fingers or toes and takes time to develop unless bare flesh is exposed to winds at low temperatures or is holding cold metal.

Treatment When cold, fingers or toes feel numb, clumsy and lose power. If it's still possible to move them they aren't likely to be freezing although at this point the skin surface can partially freeze unnoticed. If you are worried, stop and rewarm. For fingers swing your arms around to promote circulation. Pain on rewarming means either you frost-nipped or came close. For real frostbite warm slowly and evenly. Blood temperature is the optimum warming temperature and once defrosted you must promote blood circulation. Rewarming can be excruciatingly painful and blisters will probably form. When deep freezing has occurred the flesh turns white or blue and fingers or toes become wooden, incapable of movement. At this stage don't begin rewarming until in a position where refreezing cannot occur since this is even more damaging. No sensation upon rewarming means the nerves have been damaged, the most serious form of frostbite. See a doctor as soon as possible. In a wilderness situation promoting circulation with Nifedipine or alcohol until you get to a hospital can reduce the extent of permanent damage. Nifedepine (Adulat) can also be used to help prevent frostbite (5-10mg of the fast-acting type of tablets only) if your core temperature is good but the side effects are an increased heart rate that can occasionally have unpredictable results at altitude.

Boils

More common during the monsoon, these are usually the result of a staphylococcal skin infection. Non-urgent but see a doctor.

Unwelcome bed companions

If you're using your own sleeping bag then it's very unlikely you'll have problems. Renting sleeping bags always carries a very small risk of scabies but not fleas or bedbugs, and this can be further reduced by airing the bag for a day or two in the sun. If you ever use local blankets the risks increase considerably.

● **Bedbugs** Bites are normally small, itchy and in neat lines. Bedbugs do not normally live in sleeping bags because when they are aired there is nowhere to hide.

● **Fleas** All local dogs are carriers and fleas also hide in quilts, blankets and old carpets. Occasionally trekkers pick them up. The small, red, itchy bites are usually congregated around areas such as the tops of your socks, waist, armpits or sleeves. You should try not to scratch and wash yourself and your clothes thoroughly. If you can find some flea powder, use this as well.

● **Scabies** Caused by a microscopic parasite this is luckily rare amongst trekkers. It can be caught from sheets or rented sleeping bags (but only if they have not been aired properly) or contact with an infected person, sometimes another trekker. To avoid scabies you should always use a sheet sleeping bag within your sleeping bag. The itchy red spots look like pimples without the pus and may, at first, be confused with flea bites. As the parasites multiply, the marks spread widely but not usually on the face or head. Go to Khunde Hospital or the Pheriche Clinic, if possible, or visit a health post. Treatment is a head-to-toe dousing with Scabex. All clothing should be washed and thoroughly aired and your sleeping bag should be left in the sun for a several days. It takes a few days to a week or more for the symptoms, including itching to disappear, even if the treatment has been successful. Occasionally a second treatment may be necessary.

Leeches
These monsoon terrorisers are able to put a sizeable hole in you completely painlessly. Found in profusion in damp forest, leeches are adept at penetrating socks and even boot eyelets. Do not try to pull a leech off but apply salt, iodine or a lighted match and it'll quickly drop off. Leeches don't transmit disease but the wound can get infected: wash with antiseptic.

Blisters
Since you spend most of the time on your feet, looking after them properly to avoid blisters is of paramount importance.

Prevention Start with boots that have been worn in. This means not just for a short walk on level ground but with a pack in hilly country.

If a blister starts to develop while you're trekking you can usually feel it. There'll be some rubbing, localised pain or a hot spot. Stop and investigate, even if it occurs during the first five minutes of walking or just in sight of the top of the hill. The trick is to detect the symptoms before the blister develops. Apply moleskin or Second Skin, or a strong adhesive tape (Leukoplast, available in Nepal). Check that the hot spot is not being caused by the seam of a sock or a seam in your boot. Once you've applied a dressing, recheck it periodically to ensure that the problem is not getting worse.

Treatment If you develop a blister there are several approaches. If it's not painful then surround it (don't cover it) with some light padding, eg moleskin, and see how it feels. If it is painful you may want to drain it. Clean the skin, sterilise a needle by holding it slightly above a flame for a few seconds and pierce the blister. Do not cut away the blister skin until it has dried out and is no longer useful for protecting the delicate skin underneath. Put protective tape over it with some cotton wool as padding. Some people, however, put the tape straight over the blister, with no dressing.

Vaginal infections
If you have experienced these before it is worth bringing a course of the medication you were last prescribed in case the infection recurs.

FIRST AID KIT
This is a basic list to cover the more common ailments that afflict trekkers. Climbing groups, expeditions and trekkers going to isolated areas will need a more comprehensive kit. Quantities stated are for one person.

Easily purchased in Kathmandu:
● **Diamox** This comes in two forms, 250mg tablets (in Nepal) and 500mg time release capsules. One strip of 10 tablets is plenty.
● **Norfloxacin** See 'diarrhoea' above for dosage. This is a powerful drug that can also be used to treat urinary tract infections.
● **Tinidazole/Tiniba** 8-10 tablets.
● **Jeevan Jal** (oral rehydration salts) One to three packets for the replacement of salts and fluids lost by vomiting and diarrhoea. Fanta, Coke or Pepsi (with the fizz taken out) and soup are also helpful but not in excessive quantities.

You may also consider taking **Erythromycin** for skin infections or bronchitis. The dose is 250mg, four times a day.

Better purchased in the West:
● **Moleskin/Second Skin/zinc oxide based tape (Leukoplast)** – for blisters. Cheap low quality tape is available in Nepal.

● **Painkillers** Useful as for headaches, for reducing any fever and tenderness or swelling. For longer treks take plenty. Some brands are available in Nepal.

● **Plasters/Band-Aids** Assorted plasters and perhaps a stretch bandage would be useful. If you have had knee or ankle trouble previously a good support bandage is well worth bringing.

● **Betadine/Savlon** Antiseptic for cuts.

● **Throat lozenges** Bring several packets for the Khumbu cough. Available in Kathmandu.

RESCUE PROCEDURES

Assessing the situation
On a standard trek in the Solu Khumbu there are few situations where the only solution is a helicopter rescue. For severe AMS immediate descent is vital rather than even an hour or two's wait. In most cases, walking or being carried to Syangboche or Lukla is quite feasible and porters can carry phenomenal loads in short relays. During the high season, the HRA doctors can be summoned surprisingly quickly from most places in the Khumbu. In the lower reaches, the doctor at Khunde (year round) can be contacted. In addition, there are always a surprising number of doctors on treks themselves.

If somebody has had a serious accident, don't panic. If there is bleeding, apply pressure over the wound, keep them warm and take stock of the situation. Look at all your options logically and carefully.

Summoning a helicopter
The process of summoning a helicopter can take 24 hours or longer once the message reaches Kathmandu because there must be a guarantee of payment (by a trekking company, insurance company or your embassy). How quickly the helicopter comes also depends on the weather. It isn't unusual for it to take several days to reach an injured patient – there are no golden hour rescues.

There are radio posts at the National Park HQ, the HRA post and at several of the army posts. When sending a message include as much clear detail as possible: your names and nationalities, the exact location, the reason for the rescue request (this will assist the doctor sent) and an assessment of the seriousness. Helicopters require a flat area to land on, below approximately 4500m/14,764ft.

❑ **Which painkiller?**
● **Aspirin (Dispirin)** Even small amounts reduce the ability of the blood to clot, so it's useful on high altitude expeditions where dangerous blood clots occur. Aspirin reduces inflammation of the joints, a common affliction among long distance trekkers. Can also reduce fevers, though it doesn't fix the underlying problem. Better taken with food. Should not be taken at the same time as Diamox.

● **Acetaminophen (Tylenol)** As a pain killer it has fewer side effects than aspirin but it doesn't reduce inflammations.

● **Ibuprofen (Aduil, Motrin)** This is probably the best drug for tendonitis and inflammation of joints.

● **Naproxen (Aleve)** To be avoided while exercising strenuously, ie while trekking.

APPENDIX D: FLORA AND FAUNA

The best all-round guide to the flora and fauna in this region is *The Story of Mt Everest National Park* by Margaret Jefferies but it can now only be found in libraries.

FLORA

From October to the spring the Khumbu is dry and brown, almost desert-like. In contrast, during the monsoon the greenery is surprisingly intense and flowers dapple hillsides. The wide range of flora includes the rhododendron, gentian, primrose, edelweiss and the beautiful mountain poppy. The forests of the deep Khumbu valleys comprise blue pine, fir, and juniper with birch and rhododendron forests at lower altitudes. Above the tree line is dwarf rhododendron and juniper scrub. The latter is prized by the Sherpas for its fragrant and instantly recognisable smell when burnt, a scent that soon becomes very familiar. The highest plant of all is the tiny snow rhododendron.

WILDLIFE

In the Khumbu few wild mammals live above the tree line and even fewer are regularly seen.

● **Himalayan thar** A large and handsome goat adept at rock climbing. The males are around a metre high and sport a luxuriant coppery brown coat, with a paler mane. They are often seen during the first day or so of the walk above Namche, eyeing trekkers with disdain.

● **Snow leopard** Hauntingly beautiful solo cats, virtually never seen by trekkers.

● **Wolf** Rarely seen, wolves live at the top of the tree line. Their coat is thick and sandy or grey and they use their bushy tail to keep their nose warm while sleeping.

● **Weasel** Quick eyes may see a blur of tan fur around grass and rocks near villages above Namche, even to as high as 5500m/18,044ft.

● **Himalayan mouse hare** A small tail-less mammal that is surprisingly tame.

● **Musk deer** Well under a metre high, this delicate deer is occasionally seen near Dole or around Tengboche in the dark forest. It is illegally hunted for its musk, produced by a gland in the male and used for making perfume. The male has large distinctive fang-like teeth (see photo opposite p97).

● **Common mouse** At night in the lodges there's the telltale pitter-patter across the roof and the occasional scream (not of mouse origin!).

DOMESTIC ANIMALS

In the warmer lower hills a variety of animals are kept. Chickens are kept mainly as egg-producers. There are dogs; and goats are numerous, being sacrificed and eaten during important Hindu festivals and ceremonies. They are very destructive, stripping the ground and shrubs bare of leaves and are responsible for much of the deforestation close to villages. Buffaloes provide milk and meat, and pull ploughs. At high altitudes they are replaced by yaks, naks and various crossbreeds.

BIRDS

Nepal is on some major migration routes and is famed for its varied bird life. Since the local people don't hunt birds, and they are all protected in the park, with keen eyes you should seen the majority of the birds mentioned below. Serious birdwatchers should consult: *Birds of Nepal* by RL Fleming or *Birds of the Central Himalayas* by Dorothy Mierow, both usually available in the Kathmandu bookshops.

● **Lammergeier/bearded vulture** This large and beautiful soaring bird is a scavenger, often seen gliding along the mountain sides above Namche.

● **Griffon** Similar to the lammergeier, but slightly heavier with a shorter, wider tail.

● **Golden eagle** This raptor hunts pheasants, snow cocks and smaller mammals rather than being a scavenger. It is smaller and more agile than the other soaring birds.

● **Danphe/Impeyan pheasant/Monal** The national bird of Nepal, often seen in pairs. The male sports nine iridescent colours and is plump, almost heavy. The female is a plainer brown and white. Good places to spot them are along the trail to Thame and Tengboche, and around Phortse.

● **Blood pheasant** The male has a red throat, red and white tail and bright red legs. They are seen around Tengboche and Dole.

● **Tibetan snow cock** Both male and female are striped: black, white, grey and brown with orange legs. Easy to approach, they congregate in noisy groups at altitudes above Namche right up to the snow line, especially on freshly dug fields.

● **Snow pigeon** They fly in compact flocks and as they wheel around in the sky their colour alternates between light and dark.

● **Yellow-billed and red-billed chough** Black with red legs, choughs are curious and playful but have the annoying habit of attacking tents, ripping the material with their beaks. Together with crows, they are known as 'gorak' by the Sherpas.

● **Jungle crow** Black and slightly scrawny, crows are great camp scavengers.

● **Tibetan raven** ('Caw caw') Completely black, these ravens attain nightmarish proportions in the Khumbu.

APPENDIX E: NEPALI WORDS AND PHRASES

Many Nepalis, especially those used to dealing with foreigners, can speak some English. It is, however, really worth making the effort to learn even a few Nepali phrases since this will positively affect the attitude of the local people towards you and you'll be made all the more welcome.

Derived from Sanskrit, Nepali shares many words with Hindi and is also written in the Devanagari script. For many of the people you speak to (Sherpa, Rai etc) Nepali will, in fact, be their second language. Whilst Nepali is not a particularly difficult language to learn up to a basic level, Sherpa is much harder.

Nepali includes several sounds not used in English. The transliterations given below are therefore only approximate. However since pronunciation varies across the country your less-than-perfect attempts will probably be understood as just another regional variation.

Namasté

Probably the first word learnt by the newly-arrived foreigner in Nepal is this greeting, which is spoken with the hands together as if praying. Its meaning encompasses 'hello' and 'goodbye' as well as 'good morning', 'good afternoon' or 'good evening'. *Namaskar* is the more polite form.

General words
How are you?   *Bhaat khanu-boyo?* (Have you eaten your dal bhaat?)
Fine thanks   *Khai-é* (I have eaten)

Please give me	..... *di-nus*
Do you speak English?	*Angrayzi bolnoo-hoon-cha?*
Yes/no	(see below)
Thank you	*Dhan-yabad* (not often used)
Excuse me (sorry)	*Maf-garnus*
good/bad	*ramro/naramro*
cheap/expensive	*susto/mahongo*
Just a minute!	*Ek-chin*!
brother/sister	*eai/didi* (used to address anyone of your own age)
Good night	*Sooba-ratry*
Sweet dreams	*Meeto supona*

Questions and answers

To ask a question, end the phrase with a rising tone. An affirmative answer is given by restating the question without the rising tone. 'No' is translated as *chaina* (there isn't/aren't any) or *hoi-na* (it isn't/they aren't).

What's your name?	*Topaiko* (to adult)/*timro* (child) *nam ke ho*?		
My name is	*Mero nam ..... ho.*		
Where are you from?	*Topaiko/timro dess kay ho?*		
Britain/USA	*Belaiyot/Amerika*		
Australia/New Zealand	*Australia/New Zealand*		
Where are you going?	*Kaha janné?*	I'm going to	..... *janné*
Are you married?	*Bebah bo sokyo?*		
Have you any children?	*Chora chori chon?*	boy/girl	*chora/chori*
How old are you?	*Koti borsa ko boyo?*		
What is this?	*Yo kay ho?*		

Directions

Ask directions frequently and avoid questions that require only 'yes' or 'no' as a reply.

Which path goes to ....?	........*janay bahto kun ho?*
Where is ...?	.....*kaha cho*
lodge/hotel	*bhatti*
shop	*possol*
latrine	*charpi*
What is this village called?	*Yo gaon ko nam kay ho?*
left/right	*baiya/daiya*
straight ahead	*seeda jannus*
steep uphill/downhill	*bhiralo matti/talla*
far away	*tadah*
near	*nadjik*

Numerals/time

1 *ek*; 2 *du-i*; 3 *tin*; 4 *charr*; 5 *panch*; 6 *chho*; 7 *saat*; 8 *aatt*; 9 *nau*; 10 *dos*; 11 *eghaara*; 12 *baahra*; 13 *tehra*; 14 *chaudha*; 15 *pondhra*; 16 *sora*; 17 *sotra*; 18 *ottahra*; 19 *unnice*; 20 *beece*; 25 *pochis;* 30 *teece*; 40 *chaalis*; 50 *pachaas*; 60 *saati*; 70 *sottorri*; 80 *ossi*; 90 *nobbi*; 100 *say*; 200 *du-i say*; 300 *tin-say*; 400 *charr say*; 500 *panch say* ; 600 *chho say*; 700 *saat say*; 800 *aatt say*; 900 *nau say*; 1000 *hozhar*

How much/many?	*Kati?*
What time is it?	*Kati byjhay?*
It's three o'clock	*Tin byjhay*
hours/minutes	*ghanta/minoot*
today	*ajaa*

yesterday	*hidjo*		
tomorrow	*bholi*		
day after tomorrow	*parsi*		

Food and drink

restaurant/inn	*bhatti*	cheese	*cheese*
Please give me...	*......di-nus*	boiled egg	*phul*
mineral water	*khanni-paani*	omelette	*unda*
tea	*chiya*	salt	*noon*
coffee	*coffee*	spicy hot	*piro*
milk	*dood no*	chillis	*korsani china*
boiled milk	*oomaleko-dood*	sugar	*chinni*
beer	*beer*	honey	*maha*
rice spirit	*ruxi*		
Cheers!	*Khannus!*		
chicken	*kookhura-ko massu*		
buffalo	*rango-ko massu*		
pork	*sungur-ko massu*		
rice	*bhaat*		
lentils	*dal*		
vegetables (cooked)	*takaari*		
potatoes	*aloo*		
bread	*roti*		
It tastes good	*Ekdum meeto*		

APPENDIX F: GLOSSARY

ama	mother
bergschrund	gap where a glacier parts from a rock wall
bhanjyang	pass
bhatti	simple hotel
bivvy (bivouac)	small shelter for camping
Brahmin/Bahun	Hindu high priest caste
cairn	pile of stones marking a route ('stone men')
chang	home-brew made from barley or rice; also 'north'
chhu	river
chhusa	crop-growing area above main village
chimneying	climbing a vertical crack just greater than body width
chomo/jomo	mountain goddess
chorten	Tibetan stupa (see below)
chotar	prayer flag pole beside house
crampons	spikes that strap on boots to aid walking on ice
crevasse	dangerous cracks in a glacier
cwm	valley shaped like an amphitheatre (Welsh)
dal bhaat	staple meal of lentils and boiled rice
deorali	pass

dhai	curds
dingma	clearing
doko	woven, load-carrying basket
drangka	stream
ghat	river bank or bridge
goan/gau	village
gompa	Buddhist temple (literally: 'meditation')
goth 'goat-h'	shelter or temporary house
gunsa	'winter place', where early crops are grown
himal	snowy mountains
jumars	device used for climbing up a fixed rope
kang	mountain
kani	entrance arch
kharka	grazing ground (Nepali)
khola	stream
kosi	river
kund	lake
la	pass
lha	fenced herding area
lho	south
mani wall	wall of stones carved with Buddhist mantras
mantra	prayer formula
neve	smooth high snow-field, accumulation area of a glacier
nup	west
phu	high altitude grazing area at the end of a valley
piton	spike hammered into a rock crack for climbing security
pokhri	lake
prussiks	loops of cord used to climb a vertical rope
rakshi	local distilled spirit
ri	ridge or soft peak
satu	flour
serac	large block of ice typically found in an icefall
shar	east
Sherpa	of the Sherpa people
sherpa	trekking group assistant
solja/suchia	salt-butter tea
stupa	hemispherical Buddhist religious monument
suntala	mandarin orange
tal	lake
tarn	small lake without entry or exit stream
trisul	trident carried by worshippers of Shiva
tsampa	roasted barley flour
tse	peak
tsho/cho	lake
yersa	crop-growing area above main village

APPENDIX G: BIBLIOGRAPHY

TRAVEL GUIDES

Armington, Stan *Trekking in the Nepal Himalaya*, Lonely Planet Publications, Australia, 1997

Bezruchka, Stephen *Trekking in Nepal – A Traveler's Guide*, 7th edition, Cordee, UK/The Mountaineers, USA

Nakano, Toru *Trekking in Nepal,* Yama-Kei Publishers, Japan 1984/Allied Publishers, India 1985

O'Connor, Bill *The Trekking Peaks of Nepal*, Crowood Press, UK 1989

Swift, Hugh *Trekking in Nepal, West Tibet, and Bhutan,* Hodder & Stoughton, UK 1989

Nepal, Insight Guides, APA 1989

MAPS

Khumbu Himal, Freytag-Berndt und Artaria, Vienna, 1978 and 1985

Lapchi Kang, Freytag-Berndt und Artaria, Vienna, 1974 and 1985

Mt Everest, National Geographic Magazine, 1988

Planimetric Map of Satellite Images for National Remote Sensing Centre (Nepal) by Institute for Applied Geosciences, Germany 1986

Rolwaling Himal (Gaurisankar), Freytag-Berndt und Artaria, Vienna, 1981

Shorong/Hinku, Freytag-Berndt und Artaria, Vienna, 1974, 1979 and 1987

TRAVELOGUES/HISTORY

Bernstein, Jeremy *Wildest Dreams of Kew*, George Allen & Unwin UK 1970

Boardman, Peter *Sacred Summits*, Hodder & Stoughton, London 1982

Bonington, Chris and Clarke, Charles *Everest the Unclimbed Ridge*, Hodder & Stoughton, London 1983

Bonington, Chris *Everest South West Face*, Hodder & Stoughton, London 1973

Bonington, Chris *The Everest Years*, Hodder & Stoughton, London 1986

Eggler, Albert *The Everest Lhotse Adventure*, Geo Allen & Unwin, UK 1957

Franco, Jean *Makalu*, Jonathan Cape, London 1957

Gillman, Peter *Everest – The best writing and pictures from 70 years of human endeavour*, Little, Brown & Co, London 1993

Hillary, Edmund *Nothing Venture, Nothing Win*, Hodder & Stoughton, London 1975

Hillary, Louise *High Time*, Hodder & Stoughton, London 1973

Holzel, Tom and Salkeld, Audrey *The Mystery of Mallory and Irvine*, Jonathan Cape, London 1986

Hornbein, Thomas *Everest the West Ridge*, Vikas, New Delhi 1982

Howard-Bury CK *Mount Everest: The Reconnaissance 1921*

Hunt, John *The Ascent of Everest*, Hodder & Stoughton 1953

Kolhi, Capt MS *The Himalayas – Playground of the Gods*, Viking India 1983

Kolhi, Commander M S *Nine Atop Everest*, Orient Longman, New Delhi 1969

Mulgrew, Peter *No Place for Men*, AH & AW Reed, Wellington, 1964

Norton EF *The Fight for Everest: 1924*, Edward Arnold, 1925

Salkeld, Audrey *People in High Places*, Jonathan Cape, London 1991

Shipton, Eric *That Untravelled World*, Charles Scribner's Sons, NY 1969

Shipton, Eric *The Six Mountain-Travel Books*, The Mountaineers, Seattle 1985

Taylor-Ide, Daniel *Something Hidden Behind the Ranges - a Himalayan Quest*
    Mercury House, San Francisco 1995
Tichy, Herbert *Cho Oyu By Favour of the Gods*, Methuen & Co, London 1957
Tichy, Herbert *Himalaya*, Anton Schroll, Vienna 1970
Tilman, HW *The Seven Mountain-Travel Books*, The Mountaineers, Seattle 1983
Unsworth, Walt *Everest*, Oxford Illustrated Press, UK 1989
Verghese *Himalayan Endeavour,* Times of India 1962
Von Furer-Haimendorf, Christoph *Exploratory Travels in Highland Nepal*, Sterling
    Publishers, New Delhi 1989
Weir, Tom *East of Kathmandu,* The Travel Book Club
Wignall, Sydney *Spy on the Roof of the World*, Canongate, Edinburgh, UK 1996

RESEARCH

Bista, Dor Bahadur *Fatalism and Development Nepal's struggle for Modernisation,*
    Orient Longman, Calcutta 1991
Jefferies, Margaret *The Story of Mt Everest National Park,* Cobb/Horwood, Auckland
    1985
Bhatt, Dibya *Natural History and Economic Botany of Nepal,* Orient Longman, New
    Delhi 1977
Fisher, James F. *Sherpas – Reflections on Change in Himalayan Nepal,* University of
    California Press, Berkeley, 1990
Lachapelle, Paul A, *Report on human waste management in Sagarmatha National
    Park* for University of Vermont, Burlington VT and School for International
    Training, Kathmandu 1995 (kindly provided)
Mierow, Dorothy *Birds of the Central Himalayas,* 1988
Ortner, Sherry *Sherpas through their Rituals,* Cambridge UP 1978
Schaffner Urs Road *Construction in the Nepal Himalaya: the Experience from the
    Lamosangu-Jiri Road Project,* ICIMOD 1987
Sharma, Pitamber *Assessment of Critical Issues and Options in Mountain Tourism in
    Nepal,* 1989
Stevens, Stanley *Sherpa Settlement and Subsistence – Cultural Ecology and History
    in Highland Nepal* for University of California
Subba, Chaitanya*The Culture and Religion of Limbus*, Subba KB, Kathmandu, 1995
The Himalayan Journal 45 1987-88, Oxford University Press Bombay, 1988
Wilheim, Emily *Chialsa – Disappearance or Revival?*, School for International
    Training report

MEDICINE

The High Altitude Medicine Handbook, Micro-edition, Andrew J Pollard& David R
    Murdoch, Radcliff Medical Press, Oxon 1997
Medicine for Mountaineering ed. Wilkerson, 3rd edition, The Mountaineers, Seattle,
    1985
Management of Wilderness and Environmental Emergencies ed. Auerbach and Geehr,
    second edition, C.V. Mosby, Toronto 1989
Mountain Sickness, Peter Hackett, American Alpine Club

INDEX